The Fight for Maglev

The Fight for Maglev

Making America the World Leader in 21st Century Transport

James Powell and Gordon Danby,

The Inventors of Superconducting Maglev,

with James Jordan

Book cover design, 3D modeling and Illustrations created by:

Douglas Rike, Industrial Designer

*To Colleen
Best Wishes
Jim Powell*

The Fight for Maglev,

Making America the World Leader in 21st Century Transport

Copyright © 2011 James Powell, Gordon Danby & James Jordan

All rights reserved.

For permission to reproduce or transmit in any form or by any means the contents of or any part of this book, contact: james.jordan@magneticglide.com

ISBN-13: 978-1468144802

ISBN-10: 1468144804

Library of Congress Control Number: 2012900748

Printed in the United States of America

"We Do Not Ride on the Railroad, It Rides Upon Us"

Thoreau

"This is the story of a contest almost no one is watching. At stake is preeminence in the production and sale of a revolutionary new mode of transportation. It is called Magnetic Levitation – Maglev for short. It will define the coming century much as the railroad defined the last one, and the automobile and airplane have defined this one."

Daniel Patrick Moynihan, 1989

"The most effective future train system for the United States would be a maglev transit line. If such a network was in place, people in New York would be able to participate in an early-morning meeting in Washington without the bother of having to go to and from airports at both ends. Likewise, transcontinental maglev services could supersede aviation networks."

Dr. Yoshiyuki Kasai, Chairman, Japan Railways, Op-Ed, Special to The Yomiuri Shimbun 2008

"And Japan, the nation that unveiled the first high-speed rail system, is already at work building the next: a line that will connect Tokyo with Osaka at speeds of over 300 miles per hour. So it's being done; it's just not being done here."

"There's no reason why we can't do this. This is America. There's no reason why the future of travel should lie somewhere else beyond our borders. Building a new system of high-speed rail in America will be faster, cheaper and easier than building more freeways or adding to an already overburdened aviation system –- and everybody stands to benefit."

Barack Obama, April 16, 2009

Dr. James Powell and Dr. Gordon Danby,

The Inventors of Superconducting Maglev Transport

"We might be able to stimulate our way back to stability, but we can only invent our way back to prosperity."

Thomas L. Friedman, columnist and author, quote from New York Times column, "Invent, Invent, Invent", published June 27, 2009.

"To see what is in front of one's nose needs a constant struggle."

George Orwell originally published in March, 1946, and can be found in The Collected Essays, Journalism and Letters of George Orwell: In Front of Your Nose, 1945-1950, Sonia Orwell and Ian Angus, Editors / Paperback / Harcourt Brace Jovanovich, 1968, p. 125.

The Fight for Maglev

Senator Daniel Patrick Moynihan's death on March 26, 2003, at age 76, was announced on the Senate floor by Senator Hillary Rodham Clinton, who was elected to the Senate seat Moynihan had held for 24 years. She said *"We have lost a great American, an extraordinary senator, an intellectual and a man of passion and understanding for what really makes the country work."*

Known for his ability to spot emerging issues and trends, Moynihan was a leader in welfare reform and transportation initiatives and an authority on Social Security and foreign policy.

Senate Democratic leader Tom Daschle of South Dakota said *"in many respects, Pat Moynihan was larger than life,"* citing a description in the Almanac of American Politics that Moynihan was *"the nation's best thinker among politicians since Lincoln and its best politician among thinkers since Jefferson."*

Dedication

We dedicate The Fight for Maglev

to

Our families for their support and encouragement in the long fight to make Maglev a major mode of transport for the 21st Century

to

The Memory of Senator Daniel Patrick Moynihan, the Champion for American Superconducting Maglev

and to

The many wonderful people who have worked tirelessly with us to bring Superconducting Maglev to America.

Listed alphabetically, they include:

Cliff Bragdon; Gil Carpenter; Robert Coullahan; Ernie Fazio; Les Finch; Bud Gardner; Bud Griffis; Ed Harmer; John Jackson; Piyush Joshi; Chris Kempner; Otto Lazareth; Andrea Lohneiss; George Maise; John Morena; Erno Ostheimer; Judy Otto; Jim Paul; P. Philipsburg; Sal Pjerov; Jesse Powell; John Rather; Douglas Rike; Rosemary Riker; Morris Reich; Barbara Roland; Art Shennfeldt; John Skaritka; Charles Smith; Richie Tulipano; Bill Van Allen; Lou Ventre; Tom Wagner; Brian Walsh; Cindi Weavers; Rod Wickers; John Wines; Bob Worthing; Al Witzig.

With deep gratitude and thanks to all of the above,

The Fight for Maglev goes on.

The Fight for Maglev

Contents

Dedication vii

Preface xi

Foreword – How Much Time Has Humanity Got? 1

Prologue – Why Maglev is Inevitable 9

America–Once the World Leader in Transport............................21

Today and Tomorrow in America's Transport Hell..................... 37

The Message: Avoiding the 6th Extinction 53

The Maglev America Project – Our Highways to the Future.........77

Global Maglev: The Big Winners in a Much Smaller World.......101

How Maglev Works – First and Second Generation 135

The Fight for Maglev: First Round 155

Second Round – Senator Moynihan Climbs into the Ring.........189

Third Round – Decision Time for America 227

Maglev Launch: Finally, the Final Frontier...............................297

Maglev Energy Storage – The Good Sisyphus..........................327

Maglev Water Transport – A Billion Jugs A Day....................... 337

Finale - Which Song Will the Fat Lady Sing? 351

Acknowledgement.. 353

References.. 355

Index (Names) 365

Index (Places and Topics).. 369

Index (Illustrations & Credits)..377

About the Authors..381

Preface

The Fight for Maglev, Making America the World Leader in 21st Century Transport began in early 2010 when the inventors of superconducting magnetic levitation (Maglev) transport and I realized that the Obama Administration had rejected Maglev and planned to have American taxpayers invest hundreds of billions of dollars to build European style high speed passenger rail lines in the United States. We believe these obsolete, ineffective and expensive systems will cripple the United States in the years ahead. Our living standards will drop, travel will be extremely costly, and our trade deficit will continue to grow, destroying the United States as a major World economic power.

President Obama's 8 Billion dollar high speed rail program, part of the 2009 American Recovery and Reinvestment Act's nearly 1 Trillion dollar stimulus, did not include funds to demonstrate the 2nd generation superconducting Maglev, despite the President's call to action, when the High Speed Intercity Passenger Rail program was rolled out on April 16, 2009. Ironically, he praised Japan's superconducting Maglev system, which is based on the inventions of James Powell and Gordon Danby.

"And Japan, the nation that unveiled the first high-speed rail system, is already at work building the next: a line that will connect Tokyo with Osaka at speeds of over 300 miles per hour. So it's being done; it's just not being done here."

"There's no reason why we can't do this. This is America. There's no reason why the future of travel should lie somewhere else beyond our borders. Building a new system of high-speed rail in America will be faster, cheaper and easier than building more freeways or adding to an already overburdened aviation system -- and everybody stands to benefit."

It was exciting to hear President Obama praise the Japanese Superconducting Maglev System and call for America to act. In response, we created a website: www.magneticglide.com and included a video of the President's remarks to introduce Powell and Danby's 2nd generation superconducting Maglev transport system for intercity passengers and freight: http://www.readinessresource.net/maglev/2000.html.

We wrote a proposal for a grant to the Federal Railroad Administration for a Maglev Test and Certification Facility to demonstrate the performance and cost of the new 2nd Generation Superconducting Maglev System, which is cheaper, faster and much more capable than the foreign steel-wheel high speed rail and 1st Generation Maglev passenger systems. Sadly, we were ignored.

After years of trying to bring the 2nd Generation Superconducting Maglev to the attention of government policymakers, we decided to write this book to tell the public about this important new mode of transport, the first since the airplane, in hopes that voters will reject current plans to build costly "high speed" rail routes in the United States and urge their elected Federal and State government officials to support the development of the 2nd Generation Superconducting Maglev transport system for freight and passengers as a new American industry.

The approval and support of the government to use the rights-of-way of the U.S. Interstate Highway System, the vision of the late Senator Daniel Patrick Moynihan, is needed to bring Maglev to U.S. and global markets. Senator Moynihan's idea, which he strongly fought for, starting in 1987, was thwarted by the airlines in 1991. A 300 mph National Maglev Network alongside our Interstate Highways would greatly reduce highway congestion, deaths and injuries, lessen the congestion on our airways and airports, reduce oil imports and emissions of global warming gases and harmful pollutants, and dramatically cut travel costs and the costs of transporting goods.

As this book goes to press, America is experiencing serious economic problems and a rapidly declining middle class. If we are to maintain our jobs and good standard of living, America desperately needs to build domestic industries that can compete globally. An American Maglev manufacturing industry would create millions of new good paying jobs and many Billions of dollars in exports. The Interstate Superconducting Maglev Network would save every American about 1,000 dollars annually in transport costs.

Politicians and pundits talk over and over about the need to innovate, invest in new infrastructure, improve the education of our children, and expand research, so we can successfully compete in the global marketplace. So far, however, it's all platitudes and hot air, with no real plans and actions.

Transportation is fundamental to the American economy. Since the nation's founding over 200 years ago, America has led the World in new transport systems – canals, steamboats, railroads, automobiles, airplanes, and space transport – without this leadership, America would be a much less powerful, and a much poorer nation. Since the Apollo program, America has become a follower, not a leader, in World transport. Politicians are falling all over themselves to buy high speed rail trains from China, Japan and Europe. It is very sad. The foreign countries get the good jobs and a positive trade balance. America gets a few so-so jobs and a big trade deficit.

Americans have a propensity to believe the illusion that they will always have the greatest economy in the World and that they can solve any problem that comes up – not to worry. In the Prologue and first three chapters of the book we seek to lay out the *realities* of the critical problems that America and the rest of the World face in adapting to the coming decline of liquid hydrocarbon fuels and why we conclude that electric transportation is inevitable. The good news: early recognition of this reality and a commitment to action gives America the opportunity to once again take the lead in transportation.

In Chapter 4, we paint a picture of what society would be like with electric autos, and describe a Maglev America Project to build a 29,000 mile National Maglev Network for the transport of goods, highway freight trucks, delivery trucks, passengers, and autos.

In Chapter 5, we show how Maglev will be built all over the world, including some very exciting routes. Interconnecting the whole World with a Global Maglev Network will capture the World's collective imagination, much like the building of the Suez and Panama Canals did.

Then, in Chapter 6, using photos and drawings of the Maglev components, the inventors describe the 2nd Generation Superconducting Maglev transport system and how it came into being. Readers will find the inventors' thoughts about the nature of innovation interesting and relevant to America's present need to innovate in order to compete in the global marketplace. Jim Powell and Gordon Danby are exceptional people with enormous knowledge of science and natural phenomena.

Their views, after a lifetime of working at the leading edge of science and technology at Brookhaven National Laboratory, will tell the reader a lot about the nature of innovation.

In Chapters 7, 8 and 9, the "prize fight" metaphor is used to portray the three rounds of challenges in trying to bring 2nd Generation Superconducting Maglev to America. The third round is still in progress. Being a Washington based public policy person for most of my life, I tell the inside story of why the struggle has not yet been successful. Hopefully, this book will make it clear that the High Speed Intercity Passenger Rail (HSIPR) program is not only very expensive, with minimal benefits, but its existence has also shut down the effort to make Superconducting Maglev, a much better transport system, a new Made in America industry.

The final chapters describe three very important additional applications of 2nd Generation Maglev technology: using Maglev to launch payload into space (Chapter 10) and to store large amounts of electrical energy from variable power sources like wind and solar so it can be used during high demand periods (Chapter 11). Finally, we show how Maglev can move large volumes of water over long distances much cheaper than pipelines (Chapter 12). This closing chapter shows how Maglev alone will save millions of people from drought, deprivation and disease.

The clock is ticking. Unless America soon implements the 2nd Generation Maglev Systems described here, another country will, and we will import and pay an enormous price for it. To us, it seems against America's interests for our political leaders to champion importing foreign high speed rail and Maglev systems. Throwing away the opportunity to develop 2nd generation Maglev resulting in a further decline in the quality of life in America.

We strongly urge the government to fund demonstration of 2nd generation superconducting Maglev technology at a government test facility and certify it as a public carrier, (the governments of Japan and Germany financed their 1st generation systems). The resulting performance and cost data will enable 2nd Generation Maglev to compete with both the foreign first generation Maglev and the steel-wheel transport systems proposed to run on the 13 intercity passenger rail

The Fight for Maglev

Preface

routes established by the Federal Railroad Administration. Competition will benefit us all.

The questions we are often asked when we talk about 2nd Generation Maglev are "Why 2nd Generation Maglev? We already have Maglev systems operating in Japan and China, and we already have High Speed Passenger Rail systems operating in a number of countries. Why develop another system?"

The best way to answer this is to point to the history of air travel. Suppose you, the reader, wanted to take a cross-country trip by air and you were given 2 choices: 1) fly on a DC-3 or Ford Tri-Motor airplane, the best available in the 1930's, or 2) take a modern jetliner, e.g., the Boeing 777 or equivalent, which would you choose? Traveling on the 1930's airplanes, you would have a much longer trip time, much higher fares, more weather problems, a less safe trip, less comfortable seating, no rest rooms, etc., etc. One would have to either be a masochist or an incurable romantic about the past to choose a Ford Tri-Motor journey over a modern jetliner.

Similarly, traveling on 2nd Generation Maglev, which is a breakthrough advancement in transport technology, will be far superior to travel on High Speed Rail or 1st Generation Maglev, for the reasons described in detail in the book.

Briefly, with 2nd generation Maglev,

- fares will be much less;
- none of your taxes will go toward subsidizing High Speed Rail or 1st Generation Maglev routes;
- there will be a National Maglev Network with a station only a few miles from where you live, from which you can travel to any other station in the lower continental 48 States at 300 mph;
- you can take your personal auto with you on the trip, paying less than if you drove by highway, with a much shorter trip time;
- between cities you will travel at 300 mph on low-cost, elevated monorail guideway built alongside the rights-of-way of the Interstate Highway System;
- inside metropolitan areas, your magnetically levitated Maglev vehicles will travel along existing RR tracks that have been

adapted at low cost for Maglev travel to the multiple existing stations already inside the metropolitan area;
- seating will be first class;
- there will be no rail, braking or engine noise, or brake dust.

The capability to operate in a planar mode allows individual Maglev vehicles to travel with convenient non-stop service because they can electronically switch off the mainline at high speeds so that vehicles on the mainline always operate at high speed for express service.

The unique benefits of 2nd Generation Maglev go on and on.

The new 2nd generation Maglev technology will dominate 21st Century transport. America should be the leader in it!

The Maglev technology is here. Let's build it!

James Jordan is the managing co-author of The Fight for Maglev and can be reached at james.jordan@magneticglide.com

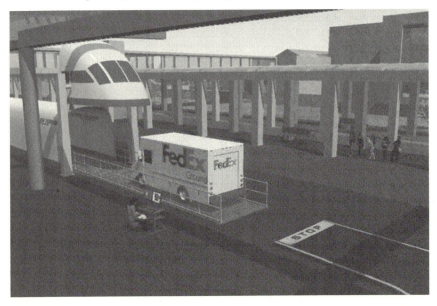

Foreword – How Much Time Has Humanity Got?

How much longer until World civilization collapses and Homo Sapiens species goes culturally, and possibly physically, extinct? We don't know – nobody knows. What we do know is that the present path that humanity is on – growing World population, dwindling resources, and continually increasing consumption of oil, coal and natural gas fossil fuels – is not sustainable much longer. Mark Twain said, "Everybody talks about the weather, but nobody does anything about it." Well, more talk about humanity's non-sustainable path would help. Instead, most people don't even think about what lies ahead and when it will happen. They only focus on the short term – getting and keeping a good job, making more money, buying stuff, family and friends, maintaining society's standards, security, helping the less fortunate, etc. Sadly, however, when evidence of looming global catastrophe caused by humanity's immense emissions of greenhouse gases is presented, people usually either ignore it, deny it, or follow Louis the Fourteenth's philosophy – "After me, the Deluge", and do nothing.

We humans are like a herd of lemmings running toward the cliff over which they will fall to their deaths. At least, lemmings have the excuse of small brain size – they can't understand the concept "cliff means death". Humans are much smarter than lemmings and don't have the excuse of small brains. We should let reason drive our actions for survival, not emotions.

To understand why our present path is leading humanity to the cliff of global catastrophe, how much longer we have before we reach it, and what actions are needed a.s.a.p. to avoid it, consider the following:

First, the evidence is conclusive that humanity's very large consumption of fossil fuels, starting in the 19th Century, has increased the carbon dioxide level in the atmosphere far faster than any natural process would. As any undergraduate chemical engineer knows, increasing the concentration of carbon dioxide in the atmosphere enclosing a hot radiating body increases its temperature by a predictable amount. True, analyzing how much the increased atmospheric carbon dioxide has increased the temperature of the Earth is more complex than analyzing a furnace, but climate models do a reasonably good job when benchmarked with temperature data for the last 100 years.

The effects of increased greenhouse gases in the atmosphere are already being felt – gone are much of the thick ice sheets in the Arctic Ocean, leaving open water; glaciers are rapidly disappearing all around the World; in the mountains, snow packs are melting fast, endangering the source of much of the World's water supply; droughts and crop failures occur more often as do severe storms and floods like the recent one (beginning in July 2010) in Pakistan; malaria, dengue fever, and other tropical diseases are spreading into the Temperate Zones, the activity of destructive bugs, bacteria, and plant plagues is increasing; ocean levels are rising, flooding low-lying coasts and islands; and on and on.

Scary as these effects are, humanity could survive them, though at a terrible price – hundreds of millions of people hungry and starving; conflicts and wars over water, arable land, and other resources; breakdown of social order; mass migrations away from flooding areas; widespread plagues, etc.

Much scarier still is what lies beyond the above effects of global warming presently projected. What are the unknown, or at least, not very well understood, effects that could lead to much greater global catastrophe? Two spring to mind – ocean acidification and the irreversible triggering of the release of tens of thousands of billions of tons of unstable deposits of greenhouse gases present in the World's oceans and permafrost regions.

First, ocean acidification. It is absolutely certain that the oceans are becoming more acidic due to the absorption of increased amounts of carbon dioxide from the atmosphere. Measurements show that over the last 150 years, the oceans have become 30 percent more acidic. It is also absolutely certain from experiments that protective shells of organisms, from microscopic cocolithophores to macroscopic mussels and oysters, will dissolve as fast as they form when the ocean becomes too acid. Much of the ocean food chain would then die and the World's oceans would become deserts, with most of its species extinct.

If humanity continues its massive consumption of fossil fuels, the oceans will die. There is no uncertainty about this. The only uncertainty is *when* it will occur. At the current rate of fossil fuel consumption, probably towards the end of this century. But nobody really knows. It could be much sooner if fossil fuel consumption per capita significantly increases. Gross Domestic Product (GDP) and the standard of living are proportional to the per capita energy consumption.

Right now, we are headed from the present 7 Billion World population to 9 Billion people by 2050 AD. As China, India and other countries industrialize at a GDP growth rate of 10% per year, their annual energy consumption is also rapidly growing. As an example of how energy consumption and our living standards are linked together, 300 million Americans consume 25 barrels of oil per person per year, 70% of which goes for transport. The average for the 6.7 Billion other people in the rest of the World is only 3.75 barrels of oil per person per year. U.S. transport emits 2 Billion tons of carbon dioxide per year, 8 percent of the World total.

As conventional oil production peaks and rapidly declines in the next 20 years, transport will shift to synfuels from coal, tar sands, and oil shale, unless new modes of transport like Maglev are adopted. Operating present types of autos, trucks, airplanes, trains and ships on synfuels will double the carbon dioxide emissions from transport.

If per capita World transport usage increased to one-half of present U.S. usage, and it is powered by synfuels, the carbon dioxide emissions from synfuels alone, leaving out electric power generation, industry, and residential consumption, would be 60 Billion tons per year, 2½ times greater than the present total World emissions from all sources.

At an annual emission of 60 Billion tons of carbon dioxide from World transport, the oceans would die not much later than 2050 AD. So, besides the uncertainties associated with the natural process of ocean acidification, we need to know how rapidly World CO_2 emissions from transport and other sources are likely to occur.

World leaders must stop making empty promises about reducing greenhouse gas emissions with cap & trade, carbon tax, voluntary reductions, whatever. We need real action, starting now!

In the area of ocean acidification, we need substantial field scale experiments, not laboratory scale, on actual marine ecosystems, deliberately making the ocean more acidic at selected and controlled locations by additional carbon dioxide in the water. Scientists then can observe what happens to the marine life, and how much of an increase in acidity will destroy the marine food chain. So far, to our knowledge, such field experiments have not been carried out. We need real data, not guesses, assertions, or denials. In Sergeant Friday's words, "Just the facts, ma'am."

Real facts are also needed about the second big unknown – will the rising global temperature in the oceans and the permafrost regions (where the temperature rise is much greater than the global average) trigger an irreversible runaway release of methane and carbon dioxide? There are 10,000 Billion tons of solid, but only marginally stable, methane hydrates in the World's oceans.

Methane is 20 times worse as a greenhouse gas than carbon dioxide. The methane in the methane hydrates will remain safely contained as long as ocean temperatures stay constant. If ocean temperatures rise significantly, the methane hydrates will decompose, releasing methane into the atmosphere that will further warm the ocean, releasing more methane, causing more warming, on and on until the Earth turns into a new Venus. In terms of global warming potential, the 10,000 Billion tons of methane hydrates is equivalent to 10,000 years of our present annual World carbon dioxide emissions.

At what global temperature and carbon dioxide level does the irreversible runaway release of methane occur? We don't know – nobody knows. What's more, there is virtually no analysis and experimentation on this question. In addition to field scale experiments on ocean acidification, we desperately need experiments on how much of an increase in ocean temperature, particularly in the methane hydrate deposits in the oceans at high latitudes, will trigger substantial releases of methane to the atmosphere. This can be done at selected controlled locations using heated water contained by thermal insulation sheets above major deposits of methane hydrates.

Finally, there is the last great unknown – the warming permafrost. As it warms, the frozen organic matter in it decomposes, releasing methane and carbon dioxide to the atmosphere. While there is less greenhouse gas release potential from the permafrost, as compared to the ocean methane hydrates, there is still an awful lot – well over 100 years' worth of equivalent annual World carbon dioxide emissions.

At what temperature level and when will that occur we don't know – nobody knows. However, it must be pretty soon, if it is not already happened, because the permafrost regions are warming very rapidly. As with the potential catastrophe of ocean acidification and methane hydrate decomposition, experimental data is needed to determine how rapidly methane and carbon dioxide will be released from the carbon deposits in permafrost soil as their temperature climbs. These experiments can be readily carried out by focusing reflected sunlight on the permafrost to increase its surface temperature, and measuring the response in greenhouse gas emissions. The experiments would be carried out over a period of several years at a wide variety of locations in the permafrost regions, so as to determine the long-term integrated response of Earth's permafrost. Such experiments may find that it is already too late to prevent an irreversible runaway of World temperatures.

A smart person doesn't wait until he or she is just about to go over the cliff before trying to develop a plan to not go over the cliff. Usually at that point, it's too late.

Humans should live up to their species name — homo sapiens, the wise ones, and not be homo saps, the stupid ones. Serious major R&D to develop and implement technologies that are technically and economically practical, and environmentally acceptable, to eliminate the large-scale use of fossil fuels must be undertaken as a high priority.

Some modest attempts are underway, but so far, all have problems that limit potential large-scale implications. Biofuels have been touted as the replacement for oil fueled transport, but the amount of arable land required is far too great to sustain our present World transport needs, let alone a future World with more people and greater industrialization. Already, hundreds of millions of people are hungry and malnourished. There is a moral choice – biofuels and starving people, or more food for the starving. Hydrogen fueled vehicles are also touted for future transport but they require enormous, impractically large amounts of electrical energy to manufacture the hydrogen. Moreover, the safety and security problems are insurmountable. Electric autos appear practical, but have very limited range and long recharge times – 40 miles for the Chevy Volt – and hours to recharge. The Volt can only make longer trips by switching to an on-board gasoline engine.

Electrical generation from wind and solar power sources is attractive, but they too have limitations. Their capital cost per kilowatt of generation capacity is very high – the usually quoted cost per peak kilowatt generated is deceptive, since the cost per average kilowatt generated is typically 3 to 4 times greater, reflecting the periods when the wind doesn't blow or the sun doesn't shine. Moreover, their power output varies widely with time, whether the wind is blowing or the sun is shining, and often does not match the power demand of the electrical grid.

So far, there are no large scale, cost effective ways to store the electric output from wind and solar plants, so as to meet the time varying demands of the electrical grid. Finally, surprisingly, there is a lot of opposition to wind and solar power sources from various groups, including environmental ones. Wind power turbines kill birds and have noise, visual intrusion, and land-use problems. Solar farms have the problems of large-scale land-use and visual intrusion.

For large-scale implementation of new technologies, it is not enough that they are environmentally better and necessary for long-term sustainability. People care about these benefits, but they focus more on how the new technologies will affect them in the short-term.

Will it cost more, be less convenient, take longer, and be less comfortable to get to work, shop, take trips, etc., than what I do now? Will I have to pay more for electric power and home heating? Will it reduce my wages? Cost me my job?

For the public to accept a new technology, it must economically benefit them and improve their quality of life. Otherwise, they will resist it. Costs twice as much to drive to work using non-fossil fuels as synfuels from coal? Forget it – virtually everyone will want the synfuels, even if it causes the oceans to die 20 years down the road.

Maglev has the unique capability to greatly reduce our future usage of fossil fuels for transport and energy, while at the same time saving the

The Fight for Maglev   Preface

public substantial amounts of money and providing a much better quality of life. That is why we fight for Maglev, the subject of this book.

Maglev will not only provide much faster, cheaper, more convenient and comfortable transport, while at the same time helping to prevent environmental catastrophe, but it will also benefit the World in many other ways.

Maglev can also store very large amounts of electrical energy at very low cost, making it practical for wind and solar power sources to efficiently match their highly variable power outputs to the time varying demands of the electrical grid. Maglev can also transport, at low cost, Billions of gallons of fresh, clean water daily over distances hundreds of miles, from water rich regions to drought areas, for growing crops and the personal needs of inhabitants.

Finally, Maglev launch-to-space will radically expand humanity's capabilities and experiences, by making the cost to go into space hundreds of times cheaper than using chemical rockets. Maglev launch will enable beaming of vast amounts of clean, very low cost electrical power to Earth from solar power satellites, large colonies on the Moon and Mars, human exploration of the entire Solar system, detailed imaging of extraterrestrial planets and their civilizations, space manufacturing and tourism, and a robust, practical defense of the Earth against asteroid and comet threats.

The major inventions in human history: fire, agriculture, animal domestication, ceramics, textiles, the wheel, the steam and internal combustion engines, airplanes, rockets, nuclear energy, electricity, telecommunications and computers, have all ushered in advances that make the World a better place and to improve our lives and the lives of others. Maglev is the next step in this continuing journey.

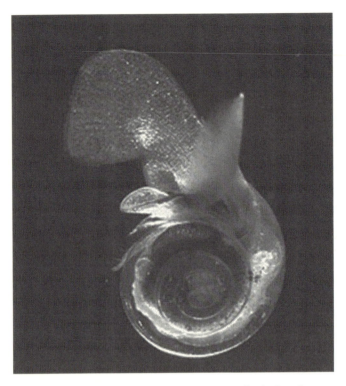

A free-swimming pteropod, _Limacina helicina_, a mollusk that forms a calcium carbonate shell made of aragonite. They are an important food source for juvenile North Pacific salmon and also are eaten by mackerel, herring, and cod. Photo courtesy NOAA

Rising levels of carbon dioxide results in a substantial increase in the release of hydrogen ions, which lowers oceanic pH levels. The release of hydrogen ions in the water combine with any carbonate ions in the water to form bicarbonate, thus removing substantial amounts of carbonate ions from solution. The saturation of seawater with carbonate ions is extremely important for marine species that construct their shells or skeletons with calcium carbonate in a process known as calcification. These species include most corals, mollusks, echinoderms, foraminifera, and calcareous algae. Not being able to form shells threatens the species and the food chain that is critical to other species.

Prologue – Why Maglev is Inevitable

"Make no little plans. They have no magic to stir men's blood and probably will not themselves be realized"

Daniel Burnham, architect of the 1892 World's Fair Exposition in Chicago, the Flatiron Building (NY City) and Union Station (Washington, DC)

We have written this book for two important reasons:

1. Greenhouse gases from oil fueled autos, trucks, airplanes, trains, and ships are already a major cause of global warming. Their emissions will increase dramatically in the decades ahead as the developing countries, particularly China and India, industrialize and their transport demand grows. Conventional oil based fuels will soon be much scarcer and more expensive, precipitating a massive shift to synthetic fuels derived from coal, tar sands, oil shale, methane hydrates, etc. This shift will double the greenhouse gas emissions from transport. There is no way to capture and sequester carbon dioxide from autos, trucks, airplanes, trains, and ships. The only way to avoid environmental disaster from global warming is to transition to electric transport – electric cars and trucks for local trips and Maglev for longer distance travel. Public understanding of this critical issue is vital. Unless World leaders begin to really act to meet the crisis, rather than just making speeches, we face catastrophe.

2. For 200 years, America led the World in major transportation breakthroughs, from the Erie Canal to the Transcontinental Railroad to airplanes, Henry Ford and the Model T, Eisenhower's Interstate Highway System, and Kennedy's space program and the Moon Landing. No more. America is now a follower in transportation, not the leader. Detroit is a disaster area. Our government wants to buy High Speed Rail trains from Europe and Asia. Our lead in aircraft technology is eroding. Millions of U.S. manufacturing jobs have gone to overseas competitors, and U.S. workers' real incomes have stagnated for decades.

Superconducting Maglev, the first new transport system since the airplane, will be dominant in 21st Century transport. Invented in America in the 1960's, it has been ignored by the U.S. Government, leaving the development of 1st generation Maglev passenger systems to Japan, Germany, and China. We tell the story of how the U.S. let other countries take the lead in Maglev, losing the opportunity for millions of new U.S. jobs, many Billions of dollars in exports of high tech equipment and greatly reduced dependence on oil. This failure to lead the World in Maglev has been a colossal mistake for America.

We further describe how a much more capable 2nd generation Maglev system has now been invented in America, and why it will revolutionize World transport. America has a second chance to regain the lead in Maglev, with its enormous environmental, energy, and economic benefits, millions of new U.S. jobs, and many Billions of dollars in exports. Will the U.S. take this second chance and lead the World in transport once again, or will it toss it away? That is the 64 Trillion dollar question. In the past our leaders – Lincoln, Roosevelt, Eisenhower, and Kennedy – pioneered new transport systems. Not anymore. Americans must demand that once again the U.S. lead the World in transportation, and not spinelessly let other nations reap the benefits in jobs and a better standard of living.

What is Maglev and why is it important? Maglev 2000 vehicles (the name we have given to our 2nd generation superconducting Maglev system) are magnetically levitated and propelled several inches above a guideway, without mechanical contact or friction, their speed limited only by air drag. They do not have engines, do not burn oil, and emit no pollutants and greenhouse gases. They are very safe, energy efficient, quiet, and comfortable.

Maglev 2000 vehicles can carry passengers, personal autos, heavy highway trucks, and freight at much higher speeds and lower cost than by highways, airways, or steel wheel-on-rail trains. When the proposed 29,000 mile National Maglev Network is built, 80% of the U.S. population, over 230 million people, will live within 15 miles of a Maglev station. From there they can reach any other station in America in a few hours at a speed of 300 mph. The Maglev routes between America's cities will operate on the rights-of-way alongside our Interstate Highways. Upon reaching the metropolitan urban/suburban areas,

Maglev 2000 vehicles will travel along existing railroad tracks that have been adapted for Maglev service. The adaptation is simple, quick, and low in cost, by attaching thin panels that contain ordinary aluminum loops to the RR crossties. Conventional trains can still use the tracks, with appropriate scheduling. The Maglev 2000 vehicles would not operate at 300 mph in urban/suburban areas, but at lower speeds suitable to the surroundings.

In America, over 40,000 people die every year in highway accidents – equivalent to a jet airliner crash daily – and hundreds of thousands more are seriously injured. World-wide, over a million people are killed annually by traffic accidents, with many millions more seriously injured. Once implemented, Maglev will save millions of people annually from death and serious injuries on the highways. Moreover, Maglev will also greatly reduce the damage to people's health from the pollutants and microparticulates presently emitted from the autos and trucks on our highways. The American Lung Association has stated that people living in areas with heavy highway traffic die on average 2 years earlier than they should.

Maglev also offers the opportunity for a major new American manufacturing industry with millions of well-paid jobs and annual exports of many billions of dollars, helping to raise our living standards and reduce the large U.S. trade deficit.

While all of these benefits are extremely important, the one thing that will make Maglev absolutely inevitable is the global warming crisis and the need to stop using fossil fuels. Without fossil fuels, human society would still be at the horse and wagon stage, with people and goods traveling at a few mph over short distances. In 1800, the annual GDP per capita for Americans was only 1,200 dollars (in constant 2007 dollars) and the annual per capita travel distance was just 1,500 miles. Today, the per capita GDP is 50,000 dollars (in constant 2007 dollars) and the per capita travel distance 15,000 miles. (1)

What happened? Fossil fuels for transport. Starting in the early 1800's, coal fired steam engines powered steamboats and railroads, followed in the early 1900's by oil powered autos, trucks, trains, airplanes, and ships. Today, our transport is completely dependent on oil. Since Edwin Drake started producing petroleum in Western Pennsylvania in 1859, the World has consumed approximately 1 Trillion barrels of oil, most of it for transport.

It's hard to comprehend how much a Trillion barrels of oil is. Try visualizing a lake of oil 1 mile square in cross section – that is, a square one mile on a side – that contains a Trillion barrels of oil. The oil lake would be 40 miles deep. Roughly, there is another Trillion barrels of oil still in the ground. When extracted it would make the oil lake 80 miles deep. That's a lot of oil.

In theory, the oil still underground could sustain the World for another 33 years at the current rate of production of 30 Billion barrels per year. In practice, though, production has already plateaued and will steadily decline over the coming decades, so the end of conventional oil will stretch out well beyond 33 years. There has been a lot of argument about when "peak oil" will occur. More significant is the increasing competition from developing countries like China and India for ever scarcer oil, which will drive up its price. Today (April, 2011), it is around 109 dollars per barrel; in a few years, analysts predict 200 dollars per barrel.

Which road will transport take in the coming decades of the 21st century, as conventional oil becomes much scarcer and more expensive? How can we maintain present living standards in developed countries, and also raise them in the poverty stricken areas of the World?

The accompanying decision tree illustrates our choices. If we continue with internal combustion engines, our autos, trucks, airplanes, ships, and most trains must shift to alternative fuels as the conventional oil dribbles away. What are the options?

The Decision Tree for Future Transport

A few years ago, there was much enthusiasm for ethanol produced from corn. However, most now realize that ethanol fuel is an impractical dream.

A gallon of ethanol has only 2/3 the combustion energy of a gallon of gasoline or diesel fuel.(2) Worse yet, by the time one deducts the fuel energy needed to plant, grow, and harvest the corn feed for ethanol production, and the energy needed to process the corn into ethanol, the net energy from a gallon of ethanol is only 1/4 that of a gallon of gasoline or diesel, based on U.S. Department of Agriculture analyses.(2)

The per capita consumption of gasoline and diesel fuels by Americans is 600 gallons per year. To match this, each American would need 2400 gallons of ethanol annually. However, an acre of corn cropland yields only 360 gallons of ethanol, based on 150 bushels of corn per acre and 2.4 gallons of ethanol yield per bushel so that each American would require 7 acres of farmland to grow corn to make the ethanol he or she needed. Today America has 300 million acres of farmland, 1 acre for every man, woman, and child in the country. If we didn't eat and used ethanol for transport we could drive, fly, and move goods 1/7 as much as we do today. The entire land area in the 48 continental states, 2 Billion acres with much of it mountains and deserts, is not enough to grow the ethanol we would need for transport. Some advocate obtaining ethanol from cellulosic materials – switchgrass, cornstalks, etc. – but the production is still much too small. Per capita, Americans consume on average 2,000 calories per day of food, and burn 50,000 calories of fuel daily in their autos and trucks. It is just not possible to grow enough plant materials to fuel America's transport needs. Rest in Peace, ethanol.

Hydrogen fuel is an even more of a fantasy than ethanol. It would take 1,000 new nuclear reactors, each of 1,000 megawatts(e) capacity – ten times the number of reactors America now operates – to make enough hydrogen fuel to equal the gasoline and diesel fuel we currently burn in our autos and trucks. A couple of years ago, there was a lot of talk about the "Hydrogen Highway" being promoted in California. There are over 200,000 gasoline fueling stations in America. Imagine over 200,000 hydrogen filling stations holding massive amounts of highly explosive hydrogen that likes to leak into the atmosphere, ready to explode from a tiny spark. Visualize filling up your car's hydrogen tank, hoping that there's not a leak in the hose attachment, or left over hydrogen, like when you used to fill up with gasoline. Imagine 70 mph bumper to bumper traffic, with each car carrying hydrogen tanks that hold the explosive equivalent of 500 pounds of TNT. The hydrogen in the tanks would either be a very high pressure (5,000 psi) gas or in liquid form at 420 degrees Fahrenheit below zero. Either way, it is not easy to keep the hydrogen inside its tank, especially in a crash.

Even worse, imagine having a terrorist or deranged person steal or carjack a hydrogen car – over 1 million autos are stolen in the U.S. every year – attach a small bomb to the hydrogen tank, and park it in a garage underneath a building, or in a shopping mall lot, or on a busy city street. The bomb could then be detonated remotely by a cellphone call, or by an attached timer causing your hydrogen tank to explode. Result? Many deaths with virtually no way to prevent such attacks. A perpetrator could carry out several attacks a day – no special skills required. The small bombs that set off the hydrogen explosions could even be bought in the black market. Fortunately, the initial enthusiasm for hydrogen fuelled cars appears to have greatly abated. Rest In Peace, hydrogen fuel.

What's left for the Internal Combustion Engine? Synfuels! Synfuels – synthetic gasoline and diesel fuel made from coal, tar sands, oil shale, and natural gas (i.e., methane) – are practical. While more expensive than today's oil, they are affordable for transport. Germany used synfuels during World War II, and South Africa's Sasol plant has produced synthetic gasoline from coal for many years. Canada produces 2 million barrels daily from its immense deposits of tar sands in Alberta and British Columbia. Methane, i.e. natural gas, can be readily converted to gasoline and diesel fuel. There are immense amounts of methane locked up in shale and frozen methane hydrates in ocean beds.

The above deposits could provide all the synfuels the World requires for many hundreds of years. The oceanic methane hydrates hold 10 Trillion tons of methane. Converted to synfuels, they could by themselves supply the World for thousands of years.

The problem with synfuels is not sustainability of supply, but sustainability of the environment. Currently, American's transport systems emit over 2 Billion tons per year of carbon dioxide from their tailpipes, 1/3 of total U.S. emissions.(3) While it may prove practical to capture carbon dioxide emissions from power plants and other industrial processes, and sequester it safely underground, it is not practical to capture carbon dioxide emissions from tailpipes.

Roughly, the total carbon dioxide emissions from synfuels are double these from conventional oil, when the carbon dioxide from the synfuels production process, is included. Using synfuels would increase U.S. carbon dioxide emissions from transport to 4 Billion Tons annually. As China, India, and other nations continue to develop, their transport emissions will increase. America's population is 300 million persons, compared to 6.3 Billion in the rest of the World. By 2050 A.D., total World population is projected to grow to 9 Billion persons. Using synfuels, if the World per capita average carbon dioxide transport emissions at that time were only one-half of today's per capita U.S. emissions, total World transport emissions would be 60 Billion tons of carbon dioxide per year, 2.5 times greater than today's total of 25 Billion tons.

World leaders call for a reduction in carbon dioxide emissions of 80% from today's level by 2050. With such a reduction, world total carbon dioxide emissions would be only 5 Billion tons annually. There is a big gap between 60 Billion tons and 5 Billion Tons. There is no way to achieve major reductions in carbon dioxide emissions, if we continue to use internal combustion engines for transport. In fact, future world carbon dioxide emissions from transport alone will be considerably greater than today's total amount, even if carbon dioxide emissions from power plants and industrial processes were cut to zero.

What are the consequences to the World if we continue to emit tens of Billions of tons of carbon dioxide annually to the atmosphere? Extremely bad. Most attention has been focused on the efforts on climate, i.e., higher temperatures, melting glaciers and ice sheets, increased droughts and food shortages, rising sea levels and flooding, species shifts and extinctions, spread of tropical diseases, etc.

Bad as these are, there are even worse effects ahead. The ocean is becoming more acidic due to its absorption of carbon dioxide from the atmosphere. Experiments(4) have shown that when the ocean reaches a certain level of acidity, calcium carbonate shells dissolve as fast as they can form, effectively killing much of the marine food chain, from microscopic plankton to large organisms. At the current rate of acidification, projections indicate that this "no-shell" point will be reached in the 2070 to 2100 time frame, with the result that there will be mass extinction of much of the ocean life.

Besides ocean acidification, there looms the "climate tipping point", in which global warming reaches a runaway condition. The increasing temperature causes methane to be released from marginally stable methane hydrates in the ocean and from organic material in permafrost areas in Canada, Siberia, and other regions. Per molecule, methane has 20 times as much global warming effect as carbon dioxide, and there are vast amounts of methane stored in methane hydrates and frozen organic matter. Methane "boils" have been observed in the Arctic ocean (5) from decomposing methane hydrates, as well as methane emissions in permafrost areas.(6) Once the runaway "tipping point" is reached, the warming process will automatically proceed, even if all man-made carbon dioxide emissions suddenly ceased. When this tipping point will be reached is not certain, but it will occur if we continue to emit large amounts of carbon dioxide. It may already have been reached, but we haven't yet realized it.

In conclusion, America cannot indefinitely sustain its present transport systems that depend on internal combustion engines. It must transition to electric transport systems that do not emit carbon dioxide as soon as possible, and not wait until it's too late.

There are 3 possible electric transport systems – electric cars, electric rail, and Maglev. Electric cars are desirable and practical, but have their limitations. The Chevy Volt, for example, which was introduced at dealers in 2011, has a maximum range of 40 miles before it must be recharged or switch to a back-up gasoline engine that extends its range.(7) Longer trips almost certainly will use the gasoline engine, because no one will want to stop every 40 miles or so and wait several hours for a recharge.

Electric cars have other constraints as well, particularly in colder regions. Batteries should not be charged or discharged when they are cold, as this may degrade them. Providing electric energy from the battery pack to heat the car in cold weather will reduce the car's range. In hot weather, using the battery to power air conditioning will also reduce range.

Electric cars will be practical for short trips. For long trips, it appears practical and desirable to have them carried on high speed Maglev 2000 vehicles, together with their passengers. Visualize a traveler driving his electric car a few miles to the nearest Maglev 2000 station, driving onto a Maglev vehicle, and then settling down in a passenger cabin while the Maglev 2000 vehicle takes the car and them to the Maglev station near the final destination. There, the drivers and their passengers get back into their cars and drive off to their destinations. During the trip on the Maglev 2000 vehicle, their electric car would be recharged, using on-board electric power.

Maglev 2000 would provide the same kind of service for long distance highway trucks. Such trucks, because of their high energy requirements per mile of travel, and their long travel distances – average haul distance for intercity highway trucks is approximately 500 miles – cannot be electrically powered, except for short distances.

With the National Maglev Network, almost all travel could be electrically powered, with Maglev 2000 providing long distance capability for passengers, autos, and trucks, while electrically powered autos and trucks handled short local trips. There would be little domestic air travel, with most flights being across the oceans and to remote areas not served by Maglev 2000.

The Decision Tree diagram shows only a very small role for electrically powered High Speed Rail (HSR). Electrically powered conventional rail will still play a role in the transport of bulk freight, etc., grain, cement, etc., but HSR's role will be virtually zero. This is because HSR only carries passengers, is inherently very expensive, and must be heavily subsidized by government.

Even in countries that possess excellent HSR systems, like France and Japan, the per capita travel on HSR is small compared to other transport modes. For example, in France, per capita, the French travel on HSR 400 miles annually and drive 7,600 miles. In Japan, per capita, they travel 400 miles on HSR and drive 4,000 miles.(1)

In America, per capita, we travel more than 10,000 miles per year by automobile, 2,750 miles by air, and 18 miles per year by Amtrak.(8) Building HSR in the U.S. would increase rail travel. However, because America is much bigger than countries like France and Japan and has much lower population densities (80 per square mile in the U.S. 871 in Japan, and 288 in France).(9) HSR travel in America would be considerably smaller than the 400 miles per year in France and Japan. Probably less than 100 miles per capita per year.

In contrast, Maglev 2000 can provide essentially all long distance travel in the U.S. for passengers, autos, trucks, and containerized high value freight, without oil and greenhouse gas emissions, at higher speeds and lower cost than existing transport systems, while saving many thousands of lives and serious injuries annually.

It is very difficult to understand why America fails to aggressively implement Maglev in view of its many benefits. Maglev is not a futuristic fantasy. Japan and Germany have both developed operating 1st generation passenger Maglev systems that have carried many thousands of passengers and total run distances of hundreds of thousands of miles. The Japanese superconducting Maglev system, now operating in Yamanashi, Japan is based on the 1966 inventions of Powell and Danby,(10) which are described later. Japan plans to extend their present system to become a 300 mile, 300 mph Maglev route between Tokyo and Osaka, which will carry 100,000 passengers daily. (11)

The principal factors holding back implementation of the 1st generation Maglev systems in America is their high construction cost, on the order of 60 million dollars per two way mile, their limitation to passenger only transport, and their incompatibility with existing rail.

Realizing this, Powell and Danby have improved their original 1966 inventions to incorporate important capabilities including:

- Much lower construction cost for the Maglev guideway
- Ability to carry high revenue highway trucks, personal autos, and freight, in addition to passengers
- Capability for levitated travel along existing railroad tracks, which have been adapted for Maglev at very low cost
- Ability to electronically switch at high speed off of the main line to off-line stations for unloading/loading operations
- Ability to be privately financed without government subsidies for construction and operation
- Ability to use the new high temperature superconductors

The new 2nd generation Maglev 2000 system does not require technology breakthroughs. The technology required already exists and is commercially available. The only requirement is to assemble operating vehicles for test and certification at a government funded facility.

For over 10 years, the authors have been fighting to have Maglev developed and implemented in America. In 1989-90 they served as co-chairmen of Senator Daniel Patrick Moynihan's Maglev Task Force preparing a detailed study of Maglev's capabilities and benefits for the United States.(12) The Senate passed a 750 million dollar R&D program to develop an American Maglev system. Had it not been killed in the House of Representatives, by lobbying from vested transportation interests, the U.S. would have saved many thousands of lives and prevented hundreds of thousands of serious injuries, greatly reduced oil imports, prevented Billions of tons of greenhouse gases from entering the atmosphere, created a major manufacturing industry in America with millions of new jobs and Billions of dollars' worth of exports, significantly reducing our trade deficit.

Our fight for Maglev still goes on. We are dedicated to fulfilling Senator Moynihan's vision of a U.S. National Maglev Network built on the rights-of-way alongside America's Interstate Highways, with U.S. developed and manufactured Maglev 2000 vehicles operating on the Network.

In the book we describe how America lost the first and second rounds in the Fight for Maglev. However, the fight, now in the 3rd and decisive round, is not over. America can still win the fight, if it acts decisively and quickly. If it does not, another country will become the World Leader in Maglev, and win the prize of millions of new jobs, and sell their Maglev systems to the other countries in the World, including the United States. That would be a sad ending to our long fight.

Chapter One

America–Once the World Leader in Transport

"Dodge, what's the best route for a Pacific Railroad to the West?"

Abraham Lincoln's first words on his first meeting with Granville Dodge, Chief engineer of the Union Pacific, in 1859

Starting in the early 1800's through the Moon Landing in 1969, America led the World in new transport technology. The breakthroughs described here radically transformed transport and dramatically raised living standards. With the Erie Canal we went from horse and wagon across rough terrain to smooth easy boat travel from the Northeast to the Midwest. Steamboats made long distance, rapid movement of goods on America's rivers possible. Cotton and other agriculture products to the North on the Mississippi, manufactures to the South in return.

East Coast to the West Coast via the Transcontinental Railroad took only days rather than months by wagon. Sailing from the Atlantic to the Pacific through the Panama Canal, avoided Cape Horn and 14,000 miles of rough ocean travel. Autos and airplanes – a whole new world of low cost, highly mobile transport for Americans and their goods, using the Interstate Highway System and our airways. Then the Moon Landing and access to space, with its scientific wonders, enhanced communications, improved weather prediction, environmental monitoring, GPS, Google Earth, etc.

Since then, however, America has become a follower in transportation, not a leader. Other countries innovate new transport technologies and reap the benefits. Our leaders plan to buy high speed trains from abroad, increasing our trade deficit and ceding the well-paid jobs to others, not Americans. Manufacturing is declining in the United States, but particularly in transport. Detroit is a disaster area.

Even worse, our existing transport systems – autos, trucks, airplanes, most trains, and ships, cannot function without oil. As more countries like China and India industrialize and vigorously compete for the shrinking world oil production, America's share will drastically decrease.

America desperately needs new transport technologies that will be sustainable in the decades ahead, that do not need oil, are non-polluting, emit no greenhouse gases, and are energy efficient, low in cost, quiet, and move people and goods quickly and safely. Maglev, the first new mode of transport since the airplane, meets these goals and will be a major mode of transport in the 21st Century. Maglev is inevitable.

America's first two revolutions in transportation were the Erie Canal and Robert Fulton's invention of the steamboat. Both changed our nation's life, making transport much cheaper, faster, and easier. Goodbye, horse and wagon. Hello, connecting New England to the Midwest by mule-drawn-barge through the Erie Canal, and the North to the South by steamboats, along the Ohio and Mississippi Rivers.

The Erie Canal was hand dug, 363 miles long, 40 feet wide, and 4 feet deep.(1) Eleven million cubic yards of digging, almost twice as much excavated volume as the "Chunnel" between England and France. Dug in 8 years, that's 4,000 cubic yards per day. No steam shovels or Caterpillar tractors, just men with shovels, and teams of mules to haul the dirt and rock away. Over 1,000 men died of swamp fever at Montezuma Marsh near Syracuse. It was an incredible feat for the times and a triumph for Governor Clinton, who fought against strong opponents to the project, including Thomas Jefferson.

View of Erie Canal by John William Hill, 1829. Watercolor on paper, 9 3/4 x 11 3/4 inches

Robert Fulton's "Clermont"

First Trip, New York City to Albany, August 17, 1807 followed by the "New Orleans" in 1811 from Pittsburgh to New Orleans (2)

Robert Fulton's invention of the steamboat, called "Fulton's Folly" by scoffers, transformed American commerce and passenger travel, starting from the "Clermont's" first trip from New York City to Albany in 1807, followed by the first trip down the Mississippi on the "New Orleans" in 1811. In 1816, (2) only 5 years later, Mississippi steamboats carried 376,000 tons of cargo. Mark Twain's "Life on the Mississippi" tells the wonderful story of how steamboats became the lifeblood of transport for the people that lived along the Mississippi.

Two of the greatest American Presidents, Abraham Lincoln and Theodore Roosevelt, made possible two of America's greatest transport triumphs, the Transcontinental Railroad and the Panama Canal. Before the Transcontinental Railroad was completed, it took months to cross the continent by wagon train; after May 10, 1869, it took only 7 days. By 1876, the fast Transcontinental Express took just 3 ½ days to travel from New York City to San Francisco at an average speed of 35 mph.(3) Today, Amtrak makes the same trip in the same time, 84 hours, at the same average speed.(4)

Abraham Lincoln made the Transcontinental Railroad happen. Stephen Ambrose's book, "Nothing Like It in the World", shows a painting of the first conversation between Lincoln and Grenville Dodge in 1859. Lincoln was a railroad lawyer running for President; Dodge was the chief engineer of the Union Pacific, the Eastern part of the railroad. Lincoln's first words were, "Dodge, what's the best route for a Pacific railroad to the West?" Throughout Lincoln's career he continually pushed for the Transcontinental Railroad; as President, he signed the 1862 Pacific Railroad Act that led to the Railroad's construction. He also decreed that the gauge of the railroad track – the distance between the rails – was to be 4 feet 8 inches, making obsolete all other track gauges operating in the United States.

Before the Panama Canal, ships sailing between New York City to San Francisco had to travel around Cape Horn, a dangerous journey of 14,000 miles. After the Panama Canal was built, the much safer journey took only 6,000 miles. The French began the Panama Canal in 1880, but gave up after 22,000 workers died. President Theodore Roosevelt, shown in the picture at the controls of a 95 ton Bucyrus steam shovel,(5) pushed hard for the Canal and restarted the work in 1904. The Canal opened for business in 1914, and became indispensable for ship traffic between the Atlantic and Pacific.

The Panama Canal

From Atlantic to Pacific, Completed August 15, 1914 (4)

Henry Ford's Model T (6) made automobile travel practical for millions of Americans, allowing them to travel almost anywhere at 45 mph – over 500 miles in just one day! You didn't have to be rich – a Model T cost only 200 dollars ($3,200 in today's dollars) and ran on gasoline, kerosene, or ethanol, though Prohibition dried up most of the ethanol. Model T production started in 1908. By 1918, the U.S. had 6 million autos, half of which were Model Ts. By the time the 10 millionth Model T was produced, 10% of all the cars in the World were Fords. Even the Volkswagen Beetle never came close to the impact of the Model T. Even today, there still are members of Model T clubs around the World who drive Model Ts.

The Wright Brothers invention of the airplane equally transformed transport. In the years, before their historic flight at Kitty Hawk (10) on December 17, 1903, many had attempted powered human flight, but none had succeeded. Why the Wright Brothers were the first to fly was a

combination of unique factors. First, they invented ways to control aerodynamic stability by wing warping, exploiting both a movable rudder and a forward elevator. Second, they measured in a small wind tunnel the aerodynamic forces – lift & drag – on wings and the aircraft body. Third, they had the extensive skills with mechanical devices – printing presses, bicycles, motors, etc. – in their machine shop, needed to build and test a practical engine for the flyer.

Amazing progress on airplanes quickly followed. In 1911, only 8 years later, the first transcontinental flight from New York City to Long Beach, California by Cal Rodgers in the "Vin Fizz", advertising America's new grape soft drink. In 1914-1918, the World War I Aces – Baron Von Richtholen, Eddie Rickenbacker, Billy Mitchell, became household names. In 1921, General Billy Mitchell sank the Ostfriesland in a bombing demonstration from the air. On December 17, 1935, the 32nd anniversary of Kitty Hawk, the DC-3 first flew, making air passenger travel practical. After World War II, jetliners, made it possible to quickly travel anywhere in the World at low cost. America has been the leader in modern air transportation.

It is difficult to imagine America without its 46,870 mile Interstate Highway System. We went from a bunch of local roads, not connected together, to an efficient high speed National Network that connects cities thousands of miles apart. The longest East-West Interstate, Interstate-I-90, runs 3,020 miles from Boston to Seattle, the longest North-South, Interstate I-95, runs 1,920 miles from the Canadian Border to Miami. About 1/3 of vehicle trips in the U.S. use the Interstate Highways. The most traveled Interstate is I-405 in Los Angeles, which carries 390,000 vehicles daily. (8)

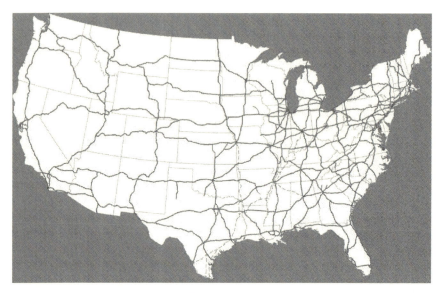

President Eisenhower personally knew why America needed a National Highway System. In 1919, he crossed the U.S. in an army convoy on the Lincoln Highway, experiencing delays, road problems, and generally low speeds on the highly variable road conditions. Then, as Supreme Commander of the Allied Forces in Europe in World War II, he saw firsthand the very fast, very efficient German Autobahn network. After he became President, he created the smooth, fast, and efficient National Interstate Highway System that has increased America's productivity and standard of living. The 46,870 mile system has cost 425 Billion dollars (in 2006 Dollars), an average of about 10 million dollars per mile. (9)

On April 12, 1961, the Soviet Union's cosmonaut, Yuri Gagarin, became the first human to orbit the Earth. On May 25th, 1961, President Kennedy announced the start of the Apollo program in a special address to Congress, saying "I believe that this Nation should commit itself to achieving the goal, before this decade is out, of landing a man on the Moon and returning him safely to the Earth." No hesitancy, no bargaining with Congress, no appointing a Special Commission – just a bold decision.

Apollo was a tremendous challenge, with enormous engineering problems. At its peak, Apollo employed 400,000 persons, and was supported by 20,000 industrial firms and universities. Eight years later, on July 20, 1969, Neil Armstrong walked on the Moon. (10) In February, 2010, NASA's Constellation program for a return to the Moon was cancelled – space exploration was no longer a priority.

Much of the Transcontinental Railroad track was laid by Chinese immigrant laborers, hired away from jobs in California and imported from China. They laid track for the Central Pacific portion of the Transcontinental RR from Sacramento to Promontory Summit in Utah, where it joined the Union Pacific line from the East. The Golden Spike at the joining of the East to the West was driven on May 10, 1869, marking the Railroad's completion.

The track and the trains that rode it were manufactured in America by American workers. That was then. Today, under the government's plan to build 13 High Speed Rail Corridors in the U.S., American workers will lay the track, and buy the High Speed Trains and associated controls, power equipment, etc., from abroad. The high tech, high paying, manufacturing jobs will stay overseas. Foreign suppliers from Europe and Japan will sell us their trains. China may also soon supply high speed trains to the U.S., an ironic twist from the 1860s.

Besides not creating jobs for Americans, and significantly increasing our trade deficit, building High Speed Rail systems in the U.S. would be a terrible mistake, as discussed later. High Speed Rail Systems would only meet a tiny fraction of our transport needs, and would require massive government subsidization to construct and operate.

Railroads and especially the Transcontinental Railroad were the first step in unifying our country and making it possible to act as a great nation. The railroads in turn were followed by automobiles and airplanes, which have further unified our country, making it more prosperous, more able to meet challenges, and more secure. It is time for the next step, a National Maglev Network that will move people and goods very efficiently at high speeds and low cost, without damaging the environment.

The Fight for Maglev   Once the World Leader in Transport

Fifty years ago, America was the Hub of World manufacturing. Steel and auto plants were the Masters of the Universe. On the Monongahela River banks leading into Pittsburgh, there were a dozen steel plants employing 50,000 workers. When I (James Powell) was growing up in Bradford Woods, Pennsylvania, in my night walks I saw the sky light up from the Bessemer furnaces in my Father's J&L Steel plant in Aliquippa, 15 miles away. My Father climbed the ladder from laborer in the Jones and Laughlin Tin Mill there to become the works manager for the whole J&L plant in Aliquippa. From there he became the plant works manager for the larger J&L Homestead Plant in Pittsburgh, and then on to be the works manager for J&L's biggest plant in Cleveland, Ohio, where he died in 1964.

At the Cleveland Plant, he managed 30,000 workers – all gone now. It was there I witnessed the beginning of the end for most of the American steel industry. I dropped by the plant one day in 1959 and walked into his office. I asked the secretary, "Where's Dad?" She answered – "He's in Building so and so, leading a tour". When I got there, Dad was talking to a group of 50 Japanese, who had rolls of blue prints under their arms and snapping photos of everything in sight. I pulled Dad aside and asked, "What are they doing here?" He answered, "J&L management has sold them all of the technology details on how to make steel, for 5 million dollars", I replied, "Are they crazy? Doesn't J&L know that Japan will be selling steel cheaper than we can make it in 4 or 5 years?" He then said, which will stay with me forever, "You know that, and I know that, and they know that. But they're capitalists, and they will take a dollar to hang themselves tomorrow, because today's more important".

While the American auto industry is still a bit better off than the steel industry, the same process is at work with them: outsourcing jobs, buying parts from foreign suppliers, selling technology, building production plants and R&D centers abroad, and so on. Unless this process stops, eventually there will be virtually no manufacturing in America.

44 years ago in 1966, Powell and Danby invented Superconducting Maglev (11), the first new mode of transport since the airplane. Maglev vehicles are magnetically levitated and propelled above a guideway without mechanical contact or friction, their speed limited only by air drag. In air, Maglev vehicles can travel at 300 mph. In air evacuated tunnels, there is no limit to their speed. As we describe later, Maglev

vehicles can even reach orbital speeds of 18,000 mph, and launch payloads into space at only 1/100th the cost of rocket launch. Maglev transport is very energy efficient, does not burn oil, emits no greenhouse gases, and is much lower in cost than existing transport systems.

Maglev is not a futuristic fantasy. 1st generation Maglev passenger systems are already operating in Japan, China, and Germany. The Japanese Maglev system – the photo shows a Japan Railways Maglev vehicle operating on the JR demonstration route in Yamanashi Prefecture, North of Mt. Fuji – holds the World record speed of 361 mph for surface transportation. The JR Yamanashi Maglev system has carried well over 80,000 passengers safely and reliably with accumulated running distances of hundreds of thousands of miles. JR plans to extend the Yamanashi Maglev system to become a 300 mile route between Tokyo and Osaka, which will carry 100,000 passengers daily with a travel time of 1 hour. (12) 60% of the route will be in deep underground tunnels.

Japan's 1st generation Maglev system is based on the original 1966 Maglev inventions of Powell and Danby. Following the publication of their inventions, groups of engineers and transport planners from Japan, Germany, and other countries visited Powell and Danby, who freely supplied details of their work to the visitors. Japan started a major development program on the Powell-Danby superconducting Maglev system, which they chose because of its large clearance of 4 inches or more between the Maglev vehicles and the guideway, and its very strong inherent and automatic stability – very important factors in Japan, a country subject to strong earthquakes.

Germany also started a major Maglev development program, but chose to follow a different Maglev path, based on using conventional electromagnets rather than superconducting ones in their 1st generation Transrapid Maglev system. The gap between the Transrapid vehicles and the guideway is much smaller than that using superconducting magnets, e.g., 3/8 inch vs 4 inches, and their magnetic suspension is inherently unstable, not inherently stable, in contrast to superconducting Maglev. The instability is overcome by fast servo control of the current in the electromagnet windings.(19) A commercial Transrapid passenger Maglev system is now operating in China, between the outskirts of Shanghai and its Pudong Airport.

As described in the later chapters, since 1966 we have continued to fight for having America become the World leader in Maglev, but without success. There were a couple of small U.S. Maglev programs that started in the late 1960's, but they closed down in the early 1970's when the U.S. Secretary of Transportation, John Volpe, decided that autos, trucks, and airplanes would meet U.S. transport needs indefinitely.

While the big Japanese and German Maglev development programs went on, we continued to try to start a major U.S. program for Maglev. In the late 1980's, Senator Moynihan became a champion of Maglev for America, and asked us to be the co-chairmen of his Maglev Task Force to provide data and reports on Maglev technology and operation.(13) His vision – which has become our vision also – was to have a National Network of high speed Maglev routes built on the rights of way of the Interstate Highway Network. He foresaw the jobs and exports it would create for America if it became a new U.S. industry.

In 1990, Senator Moynihan succeeded in having the Senate pass legislation authorizing a 750 million dollar R&D program for developing U.S. Maglev, as described later in Chapter 8. Sadly, while it passed the Senate, it died in the House of Representatives when the Chairman of the

Committee that oversaw the legislation refused to hold hearings on it. The Chairman was from Detroit.

Since then, we have continued to fight for U.S. Maglev. In particular, as described in the later chapters, we have developed the new 2nd generation Maglev 2000 system that will be much cheaper to build, is compatible with existing rail, and much more capable than the 1st generation Japanese and German Maglev systems. The 2nd generation Maglev 2000 guideways can be mass produced at a much lower cost than the 1st generation guideways. Besides passengers, Maglev 2000 vehicles can carry loaded highway trucks, personal autos with their passengers, and high value freight on the same guideway at maximum design speed.

In contrast to the 1st generation passenger only Maglev and High Speed Rail systems, the 2nd generation Maglev 2000 system has the unique ability to transport high revenue high trucks, enabling its construction and operation to be privately financed, without the need for government funding and subsidization. This is very important today when government budgets are very tight, and debt levels are stratospheric.

Full-scale components for the Maglev 2000 system – superconducting magnets, guideway panels and beam, vehicle body, etc. – have been successfully fabricated and tested and their costs validated, as described in later chapters. The remaining step is to assemble the components into complete vehicles and demonstrate their operation on a guideway. The demonstration will require government funding. After that, however, commercial 2nd generation Maglev 2000 systems can be privately financed.

Because of its energy, environmental, and economic advantages, Maglev will become the major mode of transport for the 21st Century, world-wide. As described later, it will evolve from the present 1st generation Maglev systems into the much lower cost, much more capable 2nd generation Maglev transport system, in the same way that Model-T autos evolved into today's cars, and as the 1930's DC-3 and Ford Tri-Motor airplanes evolved into the modern jet airliners.

To us it is vitally important that America lead the way in this evolutionary process, not only because of the millions of jobs and Billions of export dollars that will benefit America, if it takes the lead in Maglev, but also from the pride that it will instill in our engineers, scientists, manufacturing workers, and society. America will then once again lead the World in transportation.

While America lost the first opportunity to lead in Maglev, it still has the opportunity for 2nd generation Maglev. However, the opportunity will only last for a few more years. If the U.S. does not grasp the opportunity – and so far, it has failed to do so – 2nd generation Maglev will be developed in another country, and America will buy it from abroad.

Chapter Two

Today and Tomorrow in America's Transport Hell

"Abandon all hope, ye who enter here"

Engraving above the Gate to Hell, Dante's Inferno

The Fifth Circle: Wrath and Sullenness

Let us be your Virgil for a little while, to guide you through Today's Transport Hell, with a brief view of what Tomorrow's much worse Transport Hell will be like. You don't need to read the inscription, "Abandon All Hope, Ye Who Enter Here", and pass through the Gate, because you're already in Transport Hell.

There, we're now in the 5th Circle, "Wrath and Sullenness on the Highways" (the upper Circles are much milder, and not that interesting.) The engraving (1) shows Stradano's visualization of the 5th Circle, where the wrathful fight each other on the slimy surface of the River Styx, while the sullen just float on or beneath the surface. The photo(2) shows a typical crash scene on a U.S. Highway with one, two, or three dead or injured – now, just numbers to the government, who keeps the statistics, but doesn't do much to stop the carnage.

An awful lot of people, well over 40,000, are killed on the U.S. highways each year, equal to one jetliner crash every day and a 9/11 event every month. Six million more are seriously injured, with many horribly mangled. The economic costs – medical, emergency services, productivity loss, insurance, legal and property damage – total about 300 Billion dollars. The quality of life costs – damage to the health and the stress on the individuals involved and their families – are another 200 Billion dollars per year, making the total human cost of the accidents 500 Billion dollars per year. (3) Over a ten year period the human cost of American highway accidents is 5 trillion dollars – almost 20,000 dollars for every man, woman, and child in the U.S. Over 400,000 people die on the highways in the 10 year period, and almost 60 million people are injured, many very seriously.

While the human cost is the most important, there are also the staggering costs for highway transport. Per year, Americans spend 2.5 trillion dollars (2,500 Billion) for their automobiles, trucks, fuel, road construction and maintenance, travel time, parking, insurance, environmental effects, etc.(4). Adding in the costs of accident, the total cost of highway travel is 3 trillion dollars (3,000 $billion) annually – about 1/3 of America's disposable income, equal to 10,000 dollars per person per year.

And if that weren't enough, think of the endless hours we spend on the road, sometimes at 60 mph, but more often than not, inching along at 10 or 20 mph on congested highways. The average highway speed is 35 mph (5). Per capita passenger mile travel in America is 15,000 miles per year (1.6 passengers per vehicle). At 35 mph, on average, each of us is in a car for 430 hours a year – about 4 weeks of waking hours, assuming we get 8 hours of sleep per day.

And it's not like we can relax while we're on the road. You have to be continually alert and looking out for crazy, drunk, and careless drivers, bad road conditions, distracted car and truck drivers texting or talking on cellphones, sleepy drivers, and on and on, hoping that the car or truck ahead won't blow a tire or break down. There are a lot of good things about highway travel – being able to go to work, travel to see relatives and new places, shop, go to the movies, etc. – but overall, highway travel is definitely part of Transport Hell.

And it's going to get worse. By 2035, the vehicle flow in America's main highway corridors – I-5 and I-15 on the West Coast, I-95 on the East Coast, I-90 and I-10 across America (6) will almost double, with even lower average speeds, many more accidents, much greater transport costs, and a lot more time on the road. There will be even more reasons to be "Wrathful and Sullen."

The Sixth Circle: Heresy

Moving downwards from the 5th Circle in Dante's Inferno, we come to the 6th Circle: Heresy. In our modern Transport Hell, the 6th Circle is reserved for air travelers. There is no special relationship between

Heretics and air travelers, other than the Heretics were condemned to lie in very uncomfortable flaming tombs, while air passengers are forced to fly in very cramped, uncomfortable seats with no leg room. True, the seats are not flaming, so we should be grateful for that. However, when one is on a long cross-country or intercontinental flight, sitting trapped in the seat, waiting for a chance to go to the lavatory, it sure feels like the seat is flaming.

The latest Airbus 380 has a capacity of 853 passengers in an all economy class configuration on its 2 decks.(7) It has a design range of 9800 miles, enough to fly non-stop from New York to Hong Kong at 560 mph. It even has 18 toilets for the 873 people on the plane (853 plus 20 crew), amounting to one per 50 persons. On a 5 hour flight, this means 6 minutes average toilet time per person. Probably doable, though there have been problems with flushing airplane toilets, incontinent passengers, and other unpleasantries.

In economy class, the seat widths are typically in the range of 17 to 19 inches (though some are as narrow as 16 inches), while legroom – the distance from your seat back to the back of the seat ahead of you is typically 31 to 32 inches. Not very much – even Dante's Heretics got more room. Slouching down in your seat to get comfortable? No way. A large person in the adjacent seat? Hmm, well, it is the 6th Circle – comfort is not the idea. Able to stand in the aisle and walk up and down to prevent blood clots? Not likely. A colleague of ours says he would rather visit his proctologist than take an air trip. Understandable.

And what of flying on a smaller, regional air carrier where the pilot gets 16,000 dollars salary a year and survives on food stamps? Where he or she sleeps in the airport lounge between flights? Hmm, again. Where some flights wait out on the runaway for hours before they can take off or deplane at the gate? When flights are delayed for hours, or cancelled, because of bad weather, and you have to sit in the airport, trying to get a replacement flight? When there's only a couple of flights per day and you miss your flight because of heavy road traffic, and the only remaining flight is full? Hmm, again. Then you think about the many times a year that landing or taking off aircraft almost collide. Experienced air traffic controllers are rapidly retiring or resigning – 1,200 in 2008 alone, leaving green recruits to take over. Only 11,000 controllers serve the U.S. airways today.(8) Communications equipment between controllers and pilots is antiquated and subject to failure. Do you doubt that America's airways are a major Circle in Transport Hell?

The bright side is that the average American only takes a little over 1 airline round trip each year, and that only lasts a few hours, so the pain doesn't go on for too long – not for 4 weeks, as it does on the 5th Circle, Highways.

What's coming tomorrow on the 6th Circle? Fewer flights and higher fares, as the airlines continue to lose money. New service fees for bags, etc., including as has been proposed, a fee for going to the toilet, and a fare structure for leg room – want more leg room, you have to pay extra, even in economy. Some airlines are even proposing that passengers travel standing up and that if they want a seat they have to pay more.

Seventh Circle: Violence.

Dante's 7th Circle houses the violent in 3 rings – the inner ring, where those who are violent against persons and property swim in a river of boiling blood; a middle ring where suicides become thorny bushes and trees, to be eaten by the Harpies, and the inner ring, where blasphemers against God, sodomites, and usurers live in a desert of flaming sand.

In Transport Hell, the 7th Circle signifies America's Public Transit Systems, not because the people who ride them are violent assaulters of people and property, or suicidal, or blasphemers, sodomites, and usurers – in general, transit riders are nice, peaceful, gentle people. The only connection is that riding on public transit often feels as uncomfortable as being on a desert of flaming sand.

Urban transit has been operating in America since the early 1800's. The first horse car – a streetcar pulled by horses started operating in New York City in 1832. By 1850 dozens of cities had them. Moving on to 1900, urbanites were traveling on "safety bicycles" similar to the single speed bikes used today, and on electric streetcars in over 500 cities that averaged 11 mph. (9)

By 1950, 3 out of 5 Americans lived in urban areas – the percentage living in urban areas of 250,000 people or more climbed to 80% in 2000 AD.

Interestingly, even though the percentage of people living in urban areas increased, in 1960, 64 percent of American commuters drove to work, while 12% used public transit. In 2000, only 5 % took transit, while 87% took automobiles to work.

Why the growth in auto commuting, even though the U.S. is becoming more urbanized? Simple – until recently, automobile trips have been cheaper, more convenient, and until lately, more pleasant, while the transit systems have been typically more expensive, crowded, noisier, less convenient, more polluted, and take longer to reach one's destination. Much of the equipment is decades old. Taking the New York Subway, for example, is not a particularly pleasant experience. Lots of crowding on the subway platforms and cars, inhaling steel dust, microparticles and gases from fluids applied to enhance braking, incredible noise, making it difficult to hear and to talk, and continuous vibration and bouncing as the subway cars travel along the tracks.

Commuter rail travel, while less stressful than subways still has its problems. Average speeds are low, with a 30 mile trip taking an hour or more, service not very frequent in many areas – perhaps 3 or 4 trains a day, lots of swaying and vibration when moving, often standing room only, lots of rail noise to the riders and people living along the track.

Moreover, the fares people pay for public transit are relatively high, about 30 cents per passenger mile even with government subsidies. Typically, the actual operating costs are 2 to 3 times the fare revenues, requiring major subsidies.

The future looks dim for public transit. As government deficits grow, there are less and less subsidies available. As a consequence, transit authorities are making large cuts in commuter rail, subway, and bus service, and laying off many employees. There appears no hope of reversing this trend as long as transit authorities continue to stick with old transit technology. New technologies that will be cheaper to operate and attract greater ridership is the only solution.

8th Circle: Fraud

The Eighth Circle is a catch-all for all types of fraudulent persons, with each type residing in 10 different bolgias, or "ditches" that make up the Circle. Pimps and seducers have their own ditch, flatterers in a second (they are covered in excrement, representing their words), corrupt politicians in another ditch, and so on. It sounds like a very crowded place.

Passenger rail is not fraudulent, but it only plays a very minor role in today's transport picture. There is a lot of PR and "Field of Dreams" type of thinking – "Build It and They Will Come" – about High Speed Rail (HSR) in the government and media. Build HSR and it will solve America's transport problems? Not really.

What are the facts about conventional passenger rail in America and countries like France and Japan, where HSR lines are operating? In America, conventional intercity passenger rail (Amtrak) revenue is approximately.5 Billion dollars annually (10), about 1/1000th of total U.S. transport expenditures. There are about 25 million one-way passenger trips per year, for a total travel distance of 5.4 Billion passenger miles. Per capita, the average American travels 18 miles per year on Amtrak, and takes a round trip every 24 years.

Compare this with other modes of transport. Per capita, the average American travels 15,000 miles per year by auto, flies 2,750 miles and takes public transit dozens of times. (10) Passenger rail is not a significant part of the transport system.

While HSR is more significant in countries like France and Japan, it is still only a small player in their transport picture. Per capita, the French on average travel only 400 miles per year on HSR, equal to about 1 ¼ round trips per year, and drive 7600 miles. (9) Per capita, Japanese travel 400 miles on HSR per year and drive 4,000 miles. And this in countries that have much higher populations densities that the U.S. – 80 persons per square mile in the U.S. versus 871 in Japan and 288 in France – and much smaller in size. (11) Moreover, even the much higher speeds achieved with HSR in France and Japan – 163 mph for the Paris to Marseille run – compared to 35 mph for Amtrak – is not enough to make HSR more than a small player in Europe and Japan.

Amtrak fares average about 27 cents per passenger mile (10) and are heavily subsidized by the U.S. Government. Actual operating costs are at least double that. HSR systems in Europe and Japan are also heavily subsidized and cost about 35 cents per passenger mile. HSR is inherently very expensive because of the expensive construction cost, about 40 million dollars per two way mile, and its high operating and maintenance costs. There is no possibility of privately financed HSR lines – they will require major government funding for construction and operation, with subsidized fares. Typical airline fares are on the order of 15 cents per passenger mile. (10) For a family of 4 to fly round trip from Los Angeles to San Francisco would cost about 500 dollars. By HSR round trip it would cost about 1,100 dollars, with a subsidized fare of 35 cents per passenger mile. Driving, it would cost only 200 dollars for gas and food, plus you have a car at your destination. The choice is easy for most people – drive. It takes a bit longer; 7 hours by highway versus a couple of hours by air or HSR but the dollar savings are large. It appears very likely that the U.S. Government's proposed High Speed Intercity Passenger Rail program will not play a significant role in future U.S. transport, and will cost taxpayers dearly.

Ninth Circle: Betrayal

Now we reach the bottom and last Circle of the Inferno. No flaming tombs or desert sands here, only ice and the betrayers. The worse the sin, the more the ice that the sinners are buried in. In the center, Satan is frozen waste deep in ice, trying to escape, while his 3 faces chew on traitors, with Brutus in the left mouth, Cassius in the right, and Judas in the center mouth. Dore's engraving of Satan seems inconsistent with the usual view of Satan flying around doing his dirty work and angling to sign up peoples' souls – no Faustian bargains here.

In Transport Hell, the betrayers are not human persons, but inanimate substances – oil and the other fossil fuels, coal and natural gas. Seduced by them, metaphorically, that is, humanity has left the "paradise" of horse and wagon, first for coal fired trains, steamboats and ships, and then for oil fueled autos, trucks, airplanes, trains, and ships. (Okay, horse and wagon transport isn't exactly a paradise).

As a result, human society has become completely dependent on oil fueled transport. Without it, we would have a much lower standard of living and a much smaller population. Most of us would be subsistence farmers, and never travel more than a few miles away from our homes. In 1800, less than 6 percent of people in the U.S. lived in cities of 2,500 persons or more. Per capita GDP was only 1,200 dollars (2007 dollars) compared to today's 50,000 dollars (11).

Our oil consumption is absolutely amazing. The accompanying drawing shows the scale of "The Lake of Oil" that sustains us. Current World production of oil is 30 Billion Barrels per year, corresponding for a Lake of Oil – 1 mile wide, 1 mile long, and 1.2 miles deep. Visualize dropping the 7 Billion people now on the Earth into the Lake. They would displace only 7% of the Oil Lake's volume.

Of this annual Lake of Oil, the 300 million Americans consume 25%, or 25 barrels per person. The other 6.7 Billion persons in the World have to get by on an average of only 3.75 barrels per person per year. If they all consumed at the present U.S. average, the Oil Lake would have to be 6.6 miles deep, not 1.2 miles.

There is no way this can happen. World oil production has plateaued at about 30 Billion barrels per year, and will soon start to decline. There is no way that the bulk of the World's population can reach the U.S. level of mobility and standard of living using transport systems that depend on conventional oil. Even more quickly, however, the U.S. share of the World oil pie will start to drastically shrink as the developing nations, especially China and India, become more prosperous and buy even larger amounts of ever more expensive conventional oil.

Of course, synthetic oil can be made from Earth's much more plentiful supplies of coal, tar sands, oil shale, and frozen methane hydrates. Then there would be synfuels for centuries more – enough for everybody. However, synfuels come at a terrible environmental price because of the additional carbon dioxide emissions generated by the production process – roughly a factor of 2 increase. Today, the tailpipes of U.S. autos, trucks, and airplanes emit 2 Billion tons of carbon dioxide annually – almost 10% of total World emissions. With synfuels, the emissions would double to 4 Billion tons per year, 20% of today's World total. As world mobility grows, synfuels emissions would dominate. Because there is no practical way to capture and sequester tailpipe emissions, global warming would accelerate with devastating consequences to the environment. Oil would have then betrayed humanity into trashing the planet.

Table 1

Major Biological Extinctions in Earth's History (3)

Extinction	Years Ago	Consequences	Causes
First	440 million – End of the Ordovician Period	25% of Marine Families Extinct (No life existed on land)	Sudden Global Cooling
Second	370 million – near end of Devonian Period	19% of Families Extinct	Possible climate change
Third	245 million – end of Permian Period	54% of Families Extinct – Largest Extinction in Earth's History (90% of species became extinct)	Climate change due to plate movements (possible asteroid impact)
Fourth	210 million – end of Triassic Period	23% of Families Extinct – occurred shortly after dinosaurs & mammals evolved	Uncertain
Fifth	65 million – end of Cretaceous Period	17% of Families lost – end of dinosaurs	Asteroid impact and volcanic eruptions
Sixth	Present & Ongoing	Projected Extinction of 50% of Species by 2100 AD	Human activities (fossil fuel combustion, agriculture, over hunting & fishing, etc.)

Chapter Three

The Message: Avoiding the 6th Extinction

"For that which is common to the greatest number has the least care bestowed upon it. Everyone thinks chiefly of his own, hardly at all of the common interest; and only when he is himself concerned as an individual. For besides other considerations, everybody is more inclined to neglect the duty which he expects another to fulfill; as in families many attendants are often less useful than a few."

Aristotle, Politics, Book II, Chapter III

The 6th Extinction

Humanity is now in the early stages of the 6th mass extinction. The previous 5 extinctions were due to natural causes that disturbed the World's environment. There were basalt flood events, falling sea levels, asteroid impacts, sustained global cooling that reduced sea levels and increased global aridity, sustained global warming that released methane from unstable methane hydrates, anoxic ocean events associated with massive volcanic eruptions, and continental drift that changed Earth's land and ocean geography, like the formation of the supercontinent Pangaea at the start of the late Permian period. (1)

In these earlier mass extinctions, large percentages of the animal species died off. During the worst extinction, the Permian-Triassic transition, over 90% of Earth's species vanished. The ecosystem took many millions of years to fully recover.

The 6th extinction is very different. Rather than caused by natural events, it is human-made. We wipe out habitats, i.e., cut down rain forests, convert grasslands to farmlands, divert and dam rivers, drain lakes, and so on. We destroy animal and plant species for food, fuel, ladies hats, cute ivory objects, tiger bits for aphrodisiacs, hunting trophies, and all sorts of goodies.

We introduce invasive species into areas where they kill off the local species, and we pollute. It is estimated that by 2100 AD, over 50% of all the species present on the Earth before humankind started trashing it will have vanished.(2) What an irony – Humans are about as intelligent as a large asteroid when it comes to preserving life on Earth!

Does the 6th extinction just stop after killing off most of the species on Earth, or does it go on to wipe out humans as well? We don't know yet, but there are reasons to worry. The as yet unstoppable consumption of fossil fuels is leading mankind straight towards extinction. The process is best described as the ultimate "Tragedy of the Commons."

Tragedy of the Commons

In 1968, Garrett Hardin published his essay, "Tragedy of the Commons."(4) He discusses how unfettered access to resources by individuals not responsible for sustaining the resources, which he termed "The Commons", inevitably leads to their overuse and degradation.

This is not a new problem, as Aristotle's observation, quoted above, shows. Individuals and corporations think only of their own interests, grab as much as they can of The Commons, and don't worry about its sustainability. If someone asks who will take care of The Commons, the usual answer is "Let George do it."

Hardin tied the problem of The Commons to the need not to overpopulate Earth, a restatement of the warning by Malthus that human population increases exponentially, while resources increase linearly–if in fact, they increase at all. With unfettered access to the Commons, World resources are dwindling – oil and other fossil fuels are depleting, mineral deposits are vanishing, ground water aquifers are pumped out with water table levels dropping by hundreds of feet, and the area and fertility of the soils that grow our food are declining rapidly. Today, vast areas of the tropical rain forests are being cut down to grow food and bio-fuels. Unfortunately, as the Spanish conquistadors discovered hundreds of years ago when they tried to farm the Amazon Rain Forest, almost all of the forest nutrients were in the trees. When the trees died, their nutrients went back into the soil, to be taken up by the next generation of trees. When the conquistadors cut down the trees to grow crops, they got a few years of good yields, then nothing as the soil's fertility vanished. Today, the same process is happening over much of the World.

After Hardin published his essay, it aroused a storm of controversy, both for and against his thesis. Opponents argued that Malthus's dire prediction would never come to pass, either because new resources would always be discovered, or that some technological fix would save humanity.

Other naysayers just didn't give a damn. Like Louis XIV before them, its "*Après moi, le deluge*" or in American, "What have future generations ever done for me."

There are many examples of cultures that collapsed because they overexploited their Commons. The classic example is the collapse of the Mayan civilization. The Mayans, together with the Incas and Aztecs, were the three greatest civilizations in America before the Spanish conquistadors arrived. The Maya built large cities, beautiful temples and incredible pyramids. Unlike the Aztecs and Incas, which were destroyed by the Spaniards, the Mayan civilization collapsed by itself, hundreds of years before the Spanish came.

According to a NASA science article(5), at its peak around 900 AD, Mayan population density was 500 people per square mile in rural areas (the current average U.S. population density is 80 per square mile), with more than 2,000 people per square mile in the cities – comparable to many urban areas in the U.S.

Why did the great Mayan civilization collapse? The key appears to be that the region became almost completely deforested shortly before it collapsed. In lake sediment samples from that era, tree pollen disappeared and was replaced by the pollen of weeds, a result of the Mayan's "Slash and Burn" type of agriculture.(5) In Slash and Burn, you cut down the trees, and burn them to expose soil for crops. The ash from the burning trees fertilizes the soil, and you can grow crops for a few years until the fertility vanishes. To restore fertility, you have to let the land lie fallow for many years till a new forest grows. As part of the process, without ground cover, the fertile soil erodes and the ground temperature rises, drying out the land, further reducing crop yields.

The Spanish conquistadors practiced Slash and Burn agriculture in the Amazon, with the same results – crops for a few years, then the soil loses its fertility. Today, Slash and Burn is still practiced. About ½ of the

World's original rain forest has been cut in the last 20 years for agriculture.

It is not Slash and Burn agriculture per se that destroys a culture. If the land is not overexploited and sufficient time is allowed for it to regain fertility, the practice could go on indefinitely. What does destroy the culture is the Tragedy of the Commons – "Everyone thinks chiefly of his own, hardly at all of the common interest", to quote Aristotle. Inevitably, the land and the forest are overexploited.

Other historical examples of overuse of the land resource Commons are the deforestation of Easter Island, overgrazing of trees and plants by sheep and goats in the ancient Mediterranean Basin, and deforestation and overgrazing in the Norse Greenland Colony.

Today, we continue to exploit the forests and the land in the Amazon, where forests are cut down to grow soybeans for China, in Indonesia, to grow palm oil, and in many other areas. Chinese farmers are applying so much fertilizer to their farmland that the soil is becoming very acidic and soon will not be suitable for food production. Farmers and other water users in many parts of the U.S. are over pumping groundwater aquifers – a true Commons – so much that water table levels have dropped hundreds of feet. Water from the Colorado River is being withdrawn at such a rate that the river never makes it to the ocean. Ground surface levels in parts of the Central Valley in California have subsided over 30 feet due to overpumping of aquifers.

Tragic as these events are to those involved, they have generally been localized to a relatively small part of the World. The collapse of Mayan Civilization, the Norse Greenland Colony, and so on, did not threaten the whole World. Other civilizations, colonies, and communities took their place, until now. Now, what is new is that humanity has grown to the point that we now all share two Global Commons – the World's atmosphere and the World's oceans – that are being profoundly affected by the consumption of fossil fuels. How we as individuals and our many enterprises, release carbon dioxide and other greenhouse gases into the atmosphere and oceans affects everybody else in the World, not just us. Moreover, the effects, as serious as they are to those now alive, will be far worse to our children, grandchildren, and generations beyond, when we are long gone from the Earth.

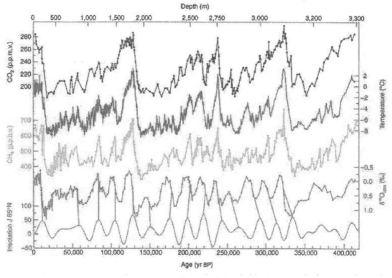

Figure 1

420,000 years of ice core data from Vostok, Antarctica research station.

Current period is at left.

From bottom to top:
- Solar variation at 65°N due to en:Milankovitch cycles (connected to ^{18}O).
- ^{18}O isotope of oxygen.
- Levels of methane (CH_4).
- Relative temperature.
- Levels of carbon dioxide (CO_2).

From top to bottom:
- Levels of carbon dioxide (CO_2).
- Relative temperature.
- Levels of methane (CH_4).
- ^{18}O isotope of oxygen.
- Solar variation at 65°N due to en:Milankovitch cycles (connected to ^{18}O).

Global Warming and Fossil Fuels – The Known and the Unknowns

Starting with the Industrial Revolution, the atmospheric concentration of carbon dioxide has increased from 280 parts per million (ppm) to the current 380 ppm.(6) This fact is confirmed by direct measurements of carbon dioxide in the atmosphere. The increase is hundreds of times faster than in any previous time in the last 400,000 years, measured by the carbon dioxide concentration in air bubbles trapped in prehistoric ice cores from the Polar Regions. The accompanying graph (Figure 1) shows how global temperature tracks global atmospheric carbon dioxide over the last 400,000 years, as measured in ice cores from the Vostok station in Antarctica. (7) Again, a fact.

A further fact. The rise in atmospheric carbon dioxide levels is due to humanity's massive consumption of fossil fuels. There are no massive eruptions of volcanoes or other sources that can account for the very large increase in carbon dioxide concentration in such a short time. A closer look at the carbon dioxide changes within the last thousand years can be seen in Figure 2 below.(8) The atmospheric carbon dioxide was measured in the bubbles from an Antarctic ice core from Law Dome near Australia's Casey Station.

The Law Dome ice core is at a location where the snow accumulation is much higher than at Vostok. Thus, the time scale for the Law Dome core is expanded and it can provide us with more detailed information about recent climate changes.

The carbon dioxide concentrations as measured by the Law Dome ice cores agree very closely with the direct measurements of the atmosphere concentrations that begin about 1950.(9) This provides strong evidence that the ice core measurements of carbon dioxide concentration are accurate indicators of concentration in the atmosphere at the time the ice core was laid down.

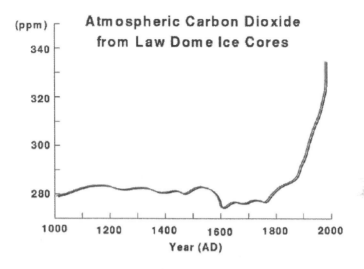

Figure 2

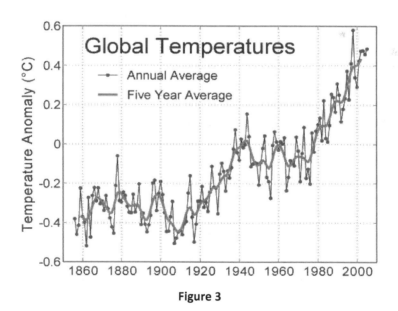

Figure 3

The next further fact. The World's average temperature is rising.(9) Over the last century, global surface temperature has increased 0.74 ± 0.18 degrees Celsius (1.33 ± 0.32 degrees Fahrenheit).(Figure 3) The temperature rise during the second half of the 20th Century was almost twice that in the 1st half.

The next fact. Carbon dioxide is a greenhouse gas. It absorbs thermal radiation, and can cause a radiating body, like the Earth, to increase in temperature. Figure 4 shows how this works. (10) Light from the Sun, being primarily at short wavelengths, passes through the atmosphere with only a small amount of absorption (assuming the atmosphere is free of clouds and airborne particulates) to the ground. A portion of the sunlight is reflected back into space, and the rest is absorbed by the Earth. The Earth then radiates the absorbed energy back to space, so that the Earth's temperature stays constant.

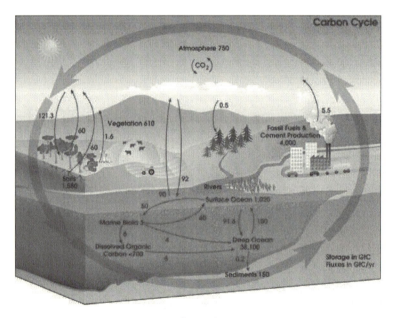

Figure 4

The radiant thermal energy emitted by the Earth is at much longer wavelengths than sunlight, and a significant fraction of it is absorbed by carbon dioxide in the atmosphere as it travels away from Earth. The carbon dioxide then re-radiates the thermal energy it absorbs, roughly 1/2 toward the Earth and 1/2 toward space. The portion radiated towards Earth is then absorbed by the Earth.

To maintain thermal equilibrium in the presence of this returning radiation from the atmospheric carbon dioxide, Earth's temperature rises to increase its thermal radiation flux to space. The more carbon dioxide in the atmosphere, the more Earth's temperature will rise, all other effects – clouds, aerosols, dust, the planet's *albedo* (reflectivity), etc. – being constant.

The radiant absorption effects of carbon dioxide are familiar to chemical engineering sophomores, who have to deal with the process when they analyze radiant heat transfer in combustion furnaces. Figure 5, using data from the Chemical Engineering "Bible", *Perry's Chemical Engineering Handbook* (11) shows the emissivity of gases containing carbon dioxide as a function of its partial pressure, Pc, i.e. concentration, in the gas; the length L of the radiation path through the gas, and the temperature of the gas, for a combustion gas pressure of 1 atmosphere.

At 380 ppm carbon dioxide concentration in the atmosphere, its partial pressure is 3.8×10^{-4} atmospheres. The total atmospheric path length (normalized to a constant pressure of 1 atmosphere), is 25,700 feet, resulting in a P_cL value of 9.77, well above the Perry data point of 5.0 ft atmosphere in the table shown in Figure 5. Extrapolating the Perry data at a temperature of 530 degrees Rankine (70 degrees Fahrenheit) and P_cL of 7.2, the carbon dioxide in Earth's pre-industrial atmosphere with 280 ppm carbon dioxide had an emissivity of approximately 0.215. At today's 380 ppm carbon dioxide concentration, P_cL is 9.77, with an corresponding absorptivity of 0.225 as future carbon dioxide concentration increases, the absorptivity will also increase, to 0.235 at 480 ppm, and 0.245 at 580 ppm.

Figure 5 Absorptivity of Thermal Radiation in air as a Function of Carbon Dioxide Partial Pressure and Radiation Path Length,

Basis: Data from Perry's Chemical Engineers Handbook, 6th Edition, McGraw-Hill (1984)

P_c = Partial Pressure of CO_2 (atm) in 1 atm air

L = Radiation Path Length

(25,700 feet in Earth's Atmosphere) normalized to constant pressure of 1 atm)

Air Temperature = 530 Degrees Rankine (70F)

P_cL (atmft)	Data Source	Carbon Dioxide Concentration (ppm)	Absorptivity of Thermal Radiation
0.2	Perry	----	0.10
1	Perry	----	0.15
5	Perry	----	0.20
7.2	Extrapolation of Perry Data	280 ppm (pre-industrial	0.215
9.77	"	380 ppm (present)	0.225
12.34	"	480 ppm (future)	0.235
14.34	"	580 ppm (future)	0.245

The gas absorptivity equals the emissivity when the absorbing gas and the emitter (i.e. the Earth) are at the same temperature.(11)   While Earth's surface temperature is slightly above its atmospheric temperature measured in degrees Kelvin or degrees Rankine above absolute Zero, the correction is small, (11) so that today's absorptivity of carbon dioxide in Earth's atmosphere is essentially equal to its emissivity, that is, gas absorptivity is also about 0.20.

Hopefully, the reader is still following this long-winded explanation (engineers love to explain things). In concrete terms, about 22 percent of the thermal radiation emitted by Earth to space, today, which keeps its temperature from continuously increasing as it absorbs light from the Sun, is absorbed by carbon dioxide in the atmosphere. A significant fraction of this absorbed radiation is radiated back to the surface of the Earth, causing its temperature to be higher than if there were no carbon dioxide in the atmosphere. The above explanation is greatly simplified to more easily convey the basics. Scientists involved in climate modeling must take into account much more complex behaviors, such as the effect of the light wavelength on absorption and emission, the effect of temperature gradients in the atmosphere, etc. However, the above basic principles still hold.

What does this mean to humanity? The more carbon dioxide goes into the atmosphere from the burning of fossil fuels, the more absorption in the atmosphere of thermal radiation emitted by the Earth, with more of it re-radiated back to the Earth, acting to increase its temperature.

Now we come to the supposed first unknown. How much of Earth's temperature rise over the 20th Century is a result of the increasing carbon dioxide concentration in the atmosphere? While carbon dioxide is a contributing factor, there are other contributors, both positive and negative, which affect global temperature. For example, soot particles and water vapor in the atmosphere, melting snow and ice in Polar Regions, which increases the absorption of sunlight, etc.

Most global warming deniers accept the fact that global temperatures are increasing, but argue that it's not caused by burning fossil fuels that generate carbon dioxide. However, there is very powerful evidence that Earth's temperatures correlate with carbon dioxide concentration as evidenced by the Vostok data (Figure 1) that shows how carbon dioxide concentration marches in step with global temperature changes.

Understanding the Global Warming Deniers

It would be nice to live in the Global Warming Deniers World. No need to worry about melting glaciers, an ice-free Arctic Ocean, the rapid acceleration of the Greenland ice sheet as it moves toward the sea, breaking off of large chunks of the Antarctic ice sheet, rising ocean levels, a string of warmest years on record, increasing severity of storms, longer and deeper droughts, tropical diseases – malaria, dengue fever, and others–spreading North and South into the Temperate Zones, the extinction of zillions of plant and animal species and so on.

Everything is hunky dory in the Global Warming Deniers World. We can go on burning as much fossil fuel as we want, for as long as we want. The effect on the environment will be zero. There is no risk of our civilization collapsing, and as for the possibility of human extinction triggered by runaway global warming – What are you? Crazy?

Unfortunately, the Deniers World is a fantasy. The above disasters, and much more, are already happening, with massive use of fossil fuels the primary cause of the process. We cannot continue dumping tens of billions of tons of carbon dioxide into the atmosphere every year for much longer before even worse disasters occur, including the extinction of the human species.

Why do the Deniers deny reality, and put forth any argument they can think of, however irrelevant, dumb or false, to deny the reality? Undoubtedly, there are many different reasons why the Deniers deny. A very human trait is to deny realities because they impose stress. Admitting that we must stop burning fossil fuels, on which our present standard of living depends is very stressful. Stress hurts and makes people unhappy. Better to believe everything is OK – no problem – at least till the Tiger bites.

Others try to avoid making decisions, which in themselves are stressful. Better to have some very confident, very forceful individual or organization tell you there is no problem, or that they're taking care of it. Just relax. Forceful, loud and confident people often convince others that their positions are correct even when they are not [Jim Powell relates an example]. I remember a long time ago an example of this process. Early on at Brookhaven National Lab, I had a friendly argument with Lou Slater, a fellow staff member in the Department of Nuclear

Engineering at the Lab. Lou was a chemist and I was a nuclear engineer, though I had received my undergraduate training as a chemical engineer at Carnegie Tech and knew chemistry pretty well.

We argued about which gas was more poisonous, and which had the lowest safe concentration in the air for laboratory workers. Lou said that hydrogen cyanide was more poisonous and had the lowest allowable concentration. I argued that it was chlorine, because I had recently read an article a few days earlier on gas safety – a topic of considerable interest to us back then because lab people used to do a lot of experiments, not like today when its mostly computer analysis and modeling. What protects workers from chlorine gas in air is that one can easily sense it, in contrast to hydrogen cyanide, which one cannot sense.

Anyway, Lou and I decided to present our arguments to Walt Becker, the Head Technician in the Technical Support Group. Lou presented his case very loudly to Walt, with lots of arm waving and facial expressions. I, on the other hand, presented my case in a normal voice, without any dramatic gestures. When I finished, I asked "Walt, which of us do you believe?" Walt sort of tried to avoid the question, not wishing to offend, but finally blurted out, "I think Lou is right." I then said "Walt, you only believe him because he's more forceful." He smiled sheepishly, and said, "yes, you're right."

In an argument, it is always more stressful to contradict the side that is more aggressive and appears very confident. One sees this all the time in TV talk shows and interviews. People tend to go with the authority type person, even if he or she isn't really an authority but just acts like one.

There are many classic experiments on people and animals that bear out this tendency. For example, a group of people has the task of judging whether two rulers are of equal length or not. However, the experiment is rigged so that everybody in the group except one, who is the actual subject, conspires to state that the two rulers, which are actually very different in length, are equal in length. The experimenter then investigates how different in length the rulers must be before the subject will speak out and say that they are not equal. In the experiments, most subjects would not disagree unless the difference in length exceeded a few inches. It took one subject a 6 inch difference before disagreeing.

A beautiful experiment on rats had them enter a tunnel that divided into two branches, one to the left and the other to the right. 50% of the time, at random, the left branch contained food, and 50% of the time the right branch, again at random. At the branch point, the rats could not view which branch would lead to the food. Moreover, they could only travel forward in the tunnel – no turning back. After a number of trials, the rat would take the left branch 50% of the time, again at random, and 50% of the time, the right branch. The result – the rat got fed 50% of the time.

Then the experimenters changed the setup. In the right branch they installed a light bulb that was not visible from the branch point in the tunnel. When the rat got to the light bulb, if it was on (50% of the time, at random) he got fed further down the tunnel. If it was off (50% of the time) he didn't get fed. After a number of trials, the rats in the experiment almost always chose the right hand branch, even though they still got food only half the time. Why? Because it was less stressful to the rat. Having someone or something decide your fate is less stressful – at least to most humans and animals – than trying to decide for yourself.

Mixed in with the Deniers who want to avoid thinking and worrying about global warming, and the Deniers who want someone to tell them what to do, is a third group, the modern Louis the XIV's.

Their philosophy? "We'll be long gone before the global warming disaster really hits!" Their only worry is, "How will the proposed actions to stop global warming affect my business, my profits, my position, and my livelihood?" Fossil fuel producers – oil, coal, natural gas – want to keep on producing fossil fuels. Manufacturers and users of motor vehicles, aircraft, fossil fueled power plants, and so on, want to keep their present systems going.

One of the realities of the American political and economic scene is that the candidate in a political campaign with the most money usually wins the election. Similarly, vested interests with a lot of money usually can thwart any effort that would harm their interests, through political contributions, advertising, consultants, media pundits, etc.

Propaganda works. The fierce campaign against people and organizations trying to stop global warming has shifted U.S. public opinion from being very concerned about it to believing that it is not real. Quoting the master propagandist, Adolph Hitler, "Through clever and constant application of propaganda, people can be made to see Paradise as Hell, and also the other way round, to consider the most wretched sort of life as Paradise."

Global warming denial is very strong in the United States, but much less so in other developed countries, because they are more objective and less swayed by propaganda, and more focused on being socially responsible to present and future generations to ensure that they have a livable World.

Consequences of Continued Use of Fossil Fuels in Transport

The total world annual emissions of carbon dioxide from all sources using fossil fuels – powerplants, transport, industrial processes, heating, etc., – is about 25 Billion metric tons(12) [1 metric ton equals approximately 1.1 short ton (2,200 lbs)]. The U.S. emits 6 Billion tons, about one fourth of the World total. Of the U.S. emissions, 2 Billion tons come from transport – autos, trucks, airplanes, most trains, ships, and barges.(13)

Per capita, Americans emit about 7 metric tons of carbon dioxide per year from their transport systems. America's current population is 305 million people. The other 6,300 million people in the World, on average, only emit about 1.2 metric tons per capita per year, 1/6 as much.

Better living standards require more transport, and more transport requires more oil consumption. Figure 6 illustrates the gallons of oil per day per capita, most of which goes for transport, for different countries around the World, as a function of their per capita GDP (Gross Domestic Product). Clearly, while there's a lot of scatter, there is a strong correlation between living standards, as measured by GDP per capita and transport use, as measured by oil consumption per capita.(14)

As countries like China and India industrialize–their combined population is 2.5 Billion people–and their living standards improve, their transport needs will climb, along with their fuel consumption. In China, highway traffic is increasing 18% annually, along with oil consumption. China now buys more cars per year than the U.S.

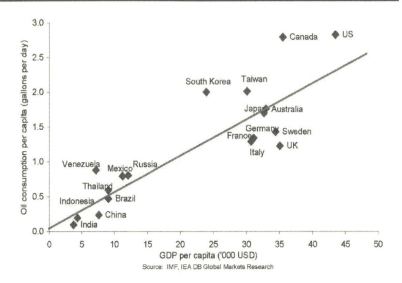

In combination with better living standards, transport carbon dioxide emissions will also grow as World population increases. The UN projects that by 2050 AD, there will be 9 Billion people living on Earth. If the average per capita transport carbon dioxide emissions were only ½ of present U.S. per capita emissions, World total emissions from transport use alone would then be 30 Billion tons of carbon dioxide per year. Wait, it gets even worse. World oil production has plateaued and will soon start to decline rapidly. Today, the World consumes 30 Billion barrels of oil per year.(15) In 2050, at the level of World transport postulated above, it would consume 75 Billion Barrels annually. There are only about 1 Trillion Barrels of oil left in the ground.(16) Right now, humans consume 10 Barrels of oil for every 4 new Barrels discovered. Conventional oil cannot sustain transport in a World with a growing population and increasing industrialization.

What about the magic alternative fuels that politicians and promoters push, i.e., biofuels and hydrogen. Both are impossible. There is hardly enough arable land on Earth to feed today's 6.6 Billion population, and its fertility is decreasing. Feeding 9 Billion people in 2050 will be extremely difficult by itself, without also trying to produce Biofuels. To produce Biofuels equivalent to the 600 gallons per capita of transport fuel that Americans consume annually would take 7 acres of farmland per person, compared to the 1 acre per person we need for our food. *There is not enough land on Earth for large-scale production of Biofuels.*

Hydrogen fuel for transport is not only an impossible dream, but would be a horrific nightmare. Producing hydrogen equivalent to the 180 Billion gallons of gasoline and diesel fuel that Americans now consume annually (17) by electrolysis of water would require building 1,000 new nuclear power reactors, each of 1,000 megawatts electric capacity. The capital cost would be about 10 Trillion dollars. The nuclear waste and safety problems would be horrendous. To achieve half of the present American transport level for the 9 Billion people living in 2050 AD would require building 15,000 new reactors, each of 1,000 megawatts capacity.

The safety and security problems of hydrogen fueled cars are even worse. Do you want to drive at 70 miles per hour in bumper to bumper traffic, where each car has a tank of high pressure (5,000 psi) hydrogen gas or liquid hydrogen equivalent in explosive power to 500 pounds of TNT? Hydrogen likes to leak and mixes readily with air, forming explosive mixtures that can be detonated by a microscopic spark or flame, resulting in a cascade of exploding cars and trucks.

Hydrogen cars would be wonderful for terrorists. Just steal or carjack a hydrogen car, attach a small explosive device with a timer or cellphone trigger to the hydrogen tank, park it in a garage, shopping mall, or busy city street, and then remotely detonate the device, releasing the hydrogen to explode with the equivalent of 500 pounds of TNT. Simple and easy to do – one million cars are stolen or carjacked every year in the U.S. *Hydrogen is not a practical transport fuel.*

The last option for transport fuel is synthetic gasoline and diesel fuel made from coal, methane, oil shale, tar sands, etc. Such synfuels have been produced in various countries for decades. Although expensive, they are practical and could support oil based transport systems for many years. However, besides the environmental problems of extraction – water pollution, habitat destruction, etc. – they greatly increase the amount of carbon dioxide. Roughly, making one gallon of liquid synthetic fuel from coal produces about 2 times as much carbon dioxide as a gallon of gasoline from conventional oil. The liquid synthetic fuels require additional carbon to generate hydrogen atoms that incorporate into the oil molecules, i.e. (CH_2) for synthetic gasoline. Likewise, synthetic liquid fuels derived from methane, tar sands, oil shale, etc., also generate additional carbon dioxide.

Researchers are working on ways to capture carbon dioxide from fossil fueled power plants and pump it deep underground rather than release it to the atmosphere. If technically and economically practical, carbon dioxide sequestration could also be used to prevent carbon dioxide from synfuels production plants from entering the atmosphere. However, unless the cost of long term sequestration is low enough, the tragedy of the commons will apply and sequestration will not occur. If synthetic gasoline costs 5 dollars a gallon without sequestration and 10 dollars with, guess which consumers and policy makers will choose. So far, economically practical methods have not been established for long-term assured sequestration.

Is it practical to capture and sequester carbon dioxide from auto exhausts before they leave the tailpipe? No. The size, cost, and weight of a carbon dioxide capture unit for an automobile would be too great. Moreover, think of going to a station after consuming a tank full of gasoline to have your big, heavy carbon dioxide capture unit removed and a fresh big, heavy unit installed in its place. It won't happen. Consumers won't let it happen. If cars and trucks continue to be powered by fossil fuels, their carbon dioxide emissions will inevitably flow into the atmosphere.

So, even if the World did eliminate all other sources of carbon dioxide emissions from power plants, industrial processes, etc., transport emissions in 2050 AD will be much greater than today's totals if we use synfuels to power our autos, trucks, airplanes and other modes of transport.

Most of the World's population lives at or near poverty level. To enjoy a better standard of living, they will require massive amounts of new transport. They already are demanding it. China's highway traffic is increasing 18% per year, and India's 12% per year. Today, there is one auto for every .04 Chinese, (17) while there is one auto for every 1.5 Americans.(18) There are 2.5 Billion people in China and India, and 305 million in America. Even if China and India grow to 1 car per 3 persons, that still would be 800 million new cars in the World. Other developing nations are not far behind. Thinking that World transport will not grow enormously in the next few decades is to stick one's head in the sand.

How fast will atmospheric carbon dioxide increase if synfuels are used for our transportation systems? The following graph (19) shows that the energy intensity of auto travel has changed very little over the last 30 years while the energy intensity of air travel has dropped by a factor of 3, due to better jet engines. However, further gains in jet engine efficiency will be small, since the technology has matured.

The relatively constant energy efficiency for auto and truck intercity travel (19) is due to drivers wanting faster, bigger, heavier more powerful vehicles that have increased frictional and air drag losses. Hopefully, better technology will reduce the energy usage per mile, though one cannot be certain.

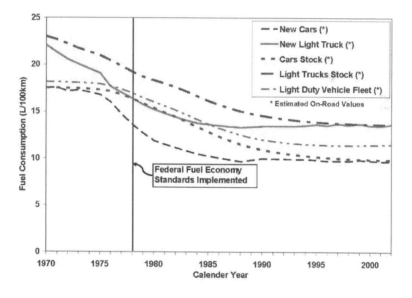

Figure 7

60 Billion tons of carbon dioxide per year from transport emissions alone (all other sources are assumed zero), 2.4 times the present total rate of 25 Billion tons annually, would increase atmospheric carbon dioxide by 5 ppm per year. By 2100, the present 390 ppm would rise to 790 ppm, a 400 ppm increase.

Climate scientists warn that the carbon dioxide concentration should actually be reduced to about 350 ppm if Earth is to have a stable climate. This cannot happen if we continue with fossil and synthetic fuels for transport. The effects of 790 ppm on climate would be devastating – massive flooding and very severe storms, droughts, crop losses, and famines, the death of much of ocean life, and very possibly triggering a runaway greenhouse catastrophe as the methane hydrates in the ocean and the organic matter in the permafrost decompose.

Table 2 illustrates the carbon dioxide emissions from just transport from 2000 to 2100, assuming the following:

1. Transport emissions per mile (or kilometer) traveled remain constant.

2. Per capita World transport emissions increase linearly from the values in 2000 to ½ of the present U.S. per capita transport emissions by 2040 AD, and remain constant thereafter.

3. Synfuels will phase in and be the primary source of vehicle fuel by 2040 AD.

4. The carbon dioxide emissions from synfuel production will not be captured, so that per mile traveled, the emissions will be *double* those of today's value.

Table 2

Billions of Tons of CO_2 Emitted per Year by World Transport	% From Transport	Year	Atmospheric CO_2 Concentration, ppm	Ratio CO_2 Concentration to Preindustrial 280 ppm
6 Billion	25%	2000	365	1.30
8 Billion	30%	2010	387	1.38
15 Billion	50%	2020	410	1.46
30 Billion	75%	2030	440	1.57
60 Billion	100%	2040	490	1.75
60 Billion	100%	2050	540	1.93
60 Billion	100%	2060	590	2.11
60 Billion	100%	2070	640	2.28
60 Billion	100%	2080	690	2.46
60 Billion	100%	2090	740	2.64
60 Billion	100%	2100	790	2.82

To better visualize how much carbon dioxide would be in the atmosphere by 2100, imagine that all of that 790 parts per million in the global atmosphere suddenly concentrated in the air above the continental 48 United States with its land area of 3.6 million square miles. The concentration of carbon dioxide in the U.S. air would be almost 5%; 10% is immediately lethal.

Another way of looking at it: if the 790 ppm carbon dioxide were liquefied, it would form a lake 30 miles square by 1.2 mile deep.

What a monument it would be to our extinction!

Actions Not Talk

Politicians and pundits offer vague promises and exhortations about the dangers of global warming and how we must do something. Somehow, however, doing something never seems to come down to specific plans and actions.

80% reductions in greenhouse gases by 2050? 20% reduction by 2020? Measured from what levels? By what countries? By what technologies? What is the schedule and cost? Cap and trade or carbon tax? Voluntary or enforced? How long do we have before the ocean dies? How long before runaway warming from carbon dioxide and methane from the rising temperatures in the permafrost and undersea methane hydrates wipe out most life on Earth? What is the maximum carbon dioxide concentration we can tolerate in the atmosphere?

Ask these question of our leaders and they blink, unable to answer except with platitudes. The pathetic legislation they introduce to limit greenhouse gases is either never passed, or if passed, watered down so much that it's toothless. Agreement among nations calling for meaningful actions to limit greenhouse gas emissions? Forget it.

The general attitude seems to be, "Maybe there's a real problem with global warming or maybe not. Right now, we can't tell. In any case, it's a long way off. If it turns out in 20, 30, 40 years, or whenever, that there really is a problem, we'll deal with it then. Meanwhile, let's go on as usual".

Unfortunately, by the time most people, including the global warming deniers and the industry lobbyists recognize and admit that the problem is real, it probably will be too late. We will have passed the point of no return, with runaway global warming and unavoidable climate catastrophe ahead.

What are the specific actions we should take now to give humanity the best chance of avoiding climate catastrophe and possible extinction?

First, we need to develop practical energy and transport technologies that do not use fossil fuels. These technologies should be commercially practical and able to be quickly implemented on a large scale, whenever the decision comes to eliminate greenhouse gas emissions and the use of fossil fuels. No waiting for 10 more years of development and testing before implementation can begin. "Be Prepared" is the motto – not "let's think about what we should do"

New technologies would include better wind, solar, and nuclear power plants, ways to store large amounts of energy from wind and solar farms, and ways to launch practical solar satellites to beam power back to Earth.

Implementation on a large scale of practical electric transport systems is needed A.S.A.P. This includes both electric cars and Maglev. The Maglev 2000 system can be commercially implemented in only 4 years. Combined with electric cars for short trips, almost all of the World's surface transport could use electrically powered vehicles with zero greenhouse gas emissions.

It is vitally important to find out what are the consequences of continued greenhouse gas emissions and their timelines. How much time do we have before the oceans become too acidic for most existing marine life? How much time before runaway global warming occurs? We need to accurately know when these events will occur as a function of the amount and types of emissions, not just by computer modeling, but also by real experiments.

Answers to these questions are crucial to humanity's future. Present World GDP is 60 Trillion dollars per year. How much is it worth spending to answer these questions? Right now, we spend a few million dollars annually – less than one-millionth of the World's annual GDP. Is that how little we value obtaining knowledge that could save humanity from global catastrophe? How about spending just 1/1000 of annual World GDP, i.e., 60 Billion dollars per year trying to pin down accurate answers to these questions?

To answer the ocean acidification question, how about isolating ocean habitats of different types at different locations and deliberately increasing their acidity by increasing the concentration of bubbling carbon dioxide in the ocean water inside the site? The site should be representative of the marine ecology and the ocean waters surrounding the site, so that the experimental results are representative of what would happen in the wider ocean. The area of the site should be several hundred acres or more. The effect of the rate of acidification and the level of acidity on marine organisms would be accurately measured.

Answering the runaway global warming questions of how warming ocean water affects subsurface methane hydrate deposits, and how warming of the permafrost affects the release of methane and carbon dioxide from the organic matter in the soil, are vital. Both of these questions should be experimentally investigated, to find out whether or not runaway global warming is a real threat.

For experiments on warming permafrost, experimenters could use solar reflectors to shine more sunlight on a site than it would normally receive, making its temperature rise faster than the permafrost surrounding the site. How much faster would methane and carbon dioxide release rates if the average temperature of the experimental site were 2, 4, 6, 8, 10 degrees Celsius hotter than the surrounding permafrost?

The area of the illuminated site could be relatively small, e.g., an acre or so. Experiments at hundreds of sites scattered around the World in different types of permafrost with different organic contents, could accurately measure how rapidly greenhouse gas emissions from permafrost will accelerate as local temperatures increase.

Experiments on the stability of sub-surface methane hydrates can be carried out at different sites on the ocean bed, using heaters to warm the water above the surface of the seabed at the site. One need not warm the entire ocean – just a thin layer of water trapped between the seabed and a thermally insulating blanket anchored above the bed. Experiments could be carried out at hundreds of different sites around the World, at a wide variety of depths and temperatures, for many different types of methane hydrate deposits.

The ability to forecast the distant future, and to act before it overwhelms us, is what separates humans from lemmings and the other animals. Right now, we are not doing very well with regard to greenhouse gas emissions and global warming. Hopefully, we will soon begin to act, and not just talk. Otherwise, we may end up as part of the 6th Extinction.

Chapter Four

The Maglev America Project – Our Highways to the Future

"This land is your land

This land is my land

From California to the New York Island

From the Redwood Forests to the Gulf Stream Waters

This Land was made for you and me" -- Woody Guthrie

Woody's great folk song got it exactly right. It is our land, with everybody an equal partner in its well-being. It doesn't belong exclusively to the rich and the powerful or the big corporations. America's land, water, air, trees, and animals – they belong to all of us.

If Woody came back today, he would be outraged at what has been done, and what is being done now, to America's environment and people. The Gulf Coast oil disaster is only one example of trashing our environment for corporate profits. How about cutting off the tops of mountains in Appalachia to remove the coal underneath, and dumping the waste into local streams, polluting the water? How about thousands of acres of toxic ash from coal burning power plants that leak into our ground water and flood our farms when it breaks out of storage ponds? How about tons of PCBs dumped into the Hudson River bed? What about the 7 Billion tons of carbon dioxide that America pours into the atmosphere every year, contributing to global warming and ocean acidification? What about the 40,000 deaths and hundreds of thousands of serious injuries on our highways every year, which cost us hundreds of Billions of dollars annually? What about the health damage and shortening of lives due to pollutants and microparticulates emitted by the cars and trucks on our highways?

While Woody would be outraged about the damage done to America's environment and people, he would be absolutely terrified at what's ahead if we do not act soon to prevent it.

Let's focus on transportation. It is absolutely critical to our national security and standard of living. Without our oil fueled cars, trucks, planes, trains, and ships, we would be back in the 1700s with horses, wagons, rafts and sails. What lies ahead if we stick with oil fueled transport? The realities are pretty scary.

Reality #1 Conventional oil will be extremely scarce and expensive

World oil production has plateaued at about 90 million barrels per day, and soon will start to decline. The demand for oil from developing countries like China and India is rapidly increasing, causing them to compete very strongly for the ever scarcer and more expensive oil. Today, the average American consumes 25 barrels of oil per year, while the rest of the 6.6 billion people in the World average only 3.6 barrels per year. When their consumption increases by only 30% to 4.7 barrels per year, America's oil share goes to zero. 10 dollars a gallon at the pump? We should be so lucky!

Reality #2 Synfuels from coal, oil shale, tar sands, etc., are the only way we can continue to use our oil fueled autos, trucks, airplanes, trucks and ships.

Expecting biofuels to meet our liquid fuel needs is not practical. Today, hundreds of millions of people go hungry because there is not enough arable land to feed them. By 2050 there will be 9 billion people in the World, not the 6.6 billion there are today. Soil fertility is degrading, water tables are dropping, the ocean is acidifying, drought areas are increasing – we will be fortunate if we can avoid mass famine, let alone make biofuels.

Today, America has 300 million people and 300 million acres of farmland, approximately 1 acre per person for food production. We consume 600 gallons of gasoline and diesel fuel per person per year. For our autos and trucks to produce ethanol from corn with a net energy equal to the 600 gallons per year of gasoline and diesel fuels would require 7 acres per person, almost the whole area of the continental 48 states. We don't have the land! Biofuels can only supply a very small fraction of our transport fuel needs.

Hydrogen fueled cars and trucks? A fantasy! Not only does it take an enormous amount of electric energy to make enough hydrogen to equal the fuel value of gasoline and diesel we burn today – 1,000 new nuclear reactors, each of 1,000 megawatts generation capacity – the safety and security problems are unsolvable. Imagine driving 70 mph in bumper to bumper traffic, with each car's hydrogen tank – either gaseous hydrogen at 5,000 psi, or liquid hydrogen at 420 degrees Fahrenheit below zero – having the explosive force of 500 pounds of TNT if it escapes in an accident, mixes with air, and detonates. Not only would the car explode, but also its neighboring cars.

Even worse, imagine a terrorist stealing a hydrogen fueled car, attaching a small penetrator device to the hydrogen tank that punches a hole in the tank, and detonates the resulting hydrogen-air mixture. The penetrator device could probably be bought on the black market. The terrorist could park the car in an underground garage, a shopping mall, or a busy city street. When the tank detonated, the shredded parts of the car would kill everybody in the vicinity, and cause a spreading cascade of explosions in neighboring hydrogen fueled cars. With time out for a lunch break, the terrorist could set off 2 or 3 cars a day.

Synfuels from coal, tar sands and oil shale are practical and affordable and have been produced in a number of countries for many years. For many years, Canada has produced one million barrels of syncrude daily from the tar sands in Alberta.

World leaders call for an 80% reduction in global carbon dioxide emissions by 2050 AD. This is impossible if we continue with oil fueled transport. An 80% reduction corresponds to reducing the present World emissions of 25 Billion tons per year down to only 5 Billion tons annually. If the World transitions to synfuels, and its average per capita transport usage in 2050 AD is ½ that of today's value, transport emissions alone would be 60 Billion tons per year.

If this happens, there will be no hope of stopping massive global warming, the ocean will acidify to the point that most marine life dies, and most of the World's species will go extinct, probably including humans.

Reality #3 The World must transition soon to electric transport, based on electric autos, trucks and 2nd generation Maglev.

Electric autos and trucks would be used for short local trips. The new Chevy Volt automobile, for example, will be able to go 40 miles between recharges. 2nd generation Maglev can transport passengers, autos, trucks and freight for long distances, at high speeds to convenient easily accessible stations near their final destinations. Autos and trucks will simply drive off the Maglev vehicle and go by highway to their destinations; passengers will use public or private transit.

High Speed Rail (HSR) is currently being touted as America's path for future transport, but it is an unsustainable proposition. It requires massive government subsidies for construction and operation, and is very expensive for travelers. It cannot carry trucks, autos, and freight, only passengers. It will not meet our future transport needs. Today, the average American takes a round trip on Amtrak every 24 years. Even in countries like France and Japan with fully developed High Speed Rail service, HSR provides only a small fraction of transport needs. The per capita HSR travel in France is only 400 miles annually, about 1 round trip per year. The per capita annual driving distance in France is 7,600 miles, 20 times greater than the HSR travel distance. The average American drives 10,000 miles annually. Even if the traveler were to equal the French HSR distance, which is very unlikely given the much lower population density and much greater size of the United States, compared to France, HSR would do virtually nothing to meet America's future transport needs.

If we want to prevent an environmental catastrophe from synfuels, America must very soon begin the transition to electric autos and Maglev. To carry out this transition, we have proposed the program called the Maglev America Project, which we describe below. The necessary technology already exists, and the required materials and manufacturing methods are commercially available. Maglev America Project is best described in terms of the answers to the following questions.

1. What is the Maglev America Project?

2. Why is it important?

3. Where and when will it be built?

4. What are its costs and benefits?

To answer the first question, the Maglev America Project will construct a 28,800 mile network of high speed Maglev routes that interconnect all of the 174 metropolitan areas in the U.S. with populations of 250,000 persons or greater, as determined by the U.S. Census Bureau. All 48 States in the continental U.S. will be served by Maglev America Project. 74% of the 304 million persons in the U.S., plus 10 million more in the Canadian cities Toronto, Montreal, and Vancouver, will live within 15 miles of a convenient Maglev station, from which they can travel at 300 mph to any other Maglev station in America. Passengers, highway trucks, passengers with their personal autos, and freight containers will all travel on the National Maglev Network.

The Maglev America Project will create America's new "Interstate Highway" system for the 21st Century, with the advantages that it will be faster, cheaper and environmentally much better than our present Interstate Highway System. It will drastically reduce our dependence on foreign oil imports, substantially reduce greenhouse gas emissions, save many thousands of lives now lost on the highways each year, prevent hundreds of thousands of serious injuries, improve public health by eliminating pollution and microparticulates from cars and trucks, and brake dust from commuter and light rail operations, reduce congestion and eliminate delays due to adverse weather. Plus, it will be much more comfortable to travel by Maglev – no road, rail, braking, or engine noise, no bumpiness and lots of very comfortable sitting room for the traveler. It will save many hundreds of hours of commuting time, be extremely reliable, and much less stressful than traveling on our existing transport systems. In the Interstate Maglev System, people will travel at high speeds to convenient, easily accessible stations near their final destinations. Autos and trucks will simply drive off the Maglev vehicle and go by highway to their destinations; passengers will use public or private transit.

The answer to the second question, "Why is the Maglev America Project important?" is simple. There are only two transport options for America in the decades ahead. Either we continue with our present oil fueled transport vehicles, using synfuels from coal, tar sands, oil shale, etc., or we transition to electric transport with the National Maglev Network.

Synfuels will lead to environmental catastrophe, maybe not within the lifetimes of America's older citizens, but very likely within the lifetimes of our young children. Do we really not care what happens to them? Judging from the collapse of many ancient societies that overexploited and wrecked their environments, like the Mayans and others, very often the existing population doesn't care. We hope that today, America and the rest of the World does care, and will chose to transition to electric transport before it's too late.

In choosing electric transport, it is important to realize that besides ensuring a sustainable society and avoiding environmental disaster, there will be major economic, social, and personal benefits in doing so, with the benefits far outweighing the transition costs.

Answering the third question, "Where and when will it be built?" requires more detail. The short answer to when? is "as soon as possible." We have laid out a 20 year program to build the 28,800 mile National Maglev Network, with all segments completed by 2030 AD. On an emergency basis it could probably be built faster, probably in half the time. The important thing is to start now, and not procrastinate.

The Maglev America Project is laid out in phases, with each phase taking 5 years. The first phase involves finishing the development and certification of the 2nd generation Maglev 2000 system. No technology breakthroughs are needed. The materials and manufacturing methods for the various components of the Maglev 2000 system are already proven and suitable for large-scale production. What is needed is to assemble and test full-scale prototype vehicles at operational conditions, certifying their safety and reliability, so that implementation of the actual system can begin. The research in Maglev has already been done, and its feasibility has been proven. The next step is engineering improvements for greater capability.

Assuming Phase 1 starts in 2011, it would be completed by December 2015. Planning for the subsequent construction phases 2, 3, and 4, obtaining environmental and regulatory approval, working out arrangements with private investors who would put up the funds for construction of the Maglev Network etc., would be carried out in parallel with the testing and certification activities in Phase 1.

Before proceeding with a description of the next 3 Phases of the Maglev America Project program, which would construct the National Maglev Network, it is helpful to discuss the nature of the highway traffic increases that the Federal Highway Administration anticipates over the next 25 years.

First, the U.S. population, some 287 million people in 2002 AD, currently 310 million people in June, 2010, is projected to increase to 390 million by 2035 AD, an increase of over 100 million people in just 33 years. This and the increase in GDP will put enormous stress on America's present highway system, as illustrated in Figures 1A and 1B.

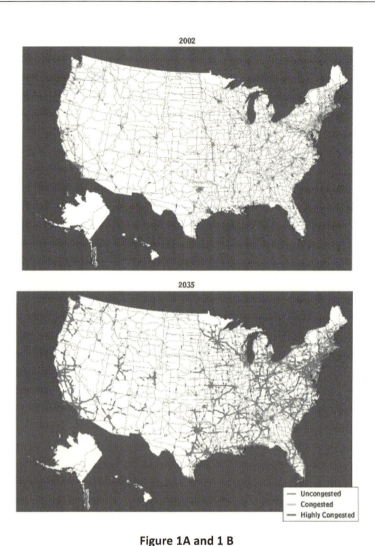

Figure 1A and 1 B

Peak-Period Congestion on the National Highway System

In 2002 only a small fraction of the Interstates were highly congested (The Federal Highway Administration definition of highly congested is that the ratio of traffic flow to traffic capacity is greater than 95%, resulting in slow bumper to bumper movement). By 2035 AD, a large fraction of the U.S. Interstates in the more densely populated states will be highly congested.

Average Daily Long-Haul Freight Traffic on the National Highway System 2002

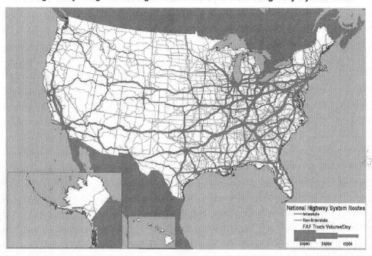

Average Daily Long-Haul Freight Traffic on the National Highway System 2035

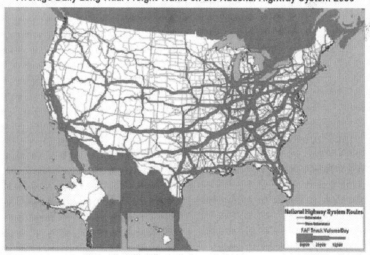

Figure 2A and 2B

Average Daily Long-Haul Freight Traffic on the National Highway System:
Comparison of 2002 with 2035

In 2002, there were only a few highway sections where the truck flow approached 20,000 vehicles per day. By 2035, again due to the increase of 100 million in the U.S. population, and the increased GDP, there are many highway sections where the truck flow is considerably greater than 20,000 vehicles per day. In some segments, truck traffic flow is approaching 50,000 vehicles per day. Think of a flow of 40,000 vehicles per day in a 2 way highway. That's equal to 1 truck passing you every 4 seconds if you stand beside a highway lane and a truck every 2 seconds if you count the truck on the other side of the highway.

Ever wonder how much damage those trucks do to our highways, and how much we have to pay every year to repair the damage? According to a Highway Research Board study, one legal heavy (40 ton) truck does as much damage to the highway as 9,600 automobiles.(1) Think of 40,000 trucks per day in 2035. That's as much damage as 384 million automobiles would cause to the highway you are standing next to.

How much does it cost to repair the highway damage done by trucks? According to another DOT study (2), one heavy truck mile of travel costs 0.41 dollars per year to repair the damage. In the U.S. in 2007, total heavy combination travel was 145 billion truck miles.(3) At 41 cents damage per truck mile, that's 60 billion dollars every year, just to fix the highway damage that trucks cause!

Want to further understand how much Americans pay for truck transport? In 2001, America's total expenditures for truck freight transport by highway trucks were 457 Billion dollars.(4) Of this, 309 billion dollars went for intercity truck transport with the other 148 billion for local truck transport. How much would that be today, with inflation and a bigger population? In 2001, the U.S. population was 285 million, today, in 2010, its 310 million.(5) The GDP deflator corrects for inflation, so that products and services can be expressed in constant dollars, not current ones that decrease in value as time goes on. In 2010 the GDP deflator is 1.21, taking 1.21 2010 dollars to buy the same things with one 2001 dollar.(6) The ratio of 2010 population to 2001 population is 310/285, or 1.09. Accordingly, correcting for inflation and the greater U.S. population would take 457 x 1.09 x 1.21, or 603 Billion dollars for truck transport in 2010 at the same real GDP per capita.

That's a lot of money, but there's still more to come. Of the 37,000 highway traffic fatalities in the U.S. in 2008, 4,200, or 11%, were killed in crashes involving large trucks. An additional 90,000 people were injured in the crashes.(7) Besides the human costs of these deaths and injuries, there are enormous economic costs, projected at more than 200 billion dollars annually. At the fraction of 12%, this amounts to more than 25 billion dollars annually.

Adding the costs of highway transport, highway damage, and deaths and injuries, the total cost of highway trucks is approximately 700 billion dollars annually. And that doesn't include the cost of health damage from the pollutants and microparticulates emitted by Diesel trucks. Studies estimate that people living in high truck traffic areas suffer extensive health problems – lungs, hearts, etc. – with their lives shortened by as much as 2 years. It is difficult to quantitatively project these health costs, but they clearly are enormous, many more billions of dollars.

So, America pays a high cost for truck transport – approaching a trillion dollars per year, today, and well over a trillion dollars annually by 2030 AD, as measured in today's dollars. The projected U.S. population in 2030 will be 373 million, compared to 310 million in 2011, and the real GDP per capita, which has grown by 30% over the last 20 years 1990 to 2010, will hopefully keep growing.

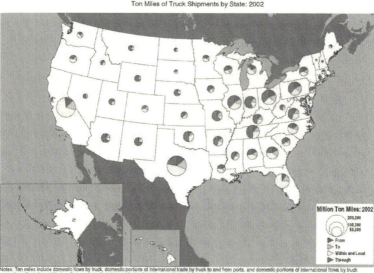

Figure 3

Ton-Miles of Truck Shipments by State: 2002 Map and Data

Lots of boring numbers, to be sure, but they deliver very serious messages:

Message #1. We must have very large amounts of truck freight transport to sustain our standard of living. Railroads, while much cheaper per ton mile, simply cannot do the job. Even though railroad costs per ton mile are 1/10th of that of truck transport, they do not carry much high value, time sensitive freight. Despite the much higher costs per ton mile for truck transport, America spends 10 times as much on trucks for freight hauling as it spends on railroad freight.

Message #2. Unless we find a practical way to get a large portion of truck traffic off the highway, in 2030 America will spend an enormous sum on truck operating costs and highway damage, along with a great cost in fatalities, injuries, and illnesses of its population. Moreover, the greatly increased congestion delays and its costs, which are not included above, will cripple our national productivity.

Message #3. There is a way to accomplish Message #2 – transport of highway trucks by Maglev. Transport costs are much less and highway damage, fatalities, injuries, and health problems are greatly reduced. Moreover, our oil imports will be greatly reduced, and greenhouse gas emissions curtailed. Very important is the amount of truck shipments correlated by state, as illustrated in Figure 3. The states with the greatest ton-miles of truck shipments are California, Texas, Florida, Illinois, Indiana, Ohio, Pennsylvania, Tennessee and Georgia. This data, together with the truck flow data in Figures 2A and 2B, guides where the Maglev routes should be located.

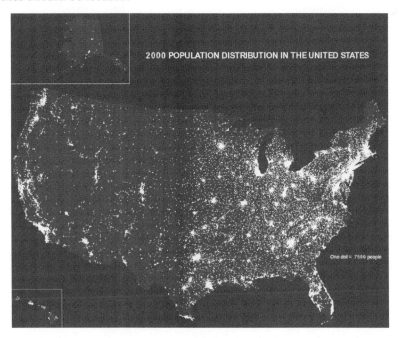

Figure 4

Also very important is where the U.S. population is located. As shown in Figure 4, most of the principal population centers are distributed along the East, West and Gulf Coasts, and in the States bordering the Great Lakes.

Waves of Maglev Construction

Phase 2, termed the "First Maglev Wave"; would be built in 5 years, starting at the beginning of 2016.

Figure 5 shows the East and West Coast Networks built in the first Maglev wave. The first wave would serve 26 States in the lower 48 continental United States, plus Vancouver, Montreal, and Toronto in Canada. Total population in the States served is 227 million. Of this population, 146 million would live within 15 miles of a Maglev Station, from which they could reach any other station in the Network in a few hours.

A total of 6,230 Maglev route miles is built in the first wave. This corresponds to 25,000 people per route mile who live within 15 miles of a Maglev station. At a construction cost of 25 million dollars per two way route mile, the construction cost per person directly served – "directly served" means living within 15 miles of a Maglev station – is only 1,000 dollars. As discussed later, this is an extraordinarily attractive deal. Not only do the Maglev riders not have to pay for the construction of the Maglev routes – they will be privately financed – but they will save at least 1,000 dollars per year in transport costs by riding Maglev. Over a 30 year period, they will save 30,000 and not have to subsidize the Maglev Network. Compare that to building a High Speed Rail Network. The population served would be much smaller, and those riding the Higher Speed Rail Network would pay much more than other modes. Plus, all U.S. taxpayers would subsidize the Rail Network, even though most would not be able to use it, which would be very unfair.

The Fight for Maglev   The Maglev America Project

Figure 5: First Maglev Wave to Be Built 2016 to 2020 AD

Maglev Network	States In Network	Population of States in Network (millions)	Population Living Within 15 Miles of Maglev Stations (millions)	Route Miles in Network
East Coast/Midwest Network	45 MN, WI, IL, IN, OH, PA, NY, MA, VT, NH, MN, ME, RI, DE, MD, VA, DC, NC, SC, GA, FL plus Toronto & Montreal	175.8 (includes Toronto, Montreal)	102.9 (includes Toronto, Montreal)	4,224
West Coast Maglev Network	CA, NV, OR, WA & Vancouver, Canada	50.9 (includes Vancouver)	43.5 (includes Vancouver)	2006
Total for First Maglev Wave (Both Networks)	26 States Plus Toronto, Montreal & Vancouver	226.7	146.4	6230
65 % of population in States Served by the Networks live within 15 Miles of a Maglev Station				

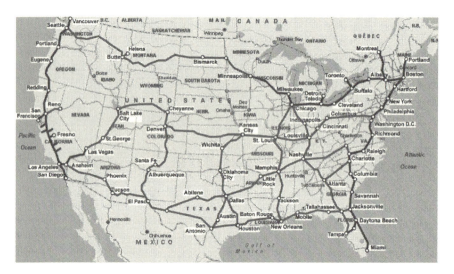

Figure 6: Second Maglev Wave completed in 2021-2025 AD

Maglev Network	States In Network	Population of States in Network (millions)	Population Living Within 15 Miles of Maglev Stations (millions)	Route Miles in Network
First Wave Plus Second Wave	45 (Iowa, Nebraska & S. Dakota not in Network) plus Toronto, Montreal & Vancouver	310 (includes Toronto, Montreal & Vancouver)	210 (includes Toronto, Montreal & Vancouver)	18,630
74 % of population in States served by the Network live within 15 Miles of a Station				

Figure 6 shows the second Maglev Wave, which would be built starting at the beginning of 2021 and proceeding through 2025. Three transcontinental routes would be built to connect the East and West Coast Maglev Networks, plus 5 North-South routes. The number of states in the National Maglev Network would increase to 45, plus Vancouver, Toronto, and Montreal in Canada. 310 million people would live in the States and Canadian cities served by the Network, with 210 million people directly served – that is, living within 15 miles of a Maglev station. 12,600 Maglev route miles would be built in the second Wave, bring the total to 18,600 miles. 65% of the total population in the served States and Canadian cities would live within 15 miles of a Maglev station.

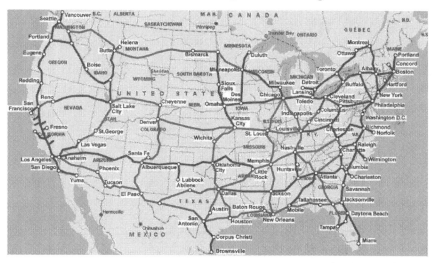

Figure 7: Third Maglev Wave completed in 2026-2030 AD

Maglev Network	States In Network	Population of States in Network (millions)	Population Living Within 15 Miles of Maglev Stations (millions)	Route Miles in Network
First, Second and Third Waves Completed	48 plus Toronto, Montreal & Vancouver	315 (includes Toronto, Montreal & Vancouver)	232 (includes Toronto, Montreal & Vancouver)	28,800
74% of population in States live within 15 Miles of a Maglev Station				

Figure 7 shows the third Maglev Wave, which would be built starting at the beginning of 2026, and proceeding through 2030. A 4th transcontinental Maglev route would be built along U.S. I-40, plus various routes to provide more efficient interconnections between the routes built in the 1st and 2nd Maglev Waves. The 48 U.S. States, plus

Vancouver, Toronto, and Montreal, would now be served by the 28,800 mile National Maglev Network, with a total population of 315 million people. Of that 315 million, 232 million of the population served would live within 15 miles of a Maglev station.

In general, the smaller Metropolitan areas, e.g., those with a population of a few hundred thousand people, will have 1 or 2 Maglev stations that serve their area. The larger areas, e.g. Seattle, Dallas, Chicago, Los Angeles, New York, etc., will have multiple stations that serve their area, with the number of stations depending on the size of the metropolitan area. Each station will be connected to all of the other Maglev stations in the high speed intercity Maglev Network.

Inside a given metropolitan area, Maglev will also provide local transport service, using existing RR trackage that has been adapted for Maglev travel. The adaptation is simple and cheap, consisting of attaching thin panels that contain loops of ordinary aluminum conductor to the RR cross ties. Maglev vehicles can then be magnetically levitated above, and propelled along, the existing RR track to serve local stations in the metropolitan area. Conventional trains can continue to use the RR trackage, given appropriate scheduling. The cost of adaptation is small – only about 6 million dollars per two way mile. Adaptation of existing RR tracks for Maglev travel can be quickly carried out without interfering with or disrupting existing conventional train schedules, and without expensive disruption of existing infrastructure.

Construction of the high speed 2nd generation Maglev 2000 intercity guideway would be simple and quick, with a minimal amount of field construction, in contrast to High Speed Rail and the 1st generation Maglev systems. High Speed Rail requires a very deep, on the order of 14 feet in depth, very stable, very straight and level on-grade roadbed. This involves a great deal of field construction, which is highly disruptive. Moreover, the on-grade roadbed must be fenced off from access, like the High Speed Rail lines in Europe and Japan.

The elevated guideways for the 1st generation Japanese and German Maglev systems do not require fencing, but do require extensive and expensive field construction, with considerable disruption to existing nearby infrastructure.

In contrast, the Maglev 2000 guideway beams are prefabricated in large factories, and shipped to the construction site by truck, rail, or along an already operating guideway. The prefabricated 100 foot long beams already have the aluminum loop panels and other equipment attached to them at the factory prior to shipment.

At the construction site, pre-poured concrete footings for the piers that support the guideway beams have already been put in place. When the prefabricated beams and piers arrive at the construction site, they are quickly erected by conventional cranes onto the pre-poured footings, and the various electrical connections between the beams carried out.

The Maglev 2000 routes can be rapidly constructed. Based on a 2 hour time period to place a guideway beam on a pier, and 4 construction teams at the construction site, with each team having a crane, a 2 shift per day schedule could construct 2 miles per week of two way Maglev 2000 guideway. This corresponds to 100 miles per year. The first Maglev wave of 6,800 miles over a 5 year construction period would have an average construction rate of 1,240 miles per year; 12 construction crews could do the whole job. In practice, because of the desire to engage local construction companies, there probably would be more construction crews operating at 8 hours per day and 2 cranes per site. In any case, the field construction requirements will be relatively modest, both in terms of cost, and in personnel.

At 25 million dollars per two way mile, the projected cost for the Maglev 2000 monorail guideway, the construction cost of the first Maglev Wave would be 150 billion dollars, about 30 billion dollars per year. To put this in perspective, the U.S. consumes approximately 180 billion gallons of gasoline and diesel fuel annually. The 30 billion dollars is equivalent to only 16 cents a gallon – a real bargain, considering it will be much cheaper to travel by Maglev than to drive.

To this construction cost must be added the cost of the intercity Maglev 2000 stations. The amortization cost of the Maglev 2000 vehicles is best included in the operating costs for transport on the network, since the number of vehicles required will depend on the volume of traffic.

When the 3rd Maglev 2000 Wave is complete, the total guideway construction cost of the 28,800 mile National Maglev Network will be approximately 700 Billion dollars at an average construction cost of 25 million dollars per two way mile. All of the 174 metropolitan areas in the 48 continental U.S. states will be served. Conservatively assuming 2 Maglev stations per metropolitan area – many areas will only need 1 station – and 20 million dollars per average station cost, again very conservative, the station cost would be about 60 billion dollars, bringing total system cost to about 760 billion dollars, including the various necessary odds and ends.

This 760 billion dollars would be provided by private investment, probably by government guaranteed bonds, at an average rate of about 30 billion dollars annually. Taxpayers would not provide any of the invested capital.

What are the revenues and benefits of the Maglev America Project? First, let us consider the revenues. The U.S currently spends about 1,500 billion dollars per year on direct transport cost, or 30 trillion dollars over a 20 year period to 2030 AD – 40 times greater than the construction cost of the National Maglev Network. However, if we continue to rely on our oil fueled autos, trucks, planes, and trains, the actual cost will be much greater. First, the U.S. population will increase from today's (2010) population of 304 million people to 373 million people by 2030. Second, the cost of fuel will be much greater as world supplies dwindle, and countries like China and India get a bigger share of the shrinking oil pie. Third, the *real* U.S. Gross Domestic Product (GDP) per capita – the measure of our average standard of living – will hopefully grow.

The real U.S. GDP per capita in 1990, 20 years ago, was 32,000 dollars per person, measured in 2005 dollars. Today, again measured in constant 2005 dollars, the real GDP per capita is 43,000 dollars per person, a gain of 1.5% per year over the 20 year period.

This translates into a substantially higher than average standard of living from that of 20 years ago. Remember, that is the average – some people are much better off, while lots of others are worse off. Americans expect their standard of living to grow with time. If it doesn't, they get angry. Assuming that the real standard of living grows by 1.5% over the next 20 years to 2030 AD, the real GDP per capita then will increase to 58,000 dollars, again measured in constant 2005 dollars.

Sounds great, *if* it happens. Now what does that increasing population and increasing GDP per capita mean for transportation outlays? In the last year of which outlay data is available from the U.S. Statistical Abstracts, 2001, the U.S. spent 309 billion dollars on intercity truck transport. As the populations grows from 285 million people in 2001 to 373 million in 2030, and as their real GDP per capita grows from 39,800 dollars in 2001 to 58,000 dollars in 2030, the intercity truck outlay will grow from 309 billion in 2001 to 500 Billion dollars. This assumes the same oil fueled truck technology in 2030 as we have today. In practice, the intercity truck outlay will be considerably greater than 500 Billion dollars, because of the rapidly escalating cost of diesel fuel and gasoline.

So, assume that in 2030 the 28,800 mile National Maglev Network carried only intercity highway trucks with their loads – no passengers, autos, or freight containers normally carried by railroad. What would be the annual transport savings for the U.S., as measured in constant 2005 dollars?

For diesel fueled intercity trucks on the highway the operating costs, including truck maintenance, amortization, energy, personnel, traffic scheduling, etc., are about 30 cents per ton mile transported. For trucks carried on the National Maglev Network, the operating costs would be about 10 cents per ton mile.

Accordingly, the annual savings in intercity truck transport outlays would be 20 cents per ton mile carried, or two thirds of the 590 billion dollars it would cost if they all drove by highway instead of taking Maglev. That's an annual savings of 390 billion dollars! From that, must be deducted the return on investment (ROI) to the private investors that put up the 760 billion dollars to build the National Maglev Network. At 10% ROI, the net savings in truck transport would be 314 billion dollars annually. At 15% ROI – remember, these are government guaranteed bonds, for which 15% seems high – the net savings would still be very large, 238 billion dollars annually.

However, there are additional sources of revenue for the National Maglev Network. These include passengers that would otherwise be flying or driving, passengers traveling with their autos, and freight containers. These sources can provide over 200 billion of additional revenue per year, making the total transport net savings enabled by the National Maglev Network more than 238 + 200 or 438 billion dollars annually, assuming a 15% ROI on the construction cost of the Network.

The above projections assume that 100% of the long distance transport of trucks, passengers, autos, and freight containers in 2030 AD is carried by the National Maglev Network. Obviously, this will not be the case. However, because of the lower cost, faster travel times, greater convenience, and environmental benefits, it appears very likely that the percentage of U.S. long distance travel that takes place in the Maglev Network will be very high, say in the range of 70 to 80 percent at least.

At a 75% utilization factor, the net transport savings received by the National Maglev Network would be well over 300 billion dollars annually, or about 1,000 dollars per person per year. Faster, better, cheaper travel – what could be more desirable?

What are the societal and environmental benefits of the National Maglev Network, which are even more important than the economic benefits?

First, the area of safety and health. Traveling by Maglev will be much safer than by highway. Today, over 5,000 deaths per year and 100,000 serious injuries are due to trucks. Highway deaths and injuries will soar in the years ahead as the roads become much more congested. Taking trucks and autos off the roads and carrying them by Maglev will save many thousands of lives and serious injuries per year. Moreover, the damage done to people's health by pollutants and microparticulates in heavily traveled areas will be greatly reduced. As an auxiliary benefit, many Billions of dollars now spent because of these deaths, injuries, and damaged health will be avoided.

Second, the linked areas of national security and economic productivity. As a nation, we cannot be secure if our economic productivity is weak, while the U.S. cannot be secure if it depends on unstable foreign sources for critical materials, such as oil. The National Maglev Network will substantially reduce oil imports – 70% of U.S. oil consumption is currently used for transport. Building the National Network will provide millions of new U.S. jobs, for both domestic and export application of Maglev. Moreover, reducing the cost of domestic transport and enabling more efficient, faster delivery of people and goods inside the U.S. will increase economic productivity and make our exports more competitive.

Third are the environmental benefits. Maglev emits no pollutants and greenhouse gases, is much more energy efficient than current modes of transport, and is very quiet with no rail, braking or engine noise.

In summary, the Maglev America Project is practical, uses existing technology, and will provide America with tremendous social and economic benefits. The 28,800 mile National Network can be completed by 2030 AD. Built by private investment, it will not require government subsidization for construction and operation.

All that is needed for the U.S. Government to bring the National Maglev Network into being is to fund a facility to test and certify the 2nd generation Maglev system described in this proposal. The funding required is extremely modest, about 600 million dollars over a 5 year period. This amounts to a per capita funding of only 2 dollars per American – about the cost of one hot dog. For this investment, the transport savings for the average American will amount to about 30,000 dollars over a 30 year period.

The Fight for Maglev	Global Maglev

100

Chapter Five

Global Maglev: The Big Winners in a Much Smaller World

"The World is Round" -- Christopher Columbus

The short answer is, "everyone will be winners." Why? There are many reasons: elimination of fossil fuels for transport, greater energy efficiency, better living standards, and much pleasanter, more comfortable travel.

OK, everybody wins, but some countries will be bigger winners than others. Who will be the biggest winners? Who will be the new Lorenzo de' Medici in the Transport Renaissance?

The biggest winner of all will be the country that develops, manufactures and exports 2nd generation Maglev vehicles, guideways, superconducting magnets, etc., to the rest of the World. The potential market is enormous. U.S. Transport expenditures are approximately 10% of GDP (Gross Domestic Product), about 1.5 Trillion dollars annually out of its 15 Trillion dollar GDP. World GDP is 60 Trillion dollars annually. At 10% of GDP, that's 6 Trillion dollars spent annually on World transport. Maglev could capture half of the transport market, amounting to about 3 Trillion dollars annually.

The 2nd generation Maglev 2000 system is designed for easy export of its equipment. 20 miles of prefabricated, fully equipped guideway beams and piers can be shipped in one large container ship, along with Maglev vehicles, electrical equipment, sensors, etc. After unloading at a port, the various components can be quickly and easily trucked to a construction site. At the site, conventional cranes would quickly erect the guideway beams and piers on pre-poured concrete footings, at very low cost. The exporting country will garner most of the profits and jobs from the manufacturing process, not the importing country.

Who will be the winning country and World Leader in manufacturing and exporting 2nd generation Maglev 2000 systems? That is a harder question to answer. For 44 years we have been working to make America the World Leader in Maglev, but without success. For the most part, America's leaders have been indifferent or opposed to developing Maglev.

For a brief moment in 1990, with the backing of the late Senator Daniel Patrick Moynihan, we believed that America would become the World Leader in Maglev. He shepherded a 750 million dollar R&D program for an American Maglev system to overtake Japanese and German Maglev. Sadly, the chairman of the Transportation Committee in the House of Representatives, who was from Detroit, refused to hold hearings on Senator Moynihan's bill, killing it. Had it become law, America would now have its National Maglev Network, and export Billions of dollars' worth of Maglev products to the rest of the World.

America still has a chance to develop 2nd generation Maglev and be the World Leader, but so far, our leaders have done nothing to win its benefits for American workers. Who will win the Maglev Race? At this point, we are sad to say, probably not the U.S. unless it acts quickly.

The World keeps shrinking in size. It's smaller than in Greek and Roman times, smaller than in Columbus's day, smaller still than in Jules Verne's novel, when Phileas Fogg went around the World in 80 days on ships and trains. Today, we can go around the World in 80 hours on jetliners, 24 times faster than in 1873.

However, there still are limits. Passengers can go around the World in 80 hours, but not most freight. To transport 1 ton of freight 1,000 miles by air costs 1,000 dollars. By truck, 300 dollars. By conventional rail, 40 dollars. By ship, 10 dollars. Three trillion ton-miles of freight are carried by truck and rail inside the U.S. per year, 100 times that carried by air.

The previous chapters described how Maglev can transport passengers and freight inside countries much more cheaply than trucks and rail. What about ships?

Today, very few people travel by ship across the oceans, because it's just too slow. Who has the time for a trip at 20 mph, when a jet aircraft will get you there at 500 mph? Yes, people take cruises to Bermuda, the

Bahamas, and Alaska, but that's for fun and relaxation. And it's too expensive for most of us.

It's a different situation for shipping freight across the ocean. Today, it's the only choice for most freight – shipping by air is just too expensive. But there are major downsides to ships. First, it takes a long time. To ship goods from China and other Asian countries to Europe takes 35 days. Second, ships consume an enormous amount of energy. World shipping consumes about 7.3 million barrels of oil per day, almost 10% of total World consumption.(1) Third, ships are a major emitter of pollutants and greenhouse gases. A big container ship emits as much sulfur oxides as 50 million automobiles (1). The 760 million cars in the World emit 79,000 tons of sulfur dioxide annually, while the World's 90,000 ships emit 20 million tons per year. A NOAA (National Oceanic and Atmospheric Administration) study (2) estimates that 60,000 people world-wide die prematurely each year from pollutants and microparticulates emitted by the World's ships. The areas most severely impacted are the Mediterranean, India, and East Asia, as well as the areas near major ports in California and Florida.

Well, the World will soon get smaller still, at least for freight, when the global Maglev routes described in this chapter are built. Using them, it will be much faster and cheaper to transport goods by Maglev, rather than by ship. In contrast to ships, the electrically-powered Maglev freight vehicles will not emit pollutants and greenhouse gases, and use less energy per ton-mile than ships.

The previous chapters focused on the Maglev America Project. In this chapter, we focus on 6 major Maglev Projects for the World:

1. Adapting the Trans-Siberian Railway for Maglev to transport freight and passengers between Europe and the Far East.

2. Construct an Undersea Tunnel across the Bering Strait to connect Asia with North America.

3. Construct a Pan-American Maglev Route from Alaska to Argentina.

4. Construct an undersea tunnel across the Strait of Gibraltar to connect Europe with Africa.

5. Adapt existing conventional rail lines in India for Maglev.

6. Adapt existing conventional rail lines in China for Maglev.

Construction of these projects would interconnect Europe, Asia, North and South America, and Africa into a single vast Maglev Transport Network that would carry freight and passenger traffic for the almost 7 Billion people living on those continents. Only the people living in Australia and the Ocean Islands, a total of only about 30 million, will not be connected together.

Before describing the construction and operation of these 6 global Maglev projects, it is useful to discuss how transporting freight by Maglev will compare with transport by ships. We have chosen the Q and A format to make the comparison.

Q1: How big is World shipping in ton-miles transported and the cost of transport? What do ships transport?

A1: World shipping transported 27.6 trillion ton-miles in 2004 (3), ten times as much as the 3 trillion ton-miles transported per year in the U.S. by truck and rail. 6.7 Billion tons are actually shipped for an average distance of 4,000 miles, resulting in 27.6 trillion ton-miles (Some shipping routes are longer than 4,000 miles, like the 10,000 mile Europe to Asia route). The total cost of World shipping is 380 Billion dollars per year, corresponding to an average cost of 1.38 cents per ton-mile. Crude oil and oil products account for 41% of the total ton-miles; coal, 12%; iron ore, 12%; grain, 5%; and other dry cargo, 30%.

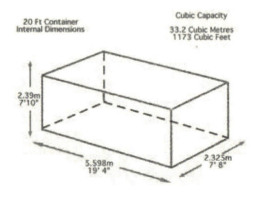

Figure 1

Q2: How are the different cargoes shipped? What is a TEU?

A2: Oil, oil products, coal, iron ore, grain, and some dry cargo is shipped in bulk form inside the ship. Most dry cargo is shipped inside discrete closed containers than can be individually loaded and stacked on a ship.(Figure 2) Containers are generally 20 or 40 feet long, 8 feet wide, and 8 feet high. The acronym TEU stands for "Twenty Feet Equivalent Unit." The maximum cargo load for a TEU is 20 short tons (1 short ton = 2,000 pounds). A TEU is basically just a steel box into which one can pack any kind of dry goods – clothing, electronic equipment, furniture, etc. One of the World's largest container ships is the Emma Maersk. It can transport 11,000 TEUs. Arriving at a port, the TEUs can be quickly unloaded as individual units onto a rail car or into a truck for transport to a destination hundreds of miles away. After unloading its TEUs the ship can then be loaded with new TEUs for shipment to another port. The total World container ship capacity is 310 million TEUs. Many of the World's ports handle 10 million or more TEUs annually.

Figure 3 Hanjin Container Ship in San Francisco Bay, Approaching Golden Gate Bridge

Q3: How many ships are in the World shipping fleet? Are there limitations on ship size? How big is the World's largest ship?

A3: There are 46,200 ships in the World shipping fleet, with a total capacity of 548 million deadweight tons (dwt). Of these, there are 18,150 general cargo ships; 11, 356 tankers; 6,139 bulk carriers; 5,679 passenger ships and 1,733 other ships (3). Ships larger than 80,000 dwt are too big to go through the Panama Canal. Called "cape size" they must go around Cape Horn at the tip of South America. The largest ship in the World has a gross tonnage of 565,765 dwt. Built in 1976 and called the "Happy Giant", over the years it has gone through many name changes and a near sinking in the Straits of Hormuz. Now known as "Knock Nevis", it has been reduced to being a floating off-shore oil storage platform near Qatar. Sic Transit Gloria Mundi.

Q4: What is the energy usage by ships, both for the ship and per ton-mile transported?

A4: Lots. The diesel power plant on the Emma Maersk cargo container ship is rated at 85 megawatts and burns 380 tons of fuel per day.(4) A typical container ship traveling at 26 knots, approximately 30 mph, burns 120 gallons per mile.(5) At that consumption rate, a ship can transport a ton of cargo approximately 750 miles on the equivalent of a gallon of gasoline. Conventional rail does about 400 ton-miles per gallon, while highway trucks do about 150 ton-miles per gallon.

Q5: How much greenhouse gases do ships emit? What percentage of total World emissions is this?

A5: As noted earlier, ships burn 7.3 million barrels of oil per day(1), corresponding to 1.3 billion metric tons of carbon dioxide emitted per year, about 5 % of total World emissions.

All in all, World shipping is great. Without it, things would cost lots more, and living standards would be much lower. Now, let's see how we can make World shipping much better.

First, how about much faster speed? Say, 300 mph instead of 22 mph. Second, eliminate the emissions of pollutants, microparticulates, and greenhouse gases. Third, reduce the cost of transport per ton-mile. Fourth, make it much easier and simpler to get goods to and from the shipping and delivery points.

Superconducting Maglev transport appears practical for achieving the above four goals on a global scale, eliminating the need for ships to cross the oceans. Now it's time for Q and A about Maglev for global transporting of freight and passengers.

Q1: Can Maglev transport the very large volume of goods that ships currently do?

A1: Yes. A single Maglev consist of 50 Maglev cargo vehicles coupled together, with each vehicle carrying 80 tons of cargo (4 TEUs) could transport 10 Billion ton-miles of cargo per year. 100 such consists operating on a single Maglev route could transport 1 trillion ton-miles per year, about 4% of the total 27.6 trillion ton-miles carried by World shipping. Traveling on the Trans-Siberian Route after it has been adapted for Maglev, the 100 Maglev 50-vehicle-consists, each containing 4 TEUs, could deliver 10 million TEUs per year, the number of units that China ships annually to Europe.

Q2: How does 300 mph Maglev compare with ships in energy consumed per ton-mile?

A2: 300 mph Maglev uses 0.030 kWh of electrical energy per ton-mile, based on 80 tons per vehicle in a multi-vehicle consist, with a skin air drag coefficient for each vehicle that is 24% that of a single vehicle (the front vehicle has a form drag coefficient of $C_D = 0.20$, based on NASA tests). At 2.00 dollars per gallon for bunker fuel, ship's energy cost is 0.25 cents per ton-mile for the thermal energy it uses, while for Maglev, the energy cost is less, about 0.18 cents per ton-mile, based on 6 cents per kWh for industrial type power.

Q3: What kinds of cargo can Maglev cargo vehicles carry?

A3: The same kinds of cargo that ships carry – TEUs, iron ore, coal, grain, crude oil and oil products, etc. Cargo containers can be very quickly unloaded from Maglev vehicles using powered roller bars inside the vehicle. Bulk dry cargo can be quickly dumped using a tilting vehicle body, while bulk liquid cargo can be quickly pumped out.

Q4: What is the cost of Maglev cargo transport per ton-mile compared to ship transport?

A4: Significantly less. The average cost for ship transport is about 1.4 cents per ton-mile, including operating cost and amortization of the capital cost of the ships. The operating cost for Maglev is 0.23 cents per ton-mile, including energy cost, vehicle amortization cost, and system personnel. Maintenance cost for the vehicles and guideway will be very low, because there is virtually no wear and tear on them – no barnacles, no corrosion, no wind and wave damage, no collision with other ships or underwater reefs, etc., etc.

One Maglev vehicle can transport 200 million ton-miles of cargo annually. Over its 30 year operating life that amounts to 6 Billion ton-miles. At 2 million dollars capital cost per vehicle the amortization cost is 2 million dollars divided by 6 Billion ton-miles or 0.03 cents per ton-mile. Personnel costs will be very small, since the vehicle consists are operated by a traffic control center, and do not have operators on-board. Including energy at 0.18 cents per ton mile, and allowing 0.01 for personnel, and a very small amount for maintenance, the total operating expense is approximately 0.23 cents per ton-mile.

Total transport expense for Maglev will include the amortization cost of the guideway. For Maglev cargo routes, in sparsely populated areas, a large fraction of the route will be constructed on-grade, for a cost of about 10 million dollars per two way mile. Portions of the route will probably use adaptations of existing railroad tracks for Maglev travel, at a cost of about 4 to 6 million dollars per two way mile, while other sections will probably be elevated monorails for a capital cost of approximately 25 Million dollars per two way mile. Based on 100 consist launches per day with each consist having 50 vehicles per consist, each carrying 80 tons (Q + A #1), the route would transport 400,000 ton-miles per day per mile of guideway, 150 million ton-miles per year per mile, and 4 billion ton-miles over a 30 year period. For an average cost of 10 million dollars per mile of two way guideway this corresponds to an amortization cost of 0.25 cents per ton-mile for the guideway.

Adding in the operating cost of 0.23 cents per ton-mile, the total cost for transport by Maglev is approximately 0.5 cents per ton-mile, about 1/3 of that by ship. So, Maglev transport is much faster than by ship, considerably cheaper per ton-mile transported, has generally shorter transport distances, e.g. 7,000 miles by the Trans-Siberian Railway route from China to Europe vs. 10,000 miles by ship; does not emit greenhouse gases and pollutants, and is easier to access by the existing rail and Maglev networks inside countries resulting in faster, better, cheaper transport. Sounds like a great deal for human society? Why not go for it?

Adaptation of the Trans-Siberian Railway Route for Maglev Transport

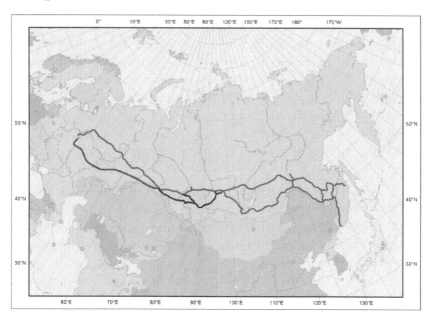

Figure 3 The Trans-Siberian Railway

The Trans-Siberian Railway runs 5,723 miles across Siberia from Moscow to Vladivostok on the Pacific Ocean. Figure 3 shows a map of the route. Approved by Czar Alexander II, construction of the Trans-Siberian Railway began in 1891, and was completed in 1916. It connects with other railroads in the Far East, as well as with other railroads in Russia and Europe.

The Trans-Manchurian Railway branches off from the Trans-Siberian Railway at Ulan Ude on the Eastern Shore of Lake Baikal, heading south to Beijing, China. The Trans-Mongolian Railway branches off 1,000 miles East of Lake Baikal, going on to Pyongyang in North Korea.

It's a long trip, 6 days and 4 hours from Moscow to Vladivostok; from Moscow to Beijing is also 6 days; and from Moscow to Pyongyang, even longer, 9 days. The first two trips average about 40 mph, while the trip to Pyongyang averages about 30 mph. Traveling on 300 mph Maglev, one could do the trip in less than one day.

Figure 4 Trans-Siberian railroad track near the town of Ust' Katay in the Ural Mountains

100 years ago, Siberia was a wild country. It still is. Figure 4 shows a 1900 photo of a Bashkir switchman standing next to the railroad track near the town of Ust' Katav in the Ural Mountains, after traveling a thousand miles from Moscow. Only 5,500 miles left to go before reaching Vladivostok!

The Trans-Siberian Railway carries freight containers from Asia to Europe, but their travel time is longer than passengers take. Current best freight travel times from Russia's Pacific ports to the Russia-Europe border is about 12 days with average speeds of 25 mph. More typically, travel times from Japan to European Russia are about 25 days.(1)

Russian Railways plans to spend 11 Billion dollars over the next 5 years on its "Trans-Siberian in Seven Days" program, to take only 7 days to transport freight from Asia to Moscow, with maximum speed capability of 60 mph by 2015.(1).

With 250 mph Maglev average speed, it would take only 1 day, not 7, to transport freight containers from Asia to Europe. At 0.23 cents per ton-mile operating cost (energy, vehicles amortization and personnel) for Maglev transport operating plus the amortized cost of the guideway capital cost of 10 million dollars per two way mile paid back in 20 years. For a total cost of 0.5 cents per ton-mile a 20 ton TEU could be transported from Asia to Europe for only 300 dollars, compared to the more than 2,000 dollars it would take to travel by ship, which would take at least a month.

At 10 million dollars per two way mile, the capital cost of the 6,000 mile Trans-Siberian Maglev line would be 60 Billion dollars. Assuming that they wanted to pay back the capital cost of the guideway in less than 20 years, say in 10 years, the transport cost from Asia to Europe would increase from 300 to 450 dollars, still a tremendous bargain compared to the cost by ship or rail, with a transport time of 1 day instead of weeks. It is difficult to understand why developers would not jump at the opportunity to make a tremendous profit using Maglev transport on the Trans-Siberian Railway.

Crossing the Bering Strait

The Gateway Between Asia and the Americas

The concept of a bridge across the Bering Strait is at least 120 years old. In 1890, William Gilpin, the first Governor of Colorado Territory talked about a "Cosmopolitan Railway" in which railways would link together the countries in the World. In 1892, just 2 years later, Joseph Strauss, the future designer of the Golden Gate Bridge, proposed a Bering Strait Bridge in his senior thesis.(1) His proposal to the Russian government was rejected.

Eventually Russia changed its mind. In 1905, Tsar Nicholas II approved a plan for a tunnel across the Bering Strait.(2) The projected cost was 65 million dollars for the tunnel. With railroads, total cost was 300 million dollars. A real bargain, even in 1906. Sadly, World War I and Lenin put a stop to the project.

Interest revived again in 1958, when T.Y. Lin, the engineer who also proposed the Gibraltar Bridge, described later in the chapter, projected a bearing bridge at a cost in 1958 of 1 Billion dollars, escalated to 4 Billion dollars in 1994. In 2005 Reverend Sun Myung Moon took up the call for the Bering Bridge and held a design competition.(1) The recent Discovery Channel television program, *Extreme Engineering*, estimated a cost of 105 Billion dollars or 5 times the cost of the Channel Tunnel, popularly called the Chunnel, between France and England.(3)

The preferred bridge route actually involves 3 bridges, one 25 mile bridge from Russia's Chukchi Peninsula to one of the Diomede Islands (See Figure 5), a second 25 mile long bridge from America's Seward Peninsula to another Diomede Island, with a short bridge connecting the 2 islands. Total length would be about 50 miles.

The Bering Strait, unlike the Strait of Gibraltar, is not very deep, with a maximum depth of 180 feet. The bridge would face problems of weather, very cold temperatures (maximum winter low temperatures of minus 60 degrees Fahrenheit), thick ice floes ramming the bridge piers, and so on.

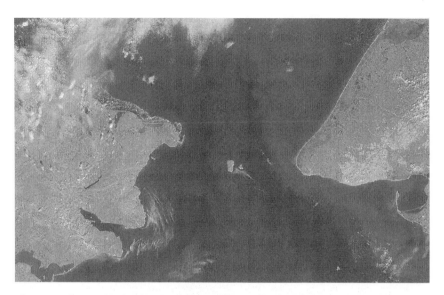

Figure 5 The Bering Strait, Separating Siberia from Alaska in the North Pacific. NASA image, taken by MISR satellite

As a result, most recent interest has not focused on a bridge across the Bering Strait but instead, on a tunnel between Alaska and Russia.

The TKM – World Link 64 mile road and high speed rail tunnel would connect Russia with Alaska. Russia's Prime Minister Putin has approved a planned mission to build a railroad to the Bering Strait as part of the TKM plan. The tunnel is projected to cost 65 Billion dollars, but so far, has not obtained firm funding commitments. In April 2007, Russian government officials told the press that the government will back the 65 Billion dollar plan, but did not promise to supply the funds.(1)

While the Bering Strait has no yet been crossed by a Bridge or a Tunnel, it has been traversed and crossed in many other ways – in 1728 by Bering, in 1989 by Kayaks, in 1998, on skis across the frozen ice, in 2006, on foot, by motorcycle, and in 2008 by an amphibious Land Rover vehicle. In 1987, a swimmer, Lymon Cox, even swam the 2 miles between the two Diomede Islands in 40 Degree Fahrenheit water.(4)

Crossing the Bering Strait with an underwater floating tunnel that carries Maglev vehicles would be a much cheaper and easier task than building a bridge or drilling a tunnel under the sea floor.

In the floating tunnel approach tube sections would be fabricated in a drydock facility with all the needed equipment attached to each section. The drydock would then be flooded, and the tube section, or sections, floated out of the drydock into open waters, to be transported by a tug to the construction site, where the tube section would be joined together to make a continuous tube across the Strait.

The interior of the tubes being towed could be empty, i.e., air filled, with sealed ends, or they could be filled with water. If empty, after joining the individual tubes into the long continuous tube, the seals would be removed, and the floating tunnel would be ready for operation. If filled with water, it could be pumped out after the individual tubes were joined together to form the final continuous tube that would cross the strait. The floating tunnel would then be ready for operation.

The floating tunnel would have positive buoyancy with upwards forces on the tube sections. These buoyant forces would be restrained by cables anchored to the sea-bed beneath. In principle, since the Bering Strait is shallow, with a maximum depth of 180 feet, the tubes could just lie on the sea-bed itself. However, because of the high speed of the Maglev vehicles using the tunnel, the inevitable up and down changes in the elevation of the sea floor would cause objectionable acceleration forces on the vehicles. By keeping the tunnel at a constant depth below the sea surface, there are no up and down vertical acceleration on the vehicles, even though the sea bed elevation may vary.

What would a floating tunnel that carried Maglev vehicles look like, and how much would it cost? Most likely, the tubes that make up the tunnel would be made of polymer concrete, not regular concrete. Polymer concrete is much stronger than ordinary concrete, by a factor of 4 or more in both compressive and tensile strength. It is not affected by exposure to salt water and freeze thaw cycling. It does not deteriorate with time, and can be cast as a slurry that hardens in place, just like ordinary concrete. It costs more than ordinary concrete, typically about 1,000 dollars per cubic yard, compared to about 100 dollars for ordinary concrete. The extra cost is well worth it. The compressive stress in the polymer concrete for the parameters given below is only 900 psi at 90 feet below the surface, a small fraction, about 5%, of the compressive strength of polymer concrete.

For a tube length of 350 feet (15 tubes to the mile), tube inner diameter of 20 feet, and a polymer concrete wall thickness of 6 inches, 430 cubic yards of polymer concrete would be required. At 1,000 dollars per cubic yard that's 420,000 dollars per tube. Adding in a very conservative fabrication cost of 1,000 dollars per cubic yard, the completed tube would cost about 840,000 dollars, or about 12 million dollars per mile for the 15 tubes. Adding in the cost of the guideway panels and monorail structure inside the tube, conservatively estimated at 5 million per one-way mile, the total fabrication cost per mile would be 17 million dollars. Finally, being very conservative and assuming it costs 1 million dollars per tube to tow it an average distance of about 6 miles to the assembly site and attach cables to the sea floor, the total cost per one way mile (15 tubes) for fabrication and installation of the floating Maglev tunnel would be 32 million dollars.

Facilities for construction of the floating Maglev tubes would be located at 3 sites – one at the Russian end of the tunnel, one at the Alaska end, and one in the middle of the Bering Strait, on one of the Diomedes Islands. The two main legs, Russia to the Diomedes, and the Diomedes to Alaska, are each about 25 miles long. The maximum tow distances to the middle of each leg from the nearest construction site would be 12 miles, with an average tow distance of 6 miles – not a difficult, long distance towing situation.

The tubes probably would be towed having an air filled interior and sealed ends. The net positive buoyancy on each tube without added ballast would be approximately 2900 short tons (1 short ton=2,000 pounds). With added ballast, e.g. bags of ordinary rocks attached to the tube, the positive buoyancy could be reduced to a nominal 1,000 tons. The cost of the tethers to anchor the floating tube would be negligible. At 10,000 psi tensile stress in the Kevlar tethers, 3% of their tensile strength, and an average distance of 50 feet above the seabed, the total cross sectional area of the tethers holding the floating tube in place would be 200 square inches, with a total volume of 69 cubic feet and a weight of about 2 tons per tube. At a very conservative price of 10 dollars per pound, the cost of the tethers would be only 40,000 dollars, about 2% of the total cost of 2 million dollars for the tube itself.

At 32 million dollars per one way mile for the 15 tubes, the 50 mile, 2 way Maglev floating tunnel systems would cost 3.2 Billion dollars. To ensure system redundancy and the capability to shut down for maintenance, 4 tubes probably would be used, providing 2 tubes each way. The total system projected cost would then be 6.4 Billion dollars. In all likelihood, the actual system cost will be less than 6 Billion dollars, because of the conservative cost assumptions.

How much does amortizing the 6.4 billion dollars the capital cost of the Bering Strait Maglev floating tunnel affect the cost of transport of freight and passengers? Start with freight containers. Transporting 10 million TEUs per year, equivalent to 200 million tons per year, based on 20 tons per TEU, from Asia to North America via the Bering Strait would cost only 1 dollar per ton, or 20 dollars per TEU – less than 1% of the 3,000 dollars cost per TEU transported by container ship. The above calculation assumes a 30 year amortization period. If the Maglev floating tunnels only carried passengers at 50,000 per day, the amortized capital cost would be only 10 dollars, a small fraction, e.g. 2% of the air fare between Asia and North America.

Since the Maglev Bering Strait tunnel system would carry both freight and passenger traffic probably at a higher flow rate than assumed above, the amortized costs per ton and per passenger traveling on the system would be considerably less than the values shown above.

Can the Maglev Bering Strait Tunnel System handle the volume of traffic flows illustrated above? Easily. A 5 vehicle consist with 4 TEUs per vehicle and 1 minute headways in a single tunnel would transport more than 10 million TEUs annually. Similarly, consists of 3 vehicles with 100 passengers in each vehicle, and 3 minute headways in a single tunnel could transport over 50 million passengers annually. Higher passenger flows would be easily handled using more vehicles per consist and shorter headway times.

All in all, the Bering Strait Maglev tunnel system appears technically practical, cost effective, and able to transport enormous volumes of passengers and freight.

The Pan American Maglev Highway – Pole to Pole at 300 mph

Well not quite pole to pole. Almost, though. The Pan American Highway runs from Prudhoe Bay on the northern shore of Alaska to Ushuaia at the tip of South America, a crow's flight distance of about 10,000 miles. It's 12,500 miles from the North Pole to the South Pole.

The Pan American Highway has a lot of twists and turns (See Figure 6), so that the actual length on the ground is about 15,000 miles. Adding in the Network of roads that connect to the Pan American Highway, and the total length of the Network is 29,800 miles.(1)

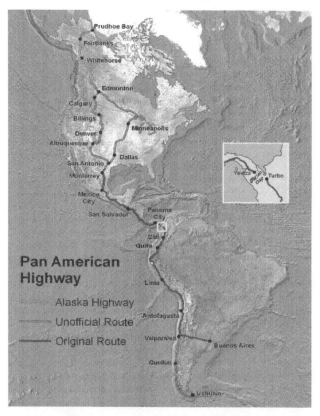

Figure 6 Map of Pan American Highway

The highway is continuous from its northern end to its southern end, except for a 54 mile gap, called the Darien Gap, located in Columbia – see map (Figure 6). The gap is intentional, with the argument being that it protects the local rainforest, and prevents smugglers, diseases, etc. from using a conventional highway to travel between North America and South America. These arguments are not valid for the Maglev 2000 system, in which closed Maglev vehicles traverse the Darien Gap on elevated monorail guideways, with no possibility of harming the rain forest or transporting drugs and diseases.

The highways alongside which the elevated Maglev monorail guide ways would be erected are generally well constructed, open highways with gentle grades and easy curves. The attached photos show sections of the Pan American Highway in City of Buenos Aires, Argentina and El Salvador.(Figure 7 and 8) The Maglev system can easily adapt to occasional small villages along the route, by simply locating the monorail guideway a few hundred feet away from the village.

Figure 7 Pan-American Highway in Argentina

Building a Maglev route along the existing Alaska Highway would be part of the Pan American Maglev Highway. The attached photo (2) shows a view of the existing Alaska Highway terminus.(Figure 9) It is broad and open, and construction of an elevated Maglev guideway alongside it would be easy.

Deducting 2,000 miles from the 15,000 mile mainline portion of the Pan American highway, since the 2,000 miles will be built anyway as part of the Maglev America Network, leaves 13,000 miles of new Maglev routes to be built alongside the Pan American Highway. However, additional mileage, about 2,000 miles of Maglev route will have to be built to connect the Bering Strait maglev tunnel to the Alaska Highway, and to the Trans-Siberian Maglev Route. This brings the total of new Maglev route construction back to about 15,000 miles for the Pan American Maglev Highway.

About 2,000 miles of the Pan American Maglev Highway would already have been constructed as part of the Maglev America Network.

Figure 8 Pan-American Highway in San Martin, El Salvador

What will the 15,000 miles cost? At 25 million dollars per two way mile, the cost for construction in the U.S., the total would be 375 Billion dollars. However, as with the Bering Maglev tunnel, one probably would want a second two way Maglev route, to provide redundancy, downtime for maintenance, etc. This would double the construction cost of the Pan American Maglev Highway to 750 Billion dollars, about the same cost as the 28,800 mile Maglev America Network.

Figure 9 Signpost at Delta Junction, Alaska marks the end of the ALCAN Highway

In practice, it is likely that the construction cost per two way mile in Central and South America will be substantially less than 25 million dollars per two way mile, since labor costs are much less. Highway construction costs in Mexico, for example, are much less than in the U.S. The total cost then would be considerably less than 750 Billion dollars.

However, even if the cost were 750 Billion dollars, it would be dwarfed by the cost of transport using conventional auto, truck, air, rail, and ship systems. Worldwide consumption of oil is 30 Billion barrels per year,

70% of which goes for transport. At 100 dollars per barrel for transport fuel, corresponding to 80 dollars per barrel for crude oil (the current price) and 20 dollars per barrel for refining, the World cost of transport fuel over a 30 year period would be 70 trillion dollars, 100 times greater than the cost of the Pan American Maglev Highway.

In just a few years, analysts predict that oil will cost 200 dollars per barrel or more. In that event, World transport fuel alone will cost 200 times more than the cost of the Pan American Maglev Highway, assuming we continue to have a fossil fueled transport system. To the costs of the transport fuel, add in the costs of buying and maintaining vehicles that have a relatively short lifetime, the environmental costs, the health and accident costs, etc. and the cost of continuing our present fossil fueled transport systems will be hundreds of times greater than the cost of the Pan American Maglev Highway system.

It seems like an easy choice – besides its many other advantages, Maglev transport will be much cheaper than the alternative.

Strait of Gibraltar

Crossing the Strait of Gibraltar at 200 mph

Europe and Africa presently connect on land through the Mid-East. It has long been a dream to join the two continents across the Strait of Gibraltar, which would connect Spain and Morocco, enabling travelers from Europe to easily reach North Africa, and vice versa.

Various bridge and tunnel designs have been proposed, but they all involve tremendous engineering challenges and all are very expensive. Arthur C. Clarke described a bridge across the Strait of Gibraltar in his 1979 science fiction novel, *The Fountains of Paradise*. Ever since, the idea of the Gibraltar Bridge has captured people's imaginations. The attached view from space shows the Strait of Gibraltar, with Spain at the top of the first photo (Figure 10) and Morocco at the bottom. A close view of the Strait is shown in the second photo (Figure 11), taken from the Rock of Gibraltar.

The Fight for Maglev Global Maglev

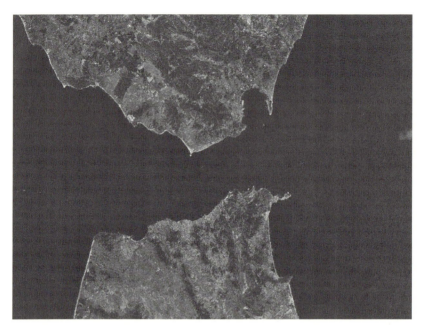

Figure 10 Strait of Gibraltar 5.53940W 35.97279N

Figure 11 View of the Strait taken from Gibraltar

The history of the area around the Strait stretches back for many thousands of years in human history. The Neanderthals arrived in the region about 125,000 years ago, and had a last stand on the Rock of Gibraltar about 24,000 years ago (1) until they were wiped out by the Cro-Magnons (that's us).

The Strait was familiar to ancient civilizations, the Phoenicians, the Greeks, the Romans, and others, because it was the gateway to the Atlantic Ocean. The Muslims crossed it when they moved into Spain over a thousand years ago, and set up the amazing cities of Granada, Cordoba, Seville and many others. If it had not been for Charles Martel and the Battle of Tours, all of Europe, and by descent, America, would now be part of the Muslim World. However, Queen Isabella had her way, and Moorish culture retreated to the southern side of the Strait.

Connecting Spain to Morocco by a fast, efficient, low cost, large scale transport capability would not only greatly enhance trade and business for Europe and North Africa, but it would also promote cultural interchange and understanding – something desperately needed today.

In 2003, the Spanish and Moroccan governments appointed a joint committee to study how to link Europe to Africa via the Strait of Gibraltar (2). To date, however, while there is great interest in a Gibraltar crossing, there has been no decision to go ahead with the project.

This is hardly surprising, given the scope and cost of such a project. So far, two approaches have been studied – bridging the Strait, or tunnel under it, like the channel tunnel (Chunnel) did between England and France.

First, the Bridge approach. At its narrowest point, the Strait is 9 miles across. That is where, in 1986, Professor T. Y Lin proposed locating a gigantic bridge to cross the Strait of Gibraltar (3). It would be by far the biggest bridge in the World. It had 2 spans, with each span 4 1/2 miles in length. Three miles of each span would be supported by suspension cables, while the remaining 1 1/2 miles was supported by rigid stays from the bridge towers. The towers were 3,000 feet high, over twice the height of the Empire State Building. The depth of the Strait under the Bridge is 3,000 feet. Luckily the water depth at the center pier, midway between the ends of the Bridge, is considerably less – there is no way that one could build a bridge pier in 3,000 feet of deep water.

Lin's Bridge has 10 lanes for motor vehicle traffic. The views driving across the bridge would be fantastic, especially if one stayed in the slow lane. However, there is pretty much universal agreement that the Bridge is just too big a job to carry off. The projected cost was 15 Billion dollars. The actual cost if it were built probably would be much greater.

A different bridge approach was proposed by a U.S. architect, Eugene Tsui.(4) Part of it floats on the surface, and part is submerged at a depth of 658 feet. The total length is 9 miles, with the first mile extending out from the coast line and then submerging for 2 miles, then sloping upwards to a 3 mile long floating island in the center of the strait, then submerging again until it approaches the Morocco end of the Bridge. The submerged portions would carry traffic in underwater tunnels. The projected cost was 10 Billion dollars, but it probably would be at least as much as Lin's bridge.

Instead of a bridge approach, the Spain-Moroccan Commission studied an underwater tunnel approach, similar to the Chunnel. The proposed Gibraltar tunnel would be 25 miles long, 980 feet deep, and constructed over a period of 15 years.(2) It would be the World's deepest undersea tunnel. Of concern is the geology of the Gibraltar Strait. An active major geologic fault, the Azores-Gibraltar Transform Fault, bisects the Strait, and severe earthquakes have occurred. Also of concern are two very deep Quaternary clay channels in the middle of the Strait, which could make construction difficult.(2) The Gibraltar tunnel would be very expensive. The actual cost of the 31 mile long Chunnel – slightly longer than the proposed 25 mile Gibraltar tunnel – was about 10 Billion dollars in 1985 prices (5), and was 80% greater than the projected cost before construction started. In today's dollars, the Chunnel probably would cost at least 20 Billion dollars. The greater construction problems for the Gibraltar Tunnel, i.e., its deeper depth (950 feet vs 250 for the Chunnel), earthquakes, and less favorable geology, could further increase cost.

An undersea Maglev tube, similar to that described earlier for the Bering Strait crossing, appears much more practical, with a projected cost of 30 million dollars per one-way mile, a four tube system providing two tubes in each direction, the 9 mile crossing, would cost about 1.1 Billion dollars, at least 10 times lower cost than a bridge or tunnel across the Strait.

About 16 million passengers travel the Chunnel per year, together with about 10 million tons of freight.(5) Traffic on the Maglev Gibraltar route would be at least as much, and probably even greater. The Maglev line can easily handle extremely high traffic loads. Using 3 vehicle Maglev consists with each vehicle carrying one hundred passengers, and 4 minutes headway between consists, the 4-tube Maglev System could carry 116 million passengers annually, 10 times the passenger traffic in the Chunnel and far more than would ever travel across the Gibraltar Strait. At 200 mph it would take less than 3 minutes to cross the Strait, so there would be only 1 Maglev consist in the tube at any given time.

Similarly, with each Maglev vehicle carrying 40 tons of freight, equal to 2 TEUs and 4 minute headways, the capacity of the 4 tube system using 3 vehicle consists would be 60 million tons of freight annually, 6 times greater than the Chunnel.

Clearly, the freight and passenger capacity of the Gibraltar Maglev system will be much greater than the actual traffic demand, so that both freight and traffic can use the system – probably 2 tubes for freight and 2 tubes for passengers.

Even for these extremely high passenger and freight traffic flows, only a small number of Maglev vehicles would be required. For a 10 minute vehicle cycle time, 3 minutes to cross the Strait and 7 minutes to unload/load passengers or cargo, a single Maglev vehicle could make 150 one-way trips per day, carrying 5 million passengers or 2 million tons of cargo per year.

With a fleet of only 40 vehicles, 20 operating (10 for passengers and 10 for cargo) and 20 in reserve, the Maglev system could carry 50 million passengers and 20 million tons of cargo per year. The capital cost of the Maglev vehicles? At 5 million dollars per vehicle, only about 200 million dollars.

The cost of crossing the Strait? Trivially small. Assuming a 30 year amortization period, and half of the amortized capital cost borne by 50 million passengers, the capital cost per passenger would only be 40 cents per trip. The energy cost? Only about 4 cents per trip.

The Gibraltar Maglev line is a tremendous bargain – tying Europe and Africa together for a very small amount of funding, while yielding tremendous benefits in reduced cost of transport and greatly increased productivity.

Converting India's Railways to Maglev

India's railway system is unique. It is ranked low in the World by number of route miles, 40,000 compared to 140,000 per the U.S. which is number 1 – (Russia is number 2, followed by China, number 3).

But India dwarfs the U.S. in passenger travel. In India, 20 million people ride the trains every day. In the U.S., 70 thousand take Amtrak every day. Adding in U.S. commuter rail, India still transports 100 times more rail passengers per day than the U.S.

What's it like to travel on India's trains? Three words – crowded, slow, and very cheap. The reader has probably seen photos of Indian trains with passengers on the roof of the railway cars and clinging to the sides. To be fair, that is not the normal way passengers travel, but it does indicate that in certain areas, India's rail systems are stretched to, and even well beyond, capacity.

India's railway system Mumbai (formerly known as Bombay) illustrates what the effect is when railway systems are stretched way beyond their capacity. The Mumbai railway system carries 6.5 million passengers daily, one-third of India's total rail passenger traffic. During rush hours, railway cars designed to carry 200 passengers are packed with 500 people, with as much as 14 passengers standing in a square yard of floor space. This is termed *Super Dense Crush Load Time*. (3)

Traveling on the Mumbai rail system is not only uncomfortable, but also dangerous. In 2007, 3,997 people died on the Mumbai rail system corresponding to 10 persons per day on average (higher during week days), and 4307 were injured. (3) One third of the deaths were due to people losing their grip on the side of the train. One half of the deaths occurred when people attempt to cross the tracks and were hit by a train. They don't want to walk a mile to a foot-bridge to get across the tracks and then have to walk back again. (3)

A smaller number of deaths, 41 per year, were due to people hitting trackside poles while hanging out of overcrowded trains. Another 21 people die annually by electrocution from overhead power cables when they sit on the roof. (4)

If a person is injured, there is a lot of red tape and time before he or she can get to a hospital. To quote T.S. Bhai, ex-superintendent of the Government Railway Police, (3) "The railways must get a stretcher, inspect a body, and then write a memo about the injury. Then an ambulance is requested. Much time is lost". Bhai started an ambulance service in 2004 after he saw an unconscious railway victim raise his hands after being left for dead on the platform for three days (3). "I've seen bodies lying in pieces unattended," he said.

India's trains are not fast, but they are cheap. For long distance travel, passengers pay about 1 cent per passenger mile; for urban travel, about 0.5 cent per passenger mile (5). Compare that for U.S. commuter rail and Amtrak travel, which averages about 30 cents per passenger mile, and High Speed Rail, about 50 cents per passenger mile.

Amazingly, Indian Railways is essentially self-supporting, with relatively modest government subsidies to cover a portion of their capital improvements. For the 2009-2010 fiscal year, Indian Railways revenue was 88,355 Rupees (18.8 Billion U.S. Dollars) with a net income of 951 Rupees (202 Million U.S. Dollars).(1) Of the revenues, 11.2 Billion U.S. Dollars came from freight, 4.6 Billion dollars from passengers, 1.1 Billion from dollars sundry other Earnings and 0.5 Billion dollars from other Coaching Earnings.

Why are the fares and the revenues so low when the Indian Railways carry 20 million passengers per day, equal to 7.4 Billion passengers per year? All of the U.S. Amtrak system only carries 26 million passengers per year, and its passenger revenues are 1/3 of the Indian railway passenger revenues. On average the Indian passenger only pays 2.60 dollars per trip!

One starts to understand why this is so, when one considers what the Indian workers are paid. The Indian Railway System is the largest single employer in India, with 1.6 million employees. The total salaries for these 1.6 million workers are 3 Billion dollars per year, corresponding to an average annual salary for a worker of 1,860 dollars. Incomes in India are much smaller than in the U.S., so their expenditures have to be much smaller also. India's annual per capita GDP is 1,030 U.S. Dollars per person, so railway workers make good salaries. (5)

India is rapidly industrializing, and will become a very important World economy in the not too distant future. The BRIC (Brazil, Russia, India, & China) report published by Goldman Sachs projects that India will be the second largest economy in the World, after China, by 2043.

India's climb to this economic level can be substantially accelerated by converting its present railway system for Maglev service. Using Maglev 2000 technology, very low cost panels that contain ordinary aluminum loops would be attached to the crossties of the existing RR tracks as described in Chapter 6. Maglev vehicles would then operate on the existing tracks, which could still operate with conventional trains, if and when appropriate.

The benefits to India would be enormous. Much faster travel speeds, triple the speed of the existing trains; much lower energy requirements and costs for transporting passengers and freight; greater economic productivity resulting from lower cost; more efficient transport; much greater transport capacity, because of faster speed; and more frequent service and much greater safety because of automatic control of the spacing between trains.

What are the issues and costs for converting India's present railway route for Maglev service? The attached map shows the India Railway Network, which totals 69,000 miles of track, and 40,000 route miles. 28% of the route miles are electrified. (1)

India does not use the standard rail gauge of 4 feet 8 1/2 inches, which is the predominant gauge for the rest of the World. Instead it uses broad gauge track, with 5 foot 6 inches between the rails. 87% of the total track length is broad gauge. (1) Most of the rest of the trackage, about 10%, uses meter gauge, 3 feet 3 1/2 inches between rails. About 3% of the track uses even narrower gauges, 2 feet and 2 feet 6 inches, mostly in hilly terrains. India is now converting its meter gauge track to broad gauge.

The main issue for Maglev conversion is whether it should install a panel system that is compatible with both standard 4 foot 8 1/2 inch gauge and India's 5 foot, 6 inch broad gauge. There probably are some cost and

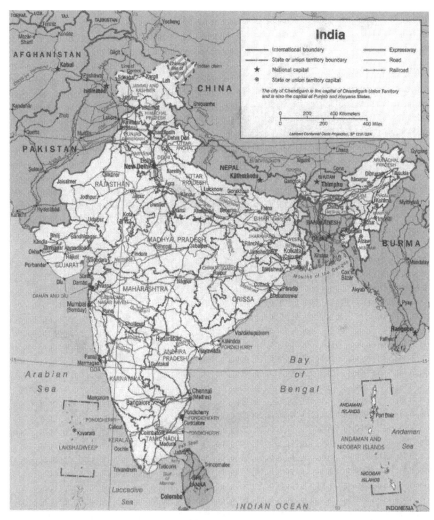

capability tradeoffs that would have to be explored before making the decision. Having different gauges in different countries, like the difference between Russia and Europe, can be a real bother.

How much would conversion of India's Railway Network for Maglev cost? In the U.S. the cost of conversion is about 4 to 6 million dollars per two-way mile, depending on local conditions. The cost for conversion in India will be substantially less, because of lower labor and manufacturing costs.

Assuming a conversion cost of 2 to 3 million dollars per mile, half of that in the U.S. appears conservative. It could be significantly lower. At an average cost of 2.5 million dollars per two way mile in India, the total cost for converting the 40,000 route miles in India would be 100 Billion dollars.

India's current GDP is 1.25 trillion dollars.(6) Carrying out the conversion to Maglev over a 10 year period would cost 10 Billion dollars annually, less than 1% of the annual GDP. The economic benefits to India would significantly outweigh the conversion cost.

Converting India's existing railways to Maglev would be much less expensive than building new High Speed Rail trains, which are currently under consideration, and it would have much greater benefit, both economic and social, than High Speed Rail.

As discussed in the paper, "Urban Transport Crisis in India", by Pucker et al,(7) "Much of the population is so poor that it cannot afford any motorized transport at all, and must spend up to three or even four hours a day for travel." Quoting the authors, "As in most developing countries, a high percentage of travel in Indian cities is by walking or cycling, mainly because much of the population is too poor to afford motorized transport. Walking and cycling are most important in smaller cities, accounting for over two thirds of all trips. As city size increases and trip distances become greater, the relative importance of walking and cycling falls to about half of all trips in medium sized cities, and about a third in the largest cities."

Maglev transport in India, with its lower cost, faster travel, and greater service access and availability, can significantly improve public transport capability so that it can serve those presently not able to afford it.

China is on the Transport March.

Not the Long March of Mao Tse-Tung (modern: Mao Zedong), but a much faster march to dominate the World with their High Speed Rail systems. China already dominates the renewable energy market, manufacturing ½ of the World's wind and solar power systems. By dominating the High Speed Ground Transport market, they will be able to export many Billions of dollars' worth of railway equipment manufactured in China, making the countries that buy their railway exports dependent on China's good will.

China has been very aggressive in developing their capability for High Speed Rail (HSR). In 2008, China initiated its first high speed passenger train service that reached 186 mph on the Beijing to Tianjin line (1). Currently (September 2010) China's HSR network totals 4,000 route miles in service, with 200 route miles operating at 220 mph (2), and 10,000 miles being constructed. The HSR Network will reach 8,100 route miles by 2012, and 16,000 miles by 2020 (1). The following map shows China's present railway system, which totals about 50,000 miles in length.

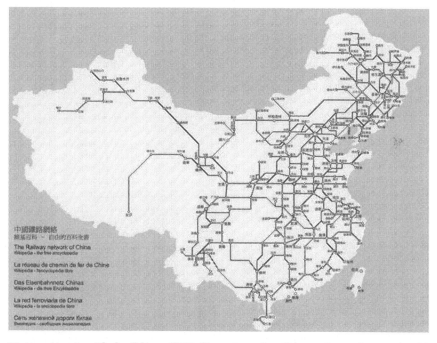

Not content with building HSR lines just in China, they plan to build them all over the World. Not just plans to do so – China is already building HSR lines in Turkey, Venezuela, and Saudi Arabia (3). In a resources deal, China is building a rail system for Burma in exchange for Burma supplying lithium, a vital component for high performance batteries for electric cars and other applications. (3)

China plans two HSR networks to connect China with Europe, one with a terminus in London and the second with a terminus in Berlin – more than 10,000 route miles. Instead of 6 days for passengers to Beijing via the present Trans-Siberian line through Russia, by 2025 travelers will take only 2 days to go from Beijing to London. The third HSR route China plans to build would connect China with Vietnam, Thailand, Burma, and Malaysia. China intends as part of its Pan-Asian railway plan to link 25 countries with a total 50,000 miles of track (3,4).

China has also signed agreements with the State of California and General Electric in the U.S. to supply HSR equipment and help finance the proposed High Speed Rail line from San Francisco to Los Angeles (3).

How has China come so far, so fast in High Speed Rail? First, by making it a national priority. America used to have national priority programs. Remember the Apollo program? From virtually nothing in space programs in 1962, when President Kennedy initiated Apollo, to landing men on the Moon in 1969, only 7 years later. When a Nation has the will and the means, it can do wonders. America seems to have lost its will, and just passively drifts along. China hasn't.

Second, by adapting and evolving existing technology into better systems. China acquired foreign HSR technology through technology transfer agreements, from foreign suppliers – Bombardier (German and Swedish Trains), Alstom (Italy/France) and Kawasaki Heavy Industries (Shinkansen Japan). (2) China then improved the foreign technology, with higher train speeds, and established the capability to manufacture the improved HSR systems in China, not just buy them from abroad. Now, they have the ability to corner the World market in High Speed Rail and replace existing suppliers, just as they are doing with wind and solar power sources.

A key objective in China's strategy to cover the World with High Speed Rail systems is to help countries acquire advanced HSR to improve their transport capabilities and boost their economies, in return for which the countries helped will make long-term commitments to supply China with valuable resources – oil, gas, minerals, etc. The agreement with Burma to supply China with lithium for batteries, in return for China building HSR in Burma is an example of this strategy.

Why is China pushing High Speed Rail so aggressively when 2nd generation superconducting Maglev is a much better choice? HSR costs much more than 2nd generation superconducting Maglev; it cannot transport heavy freight like the 10 million TEUs that China sends to Europe each year, only passengers. Its revenues will be much less than those from Maglev, because it cannot carry heavy freight; it is not as energy efficient as Maglev; it has major maintenance requirements and costs, unlike Maglev, which is virtually maintenance free; and it cannot electronically switch at high speed to off-line stations, requiring long distances between stations to maintain high average speeds. And HSR speeds are substantially slower than Maglev. Two days to go from Beijing to London by High Speed Rail? Maglev could do it in just one day. Most travelers would fly Beijing to London rather than take two days by HSR, but a large fraction would take one day Maglev rather than fly, given the weather and congestion from delays for air travel, its uncomfortable seating, and the lengthy screening process. And especially Maglev with sleeping accommodations free of the shaking and jostling of traditional rail.

The reason why China has chosen HSR over Maglev – at least for the moment – appears to be twofold. First, HSR is more developed than Maglev and can be more quickly implemented on a large scale by China, using already existing railroad trackage, both in China and in other countries.

Second, the 1st generation Transrapid Maglev System that China built and now operates in Shanghai, offers no real advantages over High Speed Rail. It costs much more than HSR, its speed is not that much greater than HSR, and like HSR, it is a passenger only system. It cannot carry heavy freight, trucks, and TEUs, the big money makers. Moreover, Germany, in contrast to the foreign HSR companies, refused to share the technology and allow source production in China, eliminating the manufacturing potential for China.(2) In addition, residents living along the proposed Maglev extension to Hangzhou protested it because they believed – wrongly – that there would be electromagnetic radiation from the Transrapid Maglev vehicles that would harm their health.

So far, the Chinese have not sought to develop 2nd generation Maglev, but they inevitably will. Once they perfect their Maglev system, which they could do in a few years after they start development, they would market it

World-wide. Very importantly, 2nd generation Maglev systems do not require new dedicated guideways. Adapting HSR trackage for Maglev would only require attaching very low cost aluminum panels to the crossties of the HSR track, and Bingo! – 2nd generation Maglev vehicles could travel above the HSR tracks at 300 mph, not at 180 mph, carry trucks and other heavy freight, with less power and at lower cost with much less maintenance than HSR. China would make a fortune carrying out the conversion to Maglev.

21st Century transport will be a mammoth industry. World GDP is currently 60 Trillion dollars annually. China's share is relatively small, only about 5 Trillion dollars [9 Trillion on a purchasing power parity (PPP) basis]. But its GDP is growing at 10% per year, while the developed countries are only growing at 1 to 2% per year. By 2020, if China's growth rate remains constant, its GDP will be 15 Trillion dollars annually, equal to America's current GDP. By 2030, China's GDP would be 45 Trillion dollars annually, assuming 10% per year growth rate. 2030 is not very far away.

Transport expenditures account for about 10% of World GDP. With 2nd generation Maglev, China will be in the catbird seat for transport. Being smart and aggressive, they soon will understand this, and start to develop 2nd generation Maglev.

Chapter Six

How Maglev Works – First and Second Generation

"A scientist discovers what is,

an engineer builds what never was"

--Theodore Von Karman

Before describing how Maglev works, it is helpful to clear up two very important points that often get lost when thinking about Maglev.

First, Maglev is not just a faster train. It is a completely new mode of transportation, the first since the airplane. Many thousands of years ago, humans walked and rode horses. Then came ships, and the wheel, both of which have evolved enormously from their primitive beginnings to today's wonders. For the wheel, from wagons to chariots, to railroads, to automobiles and trucks, to NASCAR. Then came the airplane, from the Wright Brothers to the Vin Fizz, to the Red Baron, to the DC-3, to today's modern jet airliners.

Similarly, Maglev is evolving from the 1st generation Japanese and German passenger systems to the 2nd generation Maglev 2000 system that will carry not only passengers, but also trucks, autos, containers and bulk freight, fresh water, and lots more. Moreover, Maglev will store large amounts of electrical energy and launch cargo, and eventually humans, into space.

How is Maglev different from the other modes of transport and why are these differences important?

First, Maglev vehicles have no wheels. They are magnetically levitated above and move along a guideway without mechanical contact – no frictional energy losses, no heavy point loads on the guideway from wheels. Compare that with the damage done to highways by heavy 18 wheeler trucks. There is no wear and tear on the guideway, resulting in very long lifetimes for Maglev vehicles and guideways, with very low maintenance costs.

Second, Maglev vehicles have no engines. Instead, they are magnetically propelled along the guideway by a small AC (Alternating Current) in the guideway windings that pushes on the vehicle's superconducting magnets. Vehicle speed is controlled by the frequency of the AC current – to speed up, frequency is increased, to slow down, frequency is decreased. Maglev vehicles are locked into the AC current wave as it moves along the track, much as a surfer is locked into a water wave. The distance between Maglev vehicles operating on a guideway always remains constant, regardless of whatever forces – headwinds, tailwinds, upgrades, downgrades, etc. – act on the individual vehicles. *There is no possibility of one vehicle colliding with another*, in contrast to conventional autos, trucks, trains, or airplanes. Moreover, the Maglev vehicles draw power from the grid as they accelerate to operating speed. Almost all of that energy returns to the grid when the vehicles decelerate to stop at a station, using energy efficient electrical braking, not loss by mechanical braking. Finally, Maglev vehicles do not emit pollutants or greenhouse gases, unlike autos, trucks, diesel trains and airplanes, or brake dust particles from mechanically braked wheeled vehicles.

Third, Maglev travel is very energy efficient. Driving in a 20 mpg, 60 mph automobile, 2 kilowatt hours of gasoline energy are consumed per passenger mile, assuming that the driver is alone in the car. Travelers in a 300 mph passenger Maglev vehicle that operates in the atmosphere consume only 0.06 per kilowatt hour of electrical energy per passenger mile, 1/30th as much as by auto. Granted, thermal energy is not electrical energy, but on a cost basis, at 3.00 dollars per gallon, 1 kWh of gasoline energy costs approximately 8 cents, about the same as the industrial cost of electrical energy per kWh. For a thousand mile trip, the fuel for a 20 mph auto trip that takes over 16 hours of driving is 150 dollars. For the same trip by 300 mph Maglev, trip time is a little over 3 hours, with an energy cost of only 5.00 dollars.

Fourth, Maglev vehicles do not need to travel in the atmosphere. Airplanes have to travel in the atmosphere: Maglev does not. In a low pressure tunnel Maglev vehicles speed can be much greater than 300 mph, and energy cost much less, because there is no air drag. In low pressure tunnels, a Maglev speed of 2,000 mph is practical. New

York City to Los Angeles in 1 hour and 15 minutes! That's the way to go! The electrical energy cost? 50 cents! The energy cost is not completely zero, because there are some small I^2R electrical losses in the aluminum guideway loops that carry the induced currents that levitate the Maglev vehicles, plus the AC current that accelerates the vehicle. Incidentally, once the Maglev vehicles reaches 2,000 mph, it could simply coast from New York to Los Angeles, without additional propulsion required. For the cross country trip, without propulsion, the vehicle speed would drop to 1,850 mph. It probably would be desirable to reboost speed, to 2000 mph every 500 miles, so that the average speed was 1985 mph. The increase in trip time would be very small, about 30 seconds.

Fifth, Maglev travel is noiseless and very comfortable. Highway travel is very noisy, both from the internal noise from one's own car – engine noise, tire noise – and the external noise from other cars and trucks on the highway. Trains are very noisy, from rail and engine noise. And airplanes? Exceedingly noisy.

Maglev vehicles have no rail or engine noise – only a quiet swish of air. The only noise one will hear is other people talking. The vehicle walls will be sound absorbing, so that talking will not annoy fellow passengers.

Moreover, unlike autos, trains, and planes, which are very bumpy with lots of annoying vibration, Maglev travel will be vibration free – like sitting in a comfortable chair in your home. Maglev can magnetically compensate for any variation in external force on the vehicle and any small variations in guideway construction, to achieve zero vertical and lateral vibration of the vehicle as it travels along the guideway.

For the above reasons, traveling on Maglev will be much pleasanter, much faster, much safer, and much cheaper than by present modes of transport.

Sadly, when we try to explain these advantages of Maglev to most politicians and bureaucrats, they seem to go into a trance and withdraw from the real World. One can almost hear the word, Omm, Omm, over and over. Sadly, enlightment never seems to follow the trance state. Basically, it's much easier for them to stick with the old World and less risky past. Moving to the new World of Maglev requires new thinking and risks. These attitudes are hardly limited to today's society: they are the reason that many past societies have collapsed. As societies mature

The Fight for Maglev   How Maglev Works

and become rigid, they resist the necessary changes needed to survive in a changing World. Maglev is one of those necessary changes.

The second important point is the difference between research and engineering, and how people's misconceptions about the differences affect the ability to adopt new technologies like Maglev.

People often think that new engineering accomplishments require research. They do not. Scientists do research to discover and understand new physical laws, forces, materials, etc. Engineers then use the new information and the new materials to design and build new structures.

Examples? Scientists discover carbon nanotubes and how to make them into ultra-high strength materials. Engineers then use the materials to make lightweight high strength cables for very long bridge spans. Another example? Scientists discover electromagnetic waves and how to generate, transmit, and receive them. Engineers then build radio and TV transmitters and receivers and cell phones. Maglev? Scientists discover superconductivity, first in conductors that had to be cooled by liquid helium to a few degrees above absolute zero, and more recently, superconductors that only require cooling to liquid nitrogen temperatures, a much easier task. Using superconductors and other manufactured materials based on research by scientists, engineers have now built what never was: Maglev.

Inventors are the bridge between research and engineering. The information obtained by research exists, but it is not yet been put together in a new way for engineers to "build what never was." With Samuel Morse, for example, conducting electricity through metal wires was well known, as was the sparking noise from an electrical discharge. Before Samuel Morse, nobody had put the two together, until he invented the telegraph. When we invented superconducting Maglev, superconducting magnets were being used for high energy particle accelerators, but no one had thought of applying them for levitated transport.

Today, not only are all the materials and detailed computer codes needed to build Maglev systems readily available, with no research required, but technically successful first generation Maglev systems have already been built and operated in Japan, Germany, and China. Other countries are moving towards their own systems. As we describe in this book, the new

2nd generation Maglev 2000 system will be much more powerful, efficient, versatile, and adaptable and will soon make the present 1st generation Maglev systems obsolete, just as jet airliners made propeller airliners obsolete. Engineering improvements are not research: their outcomes are usually predictable and accurate.

That is not to say that engineers cannot make mistakes and build defective things. If they are careless, do not check the accuracy of their designs and continually inspect the quality of the materials they are using, they become known as "bad" engineers, and no one will hire them. In the Old Soviet Union, according to the story – probably apocryphal – managers took a more direct approach. Following the completion of a bridge, the Chief Engineer and his deputy would be stationed under the bridge as it loaded with traffic. Defective bridge? Goodbye, bad engineers! Needless to say, we do not believe that approach will be necessary for 2nd generation Maglev.

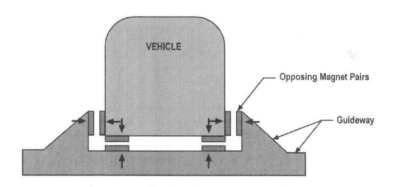

Magnetic Suspension based on the Repulsive Force between Permanent Magnets on a Vehicle

Figure 1

On to engineering Maglev, the new mode of transport. Maglev uses magnets to levitate and propel vehicles along a guideway, so let's begin with the magnet options available to the engineer. There are 3 basic types of magnets: permanent magnets, electromagnets, and superconducting magnets, as illustrated in the drawings (Figures 1, 2, 3).

Almost everyone has experience with permanent magnets, using them to hold things on a refrigerator, using them in toys, etc. In a permanent magnet, the movements of electrons in the atoms of the material are aligned by an external magnetic field during the magnet's manufacture. When the external magnetic field is removed, the electron movements remain locked in place, generating a permanent magnetic field that persists unless the material is damaged by heating, high stress, etc. No electric power is needed to maintain the magnetic field.

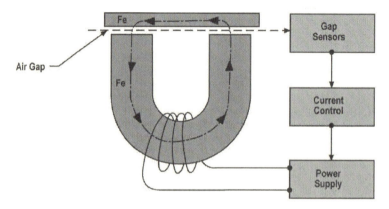

Magnetic Suspension based on Servo Control of the Attractive Force between an Electromagnet and a Ferromagnetic Sheet

Figure 2

Electromagnets create a magnetic field by passing electrical current through a loop or coil of electrically conducting wire. Electromagnets are everywhere – in electric motors and generators, transformers, and other electrical equipment. Electromagnets work as long as current keeps flowing through their conducting wires, and stop working when the current stops. As the current flows through the electromagnets conducting wire, however, it consumes electrical power, turning it into heat, because the wire has an electrical resistance. These losses, expressed as I^2R losses, where I is the current and R is the resistance, limit the practical strength and spatial extent of the magnetic field generated by the electromagnet.

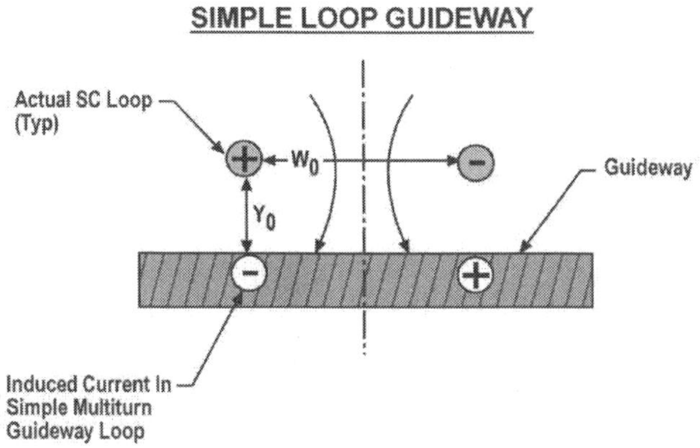

SIMPLE LOOP GUIDEWAY

Figure 3

Superconducting magnets, the third type, are essentially electromagnets that behave like permanent magnets. Their magnetic field is generated by electrical current in a coil of superconducting wire, like an electromagnet, but because the superconductor has zero electrical resistance, the current will continue to flow forever after the electrical leads that charged the superconducting magnet with its initial current are withdrawn, making it in effect a permanent magnet. There is a very small amount of refrigeration power required to keep the temperature of the superconductor low enough that it stays in the superconducting state.

Superconducting magnets are much more powerful than permanent or electromagnets, both in terms of the strength of their magnetic field, and the spatial extent of the field. As discussed below, while Maglev systems have operated using electromagnets and permanent magnets, they are very limited in their capabilities. The clearance between a magnetically levitated vehicle and the guideway using permanent or electromagnets is very small, about $\frac{1}{2}$ of an inch, and it cannot carry heavy loads, such as 18 wheeler highway trucks.

In contrast, using superconducting magnets for Maglev, the clearance between the levitated Maglev vehicle and the guideway can be much greater, e.g. 4 to 6 inches, compared to the $\frac{1}{2}$ inch for electromagnets and permanent magnets. This is very important for safety. Moreover,

Maglev vehicles with superconducting magnets can carry extremely heavy loads, e.g. fully loaded highway trucks, hundred ton concrete blocks for energy storage, and 200 ton loads of fresh water. In addition, superconducting magnets enable Maglev vehicles to be inherently and automatically very strongly stable so that no external forces, including hurricane winds, make the vehicles contact the guideway.

As an example, consider one of the 16 superconducting magnets on a 2nd generation Maglev 2000 vehicle that would transport an 80,000 pound highway truck at 300 mph for hundreds of miles to its destinations. If the superconducting magnet used ordinary copper conductor instead of superconductor, the I^{2}R power required per magnet would be 36,000 kilowatts. For the 16 magnets on the vehicles, the total power would be 500,000 Kilowatts, or ½ the power output from a 1,000 megawatt coal or nuclear power plant. Clearly impossible. A small amount of power is required to keep the superconducting magnets cold: less than 10 kilowatts. At 10 cents per kilowatt hour, that's only 1 dollar to transport the 18 wheeler highway truck 300 miles down the road.

To most people, superconducting magnets are mysterious, far-off fantasy type things. However, superconducting magnets are very real, well developed, and commercially available. There are thousands of MRI machines around the World using superconducting magnets that operate very reliably. The next time you get a MRI scan, look up at its housing and think of the superconducting magnet inside. The Japanese superconducting Maglev vehicles have carried many tens of thousands of passengers with accumulated running distances of hundreds of thousands of miles.

Figure 4

LHC Magnet in Tunnel (Credit Fermilab Visual Media Services)

The Large Hadron Collider (LHC) high energy particle accelerator at CERN (1) in Switzerland has over 15 miles (See Figure 4) of very high field, 80 kilogauss, superconducting magnets. The same total length of magnets on a fleet of 300 mph passenger Maglev vehicles would provide 700 Billion passenger miles of travel per year, equal to the total annual passenger miles of all U.S. air travel.

Moreover, the LHC superconducting Magnets are much more complex and technically challenging than those on Maglev vehicles. They operate at much lower temperatures than Maglev magnets, 1.7 degrees Kelvin above absolute zero, compared to about 35 Kelvin for Maglev magnets using high temperature superconductors. The refrigeration for LHC magnets is much more difficult, requiring vacuum pumping of liquid helium, and much greater refrigeration power than that for Maglev. The magnetic field inside the LHC magnets must be extremely precise in strength and position, and very stable. Very tiny deviations, e.g., a small fraction of a thousandth of inch, could cause the high energy particle beam that they guide to hit the magnet and destroy it. All of the approximately 10,000 magnets in the LHC thrust must function perfectly, for the LHC to be able to operate.

Such precision and reliability is not needed for superconducting Maglev. Even if some of the magnets were to fail, safe levitation would still be maintained. The probability of levitation failure is extremely small, millions of times safer than the probability of failure for a commercial airliner.

Finally, the cost of Maglev magnets will be much less than the cost of the LHC magnets, because the Maglev magnets are much simpler and easier to build. The 12 miles of the 1232 LHC superconducting dipoles cost only 600 million dollars to build. (2) Even if 12 miles of Maglev magnets cost as much, which is very unlikely, over a 20 year period, their cost for Maglev travel would be only 0.006 cents per passenger mile. A passenger traveling from New York City to Los Angeles would pay only 20 cents for the superconducting magnets on his or her Maglev vehicle.

Now that we know about magnets, how are they used to levitate and propel Maglev vehicles?

Four Maglev systems have been developed:

1. Electromagnets on the Maglev vehicle that are attracted upwards to iron rails on the guideway above (The German Transrapid System).

2. Permanent magnets on a Maglev vehicle that generate a repelling force between them and a sequence of permanent magnets located on the guideway beneath the vehicle.

3. Permanent magnets on the moving Maglev vehicle that induce currents in aluminum loops located on the guideway beneath. The magnetic interactions between the vehicle's magnets and the induced currents in the aluminum loops generate repelling forces that levitate the vehicle.

4. Superconducting magnets on the moving Maglev vehicle that induce currents in aluminum loops located on the guideway beneath. The magnetic interactions between the vehicle's magnets and the induced currents in the aluminum loops generate repelling forces that levitate the vehicle.

Systems 1, 2, and 3 are very limited in their capabilities. The gap between the Maglev vehicle and the guideway is very small, about ½ inch, and their lifting power is too weak to carry heavy highway trucks and freight. These restrictions increase their construction cost – guideway tolerances have to be very precise to maintain a ½ inch gap at hundreds of miles per hour, increasing the cost of construction.

Second, the biggest source of revenue for the American superconducting Maglev system will be the transport of heavy intercity highway trucks – not passengers. Higher construction cost and lower revenues makes systems 1, 2, and 3 unattractive for private investment.

In contrast, the much more powerful superconducting magnets for system #4 enable much greater clearances between Maglev vehicles and the guideway, e.g. 4 inches or more, compared to ½ inch, plus the ability to carry heavy highway trucks and freight. These unique advantages reduce construction cost and greatly increase revenue, making superconducting Maglev attractive to private investment.

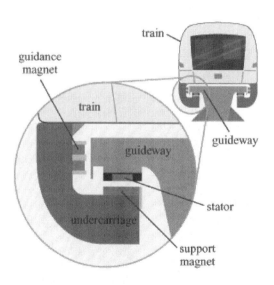

Figure 5

Besides vehicle-guideway gap and lifting power, there is a third very important difference between the four systems, that is, their stability. Systems 2, 3, and 4 are inherently stable. That is, as the vehicle gets closer to the guideway, i.e., the gap between the vehicle and guideway decreases, the magnetic repelling force automatically increases, without any need for servo control. This inherent stability enables the vehicle to maintain a safe suspension distance above the guideway even when external forces, e.g. winds, up and down grades, etc. act on it. Similarly, the geometric configuration of the magnetic suspension is designed so that the desired lateral position is inherently stable. If any external lateral forces, e.g., winds, curves, etc., act on the vehicle, opposing magnetic forces are automatically generated that maintain the vehicle's lateral position. Pitch, yaw, and roll positions are also inherently stable, allowing vehicles to safely move without resistance along the guideway.

System #1, however, is inherently unstable. As the vehicle electromagnets get closer to the iron rail above them, the stronger becomes the lift force (See Figure 5) for constant current in the electromagnet windings. If the current is not quickly reduced, the vehicles would be pulled into the iron rails, much as the force between a permanent magnet and a refrigerator door gets stronger as the magnet gets closer to the refrigerator, eventually clamping onto it.

The German Transrapid 1st generation passenger maglev system avoids this instability problem by very rapid servo control of the current in the electromagnets on the vehicle. If the gap between the vehicle's electromagnets and the iron rails gets smaller, the servo control system decreases the current in a time scale of a few thousandths of a second. If the gap gets larger, the control system increases the current, again on the time scale of a few thousandths of a second. As long as the servo control system works properly, the Maglev vehicles cannot contact the guideway.

Superconducting Maglev was invented by Powell and Danby in 1966. Following publication of their 1966 paper, they were frequently visited by teams of Japanese engineers and railroad experts to discuss superconducting Maglev. Besides Maglev's ability to operate at considerably higher speeds than their already operating High Speed Rail Systems, Japan Railways was very attracted to the large clearance and strong inherent stability of superconducting Maglev, a very important feature in Japan, which frequently experiences strong earthquakes and ground displacements. Rail trains are subject to derailment during strong earthquakes. The great 1995 Kobe earthquake in Japan occurred at 5:46 a.m., before Japan's trains began their runs. If it had occurred a few hours later, thousands of people would have died in the derailed trains.

Figure 6

Based on the 1966 Powell-Danby inventions, Japan Railways has engineered and built their 1st generation Maglev system. Figure 6 shows one of their Maglev vehicles operating on the Yamanashi demonstration guideway north of Mt. Fuji. Japan's Maglev system holds the World ground speed record for passenger transport – 361 mph! Japan Railways plans to build a 300 mile Maglev route between Tokyo and Osaka that will carry 100,000 passengers daily, with trip times of 1 hour.

The drawing, , shows how the Japanese Maglev guideway is constructed. (See Figure 7) A sequence of ordinary aluminum wire loops is located on the sides of the U-shaped guideway. The loops are not electrically powered and are individual units, with no connections between successive loops. As the moving Maglev vehicle passes the loops the superconducting magnets on the vehicles induce electric currents in them. The magnetic interaction between the induced currents in the loops and the superconducting magnets on the vehicle automatically levitate it and stabilize it vertically, laterally, and in the pitch, yaw, and roll directions. The Maglev vehicles can move freely along the guideway, with a very small magnetic drag, due to I^2R resistive electrical losses in the aluminum conductor.

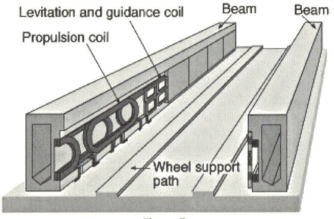

Figure 7

A second set of aluminum loops on the sidewalls of the guideway carries an applied AC current wave that pushes on the vehicle's superconducting magnets, propelling it along the guideway. The vehicle speed is controlled by the frequency of the AC current: to increase speed, the AC frequency is increased. The AC power is supplied from the electrical grid. When the vehicle accelerates, power is drawn from the grid to increase its kinetic energy. When it cruises at constant speed along the guideway, the grid supplies power to overcome air drag on the vehicle. When the vehicle slows down to stop at a station, its kinetic energy is returned to the grid by magnetic braking of the vehicle.

A very important safety feature of this magnetic propulsion system, termed the Linear Synchronous Motor (LSM) is that the vehicle's speed is locked into the speed of the AC current wave, much as a surfer is locked into a water wave. This ensures that multiple vehicles operating on the guideway always maintain a fixed distance between them regardless of the varying forces – head and tail winds, up and down grades, etc. – that act on the individual vehicles. Unlike conventional rail trains that operate on a railroad track, which do experience collisions, Maglev vehicles that operate on the same guideway cannot have collisions.

While the 1st generation Japanese superconducting Maglev system has operated very successfully and safely, it has major limitations. Its guideway is very expensive to build, the vehicles can only carry passengers -- not heavy trucks, autos, and freight, which greatly increase the revenues to the Maglev system -- the vehicles cannot travel along existing railroad tracks, and if they want to switch to off-line stations for loading and unloading, they must do so at slow speed using very big and cumbersome mechanical switches.

Realizing that these limitations have held back the large scale implementation of Maglev in America and world-wide, Powell and Danby have invented engineering improvements that make Maglev even more attractive. Their new 2nd generation Maglev 2000 system is:

- Much cheaper to build.

- Able to carry heavy highway trucks, autos and freight as well as passengers.

- Able to operate at 300 mph on elevated monorail guideways, as well as on existing on-grade railroad tracks at lower speeds.

- Able to switch electronically, not mechanically, at high speed to off-line stations for unloading and loading, thus avoiding the bottleneck of slow mechanical switches. Using "skip-stop" service Maglev 2000 vehicles can bypass stations at high speed, stopping only at scheduled ones. This enables stations to be closely spaced for convenient access, while still maintaining high average speed for Maglev service.

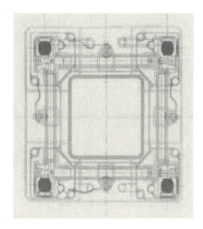

Figure 8

To achieve these improvements, Powell and Danby use superconducting Magnetic quadrupoles on 2nd generation Maglev vehicles (See Figure 8), instead of the superconducting dipole used in the Japanese 1st generation Maglev vehicles. Dipoles only have 2 magnetic poles, North and South, while quadrupoles have 4 poles, two North and two South. The quadrupole allows Maglev 2000 vehicles to travel along on elevated monorail beams, as well as travel along a flat planar surface, and smoothly transition between the two types of guideway, (Figure 9) something not possible with superconducting dipoles.

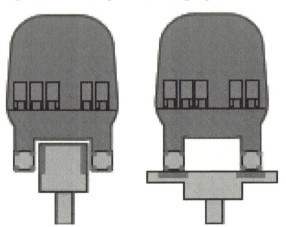

Figure 9

The construction cost of an elevated monorail is much less than that of the U-shaped guideway used in the 1st generation Japanese Maglev System. Moreover, the monorail guideway beams can be prefabricated at large factories and trucked to the construction site with all of its panels and electronic equipment already attached, there to be quickly erected at low cost onto pre-poured concrete footings, eliminating the need for expensive, large-scale field construction.

When traveling along the monorail guideway the sides of the quadrupole magnets interact with aluminum loop panels on the sides of the monorail beam, levitating and stabilizing it vertically, laterally, and in the pitch, yaw, and roll directions. A second set of aluminum loops in the panels on the sides of the monorail beam magnetically propel the vehicle.

As a vehicle approaches an off-line station, the monorail beam transitions to a planar surface on which there are two independent sets of aluminum panels. One set will be closed circuited, the other open circuited. If traffic control wants the Maglev 2000 vehicle to proceed ahead on the guideway, by passing the off-line station, it closes the panel A circuit allowing induced current to flow and open circuits the panel B circuits. If traffic control wants the vehicle to transition to a secondary guideway that leads to the off-line station, it signals the A panels to open circuit and the Panel B circuits to close. The two sets of overlapping panels physically diverge from each other proceeding along the planar switch section until they are completely separated. The planar guideway switch section then transitions to 2 separate monorail beam guideways – one is the main high speed guideway with the other being the secondary guideway, on which the vehicle decelerates to stop at the off-line station.

A similar process occurs when the vehicle leaves the off-line station to rejoin the main guideway. The vehicle accelerates on the outward bound secondary guideway to another switch section that enables it to transition to the main guideway.

Maglev 2000 vehicles can operate on existing railroad tracks as well as monorail beams, by simply attaching very low cost aluminum loop panels to the crossties of the railroad track. Maglev vehicles can then travel without wheels or mechanical contact along the tracks. Conventional trains can continue to use the tracks given appropriate scheduling.

This unique capability allows Maglev 2000 vehicles to travel between cities at 300 mph, on elevated monorail guideways, (Figure 10) and then transition to levitated travel on existing railroad tracks at moderate speed, e.g. 100 mph, inside the urban and suburban areas of the city. No expensive disruptive construction of new infrastructure is needed – just attaching thin panels easily and quickly at low cost to the crossties of the existing railroad tracks.

Figure 10

A further important advantage of the Maglev 2000 quadrupole magnet is that the strength of the magnetic fringe field that extends outside of the magnet is much smaller than the strength of the fringe field outside of dipole magnets. Using quadrupole magnets, the magnetic field strength in the passenger vehicle can be the same strength as the natural magnetic field that surrounds us on Earth, i.e., slightly less than 1 gauss.

Using dipole magnets, as on Japan's 1st generation Maglev vehicles, the strength of the fringe field inside the passenger compartment is higher than the natural Earth field, on the order of several gauss. There is no evidence that DC field strengths of several gauss are harmful in any way, but the public often tends to worry when they are exposed to non-normal environment. Maintaining passenger magnetic field exposure at Earth ambient levels eliminates such worries.

In Japan's 1st generation system, the dipole superconducting magnets are located at the ends of the Maglev vehicles, so as to reduce the strength of the fringe magnetic field in the passenger compartment. By using superconducting quadrupoles, not only can the fringe field strength be reduced to Earth ambient levels, but the superconducting quadrupoles can be located along the vehicle, and not just at its ends.

Figure 11

This greatly increases the lift capability of the Maglev vehicle, allowing it to carry very heavy loads like highway trucks, multiple autos, freight containers, heavy concrete blocks uphill to store energy, and large volumes of fresh water to drought areas. The attached drawing shows a

Maglev vehicle carrying a fully loaded 80,000 pound highway truck (Figure 11).

In this chapter we have described the general principles of how Maglev works and the engineering approach to achieve its design objectives. Chapter 8 describes in greater detail how the various components for the 2nd generation advanced Maglev 2000 system have been fabricated and successfully tested. The next step is to assemble the Maglev 2000 components into vehicles that will be operationally tested in a Maglev 2000 guideway for certification as a public transport system.

The Maglev 2000 system has been engineered to be an extremely safe form of transportation. It has a large clearance; it is very strongly inherently stable – no conceivable external force, including hurricane winds, can make it contact the guideway; it operates with multiple independent superconducting magnets, which have a very low failure rate, and even if a large fraction of them failed, the vehicles would then coast to a safe stop; its position on the guideway is locked onto the AC propulsion current wave, so that the distance between vehicles on the guideway always remains the same, even when varying head or tail winds, or up and down grades affect the various vehicles in a different manner; it can operate in ice and snow conditions; it will continue to be safely levitated even in the presence of substantial ground movements from earthquakes; and it operates on an elevated guideway when traveling at high speeds, with much less effect on existing infrastructure, in contrast to the on-grade operation of high speed rail trains, which requires fencing off the on-grade tracks.

Chapter Seven

The Fight for Maglev: First Round

"Build a Better Mousetrap and the World will Beat a Path to Your Door"

--Ralph Waldo Emerson

Yes, Emerson was right – at least at the beginning. When Gordon Danby and Jim Powell published their 1966 paper(1) describing Superconducting Maglev(Figure 1), the first new mode of transport since the airplane, it created a great buzz, even in the United States. I (Powell) remember a call from someone in the U.S. Office of High Speed Ground Transport shortly after our presentation, saying that the Office had gotten 50 calls from groups that wanted to start a Maglev program. At that time, the Office of High Speed Ground Transport was trying to develop for U.S. application a new high speed surface transport system that would travel much faster than railroad trains. The great hope under test at their facility in Pueblo, Colorado was the Tracked Air Cushion Vehicle (TACV). The TACV was basically a Hovercraft (Figure 2) traveling along a surface guideway – very noisy, consumed a tremendous amount of energy, and had lots of problems. Other proposals were even further out. I (Powell) remember a briefing by an engineer at Grumman, about a system of aircraft that flew inside tunnels.

Figure 1 Front Page of 1966 Paper

Three U.S. programs on Maglev started within a few years after our 1966 publication – Howard Coffey's program at Stanford Research Institute, a program at Ford Motor Company and Henry Kolm and Dick Thornton's Magneplane program at MIT. We were not part of the R&D mission of Brookhaven Lab and we were not involved in any of the U.S. or foreign Maglev efforts.

Figure 2 Photo of TACV

Our Maglev work was done on our own time, independent of the Laboratory. However, we welcomed visitors who came to talk about Maglev, and freely shared our ideas and work with them.

We had lots of visitors. Teams of scientists and engineers from Japan came regularly to discuss Maglev. Less frequently, we also had visitors from Germany and other countries. We continued to publish Maglev papers, describing how the Linear Synchronous Motor (LSM) magnetically propelled Maglev vehicles without an on-board engine, how iron plates on the guideway greatly increased the lifting capability of Maglev vehicles (4) and other Maglev innovations. (5,6,7,8)

Sadly, U.S. R&D on Maglev effectively ceased in the early 1970's when the Office of High Speed Ground Transport shut down, with the decision that automobiles and aircraft could meet all U.S. transport needs into the far future. That decision let other countries, notably Japan and Germany, become the World leaders in Maglev.

In our conversations with the Japanese scientists and engineers, it was clear from the very beginning that they strongly favored Superconducting

Maglev over other concepts. As they told us, two advantages of superconducting Maglev were extremely important to them.

First, the large physical clearance of 4 inches (10 centimeters), or more, between a Maglev vehicle and the guideway it traveled along. Japan has frequent earthquakes and ground movements. Large clearance enhances safety during earthquakes, and reduces guideway alignment problems caused by ground movements. In 1995 Kobe experienced a 6.8 magnitude earthquake (9). Fortunately, the earthquake occurred at 5:46 AM in the morning. Had it occurred a few hours later, thousands would have died in high speed train derailments. With regard to alignment problems caused by ground movements and the pounding of rails by heavy wheel loads, Japan Railways sends out several thousand workers every night to inspect and maintain proper alignment of the rails on its high speed routes. Superconducting Maglev will virtually eliminate these high speed rail problems.

The second important advantage was that Superconducting Maglev systems are designed to be inherently strongly stable. Using a sequence of individual superconducting loops on the vehicle and aluminum loops along the guideway, the levitated vehicle is magnetically suspended at an equilibrium point above the guideway. If an external force tries to push it towards the guideway, the magnetic levitation force increases, pushing the vehicle back to its equilibrium point; if the external force acts to push it up and away from the guideway, the levitation force decreases, causing the vehicle to return to its equilibrium point. Similarly, external horizontal forces on the vehicles are immediately countered by magnetic forces that push it back towards its equilibrium point. The vehicle is also inherently stable in the pitch, yaw, and roll directions. However, the vehicle moves freely along the guideway without hindrance. Safety is very important in Japan, and the inherent strong stability of superconducting Maglev is extremely attractive. With proper design, even hurricane force winds cannot make a Maglev vehicle contact the guideway. Also, with large clearance, construction tolerances are greater than for small clearance systems, reducing construction cost.

Initially, the German Maglev program began development of both Superconducting Maglev and Electromagnetic Maglev, but in the 1970's focused on Electromagnetic Maglev, believing it could be commercialized more quickly. Electromagnetic Maglev is fundamentally different than

Superconducting Maglev. In Superconducting Maglev the vehicle is levitated by the force between the superconducting magnets on the vehicle and induced currents in ordinary aluminum loops on the guideway. It is inherently strongly stable, with large clearances. Electromagnetic Maglev levitates a vehicle using the attractive magnetic force between conventional electromagnets on the vehicle and iron rails positioned a short distance above them on the guideway. Electromagnetic Maglev, unlike Superconducting Maglev, is inherently unstable, not inherently stable. Levitation is maintained by fast servo control of the currents in the vehicle's electromagnets, on the time scale of thousandths of a second. As the gap between the vehicles and guideway decreases, the currents in the electromagnets are quickly reduced; as the gap increases, the currents in the vehicle magnets also increase.

For Electromagnetic Maglev the gap between the vehicle and the guideway is much smaller than for Superconducting Maglev, i.e., about 3/8th of an inch (1 centimeter) compared to 4 inches (10 centimeters) for Superconducting Maglev.

After the U.S. Government dropped out of the Maglev race in the early 70's, the governments of Japan and Germany continued their major development programs. By 1990, the start of the 2nd round in Maglev R&D, and the point at which Senator Moynihan climbed into the ring, as described in the next chapter, both Japan and Germany had made great progress toward building commercially ready 1st generation Maglev systems.

At its test track in Miyazaki (10) Japan Railways (JR) had tested a series of ever more capable and sophisticated Maglev vehicles. Starting with the unmanned ML-500 vehicle through the manned MLU001 and MLU002, JR achieved greater and greater speed. By December 1987, MLU001 achieved 400 kilometers per hour (240 mph) carrying passengers. MLU002 achieved slightly lower speed in 1989, 394 kilometers per hour (236 mph).

Figure 3 shows a photo of the ML-500 vehicle; Figure 4, the MLU001 vehicle. The Japanese Maglev development effort has been extremely impressive. Over the years, they have continued to make steady progress, with a long term commitment to the thoughtful and careful development of their Maglev system.

Figure 3	Figure 4	Figure 5
ML-500 Vehicle	MLU 001 Vehicle	MLU 002 Vehicle

At its test track in Emsland, Germany also made major strides from 1970 to 1990 on their Transrapid Electromagnetic Maglev System. Figure 6 shows the evolution of the Transrapid EMS vehicles from 1976 to 2008.

Figure 6

Transrapid Vehicle

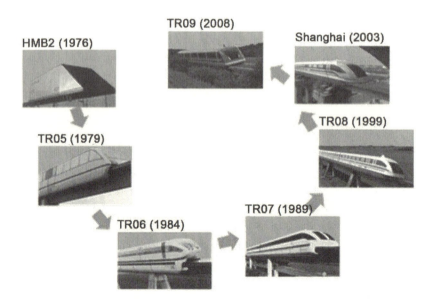

A number of earlier EMS vehicles were tested separately prior to 1974, when Krauss Maffei and MBB joined together to form Transrapid. These earlier EMS vehicles included the MBB "Prinziplahrzeng", the MBB Komet and the Krauss Maffei TR-02 and TR-04.

The speed records of the various Transrapid type vehicles tested between 1970 and 1990 are given below (11):

Transrapid Vehicle	Speed (km/hour)	Date
Prinzzipfahreg	90	1971
TR 02	164	1972
TR 04	250 (manned)	1973
Komet	401	1975
TR 06	406 (manned)	1987
TR 06	412 (manned)	1988
TR 07	436 (manned)	1989

For extended testing of the Transrapid vehicles, Germany constructed a 31.5 kilometer test track at Emsland, Germany. The single track had turning loops at both ends, permitting continuous running tests. The Transrapid vehicles through TR-08, tested in 2003, obtained power for the levitation magnets by physical contact with the track. The new TR-09 needs no physical contact with the track at any speed, but receives power by inductive transmission from the track's propulsion system. If the track's propulsion system fails, TR-09 uses on-board batteries for power to maintain levitation.

Meanwhile, in America, we observed the progress and Maglev accomplishments in Japan and Germany with great frustration. Although America had decided it didn't need Maglev transport, and was not going to do any R&D on it, we continued to work on Maglev, improving our designs and publishing papers. When Senator Moynihan became a champion of Maglev, for a brief time we thought, "We've won! America will finally enter the Maglev Race and win it, to become the World Leader in Maglev". Sadly, the "Dark Forces" – less dramatically, the vested U.S. transport interests – killed America's second opportunity to develop Maglev. Details of Senator Moynihan's efforts to have America build a National Maglev Network are described in the next chapter.

Before telling the Moynihan story, it is important to discuss what enables individuals and organizations to innovate and invent new technologies. While America has been innovative in some areas, e.g., consumer electronics and pharmaceuticals, it has fallen behind in other areas, particularly in energy and transportation.

The decline in innovation, and the reasons for it, are best understood by comparing the educational and work environments when we began our science and engineering careers more than 50 years ago, with the educational and work environments young people experience today.

In talks with individuals and groups, we are often asked the question "how did you come to invent Maglev?" Sometimes it's rather different, as when Gordon, who visited Japan in the 1980's, was asked by a Japanese scientist, "Why did you invent Maglev, when nobody told you to?"

His question pinpoints an attitude toward innovation and invention that is unfortunately becoming more and more prevalent in America. Process, i.e., obtaining approval of planned Work Breakdown Schedules before one undertakes an R&D program, with Zillions of specified "tasks" that have to be completed by a certain date at a certain cost, is very common today. When we began our careers, there was much greater opportunity and flexibility to explore new paths and innovate than there is nowadays. Later on, we describe what R&D was like at Brookhaven National Laboratory 50 years ago – a very different working environment.

Today, politicians and pundits keep making speeches and exhortations about how "America needs to innovate", as if their platitudes would actually result in greater innovation and more inventions. Managers and educators often lecture that we need to teach workers and students on "how to innovate and invent".

Get real, folks. Innovation cannot be ordered or taught!! That is what the Japanese scientist failed to understand. Teachers can inspire students, and give them training and information that will help them to innovate and invent, but they cannot teach them a set of rules that will make them innovate.

Innovation is an emotional drive, not a logical procedure. Innovators and inventors like to think of new ideas, build new devices, find out how things work, and make the World a better place. They are explorers of unknown territories – not geographic ones, but scientific and engineering ones. Theodore Von Karman, the famed aerodynamicist, said it best. "a scientist discovers what is; an engineer builds what never was."

A person who resists new ideas, hates change, and doesn't care about improving the World for others, will never innovate, no matter how often he/she is exhorted, lectured and ordered to do so. The words will simply fall on deaf ears.

Our answer to the Japanese scientist's question, "Why did you invent Maglev, when nobody told you to" is simple. "We invented Maglev because nobody told us to."

Most young people start out wanting to innovate and invent new things, but are often discouraged, blocked or sometimes thwarted by business and unexpected events as they proceed along life's path. However, the happenings are not always negative, but can be positive – encouragement and examples of success from relatives and friends, colleagues, and others, a supportive workplace, and helpful events, both random and deliberate.

Our journey to the invention of superconducting Maglev provides some interesting examples of how both positive and negative factors affect innovation in science and engineering.

When asked the usual question, "How did you come to invent Maglev?" we generally reply with the following short story.

Short Version of the Invention of Superconducting Maglev.

Jim Powell was driving up to Boston from Long Island on a Friday night in 1959 to see a girlfriend when he got stuck for 5 hours in a traffic jam at the Throgs Neck Bridge. Sitting frustrated for 5 hours in his car, he thought there must be a better way to travel. He had been working on superconducting magnets as a way to generate electrical power from high temperature gas cooled nuclear reactors, and Bingo! Why not magnetically levitate high speed trains using superconducting magnets? When he got back to Long Island, in his spare time, he developed the idea into a design concept, entitled "The Magnetic Road: A New Form of Transport", which he presented at the 1963 American Society of Mechanical Engineers (ASME) conference in Atlanta, Georgia.

The Magnetic Road concept was not practical, because it needed many miles of superconducting magnets on the guideway, in addition to the magnets on the levitated vehicles traveling above it. Gordon Danby, a friend who Powell shared a rental house with, got interested, thinking about how the Maglev concept could be made better. Gordon proposed using ordinary aluminum wire loops on the guideway instead of superconductors. As the vehicles passed over the aluminum loops, current would be induced in them by the superconducting magnets on the moving vehicle. These induced currents would magnetically interact with the magnets on the vehicles, inherently and stably levitating it several inches above the guideway.

Bingo again! Now Maglev was economically practical. Danby and Powell then worked out the details of superconducting Maglev – what the shape of the aluminum loops and superconducting magnets would be, how to refrigerate and thermally insulate the superconductors, how to magnetically propel the levitated vehicles, etc. They then presented their ground-breaking paper "High Speed Transport by Magnetically Suspended Trains" at the 1966 American Society of Mechanical Engineers (ASME) winter meeting in New York City, to be later published in the ASME magazine and patented. The rest is history. Finis.

The above "Short Story" sounds so logical and inevitable. Just one step after another to the finished innovation. In reality, all innovations and inventions depend very strongly on chance, the kind of environment you work in, who you work with and meet, what scientific articles and data you happen upon, what interruptions – meetings and "must respond" calls – interfere with your concentration on the innovation, whether you are ill or have problems at home, whether your knowledge of the technology involved is adequate, whether your boss lets you work on the fuzzy first phase of the innovation, etc., etc.

Then, of course, even if you manage to develop a promising invention or innovation, chance determines whether it will be implemented – are there funds to demonstrate it?, will your employer support it?, or if you work on your own, will some large company or organization try to squelch it because it steps on their rice bowl? Even if it is very important, is it too long-term to attract government decision makers and investors, who want results in the next 2 or 3 years?

Innovating and inventing something is not logical and inevitable. Rather, it is like going through a complex maze. Events that happened many years ago can determine whether or not you discover something new and important in the maze. Most of its twists and turns go nowhere. You don't even know if there is anything in the maze, let alone what it is.

While innovation and invention is a haphazard thing, there are ways that it can be encouraged within a society and ways that it can be discouraged. Below we give some examples of the factors that affected us on our paths to Maglev.

Jim Powell's Path to Superconducting Maglev

For me, there were 3 major areas that influenced my path to Maglev: 1) physical survival, 2) education, and 3) a very supportive work environment. Personal survival is very important – one can't innovate, if one is dead. I really tested the odds. Many times in my youth I could have been easily killed. Some examples: exploring wild caves, mountain climbing, swimming long distances alone in the ocean at night, making large amounts of gunpowder for fireworks, flying a small plane, and white water canoeing. In all of these, I was rather clumsy and not very careful.

As teenagers in Delaney's cave in Southwestern Pennsylvania, my brother and I and his friend got lost in its many underground passages. We couldn't find our way out, because we stupidly hadn't marked our way in. Luckily, we blundered out just before our carbide lamps died. In Higginbotham's Cave in Tennessee, I was alone in a dry part of the cave when I noticed my carbide lamp was about to go out. Stupidly, I had not brought any water with me. I was saved by urinating into the lamp, generating enough acetylene for the lamp's flame to make it out of the cave – fortunately, I hadn't urinated earlier.

Luck was also with me in my mountain climbing days. At MIT, though on their roster it was supposed to be the other way around, I majored in the Outing Club, and minored in Nuclear Engineering. In the Canadian Rockies in 1954, I had 3 close calls. On a free rappel down from the top of Mt. Eisenhower, a boulder the size of a gallon jug fell a few feet from the rock face onto my head and nearly knocked me out. Had it fallen a couple of feet more, I would have lost consciousness, and crashed on the rocks 2 thousand feet below, with no belay to save me. An avalanche caught me on Mt. Athabasca, but didn't kill me. Coming down from the top of Mt. Assiniboine with a heavy pack, I slipped and rolled down a steep thousand feet snow slope studded with boulders. Luckily, I missed them ending up undamaged at the bottom.

I could recount many more close brushes with death but space is limited. By the time that Gordon and I started working on Maglev, I had pretty much stopped such activities, after I finally realized that I could get killed. However, the closest call of all was yet to come, with no warning. In January 1966, just as Gordon and I were getting ready to write our groundbreaking paper on Superconducting Maglev, while sitting at my desk at Brookhaven Lab, I was shot in the chest with a shotgun. A fellow engineer at the Lab had come to believe that his testicles were being secretly irradiated by lab personnel and felt he had to kill them. He burst into the big lab in Building T-197, naked to the waist with his shotgun and 4 symbols painted on his forehead, symbolizing, I guess, the 4 people he wanted to shoot. I was the worst hit. A friend was shot in the hand as he closed the door to his office, another colleague was shot at, but the back of his chair caught most of the pellets, and the 4th target evaded the pellets completely by diving down behind a lab bench. The assailant then left the building and killed himself in the parking lot.

I still have a lot of shotgun pellets in my chest. When I get an X-Ray or CatScan, the operator asks what are these things? After my last CatScan the operator measured the distance of the pellet closest to my aorta as 1/16th of an inch. Just a little bit further, and death, with no superconducting Maglev, at least from me. Ever since then, I've been a strong advocate of gun control.

Physical survival clearly played a major role on my path to Maglev. How can society increase one's chance of survival? Well, how about much tougher gun control? More and more, students are being shot down in our schools and universities. Many witness the shootings, even if they are not directly affected, and many have friends or relatives that have been shot. It's hard to concentrate on learning, when you're in a war zone, and difficult to innovate. More safety courses in school could also help.

The second area that influenced my path to Maglev was education. I was very fortunate in schooling, first by having a wonderful teacher, Mrs. Ray, who taught the 5th, 6th, 7th, and 8th grades in my little 2-room school in Bradford Woods, North of Pittsburgh. The 20 students – 5 for each grade – in her school room got a thorough, well-rounded education. I've always been a fan of small schools for the 1 to 8 grade level. You can interact in depth with the teacher, and it's fun and educational to listen to the lessons being taught to the higher grades. After 8th grade, my Mother enrolled me in Perry High School in Pittsburgh's Northside even though I wasn't in its District (our rural high school was to be avoided). I had to hitchhike 15 miles each way to get to school, and had to start pretty early to be sure I got there on time. Sometimes coming home, I had to walk the final 2 or 3 miles if the last pickup didn't go all the way.

Perry High was a great school. An urban school but not too big, only a few hundred students in the 9th through 12th grades, with excellent dedicated teachers in Physics, Math, Chemistry, Biology, Latin, English, History and other courses. There was no teaching to tests, just teaching to the subject. The students weren't drilled by rote, but were free to ask questions and discuss the material. The teachers weren't remote, and for the most part, students were well behaved and wanted to learn. There was ample homework. I've always felt the key was that the Perry High teachers liked the subjects they taught, knew them thoroughly, were not bored and neglectful, and wanted their students to understand and learn what they were teaching. They did sometimes have quirks. Our Biology teacher really had a thing about Eugenics. He would show lots of examples of how people with mental and physical defects passed them on to succeeding generations, and how wrong this was. His obsession may have been due to his own diabetes problems. While not part of a standard Biology curriculum, it did make one think more deeply about the good and bad aspects of evolution.

After Perry High, I went to Carnegie Tech by accident. I desperately wanted to be a petroleum geologist, because I had read a lot about their adventures. So I asked Perry's guidance counselor, "Where should I go to be a petroleum geologist?" He didn't really know, but made up an answer, "Go to Carnegie Tech and take up Chemical Engineering." By the time I found out that he was wrong, it was too late to change. It turned out that it was absolutely the best thing I could have done. The Chemical Engineering staff, Professors Beckman, Monrad and Rothfus, were superb. They taught me how to analyze and put together very complex new engineering systems to achieve a desired goal, and not seek to get a pre-digested answer from a Handbook. We did have a Handbook, the chemical engineer's "bible", *Perry's Chemical Engineering Handbook*, but were taught to use it as a source of data, not a prescription.

Our homework assignments were awesome. Most weeks we would be assigned just 2 or 3 homework problems to be handed in next week. However, each problem had many complex different parts that had to fit together for the final design, and took a lot of analytical work to figure out what the parts should be and how they interacted. I spent lots of weekends from morning till night working on just two problems. It wasn't fun, but it did help one to innovate.

My second big accident that put me on the path to Maglev occurred in my junior year (1952) at Carnegie Tech. While majoring in Chemical Engineering, I minored in Physics. One day, while passing the Physics bulletin board, I saw a small notice about being a summer student at Brookhaven National Laboratory on Long Island. I had never heard of Brookhaven Lab, but thought it interesting, and applied for a summer job there.

I loved the Lab! Because I was a chemical engineer to be, my job at BNL was in their Nuclear Engineering Department. There, I experimented on ways to extract fission products from the molten bismuth-uranium fuel in the Liquid Metal Fueled Breeder Reactor (LMFBR), a big project in the early days of nuclear reactor development.

Because of the great experience at BNL, I decided to go into Nuclear Engineering. I applied to MIT, which was just starting their nuclear engineering program as a part of their chemical Engineering Department. So in 1954 there I was, the first doctoral student in Nuclear Engineering at MIT, with Professor Manson Benedict, the grand old man of Nuclear Engineering and designer of the K-25 uranium enrichment plant at Oak Ridge, as my supervisor. Although I majored in Nuclear Engineering, I had an extremely strong minor in the MIT Outing Club. We went everywhere – mountain climbing in the White Mountains, Mt. Katahdin, the Adirondacks, the Grand Tetons, the Canadian Rockies, rock climbing in the Shawangunks, white water canoeing, cave exploring, etc. A lot of us, including me, owned old hearses, which could carry 10 people or more on a trip to the mountains. Another of the great features of MIT was taking free courses at Harvard. I took a lot of very interesting anthropology courses until Professor Benedict had a heart to heart talk with me before renewing my fellowship for the 3rd year. "Jim, you have to decide – do you want to be a nuclear engineer or an anthropologist?" I chose nuclear engineering and never looked back.

Had I never noticed that small piece of paper on the Physics bulletin board at Carnegie Tech, I never would have become a nuclear engineer, gone to MIT and Brookhaven Lab, and would never have invented Superconducting Maglev. I probably would have worked as an engineer at St. Joseph Lead, near Pittsburgh, as some of my cousins did. Random events determine one's path through the innovation maze, and affect whether or not an innovation will occur.

After completing my doctoral thesis at MIT in 1956, I applied for a job at Brookhaven Lab and started there in September 1956. I worked for 40 years at the Lab, retiring in 1996. A small confession – I didn't actually get my doctorate until 1958, even though I had completed my thesis and passed the review committee, because I kept flunking my German language test. You had to translate 1 page of German scientific text to get your diploma. I kept trying every month for 2 years, and finally passed in 1958, after which I got my diploma. Passing French was easy, but German? I finally understood Mark Twain's famous essay, "That Awful German Language".

To me, working at Brookhaven Lab was a series of fantastic, incredible experiences that I cannot imagine happening anywhere else. There was no micro-management, even for young scientists and engineers starting out. I was given certain tasks to carry out, with periodic discussions with my immediate boss, Frank Miles, a great chemist and wonderful person, as how things were proceeding. We talked about the particular task on an equal level. Fresh ideas were encouraged, not resisted.

One of my very first tasks was given to me by Clarke Williams, the Head of the Nuclear Engineering Department at Brookhaven. At that time, the big research project in the Department, involving hundreds of people, was to develop the Liquid Metal Fueled Breeder Reactor (LMFBR). The LMFBR was competing with a number of other advanced nuclear reactor systems to be the next step beyond the Pressurized Water Reactors we still have today. Oak Ridge National Laboratory was working on the Aqueous Homogeneous Reactor and the Molten Salt Reactor, and the other National Laboratories were also working on new reactor systems.

The LMFBR was a very challenging concept, but with great promise. At that time in the development of nuclear reactors, uranium resources were thought to be much smaller than we now realize, so there was great incentive for breeder reactors that would generate more fissionable fuel than they consumed, enabling the nuclear industry to rapidly grow.

The LMFBR was based on using Thorium as the fuel for nuclear reactors, not the Uranium we use today. The Uranium cycle is a relic of the nuclear weapons program, where the Manhattan Project obtained enriched Uranium-235 and the new element, Plutonium-239, made by capture of neutrons in Uranium-238 in nuclear reactors. The Uranium cycle is also a legacy of Admiral Rickover's Naval Reactors Program.

The Thorium cycle is much more desirable than the Uranium cycle. Neutrons generated by the reactor are captured in Thorium in the reactor, converting it to fissionable Uranium-233, which keeps the reactor operating. Thorium fueled reactors do not generate long lived transuranics with half-lives of tens of thousands of years. Instead, they generate only short lived fission products like Cesium-137 and Strontium-90, with half lives of 30 years or so. The nuclear wastes from Uranium fueled reactors must be safely stored for many tens of thousands of years – a very challenging task – before they radioactively decay to safe levels. Nuclear wastes from Thorium fueled reactors, in contrast, decay to safe levels in a few hundred years, a much easier storage challenge.

So, my first big task after I started work at Brookhaven Lab was to review and analyze in great detail the earlier studies of the breeding ratio for the LMBR, and determine whether it was actually greater than 1.00, as believed, or was at less than 1.00. If it was greater than 1.00, then it could breed additional fuel for new reactors; if it was less than 1.00, then it would require scarce make-up Uranium-235 fuel, hindering the growth of the nuclear power industry.

After a couple of months of study, I concluded that the breeding ratio of the LMFBR was not greater than 1.00, but less – somewhere around 0.95 or so. This was a serious blow to the LMFBR. I took my results to Clarke Williams, the Chairman of the Nuclear Engineering Department at Brookhaven, and with a bit of fear and trembling, told him the bad news. I will never forget his response, "Thank you, we needed to know that."

That was the way in Brookhaven's early days. Accuracy and truth counted. There was no hype, no attempt to hide or downplay unpleasant results, and no pressure put on scientists and engineers to do so. No threats of firing, transfer, or unfavorable job review. A few years later, the LMFBR project was canceled, mostly because of corrosion problems with its liquid bismuth coolant, but the breeding ratio problem did not help.

At Brookhaven, we were encouraged to innovate and invent new ideas and approaches. We didn't have to submit elaborate proposals with detailed work breakdown structures, milestone dates and schedules, and projected costs for each milestone. We talked about our new ideas with our supervisors and got their input, and then decided whether or not to investigate them. Some were successful and led to important breakthroughs, while others went nowhere, either because they weren't practical, or while successful and useful like Maglev, were resisted by existing interests. There were never any recriminations or blame if a new idea didn't work out.

During my 40 years at Brookhaven, I worked in many different areas, including fission and fusion reactors, plasma physics, superconductivity, nuclear waste disposal, space power and propulsion, mine safety, and new approaches for civil infrastructure. Some examples of innovations and inventions, both large and small, that proved attractive and practical: solid lithium compound blankets in fusion reactors for breeding tritium fuel, instead of highly corrosive liquid lithium; using aluminum structures in fusion reactors instead of stainless steel to eliminate generating long lived radioactive waste material; generation of ball lightning in the laboratory and the discovery of why it persists for seconds after a lightning strike; the development of a much safer and geologically stable way to dispose of long lived nuclear waste from fission reactors without it entering the environment; Maglev; The Particle Bed Nuclear Rocket, which was much lighter than the NERVA (Nuclear Engine for Rocket Vehicle Application) and became a major project for SDI/DoD; a simple way to accurately monitor the movement of walls and roofs in coal and metal mines to detect dangerous conditions leading to collapse; a magnetic sensing method to detect the precise location of unmapped deep underground pipes from surface measurements.

Even though attractive and practical, innovations and inventions often do not get implemented, for a variety of reasons. For example, the fusion reactor engineering inventions were not implemented because researchers have not achieved adequate containment of fusion plasmas. However, the biggest barrier to implementation is simple inertia and opposition to change. People and organizations resist major change for many reasons: it threatens their income and position, it requires a lot of thought and effort to change, it can be risky, and it invites criticism from people who oppose the change.

Our invention of Maglev illustrates the difficulty of implementing major technology changes in the U.S. Existing transport systems, air, rail, and motor vehicles, perceive Maglev as a threat to their business, and generally oppose it. Government officials want to avoid potential risk and criticism, so they hesitate to develop and implement major new technologies – minor marginal improvements are favored. Implementing Maglev will require a lot of work by planners and regulators – what are the environmental impacts? Where will stations be located? What are the interfaces with existing transport systems? Innovating and inventing is much easier than implementing new technologies. Removing the barriers to implementation is much more difficult than removing the barriers to innovation and inventions.

Gordon Danby's Path to Maglev

I (Danby) was fortunate in my start of life. I had health issues at birth and was sent to live with my grandparents in a small town, where I remained until adulthood. This was Richmond in Ontario, Canada. We kids were free to roam the woods and farm fields. Like others, I survived close calls. I remember falling off the running board of our ancient car. We could skate for miles on the local river. Once, I went through the ice, alone, and had to go home wet for about 5 miles. It was an uncomplicated simple life, full of sports. Like Jim, I went to a small nearby school where several grades had one teacher. I was an avid reader, typically a book a day, at home, or when not at school. High School had the same shared room system. For my last year, grade 13, I went to a large high school in Ottawa, 20 miles away, which was very good and well run.

As an aside, about 20 years ago at a time when Maglev was "hot", Jim Powell and I were interviewed by two young women for television. They were dumb-founded when we said we were both educated in old fashioned, small multi-grade schools. We told them that the younger kids learned in part by listening to the older classes. Furthermore, society was much less managed. The teacher really taught with much less control over the details from management and supervisors.

Back then, I believe most teachers were competent and did a good job. It was expected of them. A problem has crept into much of modern society: over organized benefits and mediocre performance.

Next I attended Carleton University in Ottawa. I travelled to it in my 1929 Model A roadster. At that time Carleton was quite small but had an excellent staff. Today, it is quite large with a beautiful campus and is highly regarded. In 1948, it had many WWII veterans amongst the students, who tended to add an air of seriousness.

I received a good and broad education. I started as an engineering student. After several weeks my poor drawing skills led me to switch to Physics. I enjoyed the varied classes and extensive labs. I remember a particular Physics professor who held classes in his office. There were 2 or 3 students, including myself and a dear friend to this day. Occasionally a Great Dane joined our classes. I graduated with Honors and a Physics degree.

For graduate school, I attended McGill University in Montreal. I majored in physics and my activities centered primarily on the Radiation Lab with its cyclotron. Among our professors was a pioneering Nuclear Physicist who had established constants, like the lifetime of the neutron.

Amongst our professors was a teacher named David Jackson, who was a master of electromagnetism and an exceptional communicator. His teachings had a major impact on my career. (In later times, he wrote an excellent book, "Classical Electromagnetism" on the subject.)

My PhD thesis work was on isotope studies, by using spectrometry. The work used products irradiated in the cyclotron. This field was state of the art after the war. We used samples and chemistry to separate elements for study of the isotopes. The spectrometer was assembled using surplus magnetron magnets, to separate the isotopes for study electronically.

I received a good general education in a learning environment at McGill. I graduated in 1956, Summa Cum Laude. I enjoyed very much the big city and varied environment of Montreal. I lived in rented quarters near the University. I walked a lot, a pleasure in the city.

At McGill, I had one major dangerous experience. I had a colleague whose background included "sailing" with a sail on skates. He asked me to try it with him at a point where two large rivers joined. It was a brisk steady wind. Holding up the sail I took off with enormous speed, making me nervous even with my skating skills. I suddenly realized there was open water ahead and I knew I could not stop. I jumped as high as I could and held up high the sail. I just managed to clear the water, which at the time I believed was very wide with the sail normal to the wind, helping greatly. Had I missed my "glider airborne attempt" I could have been impaled on the edge of the ice. My history would have stopped suddenly.

I skated to where I could get around the opening and strongly decided to never try sailing on skates again!

After graduating I had to find a job. The times after WWII were opposite of today. Jobs were plentiful for science and technology, which had been critical to winning the war, the climate was very positive with strong public support.

I worked about one year in Canada in operations research, but I decided I wanted to do physical research. I traveled extensively in the United States at the request of several large aerospace firms who wanted to add more technical skills. When I heard from Brookhaven National Laboratory, I was very interested. I loved Canada, but my choice of interests had pulled me towards the U.S.

After a few years at BNL, I met and married my wife, Jane, who was, and is from Long Island. We moved to a nice old village, eventually bought a historic house and raised our children. I became a U.S. citizen and have lived here more than half my life. I became truly Americanized, but still have family and friends less than 500 miles away.

At the beginning of 1957, I joined, by invitation, Brookhaven National Lab (BNL). I worked on the later stages of construction of the 30 GEV Alternating Gradient Synchrotron (AGS). This was the largest proton accelerator in the world. I joined the group that instrumented and measured the precision magnets which formed the lattice of the accelerator. Later, I particularly worked on the lattice sextuple correction elements used for fine tuning.

When the accelerator was completed (~1960), I assisted in the initial commissioning. Also, I particularly enjoyed involving myself to help develop the experimental program. I became Deputy Head of the Experimental Planning and Support Division, with special responsibility for apparatus. In addition my small group worked on magnetic elements needed for extraction and on experimental beam transport. I also worked on some particle detectors. I concentrated on developing better apparatus for measurement and using harmonic analysis to most basically express the magnetic fields.

From the beginning of its physics program, BNL encouraged collaborations between staff scientists and members of the University Groups. The combined strength enhanced, in general, the experiments. A collaboration of talents was beneficial to success. I enjoyed this and it suited my temperament. The generally smaller University Groups wanted only success with their experimental goals. Larger groups in permanent positions are more prone to play "politics" and to excessively compete for position.

In addition to beam magnets of various types, we discovered new designs for septa to extract beams from the accelerator and to split external beams to different targets. We also discovered quadrupoles with no returns on the horizontal midplanes, for open access. We also devised three dimensional multipole routines where a subset of data, very accurately measured and positioned, could determine the field everywhere. For particle detector fields, where three dimensional end effects were very prominent, our method was excellent. We became a resource to many experimental groups which required our aid.

One of the first major experiments at the AGS (~1961) was to direct a beam onto a target to produce, by decay, neutrinos to direct into a large (for the time) detector. This unique experiment was suggested by Professor Mel Schwartz of Columbia University. I eagerly joined this effort and Columbia colleagues.

I remember working with Professor Schwartz on a detector with large aluminum plates interspersed with gas to light up when a charged particle traversed or was created in the gas regions. Particle traces were observed by optics and cameras.

Electronic counters were getting started. With a very slow counting rate expected, Mel Schwartz had more confidence in photographs of tracks. I agreed with him. Massive shielding was required for the beam which was first inside the accelerator tunnel and finally in the detector. The experiment produced approximately two neutrino events per day (24 hours). It proved that there were at least two types of neutrinos, produced by electrons and muons respectively.

The rate was much too slow to optimize by direct observation of the production of the events. Targeting had to be done very carefully, by logic, bad tuning while adjusting the time of accelerator apparently increased the rate, but days later there would be less neutrino events. This led me into studying beam dynamics and when the event results were analyzed.

The success of neutrino one led to a second experiment. For this, an external beam outside of the accelerator was massaged and transported over hill and dale to a special focusing device leading to the target and detector.

My study of magnet properties as a source of multipoles, plus work on the accelerator for the two neutrino experiments, increased my interest in precision beam control and extraction properties. It is necessary to remove beam orbit errors and extract high energy particles at the exact momentum desired.

It was standard to observe orbit errors and kick the beam at each of (many) magnets to reduce orbit errors. I instituted a system of kicks at the lattice. Fundamental lattice modes with distributed multipoles only, while ignoring any higher multipoles. This requires much less power and fewer correction magnets than the brute force method. We determined that this approach straightened the orbit to a few thousandths of an inch.

Using my experience with the details of accelerators and magnet properties, experimental beams, etc., I developed, with my little group, a study proposal of making future accelerator lattices using magnets separated for each function.

People at first were skeptical of using separate magnets for focusing from the bending magnets, adding complexity and costs. The rebuttal is that Fe (iron) cores with a basic single multipole symmetry can be excited to at least 1.5 times the peak field before significant saturation, compared to combined function operation. This is apart from reducing aberrations due to the greater flexibility in optical properties of variable focusing. We published in 1962 a detailed analysis for focusing a 200 GeV beam lattice, which got attention from most of the accelerator community. Since that time, almost all accelerators use separated function magnets.

Allinger, Danby and Jackson, (Joe Allinger, a wonderful engineer who started out as a machinist. John Jackson is a partner and friend to this day;) published a series of papers (G.T. Danby, J.Allinger, J.Jackson, BNL, *Separated Function Magnet Lattice for a Very High Field Synchrotron.*)

Another sideline activity was to explore cold Fe (Iron) for low temperature magnets. It was generally considered to be too brittle. We explored small model magnets with Fe laminations, bathed in liquid nitrogen (78 Degrees Kelvin) and later in liquid helium (4 Degrees Kelvin). It worked well up to high fields (~60 kilogauss) on shaped small model magnets with no fracturing.

First we explored super pure conductors especially aluminum in the lab. These can have enormous electrical conductivity, and very high thermal conductivity (25,000 times greater than at room temperature). We had a serious study of a 70 GeV accelerator ring on top of the AGS. The thermal inertial would keep the conductivity very high up to ~9 degrees Kelvin temperature rise in magnets pulsed in a helium bath. Thermal heat capacity for short time pulses for acceleration for Fe magnets in liquid Helium would have a modest resistive loss because of thermal inertia.

The community interest in storage rings came at this time instead of single beam accelerators. This killed desire for the 70 GeV accelerator ring, since for long flat tops at full field mode, the pure aluminum thermal flywheel was not workable for very long pulses.

We turned our attention in mid 60's to superconducting coils in our tiny magnets, cooled by Liquid Helium with "cold Fe" laminations. NbTi wire was coming available and also Niobium Boron ribbons were established. Our layers of Super Conductors were interleaved with pure Aluminum sheets. These magnets were successful, very stable and could be rapidly pulsed.

We got permission to plan and build an 8 degree bend with a 40 kG Superconducting Magnet System. This was a primary component of an external beam to a new area which had to work or the entire experimental program would be stopped. It was a complete system with closed cycle refrigerators. The pulsed beam of 40 thousand joules energy impulse had to traverse the magnet aperture every second, running 24 hours a day for extended periods.

This operated successfully for several years. I believe this was the first Superconducting (SC) magnet that was committed as part of a primary facility.

BNL was struggling with a 200 GeV storage ring. The wide ribbon of woven SC wire was proposed and modeled into coils by the designated SC group. The coils were contained in a cold Fe magnet frame. The test results were repeated failures.

Several prominent scientists supported my alternate proposal. Top management at a place like BNL is normally quite accepting of dissent.

With a large construction project in jeopardy, the repeated failures led increasingly to rejection of dissent.

Fortunately a 3rd party took over, changing the failed magnet coil design to a different design, which worked at another lab job. This success came too late to save the project. The successful magnet design was later resurrected in a new colliding beam project.

My group developed a full 200 GeV Collider design. We used for the lattice a two-in-one magnet design, with one aperture above the other but the magnetic fields decoupled. This was a quite compact and economical proposal. However, it was rejected in favor of the majority revised design.

We then attacked another challenge: lattice design for a rapid cycling Booster accelerator to accumulate a large number of protons, or other particles, then accelerate them and then transfer the higher current at higher energy into the AGS. This required very pure magnetic optics in order to not dilute and diffuse the beam over a large part of the aperture. Besides very precise static magnets being required, the rapid cycling gave rise in the magnets and in the vacuum chamber to large eddy currents distorting the fields and optics. Flexibility to vary the frequency was also required.

We invented the capability for magnetic self-correction. Windings around the back legs of the magnets induced currents which power the windings on the outside of the vacuum chamber. The produced fields which cancel the eddy currents automatically for any frequency design. This successful solution for relatively fast pulsing operation has since been employed at other accelerators.

I was approached by Professor Vernon Hughes of Yale to collaborate on an important physics goal, to measure the anomalous magnetic moment of the muon (g-2) in a storage ring to very high accuracy.

Very high magnetic precision was required. The g-2 Group studied a variety of approaches, including high field SC magnet rings. To demonstrate a SC high field ring would cost a large fraction of the full construction cost of the actual experiment apparatus ring. Also, the necessary ultra-uniformity, $\sim 1/3$ x.10^{-6}, would be hard to guarantee. I supported building a 156 Kilogram Fe core ring with SC excitation. This was chosen.

The outside of the ring had to be open for counters to observe the decay products. This required a C shaped magnet with the Fe return on the inside of the ring. Because of our excellent results using pure aluminum conductor for stabilization at Liquid Helium temperatures, it was fortunate that Japanese collaborators also favored this, as it was done.

Jackson and I struggled with assuring magnetic field uniformity. I proposed having an air gap at the base of the poles to fight the strong asymmetry from inside to the outside of the magnet. We also devised a shimming technique to obtain very precise magnetic field uniformity, a necessary condition for stable beam operation at a magnetic momentum.

The ring was large, 14 meters in diameter with a 15 kilogauss magnetic field to give the exact momentum required. The assembly was made operational, in an existing building at the end of a long beam line for transport, targeting, and injection. This major undertaking took many years to commission and run the experiment. Jackson and I were the principals in successfully crafting the magnet properties and tuning technique.

I personally believe because of its large cost that it could not have been built without the Japanese collaboration. Their share of total cost was modest, although technically they contributed a large share. International programs are hardest to terminate.

The experiment was a great success, with results beyond the standard model expectation. Successor experiments are planned.

This was another highlight of my career.

I continued to advise anyone who asked for help or comment. I was approaching retirement by the time my little group undertook the design of lattice components for the Spallation Neutron Source (SNS) built in Tennessee. This had similar parameter needs as for our successful work on the AGS Booster. After I left at the end of 1999, Jackson continued this effort to the end of BNL's program.

I have had a long career with accelerators, experimental areas and with physics collaborations which, I believe, has been quite fruitful. I had some failures and rejections. I also, many times, had much support by other staff members, particularly in my later years. Some opposition I believe was petty: i.e., groups that thought I was solving problems they considered in their domain. Others were simply technical differences of opinion. On balance, in a World where no one is perfect, I had a good run.

I was occasionally approached for public service requests. One in particular I remember. A gentleman who for years has had a successful business with a device for separating materials approached BNL top management. A professor at a renowned University was applying newer technology to solve the same problem. His PR implied there was nothing earlier in the field. (This problem is not totally unknown.) The owner wanted expert opinion before possibly suing to protect his business.

I was asked to study the problem and I determined that his science was sound and prescient and he was able to successfully defend his priority in the business.

After retiring, a senior engineer asked me and Jackson to solve a problem he had on the new National Synchrotron Light Source #2. We devised an orbit correction compound magnet which provides excitation for correction of several multipoles. Each were pure components, and were superior to corrections in earlier "light sources". This was an increasing need because of the very intense and "bright" beams required for the very high performance goals of the new machine.

Besides my work at BNL, I have two ongoing outside activities; Maglev and Magnetic Resonance Imaging, or MRI.

I was invited to visit a small MRI company. It turned out the president was a brilliant MD and scientist who discovered and created MRI. He published in the mid 70's creating a great buzz. His paper and experiment was visionary and correct, but was often nitpicked on details. Some opportunistic NMR academics and also medical device companies' staff treated him viciously.

He wanted my help to design new scanner configurations. I have productively continued with this activity to the present time. Our latest product (patented) is an upright scanner in which patients can sit or stand. It can operate at any angle from horizontal to vertical. The upright capability under gravity compared to lie-down scanners is increasingly being recognized as having many unique medical advantages. One example is for spine problems: our upright scans, with also spine compression and expansion positions, can fully explore the back, so surgery avoids some guesswork which occurs with lie down scans alone. Also, whip lash effects are fully revealed so that corrective surgery can be done.

I have enjoyed making real contributions to medical progress. I also have observed the extreme efforts to suppress his seminal creation and contributions to its ever expanding use in patient treatment.

Finally, my involvement with Maglev. In time, the work by Jim Powell and me on Maglev will inevitably be recognized and used everywhere for transport, because of its unique capabilities and environmental benefits.

We were young faculty scientists at BNL. In 1960, we shared a house for approximately 2 years. Naturally we discussed our respective work.

Jim was interested in SC transmission lines and magnets. He wrote a paper proposing that vehicles with on-board SC magnets could be levitated and propelled by interaction with the magnetic fields of SC cables laid along a guideway, as a conceptual design for Maglev transport.

I became interested (~1960) and suggested inductive interaction between shaped shorted loops of metal, i.e. Al or Cu wire, on the guideway with SC magnets on the vehicles passing overhead. We realized this was very practical and the most attractive approach to Maglev yet proposed. For 150 years, it was known that magnetic forces were very strong. For levitation the problem was stability. For example, a magnet near a Fe refrigerator door has a force that increases as it gets nearer, finally clamping on the door.

I recall that after my wedding in late 1962, I realized that opposing loops connected in series cancel coupled induction with the right "null flux" geometry so that at null there is no power loss in the ground coils. Partial cancellation permits the current in these coils to be any strength compared to the SC Magnet coils, which can be much stronger than the ground currents, which are resistive and lossy. We realized that large suspensions of 6" or more are practical. Other levitation proposals had coils on the vehicles, inducing almost equal current in large continuous sheets of metal or a large coil on the ground. Thus the lift force was directly proportional to the square of the magnet field current. With variable vehicle loads this is a difficult situation, the dynamics are non-linear and restoring force very soft, with large losses.

We believed we had the first really attractive and practical Maglev. We published in 1966 (bear in mind this took a few years; we both had demanding projects at BNL).

We had Worldwide interest after publication. Japan National Railways visited us on several occasions and started a serious program. They were very taken with the LSM propulsion strength potential compared with steel wheel on steel rails. The large clearance and tolerances are very attractive in an earthquake prone land. The Japanese built a system based on our patents and ideas. This has grown into their existing, very successful 1st generation Maglev system.

Germany also visited and built a demonstration. However, the decision in Germany was to go with an attractive force system, using electromagnets pulled upwards to iron rails on the guideway. This system is inherently unstable, and requires servo-control of the electromagnet currents to overcome the strong instability. They sense and rapidly change current in the vehicle electromagnet coils to produce a stable levitation. This works, but is practical only for small clearances, i.e. approximately 1 cm, with a very small tolerance of approximately 1 mm in constructing the guideway. Guideways must be very flat and stable in the presence of temperature variations. Plus, weathering and water impact on structures, etc. The guideway is very expensive for the existing Transrapid system.

In the U.S., the DOT decided that with the Interstate Highways and modern aircraft, a new transport system was not needed. Several small studies were funded that led nowhere.

When Jim and I came to BNL, it was set up to operate with a strong academic culture, influenced by basic science, as a super university that would cooperate with existing universities to create very large experimental facilities. The Lab allowed us to have private activities, and patents outside of BNL's charter, with disclosure to avoid improper conflicts. Our Maglev discoveries were patented privately. I also proposed a 3-D stable magnetic bearing, which we also patented. Unfortunately, a servo-controlled air bearing having come out first and captured the market, we did not pursue that invention.

We continue to work on Maglev transport, typically on Sunday afternoons, sandwiched between family obligations, for over 40 years. Our only real public supporter was Senator Moynihan, who launched an initiative in the late 1980s. He proposed using the Interstate Highway rights-of-way for most Maglev guideway routes. His initiative for a real program got us started in a serious way. He was unusual for a politician. He deeply explored ideas. He was not a big organization man where ideas were concerned.

Florida investigated High Speed Rail between Tampa, Orlando, plus the cities to the South, ending in Miami. Charles Smith was an experienced rail expert who worked for the Florida government on this project. He had previously been heavily involved in the rail system between Baltimore and Washington.

Smith knew Jim and me from technical meetings and respected us. Florida funded most of our Maglev development with a smaller share from the FRA. We rented a large airport building for construction in Florida. We planned a system first phase, from Titusville to Kennedy Space Center and then to the Canaveral seaport.

We developed the magnet coils and insulation, the guideway panels and a 73 foot beam with post tensioned construction for our 2nd generation Maglev 2000 system. Transportation consultants verified our low cost projections. Additional work was also done at our Long Island hangar lab.

After extensive studies, Florida decided, correctly, that the HSR project would not be cost effective. Our support also ended. We continued work at our small aircraft hangar building workplace, where magnet coils were wound and packaged in their cryostats. They were tested to full current successfully.

Basically we had almost all the technical parts ready when we ran out of money. After Senator Moynihan's health failed, we had no support. The FTA approached us to proceed with a suburban extension of our high speed work. We proceeded with this and suddenly they withdrew their

The Fight for Maglev   Maglev: First Round

funding. Afterwards, at a meeting, we were told that a Congressman took the money for an earmark. (I believe at least 80% of earmark dollars are wasted.)

We continued to think about Maglev, apart from our BNL work and family responsibilities. The original design we called the "first generation". Our later design is greatly improved, and patented. We call it the "second generation". Instead of single loop SC dipoles on the vehicles, we introduced quadrupole (4-pole) SC magnets. These provide several basic advantages. They are easily constructed as planar loops whose spacing is equal to their width, and then connected in series opposition. This produces on the sides of a square currents that flow in alternate directions.

With quadrupoles the fringing fields will be much less than for a dipole. Aided by a small amount of shielding material, the fringing field will be 1 Gauss at all points in passenger compartments as well as entering the vehicle, or outside on the walkway or street. The Japanese first generation SC Maglev vehicle design has dipole magnets at only each end, front and back well away from passengers.

The very important consequence is that multiple magnets can be located all along the vehicles, allowing heavy freight or tractor trailer trucks to be transported. The revenues from truck transport will pay for the entire system in a few years. This is not possible for passenger only high speed rail or Maglev systems in the U.S. with its low population densities. Passenger only systems will require taxpayer funding both for construction and operations including expensive track maintenance.

A further advantage of 4-pole magnets is that the electrodynamic interaction is the same for right of way panels located on the sides of, or underneath, the SC magnets. Very high speed 300 mph plus operation will be on elevated narrow beams, with the magnets on each side of the beam which has attached panels. Low speed vehicles can operate with the bottom of the magnets above planar aluminum loop panels. This also allows high speed transition from the narrow beam to a planar system that continues on all-electric transactions to stations entry ROW, or alternatively goes straight ahead. With no switch moving parts, it can be fail-safe.

185

Because the vehicles are self-propelled with LSM, one can schedule to pass most stations with single vehicles, which can be closely spaced. This "skip-stop" procedure will keep average speed nearly as large as the running speed, not possible with slow acceleration rail. Large cities are surrounded by suburban development. Sharing the railway ROW, i.e., besides some highways, is the only way, practically for city center access. This Maglev can share ROW with trains, properly scheduled for quick access using "skip stop" for suburban stations at speeds equal to or less than 150 miles per hour.

I was chiefly responsible for quadrupole magnet ideas. Jim came up with a wonderful energy storage concept. Since our design for Maglev has very low electric losses, he proposed carrying heavy weight up to one half mile of elevation to store the enormous potential energy. He worked out a system to carry large concrete blocks uphill on flatbed Maglev vehicles powered by the electric utility. The multiple block load is stored until peak demand power is needed. Then the blocks are carried down, using the LSM as a generator instead of as a motor, putting power into the grid. Solar and wind energy can be used as well as fossil fuels. This system is 95% efficient. Most storage systems are much less efficient.

Another use of Maglev 2000 that Jim Powell has studied is for transport of water, etc., long distances to receiving locations. The vehicles can be simple structures with large bladder containers attached. The advantage over pipelines is that Maglev 2000 can traverse large elevation changes easily. Pipelines have expensive problems coping with large elevation changes.

Finally, it was accidental that Jim and I came together. (This is true also for marriages). Our combined interests and talents were necessary.

Innovations and Inventions

So what are the lessons that emerge about innovations and inventions from Jim Powell and Gordon Danby's experience in developing their superconducting Maglev propulsion system. How should society encourage innovation and invention? And most importantly, how can it lower the very high barriers to their implementation?

While society cannot alter the fundamental randomness of the events that determine the shape of discoveries and inventions, it can create an environment that increases the probability that they will occur.

Lesson 1: Emphasize creativity, new ideas, critical thinking, and rigorous analysis at all education levels, from elementary grades through graduate school. Today, emphasis is on "teaching to tests", and drilling facts and accepted ideas into students – not likely to encourage innovative thinking.

Lesson 2: Stop outsourcing America's science and engineering jobs to other countries. Nothing discourages young people from science and engineering careers more than seeing potential jobs go overseas. Why should they accumulate tens of thousands of dollars of debt, if when they graduate, there may not be any jobs.

Lesson 3: Stop micro-managing R&D projects. Elaborate "Work Breakdown Structures" with large numbers of milestones to be accomplished at specific dates for specified costs, absolutely kill creativity and innovation. If a better approach comes forth, researchers dare not investigate it, lest they miss their milestones and overspend the specified amounts. And what about, innovations and inventions outside the scope of the project no matter how important? Not only forget them, don't even think about them. Your job depends on meeting the Zillion milestones on time, and on cost, not generating new ideas.

Lesson 4: Have real experienced scientists and engineers generate and carry out R&D, without the vast amount of administrative overhead and out-of-touch management that is presently involved. Not only does this lead to more innovation and invention, but things get done faster and cheaper.

Finally, how can America lower the barriers to implementation of new inventions?

Political leadership to must declare national goals and really push to make them happen. Like Lincoln, Theodore Roosevelt, Eisenhower, and Kennedy's transport revolutions. Today, America's leaders call for major programs – "ending our addiction to oil", "green energy", "80% reduction in greenhouse gas emissions", etc., etc., but do little to make them happen.

Very often, when we talk to political leaders and government administrators about why America needs to implement Maglev, we often get the answer, "The government doesn't pick winners and losers." In other words, the government policymakers don't see themselves as playing a real role in innovation – whatever happens is OK. Instead, just make meaningless speeches about "the need for innovation."

Chapter Eight

Second Round – Senator Moynihan Climbs into the Ring

[This chapter was written by James Powell with Gordon Danby]

"Fifteen years from now, when you settle into your seat for the one-hour run from Chicago to Detroit, have a look under your seat cushion. My sincere hope is that you will not find a small tag that reads, 'Maglev: invented by American scientists, made in West Germany."

Essay, "How to Lose: The Story of Maglev" by Senator Daniel Patrick Moynihan in Scientific American, November 1989.

Twenty three years ago, in 1987, we (Gordon Danby and Jim Powell) received a call from Senator Moynihan's office asking us to come down to Washington to talk to the Senator about Maglev. By coincidence, that was 21 years after we published our invention of Superconducting Maglev. Maybe there's something magic about 2 decades – it could also mark the completion of the Maglev America Network twenty years from now.

We of course, were delighted to talk to Senator Moynihan about Maglev. Before meeting with him, we asked one of his staff assistants how Senator Moynihan had learned about Maglev and us. The staffer told us that Senator Moynihan had a terrible trip on the train from New York to Washington, and wanted a better way to travel. He asked the staffer to look into this new mode of transport called Maglev, and who he should meet to discuss it. The staffer briefed him on our activities and inventions, and Senator Moynihan then asked us to come down and meet with him.

Our first meeting, and subsequent meetings, with Senator Moynihan were exciting and stimulating. He thought about the future of America and what the country should be doing, more clearly and more realistically, than any of the other people in government, both in the Congress and the various Administrations that we have met in the many years since our initial meeting.

During that first meeting, Senator Moynihan outlined his vision for Maglev in America. He was Chairman of the Senate Subcommittee on Water Resources, Transportation, and Infrastructure of the Senate, Environmental and Public Works Committee with oversight of the Interstate Highway System. He visualized building Maglev routes on the rights-of-way alongside the Interstates and other federally supported highways to create a National Maglev Network of many thousands of miles.

Prior to the meeting, we had not really thought about how Maglev systems should be implemented to best serve America. We were and still are, primarily technologists, not planners. Senator Moynihan's vision quickly became ours.

Senator Moynihan's one-page essay in Scientific American (November, 1989) sums up why Maglev will be the dominant mode of transport in the 21st Century. Quoting his first paragraph, *"This is the story of a contest almost no one is watching. At stake is preeminence in the production and sale of a revolutionary new mode of transportation. It is called Magnetic Levitation – Maglev for short. It will define the coming century much as the railroad defined the last one, and the automobile and airplane have defined this one."*

Senator Moynihan then describes America's promising start in Maglev development following Powell and Danby's 1966 invention, but, *"Then everything stopped. On February 5, 1975, a representative of the Office of Management and Budget announced that Maglev research was no longer a priority. The budget would be juggled to shore up the past century's conventional rail technology, but by this time we were not alone in the race. Other countries had been quick to pick up on Powell and Danby's idea. By the late 1960's, Great Britain, Japan, West Germany, and–can you imagine? – Romania had initiated their own Maglev programs. Japan and Germany have stuck at it"*

"By 1972 the Japanese had a model going; by 1972 they had tested a Maglev vehicles at 320 miles per hour. The full-size German

Transrapid 06 had traveled 100,000 miles on its 20 mile test track in Emsland. And these projects did not just happen. The Japanese government has poured $1 Billion into Maglev research, the West German government almost as much. By comparison, the U.S. Government spent $3 million on Maglev between 1966 and 1975; after that, nothing."

Senator Moynihan then describes how America's transportation revolutions, starting with the Erie Canal through railroads, the automobile, and the airplane have profoundly affected American society. And how there always have been political leaders that have resisted these revolutions in transport because they would "hurt" their particular interest and the people and entities that back them. In 1829, Governor Van Buren of New York, the home of the Erie Canal, wrote a strongly worded letter to President Andrew Jackson protesting the development of railroads. The letter reads,

"As you may well know, Mr. President, railroad carriages are pulled at the enormous speed of 15 miles per hour by 'engines', which in addition to endangering life and limb of passengers, roar and snort their way through the countryside, setting fire to the crops, scaring the livestock and frightening women and children. The Almighty certainly never intended that people should travel at such breakneck speed."

Senator Moynihan understood that steel wheel trains had essentially reached their limits, and will not significantly advance in future years. One wishes those who are currently pushing High Speed Rail for the U.S. were as clear in their understanding and thinking as Senator Moynihan was.

To quote:

"Since that time, the railroad has changed very little. Just last Fall, Amtrak proudly announced that its Metroliner had averaged 110 miles per hour on a special Boston to New York run ~ two miles per hour slower than the mark set by the Empire State Express No. 999 between Batavia and Buffalo in 1893! The Japanese Bullet Train and the French TGV do a little better (operating speeds range from 150 to 180 mph) but beyond this they will not advance. They have reached the upper limit for wheel-on-rail technology."

Senator Moynihan was probably a bit pessimistic about wheel-on-rail capabilities. In the last 21 years, the best routinely operating train can now travel 20 mph or so faster than in 1989, but they have hit their realistic limits. Faster operation for short distances at selected locations, with a small number of railway cars is possible, but routine operations over hundreds of miles with loaded trains? No way— occasional stunts do not mean routine travel is possible.

In his next to last paragraph, Senator Moynihan pinpoints the fundamental truth about the U.S. developing an American 2nd generation Maglev system.

"The long and the short of it is this: no major transportation revolution has ever progressed in the U.S. without substantial Federal involvement. Maglev will be no exception. And if we do not build our own Maglev system, we will end up buying it from others."

Senator Moynihan's words tell an unpleasant truth. Without substantial federal involvement, private enterprise will never develop a U.S. Maglev system on its own. Why would they undertake Maglev development if there is no real sign that the U.S. Government would push its implementation? Politicians might oppose it, or make the approval process so difficult, as is the case for nuclear reactors, that implementation would take forever at tremendous expense. Our government has created a perfect "Catch-22" situation. The government leaves it up to the free market to develop Maglev – we don't "pick winners or losers", while the free market says, "we won't risk investing in its development, when the government does not indicate that it will implement it when it's ready." This is a recipe for never developing major new technologies in the U.S. especially when the old technologies strongly oppose it.

Which brings us to Senator Moynihan's last paragraph and his statement that, *"My sincere hope is that you will not find a small tag that reads, Maglev: Invented by American Scientists, Made in West Germany."* If there is such a tag, most likely it will read Made in China, instead of Made in Germany. Senator Moynihan fully understood the crucial importance of America developing and implementing Maglev transport for the 21st Century.

We continue with the Outside Story of the 17 years between our first meeting with Senator Moynihan, and 2004, when our very small amount of funding for developing the U.S. 2nd generation Maglev system stopped.

The Outside Story: Senator Moynihan's fight to have America Develop Maglev, and the Consequent Achievements of the 2nd Generation Maglev 2000 system.

Senator Moynihan held a number of Senate committee hearings on Maglev transport, starting in October of 1987. Rather than discussing all of them, we focus on two. The first is the hearing held on February 26, 1988 (1) in which a number of witnesses, ourselves (Powell and Danby) included, testified on superconducting Maglev technology. The hearing was held by the Senate Committee on Environment and Public Works, Subcommittee on Water Resources, Transportation and Infrastructure, Senator Daniel Patrick Moynihan, Chairman.

Present were Senators Moynihan, Stafford (Vermont), Graham (Florida), John Warner (Virginia), and Durenberger (Minnesota). The witnesses, besides ourselves, were Richard Gran (Grumman), Larry Johnson (Argonne National Laboratory), Henry Kolm (Electromagnetic Launch Research), Carl Rosner (Intermagnetics General) and Richard Welch (City of Las Vegas). The Council on Superconducting for America's Competitiveness supplied a statement for the record.

Senator Moynihan's opening statement summed up, concisely and clearly, why America should develop superconducting Maglev – why it was much better than High Speed Rail, how it would reduce congestion on our highways and airways, improve safety, increase energy efficiency, shorten travel time, and be much quieter than other modes of transport. It is disappointing to think that these problems, which he so eloquently described how Maglev could eliminate, have only gotten worse in the last 22 years, with no real actions taken to solve them.

Senator Moynihan stressed how important it was that America "leapfrog" Japan and Germany's development of Maglev, and that the U.S. could take the lead fairly quickly – if we seize the opportunity. He mentioned the legislation he had introduced in pursuit of that goal – S.1794, that would provide a blue print for a federal effort to assist in the development and implementation of a U.S. Magnetic Levitation system, and S.2072, which would permit construction of Magnetic Levitation systems on the rights-of-way of the Interstate and Federally Assisted Highway System.

The use of the Interstate Highway rights-of-way for Maglev is especially important, in light of what is currently (2011) happening in the proposed High Speed Intercity Passenger Rail program. The Administration has proposed to use existing railroad trackage or new track alignments alongside the existing tracks for high speed passenger trains. However, the freight railroad companies are strongly resisting this plan for reasons of schedule disruption and safety. They say that in no way will they allow their rights-of-way and tracks to be used for High Speed Rail systems.

Maglev can readily use the rights-of-way alongside the Interstate Highways without disrupting existing traffic flow. High Speed Rail cannot use these rights of way. The construction cost for High Speed Rail would be immense, the installation process very long and disruptive to traffic flow, and being on-grade instead of elevated, unsafe because of possible accidents caused by trucks and cars on the highway. Amtrak's recently announced 117 Billion dollar price tag for a 430 mile long High Speed Rail line from Boston to Washington, DC is proof of that.

The other Senators at the hearing, Bob Graham of Florida, Harry Reid of Nevada, and Larry Pressler of South Dakota all expressed strong support for Maglev. Senator Pressler did express one concern – that the rural states in America not be left out when the U.S. Maglev routes were built. That is a real concern, as one looks at how the current air service to the smaller rural communities is being eliminated because they are not profitable. Moreover, the proposed U.S. High Speed Rail systems will only serve a small part of America, those living in large cities, and will completely ignore the small communities and rural areas. In contrast, with the 28,800 mile long National Maglev Network described in Chapter 4, 80% of the U.S. population will live within 15 miles of a Maglev station, from which they can reach any other point in America in a few hours.

All of the witnesses that testified strongly supported Maglev technology and called for the U.S. to initiate development of a U.S. Maglev system, because of the benefits for American transport and the economy. The written submission from the Council on Superconductivity for American Competitiveness called in particular for R&D in high temperature superconductors because of their advantage over liquid helium cooled superconducting magnets.

Senator Moynihan asked us (Gordon and Jim) to form and serve as co-chairmen of a Maglev Technology Advisory Committee (MTAC) to review the status and potential benefits of Maglev for the U.S., and to prepare a report for his committee. We were very pleased and honored to do so. The formal date for the establishment of MTAC was September 28, 1988, but in actuality, it was already in action well before that date.

Including ourselves, MTAC had 21 members representing a wide range of disciplines and organizations, interested in Maglev. From the scientific and engineering research world, there was Danby & Powell (Brookhaven National Laboratory); Dick Thornton (MIT); Harry Fair (University of Texas); and Howard Coffey, Larry Blow, and Larry Johnson (Argonne National Laboratory). From the industrial and commercial world, there was Richard Gran and Mike Proise (Grumman Corporation); Henry Kolm (EML Research), David Ramsey (The Magneplane Corporation); Edward Leung (General Dynamics); John Henry and Richard Zavadowski (Babcock&Wilcox); Carl Rosner (Intermagnetics General); Anthony Bright (New Technology Products); Kevin Ott (Council on Superconducting for American Competitiveness). From the environmental world, Richard Gibbs (NY Department of Environmental Conservation); from the economists' world, Tim Lynch (Center for Economic Forecasting and Analysis).

Rounding out the 21 member team, we had two consultants, Fred Robertson (McClellan, Robertson) and Bob Salter (Xerox), Bob covered the waterfront in new ideas, from playing a major role in defense satellites while at Rand, in nuclear rockets at SDI, and in his invention of the Planet Train – traveling on Maglev vehicles at thousands of miles per hour in air evacuated tunnels.

This broad range of experience and capabilities of MTAC's members ensured a thorough and objective analysis of the benefits and issues associated with Maglev, and helped Senator Moynihan formulate his legislation for a practical U.S. R&D program on Maglev.

MTAC held a number of meetings, the outcome of which is summarized in the report *"Benefits of Magnetically Levitated High-Speed Transportation for the United States" Volume 1*, the *Executive Report* appeared in June 1989.(2) The much larger, 240 page, Volume 2, *"The Technical Report"*, which described how Maglev could be developed and implemented in the U.S. appeared in March 1992, though a draft of the report was available to Senator Moynihan's Committee in 1990, prior to Senate passage of the legislation for a 750 million dollar R&D program on Maglev.(2)

The MTAC Reports were published by the Grumman Corporation, with most of the typing and drawings prepared by Brookhaven National Laboratory personnel. The cover of the reports, as shown by the accompanying figure, was a really gorgeous view of Maglev vehicles speeding along an elevated guideway located adjacent to a 6-lane highway. Even 20 years after its publication, the MTAC reports are still relevant, and provide a good introduction to Maglev transport technology, and why it is important to America.

The MTAC Reports were followed by the 2nd major Senate hearing on Maglev held by Senator Moynihan on March 9, 1990.(3) The opening statements by Senator Moynihan, Senator Graham from Florida, Senator Reid of Nevada, and Senator Symms from Idaho, were all very supportive of Maglev. In particular, Senators Reid and Graham pushed hard for building Maglev systems in their States, Nevada and Florida.

There was considerable satisfaction that the Administration had reversed the 1975 policy of not having the government engage in Maglev development, and that it had recently decided to put 10 million dollars for R&D on a U.S. Maglev system in the FY 1991 Budget to highlight this decision. Senator Moynihan had asked Elaine Chao, Deputy Secretary of the Department of Transportation, Major General Patrick Kelly, Director of Civil Works, Corps of Engineers, and Robert Page, Assistant Secretary of the Army for Civil Works to testify concerning the proposed program.

They expressed support for the Maglev program and were ready to go ahead with spending the 10 million dollars to study Maglev for the U.S. All in all, it was a lament that America was falling behind in the development of new technologies, while other nations were overtaking us in them, and American manufacturing was declining. Sound familiar? The same laments are all being uttered today – nothing has really changed in the last 20 years since the 1990 hearing.

As usual, Senator Moynihan was very direct and blunt as he laid out the issues involved. Quoting from his statements at the hearing, with regard to Maglev, "The Department of Transportation was very resistant" (to Maglev development, just like today) "The Department of Transportation has been a dead agency in the last decade. It may be coming alive thanks to Ms. Chao."

"In any event, the Japanese are spending 3 Billion dollars on their third generation of vehicles. We have just proposed to possibly, maybe, spend 10 million dollars in the next fiscal year. That is a formula for industrial decline, there is no question about it."

Later in the hearing, clearly peeved, Senator Moynihan recalled how past political leaders pushed new technologies. Senator Moynihan – "One of the first things I became involved with in Washington years ago was the question of what to do with a supersonic aircraft. President Kennedy asked then Vice-President Johnson to head up a committee. He was in charge of the Space Committee."

"I can't retrieve the energy of these meetings. Two o'clock in the morning in the Executive Office Building; it was Saturday already and you were going to go right through into Sunday if necessary to find out, should we do this?"

"By contrast we have the entropy of the last 15 years: (i.e., since 1975, and the DOT's cancellation of the Maglev program) with that sort of 'Huh?' The nearest this subject (i.e. Maglev) has gotten to the Executive Office Building is Mr. Darman's coming in "(i.e., the Director of the Office of Management and the Budget, who put the 10 million dollars for Maglev in the Budget) in response to the 'Scientific American article". (The article by Senator Moynihan, quoted earlier).

In, referring to MTAC and its reports to his Committee, Senator Moynihan stated, "The Maglev Technology Committee, established by this Committee on September 28, 1988, and issued its first report on June 12, 1989, has shown that a U.S. Maglev effort, is, dare we say, almost a moral imperative. We can leapfrog the existing foreign technologies if we have the will."

"Perhaps we have already lost the race. If the Japanese establish a 'picket fence' around the 2nd generation technology in the next few years, while we continue with studies, we certainly will have done. And we will have lost the next mode of transportation."

"Mind, we still will have Maglev. It will just be made in Japan and Germany. But we will have lost something singular, our belief in our ability to lead the way to the future. And we will have failed our pioneers – Drs. Powell, Danby, Kolm, and others."

Senator Moynihan, of course, fully realized that 10 million dollars of government funding for Maglev would not let the U.S. "leapfrog" foreign Maglev development. Accordingly, he pushed through the Senate, a bill authorizing a 750 million dollar R&D program for Maglev, as part of the overall 5-year Transportation Authorization Bill.

After it passed the Senate, the 750 million dollar Maglev program went to the Transportation and Infrastructure Committee in the House of Representatives. The Committee was chaired by the appropriately named Representative Robert Carr from Detroit (life imitates art), who refused to hold hearings on Senator Moynihan's Maglev legislation. So it died in committee, and vested transport interests breathed a sigh of relief. U.S. Government Maglev had died once again, to come briefly back to semi-life in 1997.

Meanwhile, in another arena, Maglev still struggled on. In 1991, Powell and Danby were honored to receive the "Sparky Awards" from the High Speed Rail and Maglev Association for our Maglev inventions. The beautiful bronze muscular "Sparky Men" statuettes still adorn our offices. In May of 1992, Brookhaven Lab held a 2-day workshop on Maglev on superconducting Maglev technology, organized by the lab, the New York State Energy Research and Development Authority, and the NYS Institute on Superconductivity. Sixty leading Maglev researchers attended the Workshop to review the technology and outline the development of 2nd generation Maglev for America.

The Lieutenant Governor of New York, Stanley Lundine, addressed the Workshop. He and Governor Mario Cuomo were very strong supporters of Maglev and interacted closely with us and Brookhaven Lab. BNL organized a U.S. Department of Transportation Northeast Regional meeting on Maglev, to be held in Albany in October, 1992.

We also organized a 1 day Symposium on Maglev for the American Association for the Advancement of Science (AAAS) annual meeting that was held in Chicago in February 1992. There was a lot of interest and participation in the Symposium by the public.

As always, we continued to write papers, give lectures and organize conferences on Maglev, waiting for the Big Break to actually start the development and testing of hardware for the 2nd generation U.S. Maglev system.

The Big Break came in 1996, The Florida Department of Transportation (FDOT) decided to fund an actual hardware program for 2nd generation superconducting Maglev, not just paper studies, and we were absolutely thrilled.

FDOT provided 2 million dollars funding to the Maglev 2000 of Florida Corporation to begin a Maglev development/demonstration project in Central Florida. An equal amount of "matching funds' was supplied in the form of in-kind services by the National High Magnetic Field Laboratory of Florida State University for basic research on superconducting materials, and by the National Aviation and Transportation Center of Dowling College in Long Island, for simulation studies of the Maglev 2000 system. A final report was accepted and the contract closed.

In the summer of 1999, the Federal Railroad Administration (FRA), an agency of the U.S. Department of Transportation, awarded FDOT 3,359,750 dollars to continue Maglev 2000's work, focusing on a 20 mile route from Cape Canaveral Seaport to the Titusville Airport, with an intermediate station at Kennedy Space Center.

Figure 1a shows a map of the planned Maglev 2000 route.(4) It connected together a seaport, an airport, and a spaceport, following along a highway for much of its length. Of the 5 major modes of existing transport it was intermodally connected to four – air, sea, space, and road. It did leave out railroads, however.

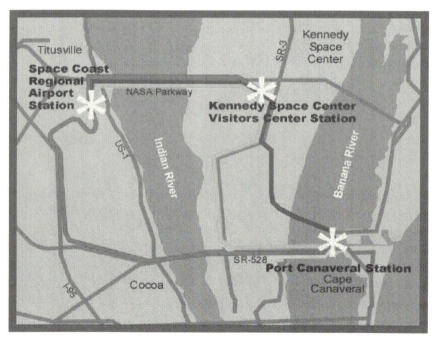

Figure 1A Maglev 2000 Route

The proposed route, if it had been built, would have been very successful, especially had it been extended 35 miles to Orlando, as was planned.

A tremendous number of tourists visit this Central Florida region to enjoy Disney World in Orlando, tour the Kennedy Space Center, and take ocean cruises from Cape Canaveral Seaport. Riding America's first Maglev line at 300 mph would have been an important part of a tourist's trip to the region.

The following artist's drawings shows a station stop for the route.

FIGURE 1B Two way Station Stop for Maglev 2000 at Florida Test Site

Study of the route was carried out by Maglev 2000 of Florida Corporation, together with the engineering and construction firms of Fredric R. Harris, Inc. and Tilden, Lebnitz, and Cooper. Additional participants included URS; Greiner, Woodward and Clyde; Solomon Smith Barney; Transportation Economics and Management Leplanes; Powell, Fragala, and Associates; Florida State University; and the National Aviation and Transportation Center.

The cost of the 20 mile Titusville to Kennedy Space Center to Canaveral Seaport route was projected to cost 600 million dollars, equivalent to 30 million dollars per two way mile. The two special bridges required to cross the Indian and Banana Rivers were a major part of the system cost.

Without the bridges, the projected cost only 14 million dollars per two way mile, for a total of about 300 million dollars.

The ridership on the 20 mile route was very conservatively estimated to be 3.2 million passengers annually in 2020 AD. With the 35 mile extension to Orlando, the projected ridership in 2020 AD was 20 million passengers annually, with a yearly revenue forecast of 336 million dollars. The capital cost of the full system could have been paid back in less than 5 years.

The Titusville – Kennedy Space Center – Canaveral route study was one of seven studies being carried out for a possible Maglev route to be built in the U.S. Ours was the only one of the 6 studies that proposed to use American maglev technology. The other 5 studies proposed buying and installing the Transrapid Maglev System from Germany. No technical work was done in these 5 Transrapid studies – just studies of the proposed route. Our study was the only one to do any technical work. A detailed 800 page final report on the Central Florida route was submitted to the FRA on June 30, 2000, and accepted. (5)

The FRA then down-selected 2 finalists out of the 7 studies. Both used the Transrapid System. One route was between Baltimore and Washington, DC, while the other was at Pittsburgh, Pennsylvania.

In the Fall of 2000, Congress designated funding of 877,066 dollars to Maglev 2000 to study a 7 mile Maglev route from the Kennedy Space Center to the Saturn V visitor area. A detailed final report was accepted by the FRA.(6)

In September of 2001, the Federal Transit Administration (FTA) awarded Maglev 2000 1 million dollars to study urban Maglev systems, with a 1 million dollar match from FDOT. A final report was submitted in 2004.

Total Awards to Maglev 2000 of Florida Corporation

Florida Department of Transportation	$7,000,000
Federal Railroad Administration	$4,236,816
Federal Transit Administration	$1,000,000
Florida Agencies	$1,050,000

The Fight for Maglev

Maglev: Second Round

To the total of slightly more than 14 million dollars add in about 0.5 million dollars of their personal funds spent by Powell, Danby, John Morena and Tom Wagner, the principals of Maglev 2000, to help keep the work going. Politicians laud small inventors and innovators, but it's very difficult being a tiny David going up against a giant Goliath, when all you have is a small slingshot and Goliath has a very big club to squash you. For every David who wins the contest, there are a thousand who get squashed.

So how did we spend the 14.5 million dollars? A lot had to go to satisfy the study requirements – lay out routes, project costs, examine environmental issues, etc., and to fund engineering/construction and other companies involved in the study.

However, we did manage to eke out some funds for actual hardware development and testing. In this we were greatly helped and very grateful to many of our technicians that wanted to work in the exciting field of Maglev. A couple were full time, but most were part time moonlighters. The pay rate was very low, and some worked prodigiously for no pay at all. Without their help, we could not have accomplished what we did.

Our total funding for hardware was at most a few million dollars– compare that with Japan and Germany, who each spent several Billion dollars in hardware development for their first generation systems – a thousand times more than our program did.

Imagine someone saying to you, "I'd like you to build a 100,000 dollar race car for the Indy 500. Here's 100 dollars. "Realizing the scope of the job, and the woefully inadequate funding, we decided that the best course was to develop and build the most important components at full size and test their performance. We could not try to assemble and test a vehicle on a guideway – the funding was just far too small to attempt that.

We set up two laboratories for Maglev 2000 development – one at the Titusville Airport in Florida, and the other at the Calabro Airport in Shirley, Long Island. Empty hangars and buildings at small airports are good places to do experimental work. They are easy to get to, have lots of parking space, good neighbors, and low rental cost. We carried out preliminary work at the Long Island facility and then transferred components to the Titusville facility for more detailed development.

We focused on the 4 main components for the Maglev 2000 system. [Details are given in Reference (7)]

1. Superconducting quadrupole magnets
2. Aluminum loop guideway panels
3. Guideway beam
4. Maglev vehicle body

Main Components for the Maglev 2000 System

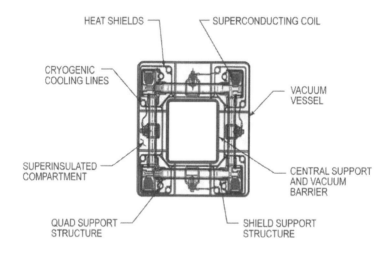

Figure 2 Cross-Section of Quadrupole Magnet

Figure 2 shows a cross section of the Maglev 2000 superconducting quadrupole magnet, the unique heart of the Maglev 2000 system. The M-2000 quadrupole magnet module has 2 superconducting loops of width W, separated by the distance W. The 2 loops carry oppositely directed superconducting currents, resulting in 4 magnetic poles, alternating as one proceeds around the circumference of the quadrupole. The 2 loops can be separate electrical circuits, or be connected together to form a single circuit. The 4 pole feature enables the superconducting quadrupole to magnetically interact with aluminum guideway loop panels positioned vertically on the sides of a monorail guideway beam, using the magnetic pole from the vertical face of the quadrupoles, or with aluminum guideway loop panels positioned on a planar guideway beneath the Maglev vehicle, using the magnetic pole from the bottom surface of the quadrupole as depicted in Figure 3.

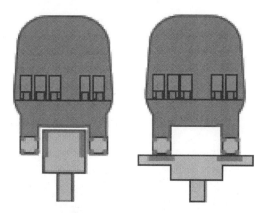

Figure 3 Maglev 2000 Vehicle on Monorail and Planar Guideway Using Quadrupole Magnets

Figure 4 Artist's Drawing of Maglev 2000 Passenger Vehicle on Monorail Guideway

Maglev 2000 vehicles can smoothly transition between the 2 types of guideway, from monorail to planar, and back to monorail. For high speed operation on elevated guideways, for most of the route (90% or more), the vehicles will operate on the monorail guideway (Figure 4). It is lower in cost, safe at high speeds, visually more attractive, and easy to erect.

At locations where switching to off-line stations is desired, vehicles would transition to a planar guideway holding 2 lines of planar guideway loops. Initially closely overlapping, the 2 lines would gradually diverge laterally. The straight ahead line of loops is the main high speed guideway, while the laterally diverging line of guideway loops leads to the off-line station.

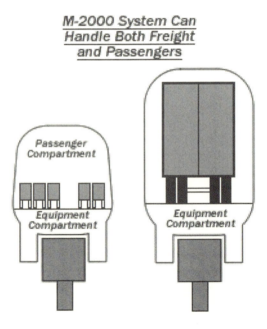

Figure 5 Maglev 2000 Passenger and Truck Carrier Vehicles on Dual-use Guideway

Figure 5 shows passenger and truck carrying Maglev vehicles on the same monorail guideway segments. Each can access separate off-line stations for unloading/loading operations.

Figure 6 Cross-Section Drawing of Levitated Maglev 2000 Vehicle Traveling on Conventional RR Track to which Aluminum Loop Panels Have Been Atached to the Crossties.

The guideway panels can also be mounted on crossties of existing RR tracks (Figure 6), enabling levitated travel of Maglev 2000 vehicles along existing RR tracks. The panels do not interfere with conventional trains, which could use the tracks for bulk freight transport, given appropriate scheduling. Maglev 2000 vehicles traveling as individual units would allow much more frequent and convenient passenger service, rather than long trains of many RR cars. Also, because Maglev loads are distributed along the vehicle and not concentrated at wheels, local track loading is much less than with conventional trains, greatly increasing track life and reducing maintenance.

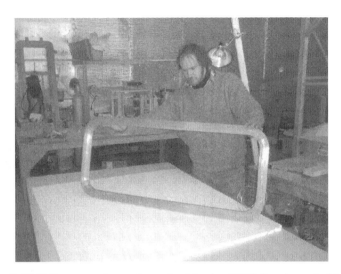

Figure 7 NbTi Superconductor Loop for Maglev 2000 Quadrupole Magnet

Figure 7 shows one of the two wound superconducting loops used for the Maglev 2000 quadrupole. The loop has 600 turns of NbTi superconducting wire. At the design current of 1000 Amps in the NbTi wire, the Maglev 2000 quadrupole has a total of 600,000 Amp turns in each of its 2 superconducting (SC) loops. The SC winding is porous, with small gaps between the NbTi wires to allow liquid Helium flow to maintain their temperature at 4.2 K, and to stabilize them against flux jumps and micro movements.

Figure 8 shows the SC loop enclosed in its stainless steel jacket. Liquid Helium flows into the jacket at one end and exits at the end diagonally across from the entrance providing continuous Helium flow through the SC winding. Before insertion of the SC loop into the jacket, it is wrapped with a thin sheet of high purity, aluminum (5,000 residual resistance ratio) to shield the NbTi superconductor from external magnetic field fluctuations. After closing the jacket, a second layer of high purity aluminum is wrapped around it for additional shielding.

The Fight for Maglev | Maglev: Second Round

Figure 8 NbTi Superconducting Loop Enclosed in Stainless Steel Jacket

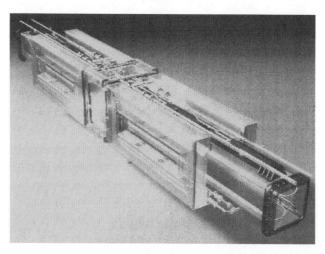

Figure 9 CAD-CAM Drawing of Maglev 2000 Superconducting Quadrupole

Figure 9 shows a CAD-CAM drawing of the complete Maglev 2000 cryostat that holds 2 superconducting quadrupoles. The magnetic polarity of the front SC quadrupole is opposite to that of the rear quadrupole. This allows levitation at lower speed than if the 2 quadrupoles had the same polarity, due to less L/R (Inductance/Resistance) decay of the currents induced in the aluminum guideway loops. The 2 SC loops are supported by a graphite-epoxy composite structure that resists the magnetic forces – due both to the forces in a loop from its self-current, and to the forces between the 2 loops – that act on them.

Figure 10 Assembly of Maglev 2000 Superconducting Quadrupole

Figure 10 shows the SC loops, support structure, and cooling currents for the Maglev 2000 quadrupole being assembled in Maglev 2000's facility on Long Island. The SC loops have a 10K thermal shield, which is cooled by Helium exiting from the jacket holding the SC loop. The SC quadrupole structure is then enclosed by an outer layer of multi-layer insulation (MLI) consisting of multiple alternating layers of glass fiber and aluminum foil. A second thermal shield encloses the SC quadrupole, and maintained at ~70 K by the helium out-flow from the 10 K primary thermal shield.

Figure 11 Completed Maglev 2000 Quadrupole Enclosed in its Cryostat

Figure 11 shows the completed SC quadrupole enclosed in its vacuum cryostat, while Figure 12 shows testing of the quadrupole magnetic levitation and propulsion forces using DC current in the aluminum loop guideway assembly beneath the quadrupole as a stand-in for the induced currents. The quadrupole was successfully tested to its full design current of 600,000 Amp turns. The magnetic forces between the quadrupole and the guideway loop assembly were measured as a function of vertical separation and lateral displacement from the centered position, and longitudinal position in the direction of movement along the guideway. The measured forces agreed with 3D computer analyses.

Since the Maglev 2000 quadrupole tests, high temperature superconductors have become much more capable, and are being commercially produced. Using YBCO high temperature superconductor wire, Maglev 2000 quadrupoles would be much simpler to construct, with much easier refrigeration. The YBCO superconductor would operate at 65K with pumped liquid nitrogen coolant and a much simpler on-board cryocooler.

Figure 12 Testing of Magnetic Forces on Maglev 2000 Quadrupole Using DC Current in Aluminum Loop Panel

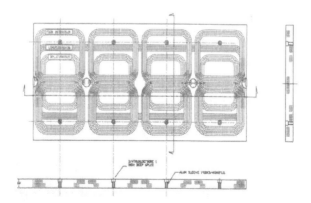

Figure 13 Drawing of aluminum loop guideway panel providing vertical lift and stability, lateral stability, and linear synchronous propulsion

Figure 13 shows a drawing of the Maglev 2000 aluminum wire loop guideway panels. It has 3 sets of multi-turn aluminum loops: 1) a sequence of 4 short independent Figure of 8 loops; 2) a sequence of 4 short dipole loops; and 3) 1 long dipole loop.

When the panels are on the vertical sides of the monorail guideway beam, the Figure of 8 loops provide levitation and vertical stability. The dipole loops on each side of the beam are connected together into a null flux circuit that maintains the vehicle in a centered position on the beam – when centered, no current flows in the aluminum null flux circuit, when an external force (wind, curves, etc.) acts to push the vehicles away from its centered position, a magnetic force develops that opposes the external force. The long dipole loop is part of the Linear Synchronous Motor (LSM) propulsion system, in which the loops on a sequence of panels are connected in series to form an energized block along which the Maglev vehicle travels. The energized block is typically on the order of 100 meters in length; as the vehicle leaves an energized block, its AC propulsion current is switched into the next block that the vehicle is entering.

For the planar guideway, the same panel design is used, with the panel laid flat on the planar surface beneath the line of quadrupoles on the moving vehicle. The Figure of 8 loops now provide lateral stability, generating magnetic restoring forces if an external force acts to displace the vehicle from its centered position on the guideway. The dipole loops act individually, with inductive currents that levitate and vertically stabilize the vehicle as it passes overhead. The LSM loops function in the same way as they do on the monorail guideway.

The planar guideway panel configuration can also levitate and propel Maglev vehicles along existing RR tracks, with the panels attached to the crossties of the RR tracks.

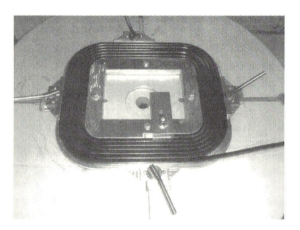

Figure 14 Wound Dipole Loop for Guideway Panel Using Nylon Coated Aluminum Conductor

Figure 14 shows a wound dipole loop, to be used in the panel. The aluminum conductor has a ~10 mil layer of nylon using a dip process to coat the conductor. The nylon insulation withstood 10 kilovolt tests without breakdown. Figure 15 shows a completed guideway loop panel with all of its 9 loops.

Figure 15 Completed Guideway Panel with Figure of 8 Dipole, and LSM Propulsion Loops

Figure 16 Guideway Loop Panel Enclosed in Polymer Concrete Matrix

The completed panel is then enclosed in a polymer-concrete structure for handling and weather protection. (Figure 16) Polymer concrete – a mixture of aggregate, cement and plastic monomer – can be cast into virtually any form as a slurry. When the monomer polymerizes (the rate of polymerization is controlled by the amount of added promoter), the resulting concrete-like structure is much stronger – a factor of 4 or greater – than ordinary concrete and not affected by freeze thaw cycles, salt, etc.

Figure 17 shows a completed polymer concrete panel left outside of the Long Island facility for 2 years. It was subjected to a wide range of weather conditions and multiple freeze-thaw cycles over the 2 year period, without any degradation. After being fabricated at the Maglev factory, the guideway panels would be attached to the sides of the monorail or the surface of planar guideway beams to be shipped to a construction site for an elevated guideway, or transported to existing RR trackage that was to be modified for use by Maglev 2000 vehicles.

Figure 17 Polymer Concrete Panel with Enclosed Aluminum Loop Exposed for 2 Years to Outdoor Environment with Multiple Freeze-Thaw Cycles

Based on fabrication experience at Maglev 2000's facilities on Long Island and Florida, using hand operated tooling, the 9 loops for a 2.2 meter long guideway panel can be fabricated in less than 1 week by one person. At 25 dollars per hour, fabrication would then cost less than 1,000 dollars per loop. Per mile of two way guideway (2,800) this amounts to less than 2.8 million dollars if made by hand. With automated tooling, the fabrication cost of the aluminum loops can be brought down considerably, to the order of 1 million dollars per mile. At 4 dollars per kg for the aluminum conductor and 1 dollar per kg for polymer concrete, the cost of the materials for the monorail guideway panels would be approximately 5 million dollars per two-way mile.

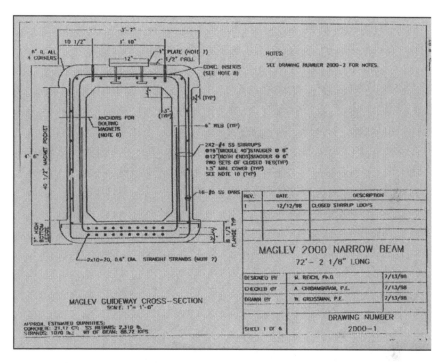

Figure 18 Design for 72 Foot Long Monorail Guideway Beam

Figure 18 shows the basic design for the monorail guideway beam. It is a hollow box beam made with reinforced concrete. Beam length is 22 meters and weight is 34,000 kg. It uses post tension construction, which allows the tensioning cables in the base of the beam to be re-tightened if some stretching were to occur. The beam is tensioned to have a 0.5 cm upwards camber at the midpoint of the beam when it is not carrying a Maglev vehicle. When the Maglev vehicle is on the beam, the beam flattens out to a straight line condition, with no vertical dip or camber along its length.

Figure 19 Photo of 72 Foot Long Monorail Guideway Beam Delivered to Maglev 2000 Facility in Florida from Fabrication Site in New Jersey

Figure 19 shows a photo of the fabricated beam after transport by highway truck from the manufacturing site in New Jersey to Maglev 2000's facility in Florida. No problems in transport by highway were encountered.

Figure 20 CAD-CAM Drawing of Aluminum Chassis for 60 Foot Long Maglev 2000 Vehicle

Figure 20 shows a CAD-CAM drawing of the aluminum chassis that was constructed for a 20 meter long Maglev 2000 test vehicle, designed to carry 60 passengers in urban and suburban service.

Figure 21 Photo of Fuselage for 60 Foot Long Maglev 2000 Vehicle

Figure 21 shows a view of the fuselage for the test vehicles. If the Maglev 2000 Florida route program had been down-selected by the FRA for continuation, the assembled vehicle would have been tested on a short section of guideway. The Maglev 2000 components are presently in storage.

Fabrication and testing of the basic Maglev 2000 components – superconducting quadrupole magnets, aluminum loop guideway panels, monorail guideway beam, and vehicle body – have been successfully carried out. The next step for the development of the commercial 2nd generation Maglev 2000 system is to test operating vehicles on a guideway.

All in all, our development work and experiments at the Florida and Long Island laboratories went very well. We built and successfully tested the quadrupole magnets, aluminum guideway panels, guideway beam, and vehicle body without any significant problems. That is unusual in most R&D projects. Doing new things often results in major problems that have to be overcome. As a colleague once remarked, "If you know that your research and development would have no problems, you wouldn't have to do it."

We did encounter one problem towards the end of our funded efforts as part of the FTA program. We had scheduled to levitate the front ends of the Maglev vehicle using superconducting quadrupoles attached to the front end, and an applied DC current in the aluminum guideway loops placed under the front end. It was a zero speed test that would demonstrate the capability to levitate the vehicles – or at least its front end, since funding was insufficient to also make the superconducting magnets for the vehicle's other end.

After successful operational testing of the superconducting quadrupole magnets and their lifting power at our Long Island laboratory, they were then shipped to our Florida laboratory to be attached to the front end of the vehicle body, which was located at Titusville.

We wanted to ship the superconducting magnets using a truck with air supported pallets that would minimize any bumping and vibration to them. As the truck took its thousand mile trip on highways strewn with potholes, bumps, cracked pavement, etc., we worried that the vacuum cryostats enclosing the superconducting quadrupoles might develop micro-cracks in the weld points in the cryostat box. Very small air leaks through micro-cracks could degrade the thermal conductivity of the multi-layer thermal insulation around the superconductor to the point where its temperature would remain above the transition temperature from the normal state to the superconducting state.

Unfortunately, program funds were not sufficient to pay the trucking company for air supported transport. We had to ship the superconducting magnets in a regular truck, and hope the resultant banging and bumping would not cause micro-cracks.

The superconducting magnets had worked perfectly at our Long Island Laboratory. However, if trucking them to Florida did develop microcracks, funding was insufficient to repair the cryostats in Florida. So we trusted to luck for a successful demonstration.

The superconducting magnets arrived in Florida and were attached to the front end of the Maglev vehicle. We then started cooling them with liquid helium, and watched the superconductor temperature steadily drop, biting our fingernails. When we reached a couple of degrees above the transition temperature, we said to ourselves, "we've made it".

Unfortunately, we hadn't. The temperature of the superconductor stopped dropping, and stood there, just shy of superconductivity. We kept at it through the night, but no luck.

As it turned out, micro-cracks in the cryostat were not the problem. When we attached the cryostat to the front of the Maglev vehicle we used a new cryostat end plate that had been fabricated to enable the attachment. Again, due to insufficient funding, we had not previously tested this end plate on a cryostat cooled with liquid helium.

Examining and testing the new end plate following the failed levitation demonstration, we discovered why the cryostat had not reached superconducting temperature. The machine shop that had fabricated the end plate had by mistake drilled an extra hole through the plate. Realizing their error, they welded an aluminum rod into the hole, and then smoothed it over so there was no visible sign of its presence.

Unfortunately, while one would not see it on the plate, air could and did leak through it into the high vacuum region inside, preventing us from reaching superconducting temperature. When we sealed the leaking hole, we were able to achieve the sufficiently high vacuum needed for the superconducting magnets. However, it was too late, and funds too inadequate to repeat the levitation demonstration.

As sad as that whole episode was, it was still even sadder a few years later when we read the evaluation of our superconducting levitation work by an observer from the FTA who was present during the failed levitation experiment. We show his evaluation below, just as it appeared in the FTA report, with our response.

His recent FTA statements about Maglev 2000's superconducting magnets and their tests, and superconducting Maglev in general, are amazingly wrong and show a complete lack of understanding of what has been done in superconducting Maglev. To quote from the FTA report,

"FTA Low-speed Urban Maglev Research Program – Lessons Learned", March 2009, by R. Hoopengardner and D. Keever, p.16; section 4.8.3.

"One of the initial goals of the FTA program was to have a team examine the possibility of using super-conducting magnets for a maglev application. The Maglev 2000 team was the only grantee to examine this concept and try to bring it to a successful demonstration phase. While the FRA had provided initial funding for this team to begin its work, the FTA grant allowed them to continue with their magnet design in the hope of at least levitating the chassis that had already been designed. This demonstration was never accomplished and this program drove home the difficulty of designing magnets that would be mounted on a guideway to provide the levitation for such a system. The team experienced one failure after another in its attempts to design and build a system that would cool the magnets to the required temperatures. These failures in a controlled laboratory environment indicated that the use of super-conducting magnets for a moving, outdoor environment is still not a viable concept."

In response,

1. The magnets are mounted on the vehicle, not "mounted on a guideway" as stated in the report. Clearly, the authors do not understand how superconducting Maglev works.

2. The Maglev 2000 superconducting magnets performed successfully in a number of tests at the Maglev 2000 laboratory in Long Island, reaching the design current of 600,000 amp turns with liquid helium-cooled NbTi superconductor. There were no problems, and the magnetic forces measured between the M-2000 magnets and powered guideway loops that simulated the currents that would be induced by the moving magnets on the vehicles agreed with the computer analyses. Bottom line: the Maglev 2000 team did not "experience one failure after another in its attempts to design and build a system that would cool the magnets to the required temperatures." The report statement is completely false.

3. "The use of super-conducting magnets for a moving, outdoor environment is still not a viable concept." Clearly, the authors have no knowledge of the Japanese Superconducting Maglev System at Yamanashi, Japan. It has carried well over 50,000 passengers at speeds up to 361 mph, with accumulated running distances of hundreds of thousands of miles. Japan plans to build a 300-mile superconducting Maglev route between Tokyo and Osaka that will carry 100,000 passengers daily with a trip time of 1 hour.

   Too bad it's not viable, according to Hoopengardner and Keever.

The authors never contacted us to find out anything about the results of our testing of the superconducting Magnets before the levitation demonstration, nor did they bother to find out what the Japanese had done with superconducting Maglev. No wonder that Maglev development has not gone anywhere in the United States.

On to more pleasant, more truthful things. During our development work on the 2nd generation Maglev 2000 system from 1996 to 2004, we had two great experiences:

- Attending the dedication of the Japanese Maglev demonstration line in Yamanashi Prefecture in April 1997.

- Being awarded the Benjamin Franklin Medal for Engineering in April 2000.

The Japanese have always been very gracious in acknowledging that their superconducting Maglev system has been based on our Maglev inventions in the 1960s, and our relationships have always been very cordial.

In February, 1997, we received invitations from the JR Railway Technical Research Institute (RTRI) to attend and be guest speakers at the April 4 dedication of the Yamanashi Maglev Test Line. To quote RTRI's invitation, *"Since our Maglev Systems have developed from your breakthrough invention of magnetically suspended trains, I believe your presence and lecture would make the opening of our test track very meaningful and successful."*

Unfortunately, Gordon was unable to attend, but I (Jim) and my wife were able to go. After the dedication and lecture I gave at the Railway Technical Research Institute about our work on Maglev, we visited Tokyo, Kyoto, Nara, Chuzenji, Nikko, and Kamakura. We had a wonderful time, and greatly appreciated RTRI's offer to meet our travel costs. We plan to revisit Japan, and this time, now that the Yamanashi line takes passengers, ride their Maglev. I would strongly urge anyone who has an opportunity to visit Japan, to do so. It is a wonderful place, with wonderful people. One of the most moving moments in Japan was when we visited the gravesites of the 47 Ronin in Tokyo, and saw how well tended they were, with fresh flowers on them, even though the 47 heroes had died hundreds of years ago.

The second great experience was when we were awarded the Benjamin Franklin Medal for Engineering in April 2000, for our invention of superconducting Maglev. The Franklin Institute, which is located in Philadelphia, Pennsylvania, was founded in 1824. It is one of the oldest science centers in the U.S. with many exhibits and education programs for the public – both adults and school children.

Since 1833, the Franklin Institute each year awards its medals for outstanding scientific and engineering discoveries. The Franklin Medals have been called America's Nobel awards. Recipients of Franklin Medals since 1833 include Nikola Tesla (1894-Engineering) for high frequency AC currents, Wilhelm Roentgen (1847-Engineering) for the discovery of X-Rays, Rudolph Diesel (1901-Engineering) for the Diesel engine, Pierre and Marie Curie (1909-Chemistry) for the discovery of Radium, Alexander Graham Bell (1912-Engineering) for the telephone, Charles Steinmetz (1913-Engineering) for his pioneering analytical work in electrical engineering, Orville Wright (1914-Engineering) for the airplane, Albert Einstein (1935-Physics) for his physics discoveries, Ernest Lawrence (1937-Engineering) for the Cyclotron, Willard Libby (1957-Physics) for radiocarbon dating, Werner von Braun (1962-Engineering) for rockets, Steven Weinberg (1979-Physics) for the unified theory of weak and electromagnetic interactions, plus many others.

We, of course, were tremendously honored to be part of such an illustrious group of scientists and engineers and thrilled to describe how Superconducting Maglev worked, and how it would become a major mode of transport in the 21st Century.(8) No words can further add to that.

Looking back on in the Second Round, from 1996 to 2004, how would we characterize Maglev's progress during that period? In our view, it was a partial success. Operation of the 1st generation Japanese and German systems proved that Maglev was technically practical, safe, efficient, non-polluting, and capable of very high speed transport. However, the cost of these 1st generation systems was too great and their revenues too small to be widely implemented. Like High Speed Rail, they would require massive government subsidies for construction and operation and their placement would be limited to a few high density corridors.

While we did not have the funds to demonstrate operation of the much more capable 2nd generation Maglev 2000 system, we were able to successfully fabricate and test the principal components for the M-2000 System. With further funding, we can assemble the components into vehicles and demonstrate the distinctive operational capabilities of high speed operation on both dedicated guideways and existing railroad tracks for both passengers and highway freight trucks, and the unique capability to electronically switch. The high revenues from carrying freight trucks, low construction and operating costs, and greater utility in closer station spacing and multiple loading docks afforded by electronic switching will be a game changer in the transport market.

Chapter Nine

Third Round – Decision Time for America

"Another dammed fat book, Mr. Gibbon? Scribble, scribble, scribble, eh Mr. Gibbon?"

Statement of King George III upon being presented by Edward Gibbon with the 2nd volume of the classic work, the 7 volume "Decline and Fall of the Roman Empire."

We know how Gibbon must have felt. Since our technical work on the 2nd generation superconducting Maglev transport system ended in 2004 when funding stopped, it's been lots of scribbling and presentations ever since.

People – politicians, bureaucrats, company employees, investors – listen, some with interest, others politely, but nothing much happens. Sadly, this seems to be the pattern for new technologies and manufacturing industries in America.

For decades, the U.S. has seen a long downhill slide in manufacturing and technology development. America once led the World in steel manufacturing. Then it started selling off the technology at the end of the 1950's to other countries like Japan, as Powell recounts in the Prologue. The resultant profits benefited the managers and owners for a little while, but devastated American workers.

The pattern has occurred in many other American industries. America created the nuclear power industry – now foreigners own almost all of America's nuclear industries. Japan is the only manufacturer of large pressure vessels for commercial power reactors, with a 5-year waiting list. American made textiles, furniture, appliances, etc.? Forget it – long gone. Likewise, television sets, telephones, and most consumer electronics.

For a while, we led the World in commercial aircraft, Silicon Valley innovations, and pharmaceuticals, but they are also slipping away.

France's Airbus is a strong competitor to Boeing. Silicon Valley jobs are being outsourced to countries like China. American corporations are setting up innovative technology centers abroad, ensuring that new discoveries will rapidly disseminate to the rest of the World, and the resulting jobs will not be in America. New pharmaceuticals are still – so far – innovated in the U.S. However, almost all drugs are produced in China and other countries.

And the rapidly growing renewable energy industries? Today, over half of the World's solar panels are manufactured in China, and almost half of the World's wind turbines. China's share will further substantially increase in the years ahead and will be the major supplier of the World's energy equipment as fossil fuels are phased out.

Millions of U.S. manufacturing jobs have already gone to other countries. Now, information technology jobs are being rapidly outsourced. Even hundreds of thousands of Wall Street manager jobs are slated to go abroad.

Why such massive outsourcing? One word – profits. Most American corporations don't care that American workers need good, adequately paid jobs. Lots of middle class jobs are rapidly disappearing, leaving mostly high level management jobs and low level, poorly paid service jobs – cleaners, landscaping, store clerks, etc., etc. American multi-national corporations typically don't worry about how outsourcing degrades the American economy and our future standard of living. They laugh at Henry Ford, the Father of America's auto industry. When asked why he paid Ford's workers on the assembly line such good wages, he replied, "So they can afford to buy my cars". When future Americans are too poor to buy the foreign produced products of America's companies, the companies too will collapse.

Our leaders pontificate about educating young Americans to compete in the World marketplace. Their empty promises are unreal. A young Chinese engineer with a Bachelor of Science makes a starting salary of 2,600 U.S. dollars per year. America's starting salary for engineers is 20 times greater. Guess which engineer American companies will hire? For 4 years of college, an American engineering student takes on a debt load of 150,000 dollars or more. Not so in China. China graduates 500,000 engineers per year. America, much less. Today, many American engineering graduates have trouble getting jobs. Who can blame young persons for seeking jobs in finance that are available and pay well?

Economists and political leaders assert that "Globalization is good for America" – goods will be cheaper, a rising tide lifts all boats, etc. This ignores reality. World resources are too limited for everybody to achieve even a small fraction of the present American standard of living. In reality, outsourcing American's jobs to lower-wage foreign workers drastically reduces America's standard of living and level of employment. Workers in the poorer countries benefit somewhat, but basically remain at the bottom of the economic barrel, to be joined by most Americans.

The second principal reason for the steady decline in the development of new technologies in America is the increasing reluctance of government and corporate leaders to take what they feel are risks. They fear risk and criticism if the new technology is unsuccessful. It wasn't always so. American leaders wanted to lead, not follow. In the past, America led the World in new modes of transport from the Erie Canal in the early 1800's through the Apollo space program in the 1960s.

Since then, the willingness to take risks on new technologies has disappeared. The Obama Administration's embrace of foreign High Speed Rail (HSR) systems is a perfect example. Our leaders love HSR because there is zero risk in building HSR. Never mind the massive government subsidies for construction and operation for a system that will only meet a tiny fraction of our future transport needs. Forget that it benefits only a small portion of the U.S. population – those lucky enough to live near a few isolated train routes, and well enough off to afford the high fares. The not-so-lucky majority of Americans who can't afford it or won't live near the routes will have to pay taxes to support them. Plus, America will buy the equipment from abroad, creating well-paid foreign jobs in other countries, and increasing our trade deficit.

Developing new technologies always involves risks. If our leaders don't want risks, then America will never develop new technologies, and will always follow other countries. Their governments invest in new technologies – European and Japanese governments developed high speed rail. The German and Japanese governments each spent several Billion dollars to develop their 1st generation Maglev systems. Not to mention their automobile and aircraft industries, etc.

When we talk to Senators, Representatives, and their staffs about the government developing a much more capable 2nd generation Maglev system, we hear the mantra, "The government doesn't pick winners and losers. That's the job of the free market". Hmmm. The Chinese government picks winners and losers and its GDP is growing 10% per year. The U.S. doesn't pick winners and losers and its GDP is growing only 1% per year. Which country is the real winner?

The unfortunate truth is today's free market also doesn't like risks. So, as new technologies evolve and make old ones obsolete, governments that aggressively push to develop new technologies are the winners, and the governments that refuse to push are the losers. In the 1950's 30% of U.S. GDP was in manufacturing. Today, it's only 10%, and will shrink even further as countries like China, India, South Korea continue to develop new technologies and take over World markets.

The third reason for the decline in development of new technologies in America is the push for quick profits. "If it takes 5 years of development before you can sell your product," private investors will say. "Get out of here. We want a return on our investment to start 6 months from now!" Likewise, politicians and bureaucrats want a quick payoff so they can take credit for it. Of what use is a payoff, no matter how great, if it occurs when the politician or bureaucrat is long gone? Major innovations generally take substantial time to develop into systems that can be implemented. They don't occur overnight.

The fourth reason, and for Maglev, very significant, is opposition from vested interests that will be hurt by the new technology. If it takes their business away, or cuts profits, look out! They will lobby the government against it, hire publicists that say it will hurt the public, pay commentators and researchers to bad-mouth it, and so on.

Maglev has a lot of enemies. Think of the major industries and groups it will negatively impact. How about airlines? Why travel by air when you can go by Maglev anywhere in the U.S. in about the same trip time, at much lower cost, much more conveniently, without travel delays due to airway congestion or bad weather, and in much greater comfort? Why drive by highway, when Maglev is much faster, cheaper, safer, and more comfortable? And, you can even take your car with you on the Maglev vehicle. Why drive trucks by highway when they can be transported at lower cost and 300 mph, avoiding the congested roads? Much less new highway construction will be required. Much less repair of highway damage from trucks. And think of the opposition from railroad companies. There will be strong public support for a National Maglev Network and its benefits, but the in-fighting against Maglev, and other innovations, hampers the implementation of new technologies.

Getting back to Mr. Gibbon and his book, "The Decline and Fall of the Roman Empire", there are broad parallels between the downward path of the Roman Empire and the American "Empire's" present downward path. The details are different, but the themes are similar.

First, historians note that in the latter days of the Roman Empire, great amounts of food, manufactured goods, and other supplies were brought by wagon into Rome. What mainly came out of Rome by wagon? Dung! In today's terms, they had a big trade deficit. America also has a big trade deficit, about 600 Billion dollars annually, 4 % of our GDP. As U.S. manufacturing declines, jobs are outsourced, and oil prices increase, the U.S. annual trade deficit will further increase. Decades ago, we had trade surpluses, not trade deficits. Today, millions of container units, called TEUs, return to Asia, not dung, but cardboard boxes and scrap metals for recycling. America's trade deficit is sustained by other countries lending us money, and buying up U.S. assets – corporations, land, roads, airports, seaports, etc. In the long term, the U.S. trade deficit is not sustainable – other countries will stop lending us money and buying U.S. assets.

The second similarity between Rome and the U.S. is the role of mercenaries. In its early days, Roman citizens fought its wars and enforced its will. Roman soldiers wiped out Carthage and sowed salt over the ruins. "Who made a desert and called it peace" in the words of an ancient historian? Romans! As time went on, however, Rome became more and more dependent on mercenaries to carry out its military actions, till at the end of the Empire, 90% of its soldiers were mercenaries. When they stopped getting paid, because Rome had no more money, they marched to Rome and sacked it.

The U.S. does not use mercenary soldiers, and is unlikely to do so. However, depending on other countries for manufactured goods has its own risks. Suppose they decide that the U.S. is a new Argentina – mired in debt, unable to repay the money they loaned us to buy their products, and they have bought up all of the various parts of America that are worth anything? Then they start to cash in their chips. What does America then do? From whom will it buy the manufactured goods it needs and the foreign oil for transport, etc.? "Don't cry for me, America."

Even the U.S. Defense Department buys a substantial portion of its military goods from abroad. The rare earth materials crucial to much of our electronic equipment comes from China. Trying to make it without foreign manufactures would be tough.

Maglev is not a panacea. It alone cannot reverse the decline of American manufacturing and economic security. More actions are needed to do that. However, U.S. development of the advanced Maglev 2000 transport system would be a very powerful force in rebuilding American manufacturing, with millions of new jobs, billions of dollars in exports, and a positive trade balance.

Introduction to the Third Round.

We now tell the story of our attempts to develop the advanced Maglev system in two parts. The Outsider's Story recounts who we talked to and the proposals we made from 2004, when technical work stopped due to lack of funding, to the present time (December of 2011). In the Inside Story, we describe our understanding of what was happening to Maglev behind the scenes. After that, we describe a future timeline, in which America fails to move forward with Maglev, but China does. The results for the U.S. are not good.

The Outsider's Story: Attempting to Start U.S. Development of the Advanced 2nd Generation Superconducting Maglev 2000 System.

The first step in selling a program is formulating a strategy. Who do you contact? What do you tell them about your program? What do you propose that they do? Who do you get to help you?

For the 2nd generation Maglev 2000 program, the answers are pretty clear. The chances of success with a given contact are pretty small, due to the large scale of the program, and the commitment required. So you contact as many entities as possible – investors, both individual and groups; corporations who would benefit from manufacturing Maglev systems; government agencies involved in transportation R&D and construction & operation of actual systems; briefings of appropriate government staffers, as well as formal proposals; meetings with political leaders, hoping to find another Senator Moynihan; meetings with civic development groups; and so on. In addition, you also write op-ed pieces for newspapers, articles for magazines, seek to be interviewed by reporters and TV personalities; give papers at conferences; and set up web-sites describing Maglev.

Over the last 8 years since funding for technical work ended, we've done all of the above numerous times. We don't want to bore the reader with a long blow-by-blow account of our many struggles to get the 2nd generation Maglev 2000 system tested and certified so that private investment can build the National Maglev Network. Rather, we recount a few selected examples that illustrate how difficult it is to innovate major new technologies and bring them to the market in today's climate.

In trying to interest American corporations in Maglev development, we have made over a dozen overtures, without success. In talks with a large aerospace corporation, the response from top management was that if the corporation worked on Maglev, they would never sell another airplane. Contact with the Director of R&D for a major automobile company drew no interest. A third major corporation wanted to work with us on a program with available funds that we had located, but only if they would acquire our proprietary patents and technology. We said no and the program opportunity disappeared. Bottom Line? Corporations are not interested if the new technology conflicts with their present business, even if it promises large future business, and they want to control and own the technology if they participate, even though they didn't innovate it.

Investors? Their Bottom Line is even simpler. "Profits are not guaranteed? There are some risks? Payoff time is more than 6 months? Forget it!" The foregoing is a bit exaggerated and unfair, but not by much. Investors generally want a quick return, with as little risk as possible. In the case of the Maglev transport system, risk not only involves technical performance, cost, and market potential, but also whether the government will certify the system and approve its implementation.

Investors often tell us that if 2nd generation Maglev 2000 was already operating on a demonstration track, with its performance and cost validated, they would invest in it. That is why government testing and certification of the Maglev 2000 transport system is essential for private investment. Major new technologies like nuclear energy, space rockets, the Internet, jet airliners, the early computers and so on, would not have happened without massive government funding. Saying that the U.S. Government doesn't pick winners and losers in major new technologies is simply not true. It does, thankfully, and America is much better off because of their choices. Once a major new technology has been demonstrated by government, the free market can take over, evolving improvements that enhance performance and reduce cost.

Besides smaller investment groups, we also tried contacting "superstar" investors like Bill Gates, Warren Buffet, Paul Allen, Sir Richard Branson, Peter Thiel, Robert Bigelow, Jim Justice, and others. The aim was not so much to present them an attractive investment opportunity, but to urge them to sponsor a new technology that would greatly benefit humanity and help avoid environmental catastrophe. So far, no response. It is virtually impossible to get past their gatekeepers.

Our efforts to get real investors have not yet been successful. However, often persons offer to get us big investors if we pony up some money for them. Having no funds or faith in these dealmakers, we say no. Some of the dealmakers make very big promises – Billions of dollars to build a transcontinental Maglev route, a Billion dollars for a Reno to San Francisco route. They come from all over the World – the U.S., China, Indonesia, South America, and so on. So far, none have come from Nigeria saying, "Just give us your bank account number so we can deposit the Maglev investment money."

We have briefed staffers at the U.S. Department of Transportation and proposed that DOT test and certify the 2nd generation superconducting Maglev system under actual operating conditions. There is some limited interest, but no action. Responses range from "DOT doesn't do R&D on transport, we only do studies on safety", to, in the case of the High Speed Intercity Passenger Rail initiative in the 2009 stimulus program, "your proposal must have the backing of a State, Interstate Compact, or Amtrak" to "that's a good idea, you should try the Department of Energy."

We have proposed 2 programs to the DOT. The big one(1) would test and certify the 300 mph 2nd generation Maglev 2000 passenger and freight carrying system for the 28,800 mile National Maglev Network (described in Chapter 4). The 5-year program would require a total funding of 600 million dollars. After its completion, the National Maglev Network would be built by private investment, at no cost to taxpayers, either for construction or operating subsidies.

The per capita cost to American taxpayers for testing and certifying the 2nd generation Maglev system would be only 40 cents per year, or 2 dollars for the 5 year program – less than the cost of a slice of pizza. The benefits to Americans when the National Maglev Network was built would be enormous – direct savings in transport costs of over 1,000 dollars per capita annually, plus millions of new jobs, large reductions in oil imports and the trade deficit, and so on. A tremendous bargain. For a cost of 2 dollars each, spread over 5 years, everyone gets many thousands of dollars in benefits over their lifetime.

Contrast that with High Speed Rail. The government proposes to spend about 4 Billion dollars to construct the 80-mile High Speed Rail line between Tampa and Orlando. It will carry about 8,000 passengers per day and require expensive operating subsidies over its lifetime. Let's be generous, and say that the subsidies over 30 years are equal to the construction cost – in practice they will be considerably greater.

Okay. The cost to U.S. taxpayers will be 8 Billion dollars for an 80-mile line that will save a few minutes driving time, and carry about 80 million passengers over a 30-year period. So U.S. taxpayers will fork out 100 dollars for each passenger trip, with the passengers themselves paying another 40 dollars or so per trip. Per capita taxes for the 80-mile line over a 30-year period? About 300 dollars, for a tiny insignificant part of the U.S. transport system, which virtually nobody will ride. It is truly crazy.

The DOT response to our proposed high-speed intercity Maglev testing and certification program? Not interested. We were declared ineligible because we did not have a State, Interstate Compact, or Amtrak sponsor. One reviewer said that they really liked our proposal but their hands were tied by the Congress. It was a matter of law. However, we note that no one at DOT took up the matter with the Congress or the White House.

The second more modest effort that we proposed to DOT was for a "TIGER" grant (2) under DOT's Federal Transit Agency's program to test and certify the adaptation of the 2nd generation superconducting Maglev 2000 system for use on existing railroad tracks. As discussed in Chapter 6, by attaching thin, low-cost, panels that contain ordinary aluminum loops to the crossties of existing railroad tracks, magnetically levitated and propelled vehicles can travel at much higher speeds and lower cost than the conventional trains that presently use the tracks. Service will be much more convenient and frequent – no need for long trains of cars pulled by a locomotive. The Maglev vehicles can travel as individual units or be coupled together into consists of 2 or 3 vehicles if the traffic flow warrants. The Maglev vehicles are also more energy efficient than conventional trains. The RR tracks can be readily adapted for Maglev service without disrupting conventional train operations, which can continue even after the trackage has been adapted for Maglev, if desirable.

Our proposed TIGER program for the testing and certification of the Maglev 2000 system for adaptation of existing RR tracks for Maglev service, to be carried out on railroad tracks at Riverhead, Long Island, was budgeted at only 60 million dollars over a 2-year period. After successful completion of the program and 1 year of running tests on a portion of the Long Island Rail Road system, the LIRR, and other railroad systems in the U.S. could be quickly adapted for Maglev service at very low cost.

The TIGER proposal was rejected. DOT wanted to construct "shovel ready" projects using existing technology, not develop a new mode of transport that would be much faster, better, and cheaper, save lives, create millions of new jobs, reduce the trade deficit and oil imports, and help to reduce global warming. It was the old philosophy. Other governments pick winners and losers, but the U.S. Government doesn't – the free market does that.

Nonetheless, we have not given up. At the time of writing, we have submitted a new proposal for the 2nd round of TIGER grants. This new proposal is scaled back from the previous 60 million dollars to 20 million. Instead of testing our levitated Maglev vehicle at full speed on a 2 mile section of adapted RR track, the test track length is only a few hundred feet long, and the speed is very low. Maybe this proposal will be accepted. (Later Note – it wasn't)

As discussed at the end of the chapter, if the U.S. Government does not very soon develop the 2nd generation superconducting maglev system, it will be developed abroad, probably by China. We then will have to buy it from them, further eroding America's manufacturing capability and the jobs that go with it.

Now to the next part of our strategy for Superconducting Maglev — meetings with political leaders and their staffs in the Congress and the Administration, with the goal of obtaining support for funding a U.S. Maglev program.

The result? Lots of interest and friendly talk, expressions of support for Maglev, but no real action. No new champion like Senator Moynihan. No legislation to fund superconducting Maglev development. Only a couple of small earmarks that died in committee.

In total, we have met more than a dozen members of Congress or their staffs, presenting the case why the U.S. should develop 2nd generation superconducting Maglev. What has been especially depressing is that none of the people we talked to in the Senate and House of Representatives has focused on how Maglev could create millions of new American jobs. That is not a priority. Political impact, positive or negative? Yes, that's important. Is it worth spending their political capital to push Maglev? Yes, that question is very important. Will it annoy senior members of Congress or the Administration? U.S. corporations? Again, very important. Nobody regards as important how investment in superconducting Maglev could create new, well-paid jobs for Americans.

Instead, Congress and the Administration are head-over-heels in love with foreign high speed rail. Buy it from abroad? No problem – American workers won't make the HSR trains and other equipment, but they will lay the track.

Politicians like California's Governor Schwarzenegger were eager to buy High Speed Rail Systems from China for the proposed California High Speed Rail Network, with the result that the good manufacturing jobs will be located in China. Even worse, he wanted China to finance the

HSR network. Of course, if China finances the HSR network, it will want its money back, with interest – lots of money back, paid for with high fares and taxes. But by that time, the politicians that made the decision for China will be long gone, along with the American jobs a U.S. Maglev system would have created.

However, China may very well decide to develop the 2nd generation Maglev system itself, and market it worldwide. China would make the Maglev 2000 systems in China and ship them to America and other countries, just like they're doing now with wind and solar power generation systems. They currently manufacture 50% of the World's wind and solar systems, and in a few years, probably 80 to 90%.

Moving on to scribble, scribble, scribble, we have submitted many op-ed pieces to newspapers, articles to magazines, proposals for TV interviews, etc. However, we have not been very successful. Two op-ed essays were published in the Washington Post, "After the Oil Runs Out", on Sunday, June 6, 2004 and "The False Hope of Biofuels for Energy and Environmental Reasons, Ethanol Will Never Replace Gasoline", on Sunday, July 2, 2006. These two op-eds frame some of the principal issues discussed in this book. Other issues that we were not able to obtain coverage for are the highway congestion, and the horrible highway fatalities and injuries, and the air quality issue. Our highways are corridors of death, full of toxic gases and micro particles that damage our health. We wrote an op-ed essay titled, "Tailpipes" to emphasize the air quality and greenhouse gases problems but it was not published.

The biofuels op-ed coincided with the oil price spike and 4 dollars a gallon for gasoline. The hard truth about biofuels is that they can only supply a tiny fraction of America's transport needs. There is simply not enough arable land in the U.S. to provide the 180 Billion gallons of transport fuel America consumes annually. Making ethanol from corn would take 2 Billion acres of cropland, the entire continental U.S. – but we only have 300 million acres of cropland.

Cellulosic ethanol and diesel fuel from algae? Also fantasies, if one expects them to fuel a major portion of America's transport.

The media's role in reporting about how America meets its future transport needs is very interesting. Lots of favorable stories about biofuels and hydrogen cars, both not real in terms of supply, and in the case of hydrogen, also safety and its potential use as bombs by terrorists. Lots of stories about High Speed Rail, but very little reporting on its high costs and the need for massive government subsidies. Lots of stories about electric cars, which are practical for short trips of 40 or 50 miles per day. But virtually no stories about superconducting Maglev, with its potential for high speed, low cost, pollution free and energy efficient travel for long distances, including carrying the family electric/hybrid car. Why so little coverage?

The 1st generation Japanese and German Maglev systems are covered but there is no reporting on how Maglev transport can evolve into future advanced systems, just as airplanes did. High Speed Rail is a mature technology, while Maglev technology can still dramatically improve. Why no coverage of the potential advances in Maglev technology?

We continue to present papers about 2nd generation Maglev at scientific conferences, describing the experimental results we have achieved, how the 2nd generation system can use existing railroad tracks that have been adapted for Maglev service by attaching low-cost aluminum wire and polymer concrete panels to the crossties, how 2nd generation Maglev can transport passengers cars for long distances at lower cost than by highway, how 2nd Gen Maglev can store large blocks of electrical energy from wind and solar power sources so that the energy can be fed to the electrical grid in periods of high demand, how Maglev can launch payloads into space at 1/100th of the cost of chemical rockets, how Maglev can transport billions of gallons of water daily to drought areas over distances of hundreds of miles at low cost, and so on.

None of the above gets reported in the media. One would think that the public would be interested in hearing about these potential solutions to America's transport, energy, and pollution problems. Evidently, the media does not agree. That's the Outsider's Story. We now come to the Inside Story of America's Maglev. We then describe how rapidly China could build the Maglev America Project, if it chose to do so, completing the "golden spike" transcontinental link of the East and West coast Maglev lines on the 150th anniversary of Abraham Lincoln's Transcontinental Railroad in 2019.

The Inside Story: Why America Has Failed to Develop the U.S. 2nd Generation Superconducting Maglev System and Manufacturing Industry.

The Inside Story is very important because the market by itself cannot introduce a major new transportation technology in the United States. Private investors say that unless it is endorsed by government, the risks are simply too great. They are right. Only the Federal government can demonstrate a game changing transportation technology. Even then, successful demonstration does not guarantee success. Remember the EV-1, General Motor's electric car? The Government financed it to reduce pollution and our oil consumption. The car was successful in trials in Southern California, but died when GM said logistics support for the cars was too tough.

Introducing superconducting Maglev, a new, innovative transport system that competes with existing transport systems for a National Transport Network is a very tall political order. Obtaining funds to develop and demonstrate the new 2nd generation system is very difficult. Typically, Government program managers say, "you haven't proved your system works." Fortunately, the Japanese have proved that Jim and Gordon's 1st generation superconducting Maglev transport system works.

We knew we had to make a strong case to Congress that Maglev could reduce highway congestion and harmful pollution, make the U.S. total transport systems more secure by reducing oil imports, and help fight the threat of global warming. Easier said than done, however.

Our "Fight for Maglev" is best told as a modern David vs Goliath story. The Biblical David killed Goliath with a stone thrown from his slingshot, and virtue triumphed. In real life, however, 99% of the time David is squashed by Goliath and the bad side wins. So far, that is our story – all our attempts to slay Goliath have failed. Bloody but unbowed, however, we still keep trying. Our attempts and why they have not succeeded are described in the following pages of this chapter, Third Round – Decision Time for America. We persist in this campaign because we strongly believe, along with many other observers, that America is being hurt by the Government's treatment of superconducting Maglev transport. The Fight for Maglev story is cause for public concern. The stakes are high. It is the future of America.

The Biblical David was lucky. He faced only 1 Goliath, who had no armor to protect him. In our fight for Maglev, we face not 1, but 3 Goliaths, all heavily armored by political supporters.

The first, and by far biggest and most powerful Goliath, is the auto/airplane/fossil fuel lobby. Like Satan in Dante's Inferno, Goliath #1 has 3 heads, all determined to chew up any technology that threatens their livelihood. Maglev would greatly reduce the demand for transport fossil fuels – conventional oil, and eventually synfuels (synthetic fuels) from coal, tar sands, and natural gas. Why fly or drive anywhere, when you can go faster, cheaper, more comfortably and conveniently by Maglev?

Goliath #2 was the 1st Generation Maglev systems developed by Germany and Japan, particularly Germany, who is aggressively marketing their Transrapid system, with the first commercial Maglev route now operating in Shanghai.

Transrapid, because of its strong lobbying power, is a formidable Goliath, but nowhere near as strong and big as Goliath #1, the auto/airplane/fossil fuel lobby.

When the third round of our fight for Maglev started in 2004, we only had to face Goliath #1 and #2. High Speed Rail was a distant Goliath, not really in the ring yet. However, when the Obama Administration took office in 2009 things changed. High Speed Rail grew into a much bigger giant, a more powerful Goliath than the Transrapid Goliath – but still much less powerful than Goliath #1. High Speed Rail then shoved the Transrapid Goliath down to position #3.

The present rankings are Goliath #1, the auto/airplane/fossil fuel lobby, Goliath #2, the High Speed Rail lobby, and Goliath #3, the Transrapid lobby. We now describe what we have tried, and how we have fared, in the 3rd round that started in 2004. Unfortunately, Senator Moynihan, who was our Maglev champion in the 1990's, passed away in 2003. There really was no one to replace him. He was a rarity in American politics, and sought to meet American's long-term needs, instead of playing short-term political games. We start with the contest between 2nd Generation Superconducting Maglev and Goliath #3, Transrapid.

The gong for the third round rang at the beginning of 2004. In one corner, we find Maglev 2000 and in the other the German Transrapid Maglev passenger transport system.

Maglev 2000's only assets were its patents, engineering designs and the full-scale components that had been successfully tested but not assembled into an operating vehicle. In contrast, full-scale Transrapid Maglev vehicles were operating on a test guideway at Emsland. And Germany and China were working hard to have a commercial system ready for the 2008 Olympic Games.

Transrapid used their test guideway very effectively as a global marketing tool. The German Maglev is appealing – smooth, comfortable and quiet. One of their marketing films shows Transrapid moving on an elevated guideway above grazing cows. The cows did not notice the train as it rapidly passed. Transrapid technology development and marketing were strongly funded and supported by the German government and a consortium of powerful industrial corporations. The effectiveness of their U.S. marketing campaign was obvious. Of the Maglev routes authorized for study by the Congress in its 1992 major transportation authorization bill, Transrapid was selected by 5 local transportation authorities who competed for the 6 routes authorized under the law.

The five Transrapid grants were used for paper studies of the routes and the environmental impacts. The funds awarded to Maglev 2000 were a small fraction of the funds awarded for the Transrapid studies. Rather than do just paper studies, Maglev 2000 used its limited funds to design, build, and test the major hardware components of its 2nd Generation Superconducting Maglev Transport System, so that its superior capabilities could persuade the U.S. Government to build a Test and Certification Facility similar to the Transrapid facility at Emsland, Germany. The theory was that once the superior cost and performance of the new 2nd generation superconducting Maglev system were certified, it would become the World Standard for Maglev transport.

Sadly, the U.S. Government chose to back Goliath, not David. 2 of the 6 Maglev routes were down-selected to continue with increased funding – both Transrapid routes. David was out in the cold. The marketing and lobbying effort made by Transrapid was intense. While Maglev 2000 was building components, Transrapid was hosting Members of Congress and their staffs with trips to its facility at Emsland. The House and Senate travel records show that members of the key committees had ridden Transrapid at Germany's Emsland Test Facility. I (Jordan) surveyed members and learned that they were impressed with Transrapid's performance and the hospitality of the Germans. In addition to the Congressional campaign, State transportation authorities were also invited to Emsland. While I did not visit the State authorities, I followed their statements in the press upon return and detected a flaw in the Transrapid's marketing campaign. The authority created to study the route from Atlanta, Georgia to Chattanooga, Tennessee determined that Transrapid Maglev would cost about twice as much as conventional high-speed steel-wheel rail train. The authority's Transrapid price per two way mile was much higher than Maglev 2000's.

Undaunted by the huge lead that Germany and Japan had in the Maglev race, failing to be selected as one of the two down-selected projects to be funded by the Federal government, and the loss of our champion, Senator Moynihan, David was bloody, but eager to get back into the fight. We then devised the following strategy.

Our strategy had seven parts, initially, and as the campaign progressed we added two more:

1. **Meet with officials in the U.S. Department of Transportation to present the national long-term energy, environment, and economic reasons why the U.S. should carry out a program to test and certify the 2nd Generation Superconducting Maglev 2000 System.**

2. **Meet with Congressional Representatives serving on committees related to transportation.** The reauthorization of transportation is contained in 6-year bills. The next 6-year bill was before the Congress in 2004. We felt that we needed to include in the bill a Maglev initiative to build a test facility, similar to those built by the governments of Japan and Germany, or it could be curtains for the new 2nd generation superconducting Maglev in the United States.

3. **Seek to appear as expert witnesses at Congressional and National Commission hearings on economically sustainable transportation.** We felt that we had a good energy, environment, public health, national productivity and export story to tell, if we could just get the opportunity to enter the dialogue.

4. **Work with local officials on Long Island to discuss a proposal for construction of a Superconducting Maglev Test Facility on the Island.**

5. **Meet with the State Department of Transportation and Other Authorities of New York.** There were strong supporters for superconducting Maglev in New York. In addition to Senator Moynihan, Governor Mario Cuomo and Lt. Governor Stan Lundine became champions of Maglev. For example, responding to all that was going wrong in the 1980s, in energy, trade, and a dramatic slowdown in economic growth, Governor Mario Cuomo appointed 28 public policy and economic leaders to a Commission on Competitiveness. Their report, *"America's Agenda, Rebuilding Economic Strength, The Critical Issues of 1992 and Beyond and What to Do about Them"*, was issued in 1992, an election year, that saw William Jefferson Clinton elected as President over George Herbert Walker Bush. Some say that President Bush was beaten by an independent candidate and fellow Texan, Ross Perot, who emphasized the twin U.S. deficits, the Federal Budget Deficit and the amount owed to the rest of the World, the Trade Deficit. Remember the colorful phrase, "giant sucking sound"[1] used by candidate Perot to

---

[1] The phrase has since come into general use to describe any situation involving loss of jobs, or fear of a loss of jobs, particularly by one nation to a rival. For example:

Mark Landler, A European Union representative spoke of worrying "about the giant sucking sound from Eastern Europe;"(2004), New York Times

describe what he believed would be the negative effects of the North American Free Trade Agreement? Mr. Perot's campaign is history. Bill Clinton won and NAFTA was passed in 1994. The twin deficit was also a principal issue cited by the Cuomo Commission.

Governor Cuomo's report became a major policy resource for us. We were pleased that the Commission had recommended Maglev for America's future. Not just any Maglev, but the 2nd generation superconducting Maglev system for passengers and freight, supporting the findings of the Moynihan study and the Senator's legislative initiative.

We quote from the report because it is instructive on how we formed our message to the government, in the articles and papers that we wrote and in this book.

From page 79 and 80, "Many observers believe that the future of transportation belongs with a new technology called magnetic levitation – "maglev" – which uses magnetism to lift and propel a vehicle along a guideway at speeds up to 300 miles per hour.

Thomas Freidman, an New York Times (2004), op-ed writer opined that "the Mexicans... are hearing 'the giant sucking sound' in stereo these days—from China in one ear and India in the other

Joe Sharkey, a New York Times columnist used the phrase (2005) "That Giant Sucking Sound" to introduce a comment about a 34% slump in employment in the airline industry.

Congressman Steve LaTourette(R-OH 14) invoked the catchphrase while criticizing the American Recovery and Reinvestment Act of 2009: "Well, today there's another sucking sound going on in Washington, D.C. And that's the tightening of sphincters on both ends of Pennsylvania Avenue as people are having to explain who put into the stimulus bill this provision of law."

Though maglev was invented by two American scientists at Brookhaven National Laboratories in 1960, the United States invested only $3 million in research between 1966 and 1975, then abandoned the effort. Meanwhile, Japan invested $1 billion and tested a model at 320 miles per hour in 1979. Demonstration maglev trains are already operating in Germany and Japan.

"In March 1992 the federal government at last created a new $700 million research fund for Maglev. A two-way maglev system on an existing interstate right-of-way could easily carry 100, 000 passengers per day at speeds of 200 to 300 miles per hour. If it is designed to carry freight also, the revenues of a maglev train are expected to cover its operating costs. But the start-up costs will be large, with several of the key technologies needing further development. The initial costs of building the lines are variously estimated between $8 million and $63 million per mile.

The task force recommends that the federal government play a major role in supporting maglev trains. It can support future R&D, work with industry to develop standards for maglev design and construction, and include high-speed railroads in national transportation plans. It should consider establishing a billion-dollar revolving loan fund to help states finance maglev projects between cities."

Because of this report, with some of the members of the Cuomo Commission's Task Force becoming senior advisors to the Clinton Administration, we were mystified that the Clinton White House did not lock onto the recommendation and make 2nd generation superconducting Maglev a real competitor for Germany's Transrapid system. But it did not. Why not? It still is a mystery as this book goes to press.

6. **Meet with investors and investment groups to seek public-private partnership in developing Maglev.** We were very aware that government funding of transportation projects has historically required some degree of private funding.

7. **Meet with transportation equipment manufacturers to seek partnerships in the development of Maglev 2000 prototype vehicles and a test track.** We felt that the Maglev 2000 system was an excellent investment opportunity for transportation equipment manufacturers. We briefed high level executives of several firms including UPS, Boeing Aircraft, Northrop-Grumman, and Ford Motors. We always had a very interested reception, but when it got down to commitment, potential partners felt that it was too risky because their involvement in Maglev would threaten their existing markets.

8. **Publish articles and seek interviews on TV, radio, and the print media, and make presentations to public audiences to explain the differences between 1st generation Japanese and German Maglev and the new 2nd Generation Super conducting Maglev Transport System and its benefits for the U.S.** We scribbled a lot, and were published sometimes. Our first successes were two Op-Eds published in the Washington Post: *"After the Oil Runs Out"* published in the Washington Post, June 6, 2004; and *"The False Hope of Biofuels, For Energy and Environmental Reasons, Ethanol Will Never Replace Gasoline"*, published in the Washington Post on Sunday, July 2, 2006. In public presentations, we made the case that the practical and lowest cost way to end World dependence on scarce oil and sustain civilization is to evolve the present oil fueled autos, trucks, rail and cargo ship systems to electric transport, eliminate emissions from coal-fired electric plants, expand renewable electric generating technologies, isolate radioactive waste from the biosphere and build 4th generation nuclear power systems.

9. **Finally, as the 7-year long campaign progressed we realized that there was another contender in the ring: steel-wheeled, European style electric rail.** Steel-wheeled high speed rail (HSR) systems are very tough competitors. HSR manufacturers of this equipment in Europe and Japan are running a very aggressive marketing campaign. During our visits to request the opportunity to appear before the House Transportation Committee, chaired by Representative James Oberstar, Jim Powell and I

attended a Committee hearing on High Speed Rail, where we learned that the capital cost of a high-speed rail system was actually greater than that for a 2nd generation Maglev system.

While our meetings have made decision makers in the private sector, the Congress, the White House and the Department of Transportation aware of 2nd generation superconducting Maglev and its benefits, so far, no commitment, Government or private, for a 2nd Generation Maglev Test and Certification program has been forthcoming.

Strategy #3 was a total bust. Despite our intense efforts we have not been invited to testify before a Congressional committee on transportation or the National Surface Transportation Policy and Revenue Study Commission. We keep trying, however.

At this point, we would like to describe to the reader some of the results of this 8-year long strategy. We welcome your ideas for how to win this decisive round. It really is the decisive round for the implementation of the 2nd Generation Superconducting Maglev Transport Network in America. Maglev is inevitable, but the United States has forgotten the Moynihan vision. Instead, our leaders want to copy foreign high speed rail, which is much less capable and requires massive taxpayer subsidies.

As we finish this book in December, 2011, it is becoming increasingly clear that the Obama Administration's High Speed Intercity Passenger Rail initiative, Goliath #2, is weakening. Governors in Ohio, Wisconsin, and Florida are rejecting HSR, and many are very skeptical about it. Because of the scarcity and uncertainty of oil and World concerns about global climate change, electric transport – Maglev and electric autos – will dominate our future transport systems. Maglev will replace High Speed Rail (HSR) for intercity passenger travel in America because advocates for building HSR in America have ignored five fundamental truths:

1. HSR requires massive government subsidies for construction and operation – it cannot be privately financed.

2. HSR fares are considerably higher than the cost of flying or driving, even when its subsidies are included. Without subsidies, the fares would be much higher still.

3. HSR meets only a tiny fraction of transport needs, even in small countries with much greater population density than the U.S.

4. HSR routes in America will be isolated and not interconnected to form a national network that can serve all Americans.

5. HSR construction and operation will be subsidized by all American taxpayers, but the travel on HSR will be available and affordable for only a small fraction of America's citizens.

Recapping the Third Round – Meeting with the Department of Transportation (Strategy #1)

We requested a meeting with the Secretary of Transportation Norman Mineta, a former Democratic Member of Congress from the State of California, who was appointed by President George W. Bush. We were disappointed to learn that Secretary Mineta had to recuse himself from the meeting because he had previously been involved in Lockheed Martin's efforts to implement the German Transrapid Maglev system. Instead, we met with Secretary Mineta's Deputy, Emile Frankel. Jim Powell and I prepared a White Paper, "The Wolf is at the Door", describing Senator Moynihan's proposal to build a national Maglev network for passengers and freight alongside the Interstate Highway System.

Clearly, our proposal was the most efficient and lowest cost strategy to expand the capacity of the Interstate Highway System. We made the case that highway and airway congestion were worsening, traffic fatalities and injuries were too high and costly, and that the global oil supply would probably "peak" in the next decade. As the result, the United States should prepare for this disruptive change by converting its oil fueled transportation systems to electrically powered Superconducting Maglev. It is especially attractive for freight and passengers because its very low operating cost per passenger mile and ton mile would attract drivers and truckers. We stressed that the 2nd Generation Maglev could carry fully-loaded highway freight trucks, earning sufficient revenues to attract private investment to build the proposed National Maglev Network. We showed the four visuals (See exhibits 1, 2, 3 and 4), in the following pages, which became the core of our message. There was a good response at the Frankel briefing and we left feeling that the next step should be a meeting with the Federal Railway Administration (FRA).

Why the FRA and not the Federal Highway Administration. Simply because the Maglev program had been placed in the FRA. Maglev is perceived as a guided rail system and not as an expansion of the capacity of our Interstate Highway System.

We then requested to meet with the FRA Administrator, and met with the FRA's Mr. Mark Yachmetz, Associate Administrator for Railroad Policy and Development, and the Deputy Administrator. As we entered the FRA's downtown D.C. office, I saw a small-scale model of the Japanese 1st generation superconducting Maglev, sitting on the top of a row of grey file cabinets. This model became our point of departure for the discussion. I introduced Dr. Powell and pointed out that he and Dr. Danby had invented Japan Railway's 1st generation superconducting Maglev system, which holds the World speed record of 361 mph. I explained that after Japan built Powell and Danby's 1st generation superconducting Maglev system, Powell and Danby had developed a new 2nd generation system that was much more capable and much cheaper than Japan's system. And we were there for Dr. Powell to brief the FRA on why the new superconducting Maglev system was much better than the 1st generation German and Japanese systems, and get the FRA's assistance in obtaining funds to demonstrate the new Maglev 2000 system.

Dr. Powell explained that their new Maglev 2000 system addressed three criticisms that transportation experts had made of both the Japanese and German Maglev systems: (1) high cost per mile for guideway construction, (2) incompatibility with existing railroad trackage, and (3) its capability to electronically switch eliminates the need to move heavy, cumbersome sections of guideway in order to switch from the mainline to off-line stations for faster, more convenient service, as the 1st generation German and Japanese systems require.

Jim Powell then explained how the new M-2000 guideway system had cut cost in half by using a new guideway design that could be mass produced in a factory and delivered to the construction site for quick non-disruptive erection with conventional cranes. We also described the capabilities of the new 4-pole magnet design, which Jim and Gordon and their Maglev 2000 crew had built at full-scale and tested on Long Island, N.Y. This new magnet gave the 2nd generation system the unique ability to electronically switch at high speeds from the mainline guideway to off-line stations for loading/unloading operations. It also enabled Maglev 2000 vehicles to levitate very heavy loads such as fully loaded highway freight trucks. We also stressed the higher energy efficiency of the superconducting magnet system over Germany's conventional electromagnet system.

The Three Themes

∀ Theme #1
  – World Oil Production Will Soon Peak and Then Rapidly Decline, Becoming Ever Scarcer and Expensive
  – Modern Society Cannot Function Without Modern Transport, Which Cannot Function Without Oil

∀ Theme #2
  – The Proposed Substitute Fuels to Oil – Biofuels, Hydrogen, and Synfuels From Coal, etc. – Will Lead to Catastrophic Consequences If Implemented On A Large Scale

∀ Theme #3
  – Electric Transport – Electric Autos For Local Trips And Maglev For Longer Distances – Is the Only Acceptable Long Term Solution
  – The Technology for Practical Electric Transport Already Exists What Is Needed Is The Will To Act

Our closing point was that if the U.S. did not switch to electric transport, it would soon have to replace the declining and increasingly expensive oil supply with synthetic fuels. This would double the already tremendous amount of carbon dioxide emissions from transport. This serious threat of global warming established the urgent requirement to get on with demonstrating this system for transportation authorities.

Americas present transport systems – auto, truck, and air – are completely dependent on refined crude oil for fuel. Without plentiful, affordable oil supplies, our economy and present living standards cannot be maintained, if we continue to depend on the oil fueled internal combustion engine. Today, oil is ever scarcer and more expensive as demand from developing countries increases, oil production plateaus, and new discoveries decline. In the next few years World oil production will peak and then steadily decline.

The only practical solution to meet the on-coming oil crisis is to electrify transport. Biofuels can only supply a tiny fraction of our transport fuel requirements, and their production has major negative impacts on rising food prices and the long-term sustainability of agricultural production. Production of synfuels from coal, oil shale, and tar sands will accelerate global warming.

Electric transport based on electric automobiles for short trips, e.g. 50 to 100 mile range, plus Maglev transport for longer distance travel, will provide sustainable, low-cost, energy efficient, environmentally clean transport for the U.S. in the 21st Century.

1st generation passenger only Maglev systems are already operating in Japan, Germany and China. The advanced new 2nd generation Maglev 2000 system, which has been developed in the U.S. by the original inventors of the 1st generation superconducting Maglev system in Japan, can be built at much lower cost than the 1st generation systems, and transport long distance trucks at much higher speed and lower cost than if they went by highway.

The high revenues from transporting trucks as well as passengers will enable the capital cost of 2nd generation Maglev 2000 systems to be funded by private investment.

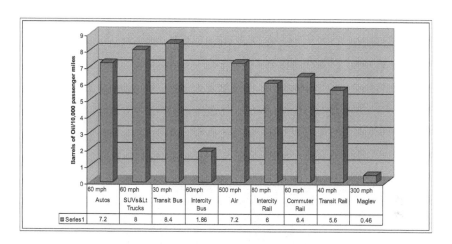

**ENERGY EFFICIENCY BY TRANSPORT MODE
IN BARRELS OF OIL OR OIL EQUIVALENT PER 10,000 PASSENGER MILES**
BASIS: TRANSPORTATION ENERGY DATA BOOK, 25TH EDITION; STACY DAVIS
AND SUSAN DREGEL, CENTER FOR TRANSPORTATION ANALYSIS, OAK RIDGE
NATIONAL LABORATORY, ORNL-6874 (2006)

The energy requirement per 10,000 passenger miles, shown above, for the different modes of transport are taken from the Department of Energy's 2006 Energy Transportation Data Book, except for the Maglev value. The Maglev energy requirement is based on a 300 mph vehicles carrying 100 passengers with a propulsion power of 2,000 Kilowatts.

Except for intercity buses and Maglev, the various modes of transport energy requirements are in the range of 6 to 8 barrels per 10,000 passenger miles. This applies to autos, airplanes, rail, transit bus, etc. Intercity buses use only about 1.5 equivalent barrels per 10,000 passenger miles, while Maglev uses only about ½ equivalent barrels per 10,000 passenger miles.

Maglev achieves its high energy efficiency because it has no mechanical contact and rolling friction — only air drag – and its vehicles are light weight. In contrast to steel-wheel HSR trains which must haul around heavy wheels, brakes and buggies. In fact, if they are not heavy the train would lose traction. Unlike airplanes, which have to carry heavy fuel, Maglev carries no fuel, but is electrically propelled. Moreover, it does not have to climb to high altitude, which is very inefficient, its propulsion system is much more efficient than jet engines and it travels at ½ the speed of jet aircraft, which greatly reduces air drag energy requirements.

The next slide in our core presentation gave emphasis to the importance of the 2nd Generation Superconducting Maglev capability to carry fully loaded highway freight trucks. Many transportation analysts fail to include the importance of highway trucking to the current U.S. economy.

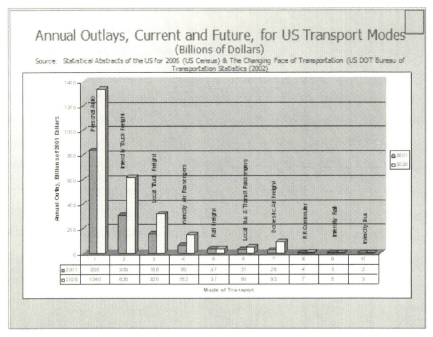

Current total U.S. outlays for truck, auto, air, and rail transport are well over 1 trillion dollars per year. By 2025 AD, based on DOT projections for passengers and freight transport, U.S. transport outlays will be well over 2 trillion dollars annually when expressed in constant dollars. Given the prospects for World oil production peaking by 2025 AD, the outlays for transport could be considerably higher.

Where do the current transport dollars go? The biggest outlay is for personal autos, over 800 Billion dollars per year. The second biggest is for truck freight transport, almost 500 billion dollars per year. Over 300 Billion of this is spent on intercity highway trucks, with an average haul distance of 500 miles. By 2025 based on US Department of Transportation projections, the outlays for intercity trucks will exceed

600 Billion dollars annually, in constant dollars. Total rail freight transport – coal, grain, containers, etc – lags far behind trucks, with a total outlay of only 37 Billion dollars annually. This will remain essentially constant with time. DOT projects that rail ton miles will be virtually constant over the next 2 decades. Even air passenger transport outlays are a small fraction of intercity trucks, 65 Billion dollars annually, compared to more than 300 Billion.

Completely lost in the pack are intercity rail and intercity bus, each at only 2 to 3 Billion dollars/year. Even if intercity rail were to increase 10 fold in passenger traffic with higher speed rail systems (an impossible dream) its outlays would still be less than $1/10^{th}$ of those spent on intercity trucks. The real revenues and transport needs are associated with developing a better way to transport intercity truck type freight. The unique 2nd Generation Maglev 2000 system offers that better way. By rapidly transporting intercity trucks hundreds of miles from their origin point to their destination, the resulting large revenues would pay off the cost of a National Maglev Network in just a few years, allowing the Network to be built by private investment, without government funding and subsidization. In addition to transporting trucks, the Maglev 2000 System can transport passengers, both intercity and locally, providing urban/suburban travel within metropolitan regions at lower cost, with zero pollution, quieter, faster and more convenient service than present systems. Finally, the Maglev 2000 system does not consume oil.

Finally, we show Maglev's impact on oil use and carbon dioxide emissions. The following table summarizes 3 possible transport futures for the United States in 2025.

Transport Demand, Oil Use and Carbon Dioxide Emissions for Three Different Futures

Transport Parameter
(Trillions/Year for Passenger Miles and Truck Ton-Miles)

	2000 AD	2025 AD		
		Massive Synfuels Future	Conservation Plus Synfuels Future	MAGLEV 2000 +Conservation Future
Auto Passenger Miles	5	8	8	4
Conventional Truck Ton Miles	1.1	2.2	2.2	0.7
Airplane Passenger Miles	0.6	1.4	1.4	0.4
Maglev Passenger Miles				5.0
Maglev Truck Ton/Miles				1.5
Transport Oil Consumption (Millions of Barrels/Day)	13	22	13	4.5
U.S. Transport, Annual Carbon Dioxide Emissions (Million Metric Tons)	2000	6800	4000	1400
Note	1) Conservation Reduces Fuel Consumption by 50% in Autos, 20% in Trucks, 20% in Airplanes
	2) Maglev provides 1/2 of Auto passenger mile demand, 2/3 of truck ton-mile demand, and 3/4 of Air Passenger demand. Also, 1/2 of remaining auto passenger miles use electric cars
Source	The Changing Face of Transportation, USDOT, BTS 00-007 (2000) and Transportation Energy Data Book, Edition 22 (September 2002)

In the first, "Massive Synfuels Future", increased demand is met by synthetic fuels refined from coal, oil shale, and tar sands for existing transport modes. In the second, "Conservation Plus Synfuels Future", reduces fuel usage in autos, trucks and airplanes by higher mileage per gallon standards. In this second future, the remaining smaller transport fuel demand is met by synfuels. In the third future, M-2000 takes over 1/2 of the passenger transport, 2/3rds of the truck ton-miles and 3/4th of the air passenger miles. Electric cars meet 1/2 of the remaining highway miles. Conservation only keeps transport oil usage at the 2000 A.D. level as demand increases. To reduce oil use below 2000 A.D. values, both M-2000 and electric autos, is needed.

In the 3rd future, transport oil usage in 2025 AD is only 4.5 million barrels daily, though transport demand in 2025 A.D. is almost twice that in 2000 A.D. This level of usage appears environmentally sustainable, even if it comes from synfuels. Carbon dioxide emissions are about 2/3 of that from transport oil in 2000 A.D.

The Next Step–Meeting with Congressional Representatives (Strategy #2).

While the meetings with the Department of Transportation were necessary and we had a good reception, they were very far from sufficient. Basically, DOT does not act independently, but follows the path laid out for it by Congress and the Administration. In Strategy #2, we focused on meetings with Representative Tim Bishop, our local Congressperson, Senator Charles Schumer, the senior Senator from New York, and Senator Harry Reid from Nevada, who had been a member of the Committee on Environment and Public Works, United States Senate, Chaired by Senator Moynihan that held hearings on the "Use of the Interstate Highway System Right-of-Way for Magnetic Levitation High Speed Transportation Systems, S.2072".

Representative Bishop was elected November, 2002 and assumed office January 3, 2003 for the district on Long Island, N.Y. where Jim Powell and Gordon Danby live. At Calverton, near the Town of Riverhead, there is a de-commissioned Navy airfield used by the Grumman Aircraft Corporation. Riverhead had received the airfield for use as an industrial park. We thought the airfield, shown in the following aerial view of Calverton, was perfect for the initial tests on the Maglev 2000 system. We talked with Andrea Lohneiss, who directed the economic development offices of Riverhead, about using the Calverton airfield for Maglev 2000 Test Facility.

Andrea was very interested and helped to arrange a meeting with Mr. Bishop and his staff. Our first meeting was with his legislative assistant, Mr. Nick Holder. After briefing him on the Maglev 2000 system, we made the case that the U.S. needed to establish a facility similar to the test facilities that had been funded by the governments of Japan and Germany, so that America could compete for the market that would inevitably develop as oil ran out. We further made the point that the guideway standard could be lost to Germany or Japan, and become the international standard, much like the standard railroad gauge of 4 feet 8 inches, did. Our final point, America runs the risk of losing the market by default and it would have to purchase foreign Maglev vehicles to conform to the international Maglev guideway gauge standard.

After several meeting with Mr. Holder, he drafted a letter for Mr. Bishop, a member of the House Transportation Committee, to send to Representative James Oberstar, who was the Democratic "Ranking" member of the committee (in 2004, Congress was under Republican control). The Transportation Authorization bill was in conference, the last stages of a bill before it becomes law.

We hoped that Mr. Oberstar would persuade Committee Chairman Don Young of Alaska that a Test Facility should be included in the new 6-year Transportation Authorization Bill. In his letter, Mr. Bishop had summarized the situation in the international Maglev competition and made a point that Germany and Japan *"have committed significant government funding to study this technology while the U.S. continues to provide little resources for research and development of this American invented mode of transportation."* He pointed out that *"in underfunding U.S. maglev technology, we have created a gap in the market that has been filled by the German Transrapid design, which has been established as an unofficial standard in the industry."*

Armed with this letter, I met with Transportation Committee Staff Members of both the Majority (Republican) and Minority (Democratic) staffs, sometimes with Jim Powell, who would fly down from Long Island, to discuss the importance of authorizing a 2nd Generation

Superconducting Maglev Test and Certification Facility. We requested an opportunity to testify before the Committee, fully confident that if we could appear before the Committee, the Members would see the wisdom of funding the testing and certification of an American Superconducting Maglev transport system. Staffers were sympathetic but there was no real action and no invitation to testify.

Sadly, the Transportation Bill did not include funds for a Test Facility for 2nd Generation Superconducting Maglev, just more funds for Transrapid.

Our next objective was to meet with New York's Senator Charles Schumer to obtain his support for a U.S. 2nd Generation Superconducting Transport Maglev System. Our path to a meeting was rather roundabout, as described in the next few pages. It started with a meeting with the Empire State Development Corporation to discuss making Maglev 2000 a tenant of the new Moynihan Station, which would expand and renovate New York City's Penn Station, the busiest rail station in America.

Senator Moynihan was intensely interested in urban architecture and development. Through his leadership, Washington, DC has a beautiful multimodal rail terminal in its Union Station near the Capitol. This project and the accompanying Pennsylvania Avenue Redevelopment would not have happened without the energy, interest, and intellectual power of Senator Moynihan. One of his last projects of great interest to Senator Moynihan, which was still unfinished when he died, was renovating Pennsylvania Station in New York City. The following photograph made in May, 1999 shows Senator Moynihan explaining the concept for the new Penn Station to President Clinton, Rodney Slater, the U.S. Secretary of Transportation, Governor George Pataki and Charles Gargano, Chairman of the Empire State Development Corporation (ESDC). The ESDC was created by Governor Pataki soon after he took office in 1995. By placing a broad range of state development agencies under the control of the ESDC, the Governor gave unprecedented authority to the ESDC's board and its chair, Charles Gargano.

In 2004, when we started this third round there was a revival of public interest in going forward with the new Penn Station.

Our intent was to become a tenant of the Moynihan Station and use office space in the Penn Station complex as the Maglev 2000 Corporate and

PHOTO OF SENATOR MOYNIHAN POINTING OUT THE FEATURES OF THE NEW PENN STATION COMPLEX TO PRESIDENT BILL CLINTON, SECRETARY OF TRANSPORTATION RODNEY SLATER, GOVERNOR GEORGE PATAKI, AND CHARLES GARGANO, CHAIRMAN OF THE EMPIRE STATE DEVELOPMENT CORPORATION. ANDREA MOHIN/ NYTIMES/REDUX

Engineering Design Center. We hoped to exhibit a full-scale prototype in the station concourse to give national recognition to this new technology and also enable our engineers to interact with railroad planners, engineers and architectural designers to incorporate the patented Maglev 2000 MERRI (Maglev Emplacement on Railroad Infrastructure) system in the new station. The Moynihan Station would also provide a natural entry into the commuter rail market: light-rail and subway cars adapted to Maglev offering the low-maintenance, energy efficient and quiet operation of Maglev.

I contacted the Empire State Development Corporation, requested and was granted a meeting with Chairman Gargano. Mr. Gargano had to cancel, but we were fortunate to still be scheduled for the lunch meeting with the President of the ESDC.

For me, it meant taking a train to Penn Station in NYC from Washington, DC. For Jim Powell, it meant coming to Penn Station from Long Island on the Long Island Railroad (LIRR). Amazingly, we managed to connect up for a cab ride to the ESDC offices.

Before departing from Washington, I received a call from Dr. F.C. "Bud" Griffis, a former colleague who I had worked with when he was the Dean of Engineering at Columbia University. My firm, James Jordan Associates, a science and technology policy consulting firm, had helped Dr. Griffis draft a book on advanced technologies for infrastructure, a project he was working on with Brookhaven National Laboratory, and pursued grants from federal and state agencies to develop some of the advanced concepts in the book. Bud, as he is known, was interested in Maglev and asked to join us for lunch. We met the President of the ESDC and his new transportation director, the former chief architect for Amtrak. We then walked to a nearby restaurant. As we were arriving, Bud rolled up in a cab to participate in the meeting. We discussed the technology of 2nd generation Maglev, its financial requirement, and how it would benefit New York State.

Our presentation went very well. However, as we walked back to the ESDC offices, the ESDC President said, "This is a great concept, a great project and a great technology, but we can't fund this project because you guys have no buzz. You need to become well known in the popular culture before we could fund a concept of this scope."

After that discouraging, but illuminating and realistic critique, Jim Powell and I headed back to Penn Station. Bud returned to the Polytechnic University of New York — he was its newly appointed Provost.

At Penn Station, Jim and I sat in the lobby waiting for our trains. I don't remember who proposed it, but we agreed that we needed to create "buzz". We would write articles for newspapers and magazines on Maglev's benefits for transportation, energy and the environment. Strategy #8 was born.

The Maglev briefing caught Bud's imagination. Bud called to propose that Jim, Gordon and I join Polytechnic University to create a Maglev Research Center. He felt that a university research center would be more likely to obtain government and foundation grants for Maglev. We agreed. Bud invited us to Polytechnic University to make a presentation to a colloquium he organized that included University and private sector, engineering, construction and design experts. The audience offered advice on how we could obtain funding to develop 2nd Generation Maglev. The key recommendation was for us to talk to the NY/NJ Port Authority, because they were the only State agency with any money.

Jim Powell, Gordon Danby, and I were appointed as Associate Research Professors at Polytechnic University. We met with Polytechnic's president and the Maglev Research Center was born.

The Maglev Research Center became a new Crusade. We met with foundations, wrote papers for engineering society meetings and published a study in a magazine format for distribution on our visits. We created a short animated film for distribution on CD's, and we created a website www.poly.edu/maglev that provided access to our papers and new animated film. Bud Griffis visited the Maglev Test Facility at Yamanashi in Japan, and became our eyewitness spokesperson for superconducting Maglev.

The Polytechnic University of NY Maglev team visited Congressional Representatives, particularly the New York delegation, asking that they support the Maglev Research Center. We also went back to the Federal Railway Administration. Bud was the former Eastern District Director for the U.S. Army Corps of Engineers. His experience in managing large projects qualified him to take the lead in presenting the case for funding Maglev. Bud participated in the meetings with the FRA, the National Academy of Engineering, the National Science Foundation, the Sloan Foundation and senior members of the NY Congressional delegation.

During a Bagel Breakfast fund-raiser for Senator Charles (Chuck) Schumer of New York, Bud talked with Senator Schumer about Maglev and the possibility of funding the Maglev Research Center to work on the new 2nd generation superconducting Maglev. Following up on Bud's efforts, I contacted Senator Schumer's office to schedule a meeting with his assistant, Mr. Andrew Lederman, to request a briefing and to request Senator Schumer's support for Maglev in America. Bud, Jim Powell, Gordon Danby and I were invited to meet the senior members of Senator Schumer's staff and Senator Schumer.

For the four of us to meet with Members of Congress on Capitol Hill was not easy. Security is tight, and parking is very difficult. Typically, on our visits to Capitol Hill, Jim Powell and Gordon Danby would fly out of

McArthur Airport on Long Island to Baltimore Washington International (BWI) airport. There, they would rent a car and drive from BWI on one of the most congested highways in the U.S. to my home in Falls Church, Virginia. Jim, Gordon and I would then drive to Union Station, park in the station garage, and meet Bud (who had taken the train from New York City) at a Korean cuisine restaurant in the station. There we would dry run our presentation before leaving for the meeting on Capitol Hill.

The tortuous logistics for our meetings made us even more committed to proposing the National Maglev Network. Just drive a few miles to your local Maglev Station, hop on a vehicle within a few minutes, and Bingo, you're on your way to downtown Washington, DC at 300 mph.

Senator Schumer's office is in the Hart Senate Office Building, the newest Senate office building. The offices surround a large atrium with a marvelous Alexander Calder sculpture symbolizing mountains and clouds. When I first saw the sculpture, I thought, why the black cloud? It should have been silver. Walking on the 3rd floor balcony passageway leading to Senator Schumer's office, visitors can look out over the open atrium and sculpture – a beautiful and inspiring sight.

Senator Schumer is a very successful politician. He has never lost a political race. Highly energetic, he is a mover and shaker in the Congress and he holds the Senate record for the most Sunday talk show appearances. We were very excited about introducing him to Maglev and gaining his support for its development.

When Bud Griffis, Jim Powell, and I showed up for the meeting, we were led by Andrew Lederman to a conference table. Joining us were 3 more members of Senator Schumer's staff: the Chief of Staff, the Chief Counsel, and the Appropriations staffer. I was very impressed with the Schumer power team. We shook hands and then Senator Schumer entered the room with his usual high energy speed. We stood and greeted him. Then, we briefed him on Maglev and our plans for it to become a major transportation system and industry for the United States, with the capability to export Maglev equipment to the rest of the World. Senator Schumer was enthusiastic about the Superconducting Maglev Network project and creating a National Superconducting Maglev Test and Demonstration Facility like those in Japan or Germany. He said to his Chief of Staff, "We can make something of this, I want to give this priority".

We were thrilled. At long last, we felt that we could see the Promised Land. I had prepared draft legislation modeled on Senator Moynihan's Maglev R&D program. He turned to me and said, "Jim what do we need to do?" I slid the draft across the table toward him. His energy and enthusiasm was wonderful.

As the year wore on and hundreds of bills made their way through the Senate, we waited for an Earmark and a Floor Statement about Maglev. Unfortunately it did not happen. The Chief Counsel, a very nice guy, met with me in the same conference room. He apologized saying that they had dropped the ball, but would get on it next year. We were unhappy, but had to accept the reality. Andrew Lederman left the staff to go off to graduate school at the London School of Economics. The appropriations staffer left for the staff of Senator Barbara Boxer of California. What was very disappointing was the loss of this powerful politician who would have become the successor to Senator Moynihan, the first champion of Maglev.

Lessons learned for David as he faces Goliath? His allies can want to help him in his fight with Goliath, but they do have their own priorities – advancing their careers, dealing with pressing near term problems, etc.,

etc. There were all kinds of issues for the Senate that were of higher priority than transportation. The aftermath of 9-11, the invasion of Iraq, the problems in Iran, threats of terrorist attacks, real and imagined. There were powerful destructive hurricanes, Rita, and then Katrina. The war in Iraq was taking a toll on lives and the Treasury. The U.S. economy was under stress. Jobs were leaving the country, unemployment was rising and as the war in Iraq dragged on, we had a super spike in the cost of oil that raised the pump price to 4 dollars a gallon from less than 2 dollars.

Strategy #7. Searching for an industrial partner in the development of Maglev 2000 prototype vehicles and a test track.

Though the Maglev 2000 organization had designed the 2nd generation system and built and tested its components, the very modest government funding was not adequate to assemble and test a vehicle on a M-2000 guideway. Accordingly, we sought to find an industrial partner who would not only provide the needed funds but also expertise in manufacturing prototype vehicles, controls and the guideway to test and certify the system for public use. There were three businesses categories: The industries that built the Japanese Maglev system was an obvious choice. The second logical group was the automobile manufacturers, Ford, GM, etc. The third group was the aircraft manufacturing industry, Lockheed-Martin, Boeing Aircraft, and Northrop-Grumman, etc. In one sense Maglev is an airplane without wings, tails, engines and fuel tanks.

Meetings with Japan Railways

Our meeting with Japanese Railways (JR) was easy to arrange. JR had opened a Washington Office to explore the U.S. market for high speed transport. I requested an appointment to have them meet Jim Powell and Gordon Danby. They were very gracious. The meeting was held at their office on Farragut Square. Washington has lots of one block square parks, usually with a statue of a Civil War General. This square is the hub of Washington's downtown and is convenient to a lot of offices, restaurants, and commercial shopping. On one side is the famous "K" street, the home of many of Washington's lobbying firms. In square's center there is a statue of David G. Farragut, a Union admiral in the American Civil War famous for rallying his fleet with the cry, "Damn the torpedoes, full speed ahead!" After the first meeting at their office, the rest of the meetings were held over lunch at the nearby Hay-Adams Hotel.

At the first meeting Jim, Gordon, and I met with the General Manager Osamu (Sam) Nakayama and the Manager Takashi Kitagawa. We were delighted by their offer of cooperation with the development of our Maglev system. We thanked them and said we wanted to brief them on improvements in the new 2nd generation design. Jim and Gordon explained the design of the 4-pole magnets and their advantages for operating in a planar as well as a monorail mode. Jim and Gordon pointed out that the electronic switching capability at high speed with this new magnet design would allow closer station spacing increasing the convenience of the passenger service. We also went over the monorail guideway design and how it could be prefabricated and erected much faster without traffic disruption. The Maglev 2000 guideway could be installed at about half the price of the U-shaped guideway for Japan's 1st generation system. Takashi Kitagawa, who had a degree from MIT, was very interested. As the meeting closed they asked how they could help us.

I proposed that we create a new private international company, and work together to develop the 2nd generation system. The new company would offer stock to raise funds to bring 2nd generation Maglev to the U.S., Japan, and the global market.

Mr. Nakayama and Mr. Kitagawa said that the proposal was appealing, but that they were a government company. To consider this, President Bush would need to speak to their Prime Minister Junichiro Koizumi about this proposal. If you remember, Prime Minister Koizumi, was a fan of Elvis Presley, and there was a big event when he visited this country and he and President Bush visited Graceland on June 30, 2006.

My response, "Do you mean me? You want me to take this proposal to President Bush? They said, "yes." I said that I would try.

How to carry out this daunting task? I had a few old Republican friends from the days when I worked as a staffer for Senator Stennis of Mississippi, a senior Democrat on the Armed Services and the Appropriations Committees. I called on them for help. One was a former colleague from Tennessee, who had worked for Senator Howard Baker, who had been appointed by President Bush as the Ambassador to Japan. I asked her for help to talk to Ambassador Baker, who I had known when he was the Majority leader of the Senate. For part of the period that I worked for Senator Stennis, Senator Baker was a member of the coalition of Senators that supported the Tenn-Tom Waterway, which connected the upper Mississippi River to Mobile, Alabama via the Tennessee and Tombigbee Rivers. I got to know him as we worked to get the many votes needed to complete that project.

Also, when Senator Baker was Majority Leader, I had met with the Western Senators on behalf of Senator Stennis to negotiate the location of the Nuclear Waste Geologic Repository as part of the Nuclear Waste Policy Act. I thought it worth a try to ask Senator Baker, the Ambassador to Japan, if he would help in arranging a joint Maglev program between the U.S. and Japan. I drafted a letter and persuaded the International Trade people at the State Department to carry it to Ambassador Baker. The letter described the proposed joint U.S.-Japan Maglev program. Unfortunately, on the day the courier arrived, Ambassador Baker had a heart attack, and was flown back to the States, never to return to Japan. Plan A had failed.

Plan B was to go for President Bush's Chief of Staff, Andrew Card. It is not easy to speak to the Chief of Staff but I persisted. He was cordial, but said, "Jim, that would be picking winners and losers, and we don't do that". He had been the Secretary of Transportation and understood the significance of Maglev but was reluctant to sponsor this initiative. I made my argument that we were not competing on a level playing field and it would take an initiative like this for our government to create a test facility similar to the facilities that had been built by Germany and Japan. I wrote to Mr. Card and made the case for asking the government to assist giving Maglev 2000 access to a *level playing field*, including reminding him of President Bush's statement on a campaign stop at Boeing in Seattle (Boeing was engaged in a legal contest in the World Trade Organization with Airbus on the level playing field issue) that he was going to work for creating a level playing field for American business. In our last conversation, I felt I was making significant progress, but next day Mr. Card resigned from the White House Staff. Plan B was dead – another failure. Ironically, as this book goes to the press, President Obama made forceful point in his 3rd State of the Union address on

Tuesday, January 23, 2011 to seek "a level playing field" for American industry. He said, *"And this Congress should make sure that no foreign company has an advantage over American manufacturing when it comes to accessing finance or new markets like Russia. Our workers are the most productive on Earth, and if the playing field is level, I promise you – America will always win."* Plan B redux?

During this period we continued meeting with Takashi Kitagawa, and made plans to create a joint effort on Long Island that would be staffed with engineers from Japan and the U.S. In a meeting between Bud Griffis, Director of the new Maglev Research Center at Polytechnic University, with Jim Powell, Takashi and me this idea was discussed. Bud planned a trip to the JR Test Facility at Yamanashi and Takashi was very helpful. Takashi is a very creative thinker and I felt that he would be a great asset in the new company if it ever came into being. He was a reminder that the new superconducting Maglev industry would need to recruit and train hundreds more young engineers.

JR is the operator of the fastest and most extensive high speed steel wheel rail system in the World, and the constructor and operator of the Maglev Test Facility at Yamanashi. The Chairman of JR, Dr. Yoshiyuki Kasai, a University of Wisconsin alumni, is a strong supporter of superconducting Maglev. In a recent article he wrote, *"the most effective future train system for the United States would be a maglev transit line. If such a network was in place, people in New York would be able to participate in an early-morning meeting in Washington without the bother of having to go to and from airports at both ends. Likewise, transcontinental maglev services could supersede aviation networks."*

Dr. Kasai recognized, as we do, that steel wheel High Speed Rail (HSR) is fully mature, and any technology advances would only be marginal. In contrast, Maglev technology is still evolving. The 1st generation German (i.e. China) and Japanese systems are still too expensive and limited in capability and revenue potential to be implemented in the U.S. Like HSR, they must be government subsidized. In effect they are like the pre-World War II DC-3 airplanes. If passenger air travel had remained at that level, instead of evolving to modern jet airliners, air travel today would be rare.

Meetings with Large Aircraft Companies

Meetings with the executives of the three largest U.S. aircraft manufacturing companies provided us with insight about the industrial partner strategy.

From the outside, large aircraft companies appear to be a perfect partner. They innovate and manufacture commercial and military aircraft and market on a global basis. 3 companies divide about 70 Billion dollars per year in government defense contracts. Investment in Maglev could be an R&D tax deduction. They agreed that their industry, product, and market were very sensitive to the price and availability of oil.

They acknowledged the threat from carbon dioxide emissions and agreed that it was unlikely to find clean, non-carbon dioxide emitting fuel. So, we said, it was essential to develop alternative transport as fast and convenient as airplanes. Again, heads nodded in agreement.

We then showed them the graph shown below to point out that the aircraft industry had probably peaked. The graph, from a research paper by Jesse H. Ausubel, C. Marchetti, and P. Meyer (1998) "Toward Green Mobility: the Evolution of Transport" European Review, Vol. 6, No. 2, pp. 137-156, depicts the peak years of the various modes of transport in U.S. history. The illustrations and the electric transport growth rate are from Powell and Jordan. The future shift around 2050 A.D. corresponds to DOE's Energy Information Agency's unrealistic estimate of when the World oil production starts to decline, a.k.a. "peak oil".

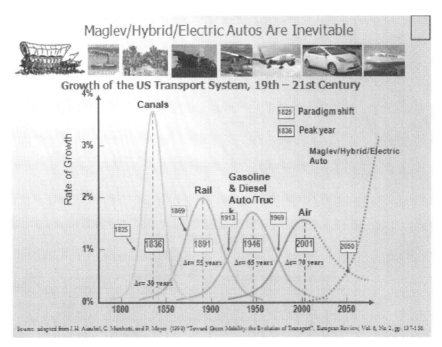

As in Chapter 1, we described the historical shifts in U.S. modes of transport over the past 200 years. Air transport is the latest mode. Future oil will be ever scarcer and more expensive, not only because its consumption rate is much greater than its discovery rate, but also as China and India industrialize, they will compete very strongly for the ever shrinking oil pie. Because of this, the next transport technologies are likely to be Maglev, hybrid/electric and all-electric autos and light trucks. Surprisingly, heads nodded in agreement, even though there were a few harrumphs.

We concluded our presentation with a proposal to jointly demonstrate the Maglev transport for passengers and freight. They seemed to take our proposal seriously. There were questions and answers, follow-on meetings and telephone conferences, especially about ferrying highway freight trucks. They realized this market was 5 times bigger than the intercity air passenger market. Maglev vehicles and equipment could fill their increasingly idle manufacturing capacity.

Despite enthusiasm for Maglev, our proposal was rejected. One company said that if they started to develop Maglev they would not sell any more airplanes.

Lessons Learned:

Large publicly traded manufacturing companies focus on quarterly performance and cannot make decisions that will disrupt their customer base. This strong emphasis on the near-term hurts U.S. competitiveness. It seems to us, after numerous briefings to executives of large manufacturing companies and investment bankers, that their myopia coupled with their enormous power to influence government policy constrains economic growth and the ability of the United States to recover from economic downturns and achieve full employment and livable income. It seems neither the private sector nor the government really takes America's long-term economic future seriously. There always are government discussions, academic studies, commissions and reports, and books concerned about America's long-term future but there is really no action on issues like our dependence on oil, climate change, and ocean acidification and the risk we are taking to put off actions to address these issues.

In *The Rise and Decline of Nations*, published in 1982, Mancur Olson, a University of Maryland professor, explains how stable, affluent societies get in trouble. In Olson's view, successful countries breed interest groups that become more and more powerful with time. The groups win government favors, in the form of new laws or friendly regulators that benefit them at everyone else's expense. Not only do they grab a larger piece of the economic pie, but *they stop the pie from growing as much as it could.* Professor Olson's thesis on the power of moneyed special interests has also been documented by Pat Choate in his books, including *Dangerous Business, the Risks of Globalization for America,* and Robert Reich in his books *Supercapitalism, The Transformation of Business, Democracy, and Everyday Life* and *Aftershock, the Next Economy & America's Future.*

Over the 1970-2010 period, there is clear evidence that America's economic growth has slowed. The U.S. economic engine, based on fossil-fueled manufacturing and transportation, peaked in the 1970's. After decades of growing dependency on foreign goods, services, and oil,

America's ability to globally compete in manufactured goods has radically declined. For example, Germany's trade per capita is almost three times that of the U.S. The U.S. has fallen to 3rd place in merchandise exports behind Germany and China.[2]

Our economic gurus keep reassuring us that the U.S. economy is strong and we are just transitioning to a service and knowledge based economy based on digital information technology. They say that the current economic dislocation is like those that occurred during the transitions from agricultural to industrial. Not to worry.

However, there is plenty of reason to worry. Our supposed strong financial sector was a house of cards that collapsed, placing the U.S. in the steepest economic decline since the Great Depression.

How does America get out of its deep financial hole? As the old saying goes, "when you're in a hole, the first thing to do is to stop digging". We need to shift away from depending on the unstable, uncontrollable, unfair and unequal financial sector path, and return back to a more self-reliant system based on American jobs, not outsourced ones, investment by the giant corporations in America, not foreign countries, increased manufacturing and exports, and transportation that does not depend on foreign oil imports that create our present huge trade deficit.

Unfortunately our leaders are not leading us to this new path even though time is limited to act on this crisis. Already current recovery and reinvestment policies give preferential treatment to the financial sector and large multi-national corporations who outsource more and more jobs. The very slow recovery from high unemployment of the 2007-2009 recession, together with the declining real wages and salaries for most Americans, the loss of value in homes, the massive number of foreclosures and the growing inequality in our society are wiping out the middle class. The American economic model is broken and the public's confidence in government's ability to solve the problem is rapidly falling.

---

[2] World Trade Organization [Trade per capita ($, 2005-2007 11,954, Germany 30,276)]

In this book we hope to make the public more aware of what an innovative Maglev transport system can do for America's economic future and their standard of living. In this connection, we obviously think that the High Speed Intercity Passenger Rail Initiative investment plan is very bad policy. It will burden an already overburdened American taxpayer with obligations to massively subsidize a system that only meets a tiny fraction of America's future transport needs.

The requirements are clear. America's long-term policies must ensure the financial security of our citizens, and optimally allocate our resources for: good health and nutrition, effective disease control, preservation of our soil, water and biodiversity, and in concert with other nations to mitigate global warming, ocean acidification, pandemics, the effects of natural disasters, and nuclear proliferation.

The long-term issues for the Congress and the Administration to consider are as follows:

- The growing deterioration of the environment: global warming, health harming pollution, loss of soil nutrition, and ocean acidification threaten the food, economic and energy security of the U.S. as well as the larger global populations.

- The realities of economics prescribe that the U.S. must become more self-sufficient in goods, services, and commodities – particularly in oil.

- The slowing rate of U.S. economic growth.

- The decline of manufacturing since the late 1980's is undermining the economic foundation of our national security and standard of living.

- Growing income inequality. Since 1975, there is a large and growing gap between the income for the top one-fifth of our society and the income for everyone else.

- The populations of the U.S., Europe, Russia, Japan, and China are aging. No one really knows the full meaning of this for our collective standard of living but it should be brought into the discussion.

Innovation and Competitiveness are Dying.

The Gathering Storm is a recent report from the National Academy of Engineering. It concluded that U.S. innovation and competitiveness is declining but its policy recommendations have been ignored. Most inventors and entrepreneurs in innovative technologies die in the "Valley of Death" that lies between discovering a new technology and actually implementing it, because of resistance from established industrial and financial power interests. The authors have experienced the "Valley of Death" first hand, not only in Maglev but also in other areas. For example, Jordan and Powell developed and tested the Advanced Vitrification System (AVS), a much simpler, safer, and cheaper way to completely immobilize nuclear waste for millions of years, until it has completely decayed to a safe, non-radioactive material, with no possibility of dispersing in the environment. The AVS was killed by powerful special interest groups pushing old waste disposal technology that could not prevent radioactive waste material from entering the environment. The influence of special interest lobbies on our government is extremely difficult to overcome.

The study in *The Gathering Storm* was carried out before the deep economic collapse in 2007 and 2008, but its findings are extremely important and must be resolved for the U.S. economy to regain its prosperity.

Quoting from *The Gathering Storm*,

"Having reviewed trends in the United States and abroad, the committee is deeply concerned that the scientific and technological building blocks critical to our economic leadership are eroding at a time when many other nations are gathering strength. We strongly believe that a worldwide strengthening will benefit the world's economy— particularly in the creation of jobs in countries that are far less well-off than the United States. But we are worried about the future prosperity of the United States. Although many people assume that the United States will always be a world leader in science and technology, this may not continue to be the case inasmuch as great minds and ideas exist throughout the world. We fear the abruptness with which a lead in science and technology can be lost—and the difficulty of recovering a lead once lost, if indeed it can be regained at all."

The Electric Transport Solution

To meet the oncoming global climate change and oil depletion crises, we must soon shift to electric transport — electric autos and Maglev for local commuter trips rather than light rail and a high-speed National Maglev Network for intercity highway freight and passengers.

If America begins now to shift to electric transport and non-fossil electric power generation, it would achieve a positive trade balance and plenty of good paying jobs in these new industries. A modest investment of only 600 million dollars for a 2nd generation superconducting Maglev Test and Certification Facility, compared to the 8.1 billion dollar small down payment for the high speed steel wheel rail initiative appropriated in the American Recovery and Reinvestment Act of 2009, would put the American 2nd generation superconducting Maglev for passengers and freight on a level playing field with the test facilities built by the governments of Japan, Germany, China and South Korea. It is wrongheaded of the United States to ultimately invest hundreds of Billions of taxpayer dollars in imported, soon to be obsolete High Speed Passenger Rail systems just because they are ready to go, while ignoring the far superior 2nd generation Superconducting Maglev that will attract private capital for construction of a National Maglev Network.

In good times the political will to get rid of harmful trade and competitiveness policies doesn't exist. A crisis enables doing things that could not be done before. New trade, investment, and regulatory policies that foster innovation, inventiveness and competitiveness are needed to benefit the American people. Now may be the time.

On several occasions before and after the election, President Obama referred to Maglev systems in China and Japan as the kind of high speed rail system that we can build in America. What he probably does not realize is the system he admires in Japan is based on the inventions of Drs. James Powell and Gordon Danby. And probably does not know that their new 2nd generation superconducting Maglev system will uniquely move freight as well as passengers at 300 miles per hour in all weather, using a very little electrical energy. Independent engineering analyses and fabrication and testing of the 2nd generation Maglev components find that it is much cheaper to construct and operate than the 1st generation Maglev and steel-wheel systems now operating in foreign countries.

Maglev eliminates the rolling friction and the rail distortion effects for the high-speed rail systems in Europe and Japan. HSR systems require frequent and expensive maintenance. GAO (General Accountability Office) recently reported that all HSR systems require government subsidies to cover construction and operating costs.[3] A 2nd generation superconducting Maglev transport system can be built and operated without government subsidies by its unique ability to carry high revenue highway freight trucks in special roll-on, roll-off Maglev vehicles plus the ability to operate on dedicated elevated guideways as well as on existing railroad tracks.

The stimulus (American Recovery and Reinvestment Act) contained 1.3 billion dollars for Amtrak and 8.1 billion dollars for high-speed intercity rail projects. The Secretary of Transportation announced a plan for the allocation of this money on April 16th, 2009.

President Obama said at the announcement ceremony, *"What we need, then, is a smart transportation system equal to the needs of the 21st century. A system that reduces travel times and increases mobility. A system that reduces congestion and boosts productivity. A system that reduces destructive emissions and creates jobs."*

"And Japan, the nation that unveiled the first high-speed rail system, is already at work building the next: a line that will connect Tokyo with Osaka at speeds of over 300 miles per hour. So it's being done; it's just not being done here."

"There's no reason why we can't do this. This is America. There's no reason why the future of travel should lie somewhere else beyond our borders. Building a new system of high-speed rail in America will be faster, cheaper and easier than building more freeways or adding to an already overburdened aviation system — and everybody stands to benefit."

---

[3] High Speed Passenger Rail: Future Development Will Depend on Addressing Financial and Other Challenges and Establishing a Clear Federal Role GAO-09-317, March 19, 2009

In light of the economic situation–high unemployment, a severe decline in tax revenues and very large budget and trade deficits–it would be disastrous to let special interest lobbies prevent the development of the American 2nd generation superconducting Maglev system.

The 2nd generation Maglev system has the following major advantages over the 1st generation Maglev and HSR systems:

- Much lower construction cost and faster, less disruptive construction, using mass produced, low cost prefabricated guideways.

- Very short payback time of construction cost, under 5 years, by transporting high revenue highway trucks as well as passengers.

- Does not require government funding and subsidy – can be privately financed.

- Can function as a 29,000-mile interconnected National Maglev Network, transporting people and goods at 300 mph to all cities in America, not just a few isolated cities.

- In combination with electric autos, can virtually eliminate the need for oil imports.

- Greatly reduces carbon dioxide emissions (today's U.S. transport emits as much carbon dioxide as our coal power plants).

- Can travel levitated along existing RR tracks to serve urban and suburban areas, by attaching very low cost thin panels that encapsulate aluminum loops to the RR crossties – no need for new expensive and disruptive infrastructure.

- Provides hundreds of thousands of new high tech jobs and many Billions of dollars of exports per year as a major new American industry (using the GAO estimate for number of jobs created by dollars of investment, we calculate that spending about 30 Billion dollars a year to construct, operate, and manufacture and equip the Maglev Network would create 1.2 million jobs and as exports of Maglev equipment and guideway components develop this number could double.)

- Greatly reduces adverse public health effects from auto & truck pollutants and microparticulates.

Powell and Danby's Maglev 2000 organization, using only a few million dollars in Federal and State funds, has successfully fabricated and tested full size prototypes of all of the components for the 2nd generation Maglev 2000 system. The next step is to assemble vehicles and operationally test them at a Maglev Test Facility, which requires government funding of about 600 million dollars (about 11 hours of oil imports). Once certified, the National Maglev Network would start construction.

The 6,000 mile first phase of the Network would build Maglev routes running along the East (Maine to Miami) and West (Seattle to San Diego) Coasts with a Maglev line from Chicago to New York. If we start this year using a small portion of the Stimulus Funds for High Speed Passenger Rail that many governors are rejecting, the first phase would be fully operational by May 2019, the 150th Anniversary of Lincoln's Transcontinental Railroad. The full 29,000 mile National Maglev Network would be completed by 2030 AD. Total cost, privately financed, is 600 Billion dollars, about the cost of 1 year's worth of oil imports.

The alternative to the National Maglev Network? Ever scarcer and more expensive oil imports from unstable foreign sources, with an inevitable shift to synthetic fuels from coal and oil shale, which will double carbon dioxide emissions and be environmentally catastrophic. There will be no hope of achieving an 80% reduction in carbon dioxide emissions by 2050 AD.

Meeting with US Senate Majority Leader Harry Reid

Meeting with the Majority Leader of the United States Senate was not easy but in 2008 it was very important to our strategy. When Senator Reid joined the Senate in 1987, he was a member of the Environment and Public Works Committee chaired by Senator Moynihan. He participated in the Moynihan hearings on Superconducting Maglev. There was a proposed Transrapid Maglev project between Las Vegas and Anaheim, CA. We hoped that if Senator Reid realized the potential of the 2nd generation superconducting Maglev technology, he might support a Test Facility and Certification of Maglev 2000 for transporting roll-on, roll-off trucks, passengers, and passenger autos.

I (Jim Jordan) went through all of the wickets for an appointment with Senator Reid, starting with a letter requesting a meeting, which led to an appointment with Robert Herbert, Senior Policy Advisor and Appropriations Assistant. Jim Powell flew down to Washington to join me for a briefing of Mr. Herbert in Senator Reid's Hart Building Office on the 5th Floor. Our briefing led to a scheduled meeting with Majority Leader Reid in his Capitol office, S-221.

Visiting the Capitol for a meeting is strenuous. You can't take a taxi or an automobile to the door. It has its advantages, however. You get a great walking tour of Capitol Hill's office buildings and streets. The Capitol is very imposing and the Senate wing, which was built in the 1850s, is an elegant classical structure. You first enter a small wooden security building where Capitol Hill police inspect your bags. Jim Powell, like most engineers, had a shirt-pocket full of pens and pencils that had to be removed before he could be scanned. After passing through the security house you then walk up a ramp to the 1st floor of the Senate Wing. There, guards direct you to a mahogany reception desk where you identify yourself, and what office you have an appointment with. The very pleasant smiling ladies behind the desk call the Majority Leader's office to confirm your visit and issue you a badge and then direct you to the elevators for the second floor.

Thoroughly tagged and guided, we then walked along the elegant 19th century tiled hallways with high vaulted ceilings and walls decorated by Italian artist, Constantino Brumidi. The decorations are stunning. Brumidi used a full palette of colors creating beautiful paintings in the technique of the Renaissance painters where the pigments are applied to the plaster while it is wet. Ornate bronze lighting fixtures that were once gas lights with etched glass globes, now converted to electricity, complete the décor. On the walls, Brumidi depicted American flowers, birds and animals, and scenes from American history. Many of the paintings are done in the "lunettes" over the doorways. As you walk to the elevators, before reaching them you pass through the Brumidi Corridor, as it is now known. There are paintings of Benjamin Franklin, Robert Fulton, with his steamboat, the Clermont steaming on the Hudson River in the background. This beautifully decorated room is a wonder of color.

Walking down these halls surrounded by beautiful art and statuary is like a trip through a art museum of America's history. Recent history is also depicted by artists, who followed after Brumidi's death in 1880. For example, there is a painting of the moon landing. It could be imagined that someday there would be a painting of Jim and Gordon working on the superconducting quadrupole magnet modules with scenes of the Maglev vehicles traveling on elevated guideways alongside an Interstate Highway. Clearly, Maglev is the first new mode of transport since the airplane, and there is a painting of the Wright Brother's first flight at Kitty Hawk in the Capitol and Maglev will be of similar importance to the World economy. You have to be patient but if you can envision something it will happen.

Taking the elevator to the 2nd floor, we were directed to S-221. S-221 is across the hall from the Senate Chamber, a large room full of 100 mahogany lift-top desks. This is what you see televised on C-SPAN, when the Senate is in session. We walked in and were led to a conference room, equally decorated in the elegant and ornate style of the 19th Century. We met Bob Herbert in the room. After we were seated, Senator Reid entered the room and shook hands with Jim Powell and me. He turned to Jim Powell and said, "I have always wanted to meet you," Jim Jordan spoke of Jim's appearance before Senator Moynihan's Committee. Senator Reid said, "Pat Moynihan was my mentor," and added, "he should still be here. You know he died of appendicitis, it was unnecessary." Jim Jordan restated the purpose of this visit, he said that we wanted to get Senator Reid's support for this new Maglev system, which would not need government subsidies, once demonstrated, by carrying high revenue trucks as well as passengers. Jim continued that it would be of special importance to Las Vegas, because it could deliver fresh produce from California along with tourists and their autos. He was very interested and got out a pencil to calculate, along with Jim Powell, the difference in delivery cost and the profit realized for food delivery.

We showed him our plan to build a transcontinental Maglev network and complete it by the 150th anniversary of the original "Golden Spike" at Promontory Point in Utah. The Golden Spike Map became our message. The meeting closed with a heartbeat skipping conclusion when he turned to Bob Herbert and said, "get a hold of Obama, I want to make something of this." We felt that we had reached the Promised Land.

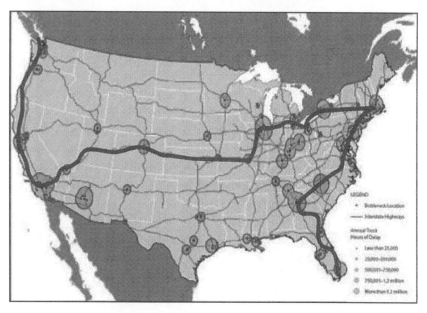

Leaving, I told Bob Herbert that I would stay in touch. As 2008 moved toward the election, our ears were tuned to Maglev and Senator Obama. He mentioned Maglev once in a C-Span televised campaign stop. It was clear that Senator Obama must be elected. Maglev's future was in better hands with Senator Obama.

Next, we started planning for a Maglev effort in Nevada. Jim Jordan called Robert Coullahan, a former business colleague, who had an emergency management and security business in Las Vegas. Jim asked him for help in creating a plan for a Maglev Test and Certification Facility in Nevada. Mr. Coullahan is a very capable and creative thinker, who works very fast. We described what we needed for the Maglev Test and Certification Facility. Within a week, he began to generate the Test Facility Concept. He had a great idea to do more than just test the passenger and freight system but to integrate it with Jim and Gordon's Maglev systems for storing electrical power and carrying large volumes of water. He called the concept SUMMIT (**SU**perconducting **M**aglev **M**ulti **I**ntegrated **T**esting) facility. It addressed 3 areas of major concern for future U.S. transport and energy generation:

1. Reducing the cost and energy of long-distance truck transport together with reducing the pollution and highway damage that trucks cause.

2. Efficient, low cost storage of electrical energy generated by clean, non-polluting, intermittent, renewable energy sources like wind and solar power.

3. Low cost (less than by pipeline), energy efficient long-distance transport of large amounts of fresh water to regions with insufficient water resources, especially the U.S. Southwest.

Bob Coullahan, Jim Powell and Gordon Danby wrote the SUMMIT White Paper and sent it to Robert Herbert. It said, "The three areas are of particular importance to Nevada. The Interstate-15 (I-15) highway corridor is heavily congested, with long distance trucks being a major contributor to the congestion. They emit large quantities of pollution, especially diesel particulates that are very harmful to peoples' health. The highway trucks cause extensive damage to highways, shortening their life, and increase highway maintenance and repair costs. A single 18-wheeler highway truck causes as much damage as thousands of autos, according to estimates from transportation experts.

They added: "wind and solar renewable energy resources hold great promise in supplying large amounts of clean energy without the greenhouse gas emissions that are contributing to global warming. Nevada is a very attractive location for large amounts of wind and solar power. However, wind power is highly variable, and only blows about 20% of the time, frequently blowing when electrical demand is low, and frequently not blowing when demand is high. Solar power is more regular, but at low output during peak demand periods in the morning and in the late afternoon. If wind and solar power are to become a major source of energy for the U.S., a low cost, efficient way to store large amounts of electrical output from them must be developed, so that the energy can be delivered to the electrical grid when needed.

"Finally, Nevada and the Southwest in general are very short of water. Water flow down the Colorado River is diminishing, Lake Mead is drying up, and underground water table levels are rapidly dropping. There is abundant fresh water in the Columbia River, but pipeline delivery from it would be much too expensive for Nevada, Southern California, Arizona, and New Mexico."

Bob Herbert called and said he was interested in the Water Carrier Project.

Later, after the November, 2008 Election, the economy was in "freefall" and unemployment was reaching very high levels. There was a lot of talk in Washington about an emergency bailout and a stimulus package. We thought the Maglev Test and Certification facility was a perfect project to help insure long-term economic recovery.

We summarized the SUMMIT concept in an email to Bob Herbert when the House and the Senate were considering the American Recovery and Reinvestment Act during the first months of President Obama's term.

"Bob,

I respectfully recommend that $330 million be included in the new Jobs Bill. This will lead to an immediate 100 test facility jobs in Nevada, new construction work jobs and will serve as a magnet to attract a manufacturing industry to fabricate the guideway plates, and the components of the vehicles.

We believe that this could be a powerful message for Senator Reid to give to the citizens of NV because of its great potential for new jobs, making NV a center for the storage of wind and solar energy generated in the Southwest, and the long-distance delivery of fresh water from the Columbia River and other sources to drought stricken areas in the American Southwest.

*The attached SUMMIT (**SU**perconducting **M**aglev **M**ulti **I**ntegrated **T**esting) facility proposed by Bob Coullahan, President & Chief Operating Officer of Readiness Resource Group, Inc., 4055 S. Spencer Street - Suite 222, Las Vegas, Nevada 89119 addresses 3 areas of major concern for U.S. transport and energy generation:*

1. Reducing the cost and energy required for long-distance truck transport, together with reduction of the pollution and highway damage that they cause.

2. Efficient, low cost storage of electrical energy generated by clean, non-polluting renewable energy sources.

3. Low cost, energy efficient long-distance transport of large amounts of fresh water to regions with insufficient water resources, especially the U.S. Southwest.

His very cost effective proposal creates a testbed for the American invented Maglev 2000 2nd generation superconducting Maglev for demonstrating the superior performance and cost of Maglev. The total cost for the 5-year plan is $330 million, only 55% of the previous engineering projection for the cost of demonstrating the Maglev.

Moreover, Bob Coullahan's plan includes the energy storage and water transport functions as well as the passenger and heavy truck transport.

The Nevada facility achieves its cost-effectiveness by testing the system on-grade, avoiding the high cost of an elevated guideway. We will be able to show that the Maglev alternative is a better option for the future U.S. land transport. The guideway will be identical to the elevated guideway but it will be on-grade including a demonstration of the unique planar operating capability of the Maglev 2000's 4-pole magnets on a rail-road track section of the test facility and electronic switching."

As the 2010 election year progressed, Senator Reid, who was up for reelection, announced that he was supporting a privately financed high speed rail project that would run from Las Vegas to Victorville,

California. He said that he had been waiting for Maglev, but that no one had really done any work. We were stunned by the news. No Promised Land for us – yet. But we are not ready to roll over and die. We are confident that if we continue on with our strategy and continue to respond to opportunities. Maglev will come to pass.

Finally, a very recent example of seizing an unexpected opportunity is described next because it reveals a very important new capability that may pave the way for Maglev's successful entry in the market.

The MAPS Excursion to Schenectady – Following Tom Edison's and Charles Steinmetz's Footsteps

Last summer (July 2010), our colleague in Las Vegas, Bob Coullahan, was exploring electric power and energy websites for ideas on how to graphically depict the MAPS system. Bob was working with Douglas Rike, an engineer with extensive computer aided design ability and skill in advanced computer graphics and animation design, to develop ways to present MAPS to potential investors. In surfing the web, Bob found the G.E. Ecomagination Challenge website that announced a competition for innovative green energy ideas, with a significant prize and promise of contact with G.E. Capital and other venture capital firms. Applications were due by the end of July. Bob notified us of the opportunity on July 13th 2010. General Electric is the perfect large manufacturing company, with a 132 year industrial history. It could implement Superconducting Maglev technology in the U.S. and worldwide. G.E. was a significant wind generator manufacturer and MAPS was a great fit for their market.

Bob and Doug went to work and came up with a great proposal for a MAPS System installation to be located in the mountains near Las Vegas. The site was located in an environmentally approved site for green energy applications with access to the grid. Bob, Jim Powell and Gordon Danby put their heads together and prepared an application. Later, we were notified that our MAPS entry had been accepted to be a potential finalist for the Challenge.

After several telephone interviews we learned that we had been selected to be one of the 8 to 10 promising energy storage technology teams invited for a presentation at G.E.'s Global Research Center in Schenectady, NY. We felt that the Tom Edison entrepreneurial spirit and the genius of Charles Steinmetz had touched Maglev. I was confident that we would win the prize and become a G.E. business partner. Why so confident? There were a number of reasons. GE is an ideal large industrial partner for Superconducting Maglev development. They manufacture MRI (Magnetic Resonance Imaging) equipment, which use superconducting magnets. They had been manufacturers of superconducting wire but spun off this division to create a company that is a major supplier of high temperature superconducting wire. G.E. is very big in rail transportation, and were promoting a new hybrid diesel electric locomotive for the Tampa to Orlando HSR route. There were negatives like G.E.'s alliance with Alstom, the major European steel wheel rail locomotive manufacturing consortium, which was vying to participate in the Obama Administration's high speed intercity passenger rail initiative, and the importance of their jet engine business with the aircraft industry. Despite the negatives there were two pluses which, in my view, balanced the negatives.

First Plus: Jeff Immelt, G.E.'s Chairman and CEO, wrote an opinion piece for the London based Financial Times, July 8, 2010, which committed G.E. to a stronger export position. Mr. Immelt, Chairman of the President's Economic Recovery Advisory Board, likely agreed with the President's goal of doubling U.S. exports in 5 years. G.E. is America's second-largest exporter, after Boeing.

We wanted to take Mr. Immelt at his word, and the Ecomagination Challenge as a serious effort to stimulate homegrown technology and jobs. The reader will see his analysis and remedy follows very closely those that we have recommended in this book and also had recommended to officials in the White House.

"Innovation can give America back its greatness

By Jeff Immelt

Published: July 8 2009 18:31 | Last updated: July 8 2009 18:31 Financial Times [spelling is British]

Over the past few decades, many in business and government bet that the US could transform itself from an innovative, export-orientated - powerhouse to an economy based on services and consumption – and that we could still expect to prosper. For a time, it looked like a can't-miss bet.

Then we missed – badly. Trillions of dollars vanished, along with America's competitive edge. An economic hurricane shook our financial system to its foundation, leaving our middle class hurt, bewildered and looking for cover. General Electric was not perfect through all of this but, throughout our 130-year history, we have adapted and remained competitive.

The challenge ahead is not impossible. The first step is recognising that we cannot simply go back to the way things were. This downturn is not simply another turning of the wheel but a fundamental transformation. We are, essentially, resetting the US economy.

An American renewal must be built on technology. We must make a serious national commitment to improve our manufacturing infrastructure and increase exports. We need to dispel the myth that American consumer spending can lead our recovery. Instead, we need to draw on 230 years of ingenuity to renew the country's dedication to innovation, new technologies and productivity.

GE plans to help lead this effort. We have restructured during the downturn, adjusting to market realities, and have continued to increase our investment in research and development. We are reinvesting in American jobs in places such as Michigan and upstate New York. We plan to launch more new products than at any time in our history.

One place where GE is reaping the benefits of this strategy is our plant in Greenville, South Carolina, where we make turbines for gas and wind power generation. We are now selling their products around the world. In fact, their biggest customer is Saudi Electric Corporation.

Some people subscribe to a Darwinian theory of economic evolution – that America has naturally evolved from farming to manufacturing to services. We should pay attention to the example of countries that are growing rapidly by emphasising technology and manufacturing, especially China. They know where the money is and where the opportunities reside and they aim to get there first.

America has to get back in the game. Renewing American competitiveness will not be accomplished through protectionism, but by rebuilding American technology, manufacturing and exports. To get back to making great things, we should clearly strive for a manufacturing workforce that is growing.

To do this, the US government can play a catalytic role. America has a long history of spending that prepares new industries to thrive for generations. Today, my country needs an industrial strategy built around helping companies to succeed with investment that will drive innovation and support high-technology manufacturing and exports. And it needs a robust trade policy that seeks to open markets abroad for US companies while being fair to international competition.

I consider myself to be the chief executive of a global company that is headquartered in the US. We are firmly committed to globalisation. Our employees – in India, in China, in the US and the UK – deserve to be able to compete and win around the world. At the same time, American business leaders have a responsibility to drive competitiveness in their own country.

On a personal note, I would hate to think that the lasting impression of this generation of American business is the one that exists today. We can do better. We have made our companies globally competitive; now we must do the same for our country. We can help solve difficult problems and create an optimistic future.

The reset economy has clarified the scope of the American challenge and offered us a chance for renewal. The best companies will concentrate on real value and real needs and invest for the long term, creating a firm, new foundation on which a stable, strong economy can grow.

The US has faced difficult odds many times. We have beaten them throughout history. With a commitment to technology and manufacturing-driven exports leading the way, America can do so once again.

The writer is chairman and chief executive of the General Electric Company

Second Plus: the "Sign"

My colleagues did not know about my childhood but it is worth telling so that the reader can appreciate why I (Jordan) felt that the G.E. invitation was sort of a remembered "Sign" that quickened my interest.

As a young boy in Ceasar Cone Elementary School built by the Cone Mills Corporation for the children of its mill workers, in Greensboro, North Carolina, once America's center for textiles, I had some wonderful teachers who let you read anything that you wanted in the school library. I didn't dote on the text books. The library was my secret pleasure. I explored the library during the "reading periods" and checked out books that interested me. When new books arrived my teachers would suggest books that they thought would interest me. One book, which had a lifetime influence on me, is the biography of Charles Steinmetz and the account of his work at G.E. Steinmetz was a mathematician and electrical engineer. He fostered the development of alternating current that expanded the electric power industry in the United States and formulated mathematical models for engineers. His ground-breaking discoveries in understanding hysteresis enabled engineers to design better electric motors for industry. Steinmetz also helped build the firm that developed transformers for electrical power transmission. In 1893 the company, along with his patents and designs, was bought by Thomas Edison's newly formed General Electric Company. Later Steinmetz founded the G.E. Research Lab.

I drew a parallel between Tom Edison and Steinmetz and Jeff Immelt and Powell and Danby. It seemed entirely possible that G.E. would see the value of the Powell and Danby patents and would fold the effort into G.E. with their new commitment to developing home grown products for export.

At G.E.'s Global Research Center

Bob Coullahan and Doug Rike put together a great PowerPoint presentation with terrific embedded animations. The presentation was designed to integrate presentations by Jim Powell and Gordon Danby about the system, how it works, and its economics; then Bob would describe the Nevada Test Facility and how it worked.

We arrived at the G.E. Global Research Center in Schenectady on a cold winter day for a dinner with the other contestants, G.E. executives, and participating venture capital representatives. Our presentation was scheduled for the next day and Jim and Gordon drove up from Long Island for the afternoon presentation. The presentation was 20 minutes with 20 minutes for more questions and answers. It was a tight schedule but doable.

While waiting to make the presentation, we viewed Tom Edison's desk, which is displayed in the lobby. A glass enclosed ticker tape on the desk is a reminder that G.E.'s fortunes depend on the stock market, a reality that would not likely change.

The presentation went very smoothly. Watching eyeballs, I left with the feeling that we had caught the attention of the audience, but uncertain whether G.E.'s Executives would see the value of this technology and how it would fit with their windmill business and would give the award to us.

Before heading for home, Bob Coullahan found the City Museum of Schenectady. What a thrill. Upon entering the museum, there was the Steinmetz desk and an exhibit devoted to Charles Steinmetz. This genius held 200 patents upon retirement. He was an early worker on Alternating Current. Maglev vehicles are propelled on a wave of an AC current. Increasing the frequency of the AC waves increases the speed. If he had been at our presentation, he would have appreciated Powell and Danby's use of Alternating Current and would have been fascinated with the phenomenon of zero resistance in superconducting material.

About a week after leaving the GE Global Research Center, G.E.'s Senior Vice President contacted the Maglev team. "Your presentation was very well received by the GE group, but after our internal discussions the Maglev opportunity wasn't one of the 3 that made it to the top of the list. I'd say this is mostly because of the early stage and substantial capital and time required for the demonstration project. Several of us were intrigued by the technology's high efficiency and inherently large scale so we would definitely like to keep in touch as you develop your demonstration project in Nevada."

He offered several specific contacts with power project developers, pumped hydro developers, the top global Architectural-Engineering firms, and several private equity firms.

Peering into the Future.

Now that we have finished the inside story of how America has failed, so far, to take the World lead in Maglev, with all its economic and environmental benefits, what's next? Which country will take the lead? It probably will be China. They have captured the lead in wind and solar power, and are building lots of new reactors. While the U.S. fiddles, they soon will dominate World manufacturing. Clearly, Maglev will evolve from the first generation Japanese and German systems into a more capable, much lower cost, advanced 2nd generation system. This evolution will happen in the next few years. The new Maglev 2000 system cannot be kept in a safe.

Which country will build 2nd generation Maglev, and reap its benefits in lower costs and less energy transportation, millions of new jobs, Billions of dollars in exports, and a less polluting environment? Will it be America, as we hope, or some other country? The decision time is now. If the U.S. fails to seize the opportunity, which country will?

China, Russia, India, South Korea, Germany, France, Britain, Brazil, among others, are possibilities. The most likely is China. Currently, China produces half of the World's concrete, 40% of its aluminum and 38% of its steel, the major materials for the Maglev guideway beams and piers. China could easily mass produce prefabricated guideway beams with the aluminum loop panels and electric equipment already attached, pre-fabricated piers to accommodate terrain elevation changes, ready to operate Maglev vehicles with their superconducting magnets, and refrigeration equipment.

All of the Maglev components could be manufactured in China, and transported by container ship to the U.S. and other countries, as decided by China. China is the World leader in container ship exports. One large container ship could transport 20 miles of prefabricated elevated monorail guideway, piers, vehicles, etc. to seaports near the Maglev construction site, at low cost. After unloading at the seaport, the prefabricated beams and piers could be quickly transported by highway trucks to the Maglev construction site, again at low cost, there to be quickly erected by conventional cranes onto pre-poured concrete footings. The jobs? Almost all in China. Cost of the Maglev system?

The Fight for Maglev   Maglev: Third Round

Considerably less than in the U.S., because of China's much lower labor costs.

How much raw materials are required for the 2nd generation Maglev 2000 guideway per two way mile, and how much do they cost? The following table shows the amounts required and their 2010 costs. Amounts of material are based on detailed 3-D computer analyses and fabrication of a full-scale prototype beam.

Material Amounts and Costs Per two way Mile for the Advanced 2nd Generation Maglev 2000 Guideway System

Basis: 100 foot long Guideway beams; 106 beams per two way mile 30 foot average pier height; piers use ½ of beam materials used in a 100 foot beam. The beam uses 30 cubic yards of concrete, 1.6 tons of stainless steel rebar, 3.1 tons of aluminum conductor, and 4 cubic yards of polymer concrete.

Note: 1 ton =2,000 pounds = 0.9 metric tonne; 1 metric tonne = 1,000 kg.

Guideway Beams and Pier Materials

Amt/two way Mile	Unit Cost	$ Cost/two way Mile
Beam – 3,000 cubic yds concrete	$100/cubic yd	$300,000
Pier – 1500 cubic yds concrete	$100/cubic yd	$150,000
Beam – 420 cubic yds polymer concrete	$800/cubic yd	$340,000
Beam – Stainless Steel Rebars – 170 Tons	$4500/ton	$760,000
Piers – Stainless Steel Rebars – 85 Tons	$4500/ton	$380,000
Beam – Aluminum Loops – 330 Tons	$2,200/ton	$730,000
	Total Materials Cost	**$2,660,000**
Transportation Cost		
China to the by Container Ship – 10,600 tons	$100/Ton	$1,060,000
Truck Transport for 200 miles in	$0.30/Ton Mile	$640,000
	Total Transport Cost	$1,700,000
	Total Cost, Materials + Transport	**$4,360,000**

The total of $4,360,000 does not include the additional costs of manufacturing labor, operating cost of manufacturing equipment; electronic power switches for the Linear Synchronous Motor Propulsion

System, pre-poured concrete footings, and erection of the beams and piers by conventional cranes at the Maglev construction site. The major portion of this additional cost is if manufactured in the U.S., adding the above material costs, to the labor cost, switch cost, etc., and emplacing them on the rights-of-way of the Interstates, our projected cost per 2-way mile is 25 million dollars, roughly 10 times the cost of materials.

Manufacturing the guideway beams and piers in China, with their much lower labor costs, and adding in the above extra costs for electronic switches, etc., plus the cost of shipping the components and piers to the U.S. by container ship, the projected cost of the Maglev America Project, if it were built by China, would be approximately ½ of the cost of manufacturing it in America, e.g., about 12 million dollars per mile. The entire 28,800 mile Maglev America Project would then cost only $340 Billion, compared to the all-American project cost of about $700 Billion.

How fast could China build the Maglev America Project? Very fast. With a target date of May 10, 2019, the 150th Anniversary of the completion of Lincoln's Transcontinental Railroad at Promontory Point, Utah, China would probably be ready to start construction of the Maglev America Project in 2015, following a 30 month testing and certification period starting in the Spring of 2012. (China could complete its testing much faster than we could in the US because of a more rigorous safety testing program which would be required by the US)

Over the 5 years following 2014, China would manufacture, ship, and erect almost 5,000 miles of guideway annually. Could they physically do it? Yes! China produces roughly 3 Billion tons of concrete annually, 60 times greater than the annual amount required for a 6 year construction period of the Maglev America Project. China produces 18 million short tons of aluminum annually, 10 times greater than the annual amount needed for the 6 year Maglev America Project construction period. China produces 10 million tons of stainless steel annually: 8 times the amount required for the 5,000 miles of the Maglev America Project constructed each year. China ships over 400 million tons of goods by container ship annually, 8 times more than the tonnage shipped for the Maglev America Project. In the U.S., intercity highway trucks transport 1.5 Trillion ton-miles per year of goods, 150 times greater than required for the Maglev America Project.

The Maglev America Project built by China? While not exactly a piece of cake, they could do it with an economy whose GDP is growing 10% per year. China graduates hundreds of thousands of engineers each year. The starting salary for a young Chinese engineer with a BS is only 2,600 dollars per year, 1/20 of a starting American engineer. China has the talent, an extremely large work force, and the very low manufacturing cost to pull off the Maglev America Project by 2019, if they would choose to do so.

Would China choose to do so? That is a much more difficult question to answer. China built and now operates in Shanghai the 1st generation German Transrapid Maglev System. China does not appear to be moving ahead with more Transrapid routes, probably because of its very high capital cost. Instead, China appears to be focusing on High Speed Steel-Wheel-on-Rail Systems for their own use and export. There are indications that they might help finance the proposed HSR System in California.

So far, China has not realized that the 2nd generation Maglev System offers much greater benefits and opportunities than High Speed Rail and the 1st generation Maglev systems. Once China understands that 2nd generation Maglev is much superior to HSR and 1st generation Maglev, we believe that it will enter the Maglev Race.

Second, does China have the financial muscle to build the Maglev America Project, and is the return on investment attractive enough to make China interested in doing it. Most emphatically, yes! The 340 Billion dollar construction cost of the Maglev America Project over a 6 year period, if carried out by China, is only 58 Billion dollars per year. While this is a lot of money, it is dwarfed by the Trillions of U.S. dollars held by China in American bonds. China would barely notice the reduction in their holdings of American debt, if they were to use a portion of it to build the Maglev America Project.

From a return on investment point of view, China would hit the jackpot with the Maglev America Project. For a 340 Billion dollar investment, the net revenues back to the investment group that financed the construction would be on the order of 300 Billion dollars per year, assuming that China charged the same transport fares that airlines and trucking companies currently charge. Over a 30 year period, the investment group would receive 9 Trillion dollars of profit for a 340 Billion dollar investment.

Of course, the net revenues would probably be somewhat less, say 150 Billion dollars per year, with the difference going to lower fares on the Maglev Network to attract users away from the other modes of transport, plus fees to U.S. Government entities, federal, state, and local, to ensure happy cooperation.

Okay, China could physically build the Maglev Project in just a few years, it has scads of funds to do the project, and it would be a real money maker. What else would they want?

Now we get into the strategic political and business aspects. Would China really want the U.S. to have a 21st Century national transport system that greatly increased American productivity, export potential, and World power? Probably not. Why build up competitors? America has done that for the last 50 years and it's been disastrous.

Better for China to rapidly build the 21st Century transport system in its own country as fast as possible and other countries from which it can get shipments of fuel, minerals, food, and other resources. They would depend on China for modern transport and China would capture their ever scarcer and more expensive resources, with America out in the cold.

The smart strategy for China would not be to totally refuse 21st Century Maglev technology to the U.S., but rather employ a "slow-roll" policy. Promise the U.S. to build Maglev in America and help it acquire the technology but drag out the process for many years. Yes, America will get a Maglev Network with help from China, but it will take 40 years to achieve. This keeps the U.S. hobbled in obsolete 20th Century transport systems, and helps to keep America from developing its own Maglev system.

Great strategy! We only hope that America's leaders are too smart to fall for it. Already, California is embracing China's offer to help build and finance a High Speed Rail system in the State. Not a good sign.

America is at the crossroads for 21st Century transport. Will we develop our own path that benefits the country, or just accept obsolete and expensive technology that does not meet our Nation's needs?

Chapter Ten

Maglev Launch: Finally, the Final Frontier

"It is morning. I stand by the mirror
And tie my tie once more.
While waves far off in a pale rose twilight
Crash on a white sand shore.
I stand by a mirror and comb my hair:
How small and white my face!—
The green earth tilts through a sphere of air
And bathes in a flame of space.

There are houses hanging above the stars
And stars hung under a sea...
And a sun far off in a shell of silence
Dapples my walls for me...."

Senlin: A Biography – Part II

Conrad Aiken

The Earth is a tiny, tiny, tiny part of the Universe, and humanity is a tiny, tiny, tiny part of life in the Universe. One would think that we humans would be consumed with the desire to find out what's out there – to have our small faces looking at what's on the Moon, Mars, Europa, Pluto, Venus, the asteroids, and all the other bodies in the Solar System. Using very large telescopes to directly image in detail what is happening on the planets around distant stars. Using microwave and laser beams to communicate with extraterrestrial civilizations. To understand how the Universe began, what other kinds of life are out there, where we're headed, and so on.

One would think so. Instead, what things are most important to people today? Watching mind numbing TV shows and movies, reading about celebrities and sex scandals – just check out the Magazines in your local supermarket – buying stuff to impress friends, relatives, acquaintances, neighbors, co-workers, and strangers, climbing the money/power ladder, fighting other cultures and countries for political domination, and so on. Yes, still a little bit of interest in what's beyond Earth, but not much.

The enthusiasm for space exploration was stronger 40 years ago when Neil Armstrong stepped onto the Moon, but has declined steadily since then. Why? And can that past enthusiasm be recovered, and become even stronger?

Before answering these questions, let me (Powell) make a small confession. As a youngster in the 1940s and 50s. I devoured the stories from the grand masters of science fiction –Asimov, Heinlein, A.E. Van Vogt, H.G. Wells, Del Rey, Jack Williamson, Frederik Pohl, Arthur Clarke, Kuttner, C.L. Moore, Hubbard, Shiras, Tiptree and even E.E. Smith. They were far more exciting than listening to the Green Hornet, the Lone Ranger, Jack Benny, Fred Allen, The Life of Riley and others on the radio even though I enjoyed their programs.

But in the great science fiction stories, rockets were the key. Rockets quickly took you wherever you wanted without problems. You didn't have to spend vast sums of money and take years to get a rocket. You just jumped on-board and took off. Rockets were always there for the encounters with aliens, saving the Earth, etc.

However, in the real World of space exploration and travel, rockets are not a tiny part of the story, they ARE the story! Today, it costs 5,000 dollars to put a pound of payload into Low Earth Orbit (LEO). A pound in Geosynchronous Earth Orbit (GEO) costs about 10 times as much. To the Moon or Mars, or beyond, don't ask. The extremely high cost of rockets effectively chains humanity to the Earth.

This is why we need a new way – Maglev Launch – to reach space. Maglev Launch can deliver payloads to LEO at 50 dollars per pound, 1/100 the cost of rockets, and less than 100 dollars per pound to GEO. It can launch hundreds of thousands of tons of payload per year, compared to the present World launch rate of a few hundred tons per year, with the failure rate for Maglev Launch far smaller than that of rockets. Maglev Launch does not use propellants. Instead, it electrically accelerates spacecraft carrying cargo and humans to orbital speeds on the surface of the Earth, from which they coast up into space. The cost of the electricity used is trivial, only 50 cents per pound of payload.

Rocket launch costs are very high because the big, very expensive rocket is thrown away after the launch. Imagine delivering refrigerators by helicopter, and throwing the helicopter away after it delivers its load. The cost of refrigerators would be enormous. Now imagine that you deliver refrigerators using a truck that can make thousands of deliveries, at much lower cost per refrigerator. Maglev Launch is that truck. All the expensive equipment remains on the ground to be used over and over again for launching. The spacecraft that carry cargo into orbit use lightweight, simple, low cost structures with a payload fraction that is much higher than possible using rockets.

Before describing how Maglev Launch works, here are some examples of major new capabilities in space that Maglev Launch can do and that rockets cannot, in Q and A format with accompanying figures:

Q1: Can Maglev Launch protect Earth from deadly asteroid and comet impacts?

A. Yes, for 100% protection, we will need large numbers of high resolution telescopes and high velocity interceptors in orbit. Asteroid (Figure 1) and comet threats must be detected far away at great distances so that they can be intercepted without endangering Earth. Multiple interceptors are required in case some fail or miss the target. Second and third waves of interceptors are needed to intercept debris threats. There is no way rockets can station enough detectors and interceptors in orbit to guarantee 100% protection.

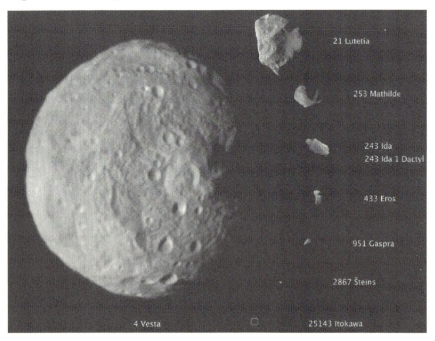

Figure 1 This Composite Image Shows the Comparative Sizes of Eight Asteroids

Q2. Can Maglev Launch enable solar power satellites to beam electric power down to Earth?

A. Yes. Beaming power down to Earth from solar power satellites in GEO orbit (Figure 2), as proposed by Glaser in 1979 (1) can supply all of Earth's energy requirements in a clean, environmentally safe manner. No need for fossil fuels, nuclear reactors, or expensive renewable energy sources. Beaming power at distances of almost 100 miles has already been demonstrated in the Hawaiian Islands (2). The cost of launching space solar satellites into GEO orbit using rockets is prohibitive – about 500,000 dollars per kilowatt of delivered power, based on a 4 kilogram per kilowatt solar power satellite. This is 100 times greater than the cost per kilowatt for power plants based on Earth. With Maglev Launch the cost to place solar power satellites in orbit will be only about 1,000 dollars per kilowatt.

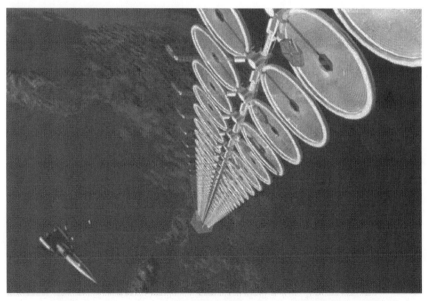

Figure 2 Sun Tower – Solar Power Satellite System (Credit NASA)

Q3: Can Maglev Launch put sun shields in space to stop global warming?

A. Yes. Placing lightweight, thin film structures at the Lagrange 1 point (Figure 3) between the Earth and the Sun, as proposed by Angell (3) and others, could block out 1 to 2% of the sunlight that would otherwise fall on the Earth enough to stop global warming. The concept is valid except that the launch cost using rockets is enormous, many Trillions of dollars. Using Maglev Launch, the cost would be on the order of a Trillion dollars, 1/60 of current annual World GDP. This appears an acceptable price to save the Earth from global catastrophe.

Figure 3 The Basic Function of a Space Lens is to Mitigate Global Warming.

Q4. Will Maglev Launch let us set up colonies on Mars? Explore Europa's oceans? Mine the asteroids?

A. Yes. The hundreds of thousands of tons per year that Maglev Launch will send into space will allow astronauts travel to and from permanent large colonies on Mars (Figure 4), land on Europa to see if there is life in its sub-surface oceans, mine the asteroids for precious metals, and many other activities that could never be accomplished by rockets. The North Polar Cap on Mars is ideal for colonies. With water from the mile thick ice sheet and the carbon dioxide from the Martian atmosphere, the colonists can manufacture virtually all of the supplies and food they require.

Figure 4 Artist impression of a Mars settlement with Cutaway View

Credit NASA Ames Research Center

Q5. Can Maglev Launch enable us to detect and view life on planets in other star systems?

A. Yes. Using Maglev Launch to place very large telescopes in space – much bigger than the Hubble Telescope (Figure 5) – we will be able to image in great detail extraterrestrial planets to see if there are structures and other evidence of alien life and intelligence. Imagine gazing at an Empire State Building on a distant planet light years away.

Figure 5 Hubble Space Telescope (Credit NASA)

Q6. Will Maglev Launch make it possible for ordinary folk to go into space and stay at space hotels? Even travel to the Moon?

A. Yes. So far, a few tourists have visited the International Space Station (ISS) at a round trip ticket cost of 20 million dollars each. When Gen-2, the second generation of Maglev Launch starts operation, the round trip ticket to a space hotel orbiting the Earth (Figure 6) will be about 20,000 dollars – expensive compared to a cruise ship, but worth it for many people as a once in a lifetime experience. A round trip to the Moon? More expensive, maybe 100,000 dollars. After reaching low-earth orbit, travelers would board a "moon taxi", which would orbit between the Earth and the Moon, skimming over the Moon's surface every 28 days.

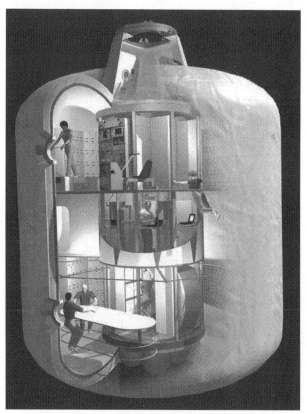

Figure 6 Space Hotels Orbiting the Earth

(Credit: NASA)

The above examples are only a small fraction of the new and wonderful things that humans will be able to do in space when Maglev Launch is built. So we come back to the fundamental question. Will humanity want to explore and expand into space when Maglev Launch makes it feasible, or will it just shrug and say, `that's nice' and stay rooted to, and only interested in, what happens on Earth.

Many argue that humanity should focus on Earth and not space, and that humans don't need to, and should not, go into space – that robot probes can do everything and do it better. Others, ourselves included, argue that man's destiny is to explore new worlds and discover unknown things.

The argument, not new, repeats human history. There have been many past societies that closed themselves off from the World around them – old China, Japan, etc. — and many societies that eagerly explored and developed new lands – the Romans, European nations, America, etc. Think of the known explorers – Julius Caesar, Alexander the Great, Marco Polo, Zheng He, Magellan, Vasco de Gama, Columbus, Champlain, Hudson, Lewis and Clark, De Soto, Cortez, Pizarro, Scott and Shackelton, Nansen, Heyerdahl and Amundsen, and on and on. And for every famous explorer, there have been hundreds of forgotten ones.

We have no doubt that once it becomes possible for humans to travel into space in much greater numbers and at much lower cost, there will be many thousands of persons wanting to explore and develop the Solar System.

The next questions are: How does Maglev Launch work? What can it do? What are the technical challenges? How soon can it start launching? How much will it cost to build? To operate?

And most important of all – Who will control it? Will it be peaceful or start an arms race in space?

Answers to the first set of questions can be arrived at since they are technical and non-emotional. Answers to the last questions are much more difficult, since they depend on human attitudes and emotions. Throughout history technological breakthroughs have produced both good and bad outcomes. Gunpowder, atomic energy, rockets, aircraft, and so on.

The Fight for Maglev   Maglev Launch

Maglev Launch must be developed cooperatively by the World's nations and operated as international facilities, open to all for peaceful applications. Developed by competing nations in an arms race to dominate space, it would result in greater world tensions and increase the risk of conflicts. Time will tell which path Maglev Launch will follow.

Maglev Launch Systems

There are two Maglev Launch systems. Gen-1, the first that will be built, is a high g (acceleration) cargo only launch system. After reaching orbital speed, Gen-1 cargo vehicles leave the acceleration tunnel which is located in high altitude terrain. The vehicles then coast up to orbit through the remaining atmosphere, experiencing strong but manageable aerodynamic heating and deceleration forces. Protective coatings and coolants for the cargo craft do not significantly increase launch cost.

The second generation Gen-2 system launches both passengers and cargo. Gen-2 spacecraft accelerate at only 2 to 3 g instead of 20 to 30 g

Table 1 Two Maglev Launch Systems.

Two StarTram Systems

Gen-1 System	Gen-2 System
• Cargo only, non reusable vehicle	• Passenger & cargo reusable spacecraft
• High acceleration (30 G)	
• Short acceleration tunnel (~100 km @ 8 km/sec)	• Low acceleration (~2 to 3 g)
• Launch from surface into atmosphere @ high elevation (> 4000 meters)	• Long acceleration tunnel (~1000 km @ 8 km/sec)
	• Launch into atmosphere @ > 20 km altitude
• Coast upwards thru atmosphere to orbit	• Coast upwards thru magnetically levitated, evacuated launch tube to > 20 Atm before entering atmosphere
• Substantial aerodynamic deceleration (~10 G) and heating rates (~25 KW/cm² at Stagnation Point)	• Modest aerodynamic deceleration (~1 G) and heating rates (~3 KW/cm² at Stagnation Point)
• Near term (next 10 to 20 years)	• Longer term (20 to 30 years)

for Gen-1, in a longer acceleration tunnel. To avoid the high aerodynamic heating and deceleration forces experienced by Gen-1 cargo craft, the Gen-2 spacecraft transitions from its ground level evacuated acceleration tunnel into an evacuated magnetically levitated launch tube that ascends to very high altitude, e.g., ~20 km (65,000 feet), where it enters the atmosphere. At this altitude, air density is only a few percent of that at ground level, resulting in low aerodynamic heating and deceleration forces.

The technology base for Gen-1 systems – Maglev, superconductors and vehicle structures capable of withstanding high heating rate – already exists. A Gen-1 facility could begin operation in the next 10 to 20 years. The Gen-1 and Gen-2 Maglev Launch systems (4,5,6,7,8) use the same approach for levitating and accelerating spacecraft to orbital speed, with the principal difference being the acceleration level. At the Gen-1 tunnel exit, the cargo craft enters the atmosphere through an "MHD window". A mechanical shutter closes off the evacuated tube between launches, opening a few seconds before the launch minimizing air leakage through the MHD window. To reduce aerodynamic drag and heating of the Gen-1 craft as it travels in the atmosphere, the altitude of the exit point is typically in the range of 4,000 to 7,000 meters (13,000 to 22,000 feet). Atmospheric drag and heating analyses find that the cargo craft can coast up to orbit without damage.

TABLE 2

Gen-1 StarTram Features and Capabilities

- Gen-1 Maglev levitation and LSM propulsion design based on Powell-Danby inventions and Japanese operating Maglev system
- Uses mature reliable, low cost Nb-Ti superconductor and cryogenic system technology
- Electrical launch energy generated by conventional power plant and stored for acceleration in Superconducting Magnetic Energy Storage (SMES) loops
  - Stored DC energy converted to AC power for LSM propulsion during acceleration using electronic inverter devices
- Exit of evacuated acceleration tunnel is closed to atmosphere by mechanical shutter and outer thin plastic film
  - After Gen-1 cargo craft exits external air leakage into tunnel while shutter is closing is minimized by "MHD Pump" that forces ionized air outwards
- Gen-1 cargo craft reference design
  - 2 meters OD, 13 meters long, 8 km/sec launch velocity
  - 40 metric ton total weight, 35 ton payload
  - 10 launches daily, 128,000 tons of payload per year
  - 30 G acceleration

The larger, lower g Gen-2 passenger/cargo spacecraft enter an evacuated, magnetically levitated tube and coast upwards to ~20 km (65,000 feet) where they enter the atmosphere. The launch tube has high current superconducting (SC) cables that magnetically interact with a second set of high current SC cables on the surface beneath, creating a levitation force of several metric tons per meter of tube length. The levitation force is greater than the weight of the launch tube plus its SC cables and tethers, resulting in a net upwards force on the tube. In turn, the levitated tube is anchored to the ground by high tensile strength, lightweight Kevlar or Spectra tethers. (Figure 7) For insertion into LEO orbit, a ΔV (change in velocity) of 0.34 km/sec to finalize the orbit is easily supplied by a small rocket on the Maglev Launch spacecraft. For a GEO orbit, the ΔV burn is somewhat larger, 1.5 km/sec.

The Gen-1 system launches cargo craft directly into the atmosphere from the end of the ground acceleration tunnel. Table 2 summarizes the principal features and capabilities of the Gen-1 Maglev Launch system. The cargo craft has a nominal diameter of 2 meters and a length of 13 meters, with a total weight of 40 metric tons comprising a 35 ton payload and 5 ton structural weight. The cargo craft has 12 lines of superconducting (SC) loops, with each line of loops occupying a 30 degree section of the surface. Each line has 12 independent SC loops of alternating magnetic polarity. Each loop has a width of 0.50 meter and a length along the cargo craft of 1.0 meter.

The superconducting loops on the Gen-1 cargo craft magnetically induce currents in aluminum loops on the walls of the acceleration tunnel, levitating it as it moves along the tunnel. A second set of aluminum loops in the tunnel will carry AC currents that magnetically accelerate the craft. The cargo craft essentially ride the AC current wave, increasing its speed as the speed of the AC current wave increases due to the increasing AC frequency, the same method as used in the 1st generation Japanese passenger Maglev system.

Figure 8 compares the sizes of the Delta IV Heavy rocket which can deliver 23.5 metric tons to LEO (Low Earth Orbit) with the Gen-1 Cargo Craft, which can deliver 35 metric tons of payload to LEO. The difference in size is a result of not having to use rocket propellant to reach orbit.

StarTram Emerging from Launch Tube

Figure 7 Maglev Launch Vehicle Emerging from Launch Tube.

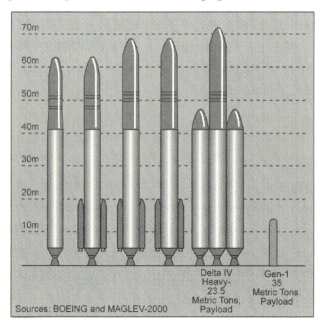

Figure 8

At orbital speed, 8 km per second, the 40 metric ton cargo craft has a kinetic energy of 1280 gigajoules, corresponding to 20 minutes of output from a 1,000 MW(e) power plant. At 6 cents per kWh, the energy cost is only 21,000 dollars for the 40 ton cargo craft. Storing and delivering the energy in less than 30 seconds to the cargo craft as it accelerates at 30 g to orbital speed is the challenge. Superconducting magnetic energy storage (SMES) is the best approach. Recent advances in superconducting (SC) and cryogenic technology make it attractive for the Gen-1 system. A circular loop of SC cable 250 meters (800 feet) in diameter with 10 megamp turns of current stores ~50 gigajoules of electrical energy. 60 such loops would store 3,000 gigajoules, almost 3 times the energy needed. The SC energy storage loops would be located along the 110 kilometer acceleration tunnel, to deliver the stored energy to the LSM windings propelling the cargo craft. The total current of 10 mega amps would be carried by multiple independent superconductors positioned on a support tube. Current densities in commercially available superconductors are millions of amps per cm² of superconductor. The total length of the 60 SC energy storage loops for Gen-1 is approximately 50 kilometers, comparable to the total length of SC magnets in high energy particle accelerators. The Large Hadron Collider at CERN, in Switzerland, for example, has 54 kilometers of SC magnets. The Superconducting Super Collider (SSC), if it had been completed, would have had 144 kilometers of SC magnets. The SC magnets in these facilities are much more complex and technically challenging than the Gen-1 SC energy storage loops, requiring extremely precise field homogeneity and conductor positioning, and reproducibility, much higher fields, and much more difficult thermal insulation. The thousands of SC magnets in the many kilometer long beam line must all function perfectly; otherwise, the particle accelerator could not operate.

The SC cost for the Gen-1 energy storage system is very low, only one billion dollars. Amortized over 10 years, with 10 launches of 35 ton payload per day, it amounts to only 50 cents per kg of payload. The refrigeration cost for the SC energy storage loops is even smaller, less than 10 cents per kg of payload.

As the Gen-1 cargo craft exits the acceleration tunnel and climbs to orbit, it experiences strong aerodynamic heating and deceleration forces. Though not as strong as re-entry vehicles (RVs) which go through all of the atmosphere on their way to their targets. Gen-1 cargo craft start from high altitude where the air density is only half that at sea level. RVs survive their trip through the atmosphere and so will Gen-1 cargo craft.

Because of atmospheric drag, the cargo craft will lose a small fraction of its initial velocity, as it ascends to orbit. The required velocity as it leaves the atmosphere is 8,000 meters per second. By launching at 8500 meters per second as the cargo craft exits from the acceleration tunnel, the velocity loss through the atmosphere can be compensated for.

The parameters for a reference Gen-1 system are given in Table 3. At 10 cargo craft per day, one Gen-1 facility could launch 128,000 tons of payload per year. With launch rates of 20 per day and a somewhat heavier vehicle, a Gen-1 facility could launch 300,000 tons annually for space commercialization and exploration requirements that do not involve large numbers of humans going into space as tourists and colonists.

FIGURE 9

Table 3. Parameters for the Maglev Launch Gen-1 Reference Design

Parameters	Reference Design Value	Range of Potential Designs
Cargo craft diameter, meters	2	1.5 to 2.5
Cargo craft length, meters	13	10 to 15
Cargo craft total weight, MT	40	30 to 50
Cargo craft payload weight, MT	35	25 to 45
Cargo craft acceleration, g	30	20 to 50
Launch velocity, km/sec	8.78	8 to 10
Altitude @ entry into atmosphere, meters	6,000	4,000 to 8,000
Launch angle, degrees	10	10 to 15
Acceleration tunnel length, km	110	100 to 150
Cargo craft velocity @ 30 km altitude, km/sec	8	7 to 10
Drag coefficient	0.09	0.05 to 0.12
Deceleration rate @ atmospheric entry, g	18	15 to 25
Nose heating rate @ atmospheric entry, kW/cm^2	30	20 to 40
ΔV loss thru atmosphere, meter/sec	780	400 to 1,000
Launch rate, #/day	10	5 to 20
Average power generation, MW(e)	210	100 to 400

Electrical energy per launch, GJ(e)	1540	1,000 to 3,000
Acceleration time, seconds	30	20
# of superconducting storage loops	40	30 to 80
Maximum AC frequency of LSM power, kilohertz	4.4	4 to 6
Payload launched per year, MT	128,000	50,000 to 300,000

What are the technology status and costs of the sub-systems for the Gen-1 and Gen-2 Maglev Launch Systems?

The principal sub-systems for Gen-1 Maglev Launch System are:

- Superconducting Maglev levitation and propulsion systems
- 110 km, 3 meter diameter evacuated acceleration tunnel
- Aluminum guideway loops in acceleration tunnel
- Superconducting energy storage and refrigeration
- Power conditioning/switching for Gen-2 acceleration
- Superconducting loops on Gen-1 cargo craft
- Gen-1 cargo craft structure
- MHD window sub-system for entry into the atmosphere
- Cooling system for ascending cargo craft as it ascends

The Gen-2 Maglev Launch System has the same sub-systems as Gen-1 with the addition of the:

- Levitated launch tube
- Superconducting cable systems to levitate the Gen-2 launch tube to high altitude
- Re-usable passenger/cargo spacecraft

Superconducting Maglev passenger vehicles are already being operated by Japan Railways. JR vehicles achieve 360 mph, limited only by air drag. In an evacuated tunnel, JR vehicles could reach orbital speeds. JR has operated five vehicle consists with a total levitated weight of about 150 metric tons.

The Maglev cargo craft accelerates in a 110 kilometer (16 miles) straight underground tunnel. Long tunnels are practical and their cost for a Maglev launch system is modest. The Large Hadron Collider (LHC) particle accelerator at CERN has a tunnel circumference of 27 kilometers. The planned Japan Railways Maglev route between Tokyo and Osaka is 500 km in length, 300 km in deep tunnels. The 72 km SSC tunnel, of which several km was constructed, had a diameter of 5 meters, compared 3 meters for the Gen-1 tunnel. The projected SSC tunnel cost was about 2 billion dollars. The cost of the 110 km mile Gen-1 tunnel will be comparable; while somewhat longer (110 km vs 72 km), its diameter is smaller (3 meter vs 5 meter). The present Japanese undersea railway tunnel between Honshu and Hokkaido is 50 km in length. The 3 Chunnel type tunnels have a total length of 93 miles. All of tunnels are considerably larger in diameter with much greater excavation volume than the Gen-1 tunnel. The tunnels had an excavation volume of 5.4 million cubic meters compared to only 1/7 as much for the Gen-1 tunnel.

The aluminum guideway loops are similar to those in the Japanese Maglev Passenger System. Even assuming a very conservative $20/kg, 10 times greater than commercial aluminum, they cost only 0.4 billion dollars. The total circumferential length of the 60 superconducting (SC) loops in the Gen-1 energy storage system is 50 kilometers, less than the 54 km length of SC magnets now operating in the Large Hadron Collider (LHC). The SC magnets for the LHC are much more complicated and difficult than the Gen-1 SC loops. The LHC magnets require extremely high magnetic field precision, and substantially higher field strength than the Gen-1 SC loops. In addition, their refrigeration requirements are considerably greater, since their thermal insulation is much thinner than that for the Gen-1 SC loops. The LHC uses liquid helium cooled superconductor which operates at 1.7 K, with very high refrigeration power requirements. The Gen-1 SC energy storage loops operate at 4.2 K with much less refrigeration power. The SC loops on the Gen-1 cargo craft use high temperature superconductor operating close to liquid nitrogen temperatures. They are cooled down just prior to launch, with a small quantity of stored coolant that keeps them cold during the few minutes needed to position the craft in the tunnel and accelerate it. The thermal insulation requirements are very modest. High temperature SC magnets have already been used on the Japanese Maglev vehicles. The Gen-1 cargo craft structure is costed at a conservative 100 dollars per kg and it would use a high strength, high temperature composite material, probably with an inner shell of stainless steel or titanium.

The MHD window uses technology similar to the 1960s large MHD generators, except that it prevents atmospheric air from entering the evacuated tunnel, instead of operating as a generator, in which hot combustion gases flow through a transverse magnetic field to generate electric power. In the MHD window, applied DC electric current flows through ionized air in the pump region, pushing it outwards to prevent it from entering the acceleration tunnel. The air would be seeded with a small amount of alkali metal vapor, e.g., cesium, ionized by a RF input and I^2R losses from the DC current. Cooling the Gen-1 cargo craft as it ascends through the atmosphere would be easier than cooling the present intercontinental re-entry vehicles (RVs) launched by ballistic missiles. RVs traverse the full atmosphere, while a Gen-1 cargo craft traverses about $\frac{1}{2}$ of the atmosphere. Moreover, unlike re-entry missiles, the much heavier Gen-1 cargo craft can carry large amounts of transpiration coolant, making it much easier for Gen-1 cargo craft to traverse the atmosphere.

The Gen-1 launch facility cost will be very small compared to its economic benefits. Consider launching space solar power satellites, which are not economically practical using rockets. Launching 50 GW(e) per year (5,000 launches/year) of SPS satellites would enable 1,000 GW(e) of electric power in space after 20 years. At 6 cents per kWh, the annual revenues from the SPS satellites would be 500 billion dollars. Over 20 years, total revenues would be ~5,000 billion dollars, 250 times greater than the projected construction cost of 20 billion dollars for the Gen-1 facility. Even if the Gen-1 facility cost was double or triple, which is very unlikely, its cost would be tiny compared to its economic benefits.

The Gen-2 system is much more technically challenging than the Gen-1 cargo only system, and more expensive, with a projected cost of 67 Billion dollars. The levitated launch tube uses existing superconductors, but will require considerable development. Gen-2 would enable large-scale human activities in space, including tourism, manufacturing and exploration. Large scale human activity in space is not economically possible using rockets. Supporting the development of Gen-2 to enable large numbers of humans to live and work in space, and to experience its wonders, depends on one's values. We believe that the cost is worth it, whether it is 67 billion, 100 billion or even 300 billion dollars (which is only 1/2% of annual World GDP.) It is part of human destiny.

The cost per kilogram of payload depends on three factors: 1) Construction cost of the facility and amortization period; 2) Payload tonnage launched annually; 3) Operating cost and payload per launch. Construction and operating cost can be projected by estimating the individual costs of the various materials and operations involved based on existing experience as benchmarks. A launch rate of 130,000 tons per year and a 10 year amortization period are assumed. Table 4 shows the projected construction and operating costs for the first Gen-1 facility. There are two acceleration tunnels, enabling one to shut down for maintenance and repairs, while the other continues operating. Each tunnel is 110 km in length, with an interior diameter of 3 meters. Added to this is 47 km of energy storage tunnels for the 60 superconducting energy storage loops.

The major contributor to construction cost, ~½ of the total 20 billion dollars, is the power conditioning system that converts the DC energy stored in the SC energy loops to kilohertz frequency AC power that accelerates the launch vehicle. The projected unit cost for the electronic switches, controls, etc. is $100/kW(e), for a total cost of ~10 billion dollars. The power conditioning sites will be located along the 2 acceleration tunnels, which will share the equipment. Handling the enormous power load of tens of gigawatts of AC power during the 30 second acceleration period will require many distributed electronic units operating in parallel. The full assembly will be highly reliable, since if some individual units fail, other units would take over their load.

Table 4. Projected Capital and Operating Costs for Gen-1 Maglev Launch

Basis: 35 ton payload per launch; 10 launches per day.

Capital Cost Component	Cost (Billion $)
Excavate/line 2 acceleration tunnel and 60 energy storage tunnel (265 km, 3 meter, $1500/m3)	3.00
Aluminum guideway loop @ $20/kg (incl. placement)	0.44
Superconductor for energy storage loops (60 loops @ 250 meter diameter, $2/KA meter)	0.94
SC cable & cryopipe manufacture and installation	0.94
Power conditioning, DC to AC @ $100/kW(e)	10.00
Vacuum & monitoring equipment for tunnels	1.00
Refrigeration systems	0.03
Prime power plant, 300 MW(e) @ $3,000/kW(e)	0.90
Launch buildings & operational facilities	2.00
Total construction cost	19.25 B$
Operating Cost Rev Launch of 35 Ton Payload	Cost (M $)
Cargo craft structure (5 MT) @ $100/kg	0.50
Superconducting loops on craft @ 2$/KA meter	0.43
Personnel @ 50 man days @ $500 per day	0.025
Energy operating cost @ 6 cents/kWh	0.021
Total operating cost/launch	0.98 M$
10 year amortized capital cost (3650 launches/year)	0.52 M$
Total cost/launch	1.50 M$
Total cost/kg of payload	43 $/kg

The 20 billion dollar Gen-1 facility cost has an amortized cost of ~15 dollars per kg of payload for a launch rate of 128,000 tons annually. Adding the cost of the cargo craft structure and its superconducting loops, energy and operating personnel – the facility would have a staff of approximately 1,000 – total unit cost is 43 dollars per kg (20 dollars per pound) of payload launched. The 20 billion construction cost is small compared with other government programs. The NASA Constellation program for the return to the Moon is ~100 billion dollars. Gen-1 is approximately 2 weeks of the U.S. defense budget. The economic benefits will greatly outweigh its cost.

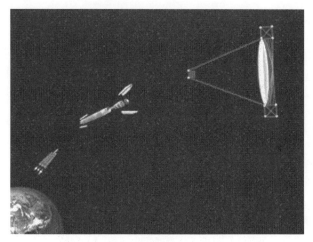

Figure 10

MIC Launch and Deployment Sequence

The capital cost for the Gen-2 system is projected at 67 billion dollars, over 3 times the cost of the Gen-1 system, even when large reductions in component costs are projected. For example, the superconductor in the levitated SC cables attached to the evacuated launch tube is projected at only 20 cents per kA meter, compared to the present 2 dollars per kA meter. Such large reductions appear possible using thin film High Temperature Superconductors (HTS) which have current densities of over 10 million amps per cm^2 in the superconducting film. The launch volume for the Gen-2 system is enormous – over 300,000 tons of cargo and 400,000 passengers annually. Even so, with a World population of 9 billion persons in 2050 AD, this corresponds to only 1 person in 500 going into space once during a 50 year period of their lifetime. In practice, probably many more would want to experience spaceflight. Over a 50 year period, 13,000 dollar cost per trip would only be an annual equivalent of 650 dollars – well within the reach of many people.

Space solar power satellites are the largest industrial market for Maglev launch. To launch 50 GW(e) per year, about 2% of present world electric generation, a launch rate of 5,000 SPS satellite cargo craft per year would be required, at a specific weight of 4 kg/kW(e) for SPS units. SPS satellites can potentially supply almost all of Earth's needs for clean, non-polluting energy. However, the high cost of rockets prevents SPS's from being practical. Even with an unrealistically low specific mass of 1 kg/kW(e) for the satellites, placing SPS in GEO would cost 100,000 dollars per kW(e) assuming 100,000 dollars/kg of payload to GEO, compared to ~3 thousand dollars per kW(e) for fossil and nuclear plants on Earth. A new concept (8) for very large, self-deploying solar power satellites, termed MIC (Magnetically Inflated Cables), is based on launching a compact package of coiled high temperature superconducting (SC) and high temperature superconducting (SC) cables that support a tether network which in turn supports a network of thin film solar cells.

Once in orbit, the SC cables would be electrically energized. (Figure 9) The outward magnetic forces on the SC cables cause MIC to expand to full size, with its shape determined by the tensile tethers restraining the outwards magnetic forces on the SC cables. For solar electric power MIC can be a simple circular loop with a planar 2-D tether network restraining the outwards radial forces on the SC cable. The solar cell array is located on the planar 2-D tether network. Using multiple SC cables, MIC can be configured as a curved solar reflecting mirror, with thin aluminized film supported by the tether network that concentrates and focuses sunlight onto a smaller solar cell array. Each cargo craft MIC launch would produce a solar collector unit of ~330 meters in diameter. At a solar cell efficiency of 20%, each unit could generate ~20 MW(e).

A number of modules would then attach together to form a larger power unit, which would beam power down to a designated location on Earth. A 20 module unit would beam down 400 MW(e), for example; a 50 module unit would beam down 1 GW(e). At 5,000 launches per year, 2,500 for the solar electric modules and 2,500 for power conditioning and beaming equipment, a Gen-1 facility could deploy 50 GW(e) of solar power annually or 500 GW(e) over a decade. At 6 cents per kWh, the present U.S. average production cost, the power production from 500 GW(e) of SPS satellites would be worth 260 billion dollars per year. For 10,000 launches per year, the resultant annual power production would be worth over 500 billion dollars with 1,000 GW(e) deployed in 10 years. The corresponding annual cost for Maglev launch is only 15 billion dollars. Using Gen-1 and MIC, many other applications are possible, as illustrated in Figure 10.

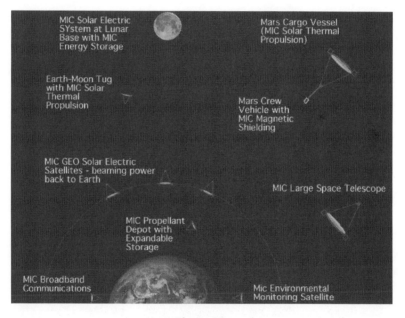

Figure 11

Gen-1's ability to launch massive amounts of supplies and construction material would greatly expand space exploration. Figure 11 outlines the exploration capabilities made possible by Gen-1, including large manned bases on the Moon and colonies on Mars. Robotic probes would explore all the planets and moons in the solar system, searching for evidence of past or present life in the oceans of Europa and other Jovian moons, and long term flight in the atmospheres of Jupiter and the other giant planets, using nuclear powered ramjets. Large samples from the other bodies in the solar system could be returned to Earth. Ultra large MIC telescopes with diameters of several hundred meters could provide detailed images of terrestrial type planets around distant stars.

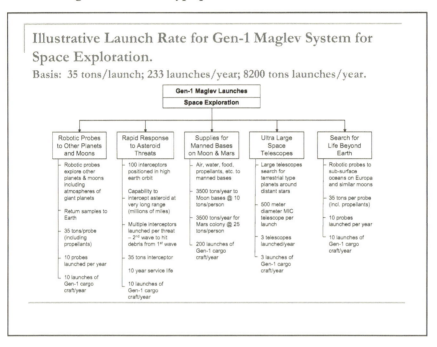

Figure 12

A very important application is the positioning a fleet of high velocity interceptor rockets in orbit to quickly intercept asteroid threats far from Earth. Rapid response and multiple interceptors to ensure intercept is crucial to protect Earth from catastrophic impact events. The asteroid defense fleet needs to intercept dangerous debris from the initial intercept, using second and third waves of interceptors. The Gen-2 system has the capabilities of the Gen-1 system, plus the ability to launch tens of thousands of travelers into space per year at affordable cost. The travelers could visit space hotels in Earth orbit, or bases on the Moon.

For the Gen-1 Maglev Launch system, the potential sites should meet the following criteria: 1) Launch altitudes of 4,000 meters or more; 2)

Remote location with very low population density; 3) Minimum flight length over land. Criterion #1 minimizes aerodynamic drag and heating, and ΔV loss during ascent through the atmosphere. Criterion #2 avoids disturbing people with the very intense sonic booms that would accompany launches. Criterion #3 minimizes hazards to population from debris if a cargo craft disintegrates during its ascent to orbit.

What are some possible launch sites for the Gen-1 facility? An ideal site for polar orbit launch is Antarctica. The Vinson Massif in Marie Byrd Land reaches 5,140 meters altitude. From there a launch vehicle would travel over the open Pacific to Alaska – halfway around the World before passing over land. There is no local population and no objection to sonic booms. The only drawback is its isolation from existing World transport routes, though existing container ships could service Antarctica. Other possible isolated sites for polar launch are listed in Table 5. The exit altitude of the acceleration tunnel will be below the top of the mountain range that houses it. A value of 500 meters (1,650 feet) is assumed for the altitude difference. The Gen-1 acceleration tunnel curves upwards to its exit. Three of the Gen-1 sites – Alaska, Greenland, and Kamchatka, have very long downrange flights over the ocean, i.e., 14,000 km or more, before reaching Antarctica. After Antarctica they have thousands of kilometers of additional flight over the ocean before reaching land again. For the Kamchatka site, the second land mass is Greenland, with a flight distance of 20,000 kilometers before reaching it.

There are few high altitude locations for an equatorial launch of Gen-1. Launch altitudes of 6,000 meters appear possible in the Andes. Africa's launch locations are at lower altitudes, ~4,000 meters. For a Gen-2 launch facility, the exit of the acceleration tunnel can be at low altitude since the magnetically levitated evacuated launch tube exits at high altitude. Low population density, isolated land areas are desirable for Gen-2, with long down range flights over the ocean. Antarctica and Greenland are attractive, as are sites in Alaska, Kamchatka, Northern Siberia, Australia, Brazil, Argentina, etc. Using two different Gen-2 sites, it could launch into both polar and equatorial orbits.

Table 5. Features of Potential Sites for a Gen-1 Maglev Launch Facility.

Feature	United States	Russia	China	Greenland (ECI is Host)
Name/location of mountain peak	Mt. St. Elias, Alaska	Klyudevskaya Sopka, Kamchatka Peninsula	Gongga Shan Szechwan Province	Highest point in Greenland ice sheet
Altitude of peak, meters	5,489	4,750	7,556	3,220
Altitude of exit point from acceleration tunnel, meters	4,989	4,250	7,050	3,220
Launch angle (LA), degrees	10	10	$10 \leq LA \leq 15$	10
Flight distance to reach first land flyover beyond host country	15,000 km flight over Pacific Ocean	14,000 km flight over Pacific Ocean	600 km flight over China	18,000 km flight over Atlantic Ocean
Location of first land flyover	Rockefeller Plateau Antarctica	Wilkes Land, Antarctica	Vietnam	Filchner Ice Shelf, Antarctica
Notes:	Second land flyover is 13,000 km farther downrange (Africa)	Second land flyover is 20,000 km further downrange (Greenland)	Second land flyover is 3,000 km further downrange (Indonesia)	Second land flyover is 5,000 km further downrange (Australia)

In summary, Maglev Launch, a radically new way to launch large amounts of payloads into space at very low cost, will result in a New Age in space, with capabilities that are impossible using rockets. The Maglev Launch system uses magnetically levitated vehicle technology similar to that now operating for passenger transport in Japan. Two Maglev launch systems are possible. The near term Gen-1 system launches 40 ton cargo craft in high altitude terrain ($\geq$4,000 meters) and ~8 km/sec from an evacuated acceleration tunnel. The cargo craft then coast up to space through the atmosphere. Aerodynamic heating and deceleration loads are acceptable. A Gen-1 facility can launch 100,000 tons or more of payload annually, at a unit cost of less than 50 dollars per kilogram and be operating by 2020 AD. The longer term Gen-2 system would launch humans and cargo into space, using an evacuated magnetically levitated launch tube that ascends to an altitude of ~20 km where the passenger/cargo craft enter the very low density atmosphere at that altitude. Gen-2 can be operating by 2030 AD.

Applications for Maglev launch include commercial development and exploration of space. The major commercial application is solar power satellites that beam continuous electric power to Earth from GEO orbit. Maglev launched SPS satellites could beam hundreds of gigawatts of power to Earth at less cost than fossil fuel and nuclear power plants. Maglev launch would enable large manned bases on the Moon and colonies on Mars. Using low cost robotic probes, the outer solar system could be explored in great detail, and samples returned to Earth for analysis. Maglev launch would provide a very robust defense against impact threats from asteroids and long period comets.

The Fight for Maglev   Maglev Energy Storage

This is the Cover of the White Paper Presented at The 2010 Advanced Energy Conference at General Electric's Global R&D Center at Schenectady, New York on November 8 and 9th, 2010. Entitled, Maglev Energy Storage and the Grid, A new approach, the MAPS (MAglev Power Storage) system. MAPS uses magnetically levitated and propelled (Maglev) vehicles to transport heavy masses from lower to higher elevations. MAPS is very efficient. Over 90% of the input electrical energy drawn from the grid and stored is returned to the grid on demand. A MAPS system can store thousands of megawatt hours of electrical energy at very low cost, in the range of 2 to 3 cents per KWH. MAPS has potential annual revenues of hundreds of Billions of dollars in the World market. MAPS is much more efficient and lower in cost than pumped hydro. Moreover, it does not have the environmental concerns and site limitations that pumped hydro has.

Chapter Eleven

Maglev Energy Storage – The Good Sisyphus

"The struggle itself ... is enough to fill a man's heart. One must imagine Sisyphus happy"

The Myth of Sisyphus, Albert Camus.

Sisyphus was one of the really bad guys in Greek mythology. Founder and first King of Corinth, he killed travelers and guests, an unspeakable crime in ancient Greece, just to show how tough and dominant he was. He seduced his niece and grabbed his brother's throne. Worst of all in terms of a career move, he snitched on Zeus, who had abducted Regina, daughter of the River God Asopus, and told him that Zeus had taken his daughter.(1)

To punish Sisyphus, Zeus ordered Thanatos (Death) to chain him in the underworld. However, Sisyphus was smarter than Thanatos, and suggested that Thanatos first try them on to show how they worked.

Sisyphus then secured the more gullible Thanatos instead of himself. With Thanatos chained no human could die, even if they were chopped up in battle. Ares, the God of War, was very angry. He freed Thanatos and sent Sisyphus back to the underworld. Sisyphus then persuaded Persephone, the Queen of the Underworld, to let him return to the upper World to see his wife. When he got there, he refused to go back to the underworld. Hermes came and forcibly dragged him back, this time permanently.

The Gods then concluded that Sisyphus needed a special punishment. He was condemned to roll a very heavy rock uphill.(2). However, just before he got to the top of the hill, the rock would roll down to the bottom, and he would have to start over again, forever. Moving on, we leave Bad Sisyphus at his task – he certainly deserved it, though Titian's painting (Figure 1) does tend to invoke some pity for him.

Going on, Maglev energy storage (3) is the Good Sisyphus. In the MAglev Power Storage (MAPS) system, heavy concrete blocks are transported up and downhill on a guideway to store electrical energy. When the electrical power being generated, whether by wind or solar farms, or by coal and nuclear plants, exceeds demand, it is desirable to store the electrical energy for later use when demand increased and the supply was not able to meet it.

As described later, MAPS energy storage appears to be the best way to store electrical energy and is much more efficient than other approaches, returning over 90% of input electrical energy fed to the MAPS energy storage facility as output electrical energy back to the grid. The energy storage efficiency is considerably lower for other energy storage approaches, typically in the range of 60% to 70%. Moreover, the cost of energy storage using MAPS is much less than with other approaches.

The accompanying drawing shows a MAPS vehicle with a 100 metric tonne concrete block loaded on its flat surface. Transported uphill for an altitude gain of 1 kilometer (3,040 feet), the magnetic propulsion system would consume 260 kilowatt hours (kWh) of electric energy to lift the block, plus a few more kWh to overcome resistive power losses in the levitation and propulsion aluminum loop panels installed on the guideway.

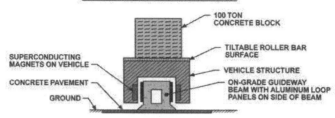

UPHILL OR DOWNHILL DELIVERY OF ENERGY STORAGE BLOCK

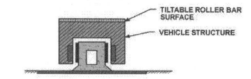

VEHICLE RETURN TRIP AFTER DELIVERY OF CONCRETE BLOCK

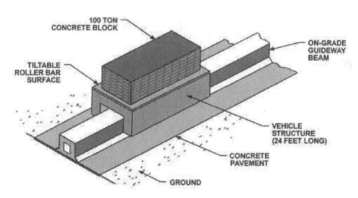

At the top of the guideway, the concrete block rolls off the MAPS vehicle into a storage yard. It remains there, with a gravitation potential energy of 260 kWh. No energy is lost as it sits in the storage yard – it can wait there for one day or one month, and still keep the same potential energy.

When the electrical grid cries out for additional electric power – "Demand is too great, our power plants can't generate enough power" – the MAPS vehicle picks up the 100 tonne concrete block at the top of the guideway and carries it downhill, returning 260 kWh (minus a few kWh of electrical losses in the aluminum levitation and propulsion loop panels on the guideway).

During the MAPS vehicle's ascent, the Magnetic propulsion winding acts in the Linear Synchronous Motor (LSM) mode, taking electric power from the grid to push it and the 100 Ton concrete block it carries uphill. During the vehicles' descent, the magnetic propulsion winding acts in the Linear Synchronous Generator (LSG) mode, feeding electric power back into the grid.

The amount of electrical energy stored by carrying the concrete block uphill is proportional to the altitude gain and the weight of the concrete blocks. Pushing a 100 tonne block 2 kilometers (6080 feet) uphill will store 520 kWh, pushing it up 500 meters (1520 feet will store 130 kWh. Similarly a 200 tonne block will store twice as much energy, while a 50 tonne block will store only ½ as much energy.

The concrete block need not be a solid block of concrete. It can equally well be a concrete box filled with rocks, which would be cheaper. A nominal 100 tonne concrete block would be 3.5 meters (11.5 feet) in width, 2.5 meters (8.2 feet) in height, and 4.5 meters (14.8 feet) in length. Fabricated at 100 dollars per cubic yard, a 100 tonne block made entirely of concrete would cost 5,500 dollars. Fabricated as a concrete box and filled with rocks it would cost on the order of 2,500 dollars.

How much would such a concrete block cost in terms of cents per kWh over a 30 year period? Not much. Assuming that it stored 260 kWh every day for 30 years (11,000 days), the cost of the block amortized over a 30 year period would be only 0.08 cents per kWh – less than 1% of the typical cost of 20 cents/kWh for cost for peaking power. The cost of Maglev transport systems is discussed later. While greater than the cost of the blocks, it is still much less than the cost of generating peak power.

The next drawing shows how the MAPS energy storage system operates. In the energy storage mode, the MAPS vehicles move upward on the left hand guideway and transport the concrete blocks from the lower storage yard to the upper storage yard, where they quickly roll off the vehicles to a designated spot in the yard. The unloaded vehicles then travel down the right hand guideway to the lower storage yard, where they pick up the next block to be transported to the upper yard.

Depending on the amount of the elevation change, the inclination angle of the MAPS guideway and operating speed, a MAPS vehicle will make 10 to 20 round trips per hour. Greater elevation change, lower inclination angle for the guideway and slower vehicle speed result in fewer round trips per hour. Typical guideway elevation changes are on the order of 1 kilometer (3,000 feet) guideway with an inclination angle in the range of 20 to 30 degrees, and speeds in the range of 60 to 140 mph.

During both the energy storage and energy delivery traveling periods of the MAPS facility, the number of vehicles on the guideway and their speed would be controlled so that the power input/output to the facility would always be continuous and match the needs of the electrical grid and power sources that were connected to the MAPS facility. The inverter/rectifier electronic systems in the facility would ensure that the input and output power, cycle frequencies and phases are correctly matched.

MAPS facilities can be designed to meet a wide range of power and energy storage needs, and are very flexible and rapidly responsive in input and output power requirements. For high power applications a practical MAPS facility can be designed to handle input/output power of 1,000 megawatts or more, with energy storage capacities of 10,000 MW. For lower power storage applications, practical MAPS facilities can be designed to handle 50 megawatts or so, with energy storage capacity on the order of 100 megawatt hours.

MAPS is similar to the 2nd generation Maglev 2000 system described earlier that transports passengers, highway trucks, autos, and freight containers on an elevated monorail guideway, but there are significant differences.

First, MAPS vehicles travel on a monorail guideway beam, but the beam is on-grade rather than elevated above the surface and mounted on piers. Having the guideway monorail beam on-grade greatly reduces its cost, from 25 to 30 million dollars per 2-way mile to about 10 million dollars per 2-way mile. While it may be necessary to occasionally elevate the MAPS monorail beam to accommodate local dips in the terrain, the majority of the guideway will be on-grade.

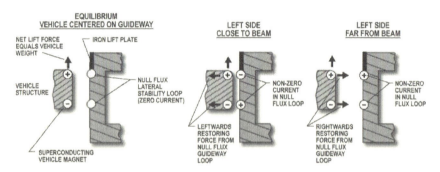

Second, iron plates positioned at the top beam provide a major portion of the MAPS vehicles lifting capability. This "iron lift" feature is attractive in two ways. The vehicles superconducting magnets are physically attracted upwards to the iron plates above them, producing lift without I^2R losses in the aluminum guideway loops, which is attractive for the design, because it increases the output/input energy efficiency of the MAPS system.

The iron lift feature is vertically stable, because as the MAPS vehicle moves upward, the lift force from the iron plates decreases. If the MAPS dipole loop were vertically centered on the iron plate, the lift force would go to zero. The "Figure of 8" aluminum loop panels on the sides of the monorail beam provide additional vertical stability to the desired design value.

However, the iron lift feature is horizontally unstable, since if the MAPS vehicle moves off center from the beam, the dipole superconducting magnet that is close to the beam will experience a stronger force drawing it towards the beam than the one that is further away. To prevent the vehicle from hitting the guideway beam, a null flux circuit consisting of 2 cross-connected aluminum loops is positioned on the sides of the beams. If the vehicle moves to the left or right of its centered position, an induced current is automatically created in the null flux circuit, creating a strong magnetic force that pushes the vehicle back towards the center position, preventing it from hitting the beam.

Third, MAPS can use lower cost dipole superconducting loops on the vehicle in place of the quadrupole superconducting loops used for the 2nd generation Maglev 2000 system. Since the MAPS vehicles do not carry passengers and do not stop at stations, minimizing magnetic fringe fields is not a requirement.

The power outputs from wind and solar facilities are inherently highly variable, both in time and magnitude. On average, wind farms only operate at 20 to 30% of capacity – that is, a wind farm with a quoted output of 100 megawatts can only deliver a time average of 20 to 30 megawatts because the wind does not blow all the time. Moreover, it may well blow at night, when its power is not really needed. Similarly, solar farms generate most of their power in the middle of the day, when power demand is less than earlier and later in the day. MAPS would take the extra power from a wind or solar farm and store it to meet peak demand when required.

So far, wind and solar power generation has been only a very small portion of total U.S. power consumption, so that the electrical grids can absorb it without much problem. However, wind and solar power cannot grow to become a major supplier of U.S. power generation unless a practical cost-effective method of storing electrical energy is implemented.

Pumped hydro has traditionally been used to store electrical energy. Like MAPS, to store energy, it moves mass by pumping water, not transporting concrete blocks from a lower to a higher elevation. To deliver electrical energy back to the grid, pumped hydro then has the water flow back downhill through a turbo generator.

Pumped hydro, while practical, has major disadvantage compared to MAPS in the areas of electrical efficiency, cost, siting capability, and the impact on the environment. The Raccoon Mountain pumped hydro facility operated by TVA (4) has an upper water reservoir of 528 acres, almost a square mile in area. The dam impounding the reservoir is 230 feet high and 1.1 mile long. Water is pumped from the reservoir on the Tennessee River near Chattanooga to the upper reservoir to store electric energy, and then run through turbines back to the Tennessee River to generate power for the grid. The facility has a maximum power output of 1600 megawatts electric.

A MAPS facility could store and deliver the same amount of electrical power with a much smaller environmental foot print, at much lower cost, with much less energy losses. A pumped hydro facility will return only 70% of the power that is fed into it, while a MAPS facility will return over 90% of the input power back to the grid. To deliver 1 million kWh back to the grid, the pumped hydro facility has to take in about 1 ½ million kWh from the grid, and loses almost ½ million kWh in the process. In contrast, MAPS will be over 90% efficient, needing to take in only 1.1 million kWh from the grid, with a much smaller loss of 1/10 of a million kWh. As a consequence, totaling just the losses due to storage inefficiency, pumped hydro will increase the delivered cost of electric power by 50%, while MAPS will only increase it by 10%.

Further, because the construction cost of a pumped hydro facility will be much greater than that for MAPS, e.g., about 1,500 dollars per kilowatt for pumped hydro compared to about 500 dollars per kilowatt for a MAPS facility, the differential between the cost of electrical storage for the two technologies will even be greater.

At a base cost of 10 cents per kWh of input power, the output cost for a pumped hydro facility will be about 17 cents per kWh, taking into account electrical losses, amortization over 30 years, personnel, and maintenance. The corresponding cost for a MAPS facility will be much less, about 12 cents per kWh.

Moreover, MAPS can be sited at a much wider range of locations. It does not require water and can be easily built in arid regions. It will not affect local water quality and aquatic life, will be much smaller in area, and much more acceptable to environmentalists.

Finally, a MAPS facility can be built quickly, in 2 or 3 years at most, with assurance that it will come on line at the planned time. Construction time for a pumped hydro facility will be at least 5 years or more, and subject to delays from lawsuits by environmental groups and approval by regulators. Wind and solar power facilities would be greatly distressed if the planned-for electrical storage capacity was delayed for long periods, or even stopped from going forward. The effects in their ability to meet grid power demands, and to deliver power at the projected cost, would be very seriously impacted.

Given a strongly funded development and testing program, MAPS facilities could be implemented within 5 years from the start of the program.

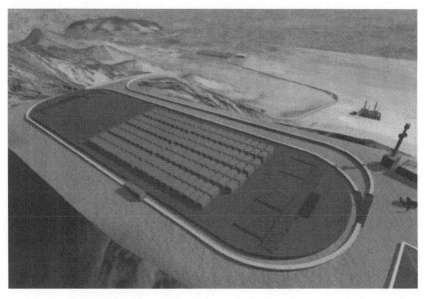

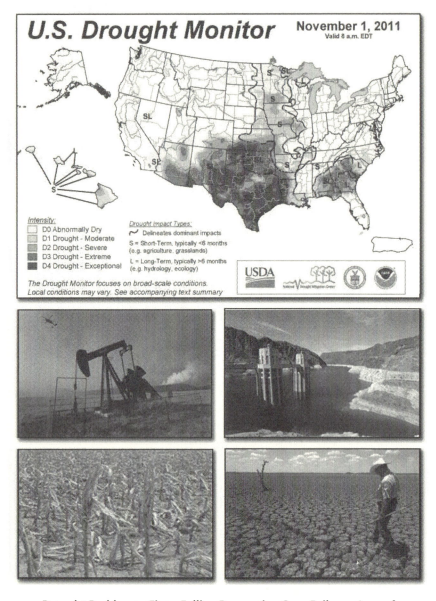

Drought Problems: Fires, Falling Reservoirs, Crop Failures, Loss of Rangeland and Soils Negatively Impact Energy, Food, and Economic Security.

Chapter Twelve

Maglev Water Transport – A Billion Jugs A Day

"A Book of verses underneath the Bough
A Jug of Wine, a Loaf of Bread --- and Thou
Beside Me Singing in the Wilderness--
And Wilderness were Paradise enow!"

The Rubaiyat of Omar Khayyam,

Quatrain XI, Edward FitzGerald, 5th edition.

Omar Khayyam's beautiful quatrain stirs one's soul and appreciation of the really important joys in life – companionship, poetry and literature, food and drink, and expressing feelings. A small quibble, however. Does one really want wine in the Wilderness? Wouldn't some jugs of water be better, and more useful for survival, particularly if you didn't know where the next water would come from and when? Wine is not a good idea in a Wilderness, particularly if it's dry and hot, because drinking it just makes you more thirsty.

How long can one survive without water in Death Valley in the summer? About 1 day in the sun, maybe 2 days if you can find shade (there's not much shade in Death Valley). In New York City, maybe 5 days without water, assuming you don't get mugged first.

People can live much longer without food. David Blaine, the magician, survived without food for 44 days in September 2003 when he lived in a suspended plastic cage above the Thames River in London (1). He drank 4.5 liters of water daily, which kept him alive, but he lost 25% of his body

The Fight for Maglev   Maglev Water Transport

mass. Political and war prisoners, and people in concentration camps, have survived for similar periods.

However, to grow the food we need water, lots of water, much more than we drink. A gallon jug of drinking water per day is enough to stay alive in the Wilderness, unless it's Death Valley. Eating a couple of hamburgers per day, along with a pound of plums and cherries, takes 1,500 gallons of water to grow and process the delicacies. Table 13.1 below lists the amounts of water need to grow and process some common foods, as given by National Geographic magazine (2).

Table 1

Water Requirements to Grow and Process Consumer Foods

Food	Gallons of Water Per Pound of Food
Beef	1,857
Pork	756
Chicken	469
Sausage	1,382
Process Cheese	589
Eggs	400
Hamburger	634
Figs	379
Plums	193
Cherries	185
Bananas	103

The Fight for Maglev   Maglev Water Transport

There is plenty of fresh water in the World. The Amazon River discharges 4.5 Trillion gallons of water daily. If apportioned out evenly to everybody on Earth that would be 700 gallons per person per day, more than sufficient for their needs for drinking, bathing, growing food, sewage disposal, etc. And the Amazon discharge is only 15% of the World's total river runoff.

The problem is not lack of fresh water, but its distribution. Some regions have much more than they need, while others suffer severely from lack of water. The U.S. Southwest is very short of water, and conditions are getting worse. Lake Mead is drying up, there are disputes over who gets the diminishing flow of the Colorado River, water tables have dropped hundreds of feet in California, Arizona, and Nevada, farmers don't have enough water to grow crops, and on and on.

The water shortages of the American Southwest area mirror the severe water shortages all over the World, in Australia, China, the Mideast, Africa, etc. Global warming is rapidly melting glaciers and high altitude snow packs, diminishing river flows during the summer, when the water is most needed. Many regions now existing on the margin for their water needs will soon start to experience severe droughts as global temperatures continue to rise, imperiling Billions of people.

What are the options to meet the mounting needs for fresh water in the regions that presently subject to droughts, or soon will be? There are not many. For fresh water sources, the options are:

- Desalination of sea water

- Rivers

- Lakes

- Aquifers

For the transport of fresh water from a source to a user, the options are:

- Tankers

- Canals and Aqueducts

- Pipelines

- The Maglev Water Train

339

Desalination plants presently operate at a number of locations around the World. The total world production of fresh water from the desalination plants is 12 Billion gallons per day (3), 400 times smaller than the daily discharge of the Amazon River. The bulk of the desalination output is in the Mideast, with the World's largest plant, the Jebel Ali unit in the United Arab Emirates producing 200 million gallons daily. (4)

Desalination is not cheap. There are various processes, multiple effect distillation, reverse osmosis, etc., but on average, the quoted cost is about 1 dollar per cubic meter, or about 4 dollars per thousand gallons.(5) The cost factors are not very clear – are there hidden subsidies, extra low interest rates, favorable fuel energy costs and so on.

Taking the 4 dollars per 1,000 gallons at face value, however, it is still quite expensive to desalinate. People in well-off countries like Israel, Saudi Arabia and the United Arab Emirates can afford it, though farmers probably will complain, but for most of the poorer countries, the costs will be too great.

Even if a country can afford desalination, most of the time the fresh water produced will have to be transported to other parts of the country. How do the transport options compare?

Tankers are of very limited usefulness. They can only travel from one port to another, not inland. Moreover, the transport costs are very high. At a typical shipping cost of 1 cent per ton-mile, transporting 1,000 gallons of water a distance of 300 miles would cost 12 dollars per 1,000 gallons, three times the cost of desalinating it. Only in rare cases does shipping large amounts of water by tanker make sense.

Leaving out tankers, we are left with 3 transport options: canals/aqueducts, pipelines, and the Water Train to convey fresh water from various sources – desalination plants, rivers, lakes, and aquifers. In general, the transport systems will be on land and operate under a wide range of conditions: transport distance, volume to be transported, type of terrain traversed, e.g. flat or hilly or mountainous, rock, sand or normal soil, temperature and climate, e.g. hot or cold, dry or wet, etc.

In some cases, canals/aqueducts will be the best water transport systems, in other cases, pipelines, and in still others, the Maglev Water Train. Let us examine how the World's largest aqueduct and pipe line systems, to see how they would compare with the Maglev Water Train, if it were to do the same job. Then we will see what unique water transport capabilities are enabled by the Maglev Water Train.

Before comparing the 3 water transport options, what is the Maglev Water Train, and how does it work? Briefly, the Maglev water train operates very much like the Maglev Energy Storage System described in the previous chapter, with some differences.

The guideway for the Maglev Water Train is on-grade like that for the Energy Storage System (Chapter 11). The main difference is that the Energy Storage vehicles operate as individual units or at most, a few vehicles coupled together to form a small consist, while the Maglev Water Train operates as a long train of many vehicles connected together. A typical Water Train will be 2 kilometers in length or more, with 70 or more vehicles in the train.

Instead of a heavy concrete block on top of a flat surface, the configuration used for Maglev energy storage, the Maglev Water Train vehicles have expandable bladders on a curved surface, as shown in Figure 1.(6) On the out-bound water delivery trip, the bladder is filled with water. After delivery, the bladder is collapsed, reducing the vehicle's frontal area and its air drag.

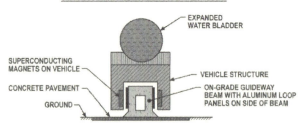

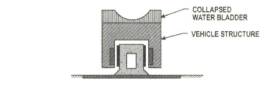

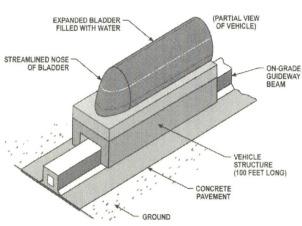

Figure 1

Having the Water Train vehicles operate as a long train has two big advantages over operating them as single individual units. First, the propulsion power requirements per vehicle are reduced by a factor of approximately 4 when they operate as a long train, compared to operating individually. This effect is familiar to anybody who has taken advantage of the "draft effect" when you ride behind a vehicle that travels ahead of you. One sees bicyclists doing this in races – the bicyclist will save energy by riding just behind his rival for a long distance, reducing the air drag on himself and saving energy, and then pull ahead of his rival just before the finish line, because he's not as tired and has more energy for the final push. In the early 1900's there was a famous stunt on Long Island, in which a bicyclist reached 90 mph when he bicycled just behind a Long Island Railroad train.

The physical reason for the "draft effect" is simple. The frontal area of the first vehicle displaces the air ahead of it, which then flows around the following vehicles without having to be displaced. There are frictional drag forces on the following vehicles as the displaced air flows over their surfaces, but these forces are much less than if they were traveling as individual units, and the air ahead of them had to be pushed away from its front.

The 69 vehicles behind the first vehicle in a 70 vehicle water train traveling at 150 mph, will each experience an air drag force of only 272 pounds of force. The fully loaded Water Train vehicles weighs 640,000 pounds (290 Metric Tons), corresponding to a lift/drag ratio of about 2300/1. For comparison, airplanes have a lift/drag ratio of about 20/1, requiring 100 times more propulsion energy per unit weight than the Maglev Water Train. Automobiles and rail trains are a bit more efficient than airplanes, but still have lift/drag ratios (tire friction for autos, rail friction for railroad trains) of approximately 100/1.

To sum up, the Maglev Water Train is 100 times more energy efficient in transporting material than an airplane would be, and 23 times more energy efficient that trucks or rail trains would be in transporting water. As a result, trucks and rail trains are only practical for short distances, e.g., a few miles. The above calculations do not include I^2R losses in the Maglev guideway loops. However, these are much smaller than the air drag losses, because the iron lift plates provide the bulk of the lifting power with minimal energy losses. The iron in the composite plates is in the form of fine wires in a polyester matrix, to minimize I^2R losses.

The very high lift/drag ratio for the Water Train vehicles yields 3 very important benefits:

First, on level terrain, the cost of propulsion energy per 1,000 gallons delivered is very low. For a 300 mile delivery distance, it only costs 22 cents per 1,000 gallons for the propulsion energy, assuming a unit cost of 10 cents per kWh, which is conservative. At a more likely cost of 5 cents per kWh, the propulsion energy would only cost 11 cents per 1,000 gallons.

Second, if the water delivery route is down grade because the water source is at a higher elevation than the user – a common situation when the water comes from snow packs in the mountains – the Water Train needs less propulsion energy as it coasts downhill to the user. Given a grade of only 22 feet per 10 mile distance, the Water Train needs no propulsion energy at all, but simply coasts to the delivery point. Rivers generally have steeper grades than 22 feet per 10 miles. If the grade is steeper, the Water Train would generate electric power into the grid, rather than taking power from it. Over a 300 mile distance, if the water source is 660 feet higher in elevation than the user, no propulsion power for the 150 mph Water Train would be needed for water delivery. To be fair, some small propulsion power would be required for the return trip, but because the water bladder would be collapsed, the power requirement would be small compared to the power needed with a full bladder.

Third, the coasting distance between successive propulsion "kicks" is extremely long for the Water Train. Assuming the Water Train average speed is 150 mph, but after propulsion "kick", its speed increases to 160 mph, and then gradually coasts down in speed to 140 mph before it gets the next propulsion "kick". How far does it coast until the next kick at 140 mph? Remarkably, 87 miles between propulsion kicks. This helps to reduce guideway cost, since the propulsion windings only have to be located on a small fraction of the guideway, with the distance between propulsion sections being approximately 90 miles apart.

How far would a 150 mph rail train go between propulsion "kicks"? Not very far. With its drag coefficient being 23 times greater than the Water Train, the 150 mph rail train would drop from 160 mph down to 140 mph in less than 4 miles. And that only considers rail drag. Add in air drag, and the 160 to 140 mph coasting distance for the rail train would be less than 2 miles. And the 75 mph auto? How far would it coast without propulsion from 80 mph down to 65 mph, the same proportional drop in speed as the Water Train? Adding in air drag, the coast distance would be only a quarter mile or so.

Having the propulsion sections so far apart for the Water Train not only saves on the cost of the guideway, but also on the cost of the transmission power lines that lead to the widely separated propulsion sections.

Finally, because of the high kinetic energy of the high field Water Train vehicles, they can coast up and down high hills without needing propulsion power. Climbing up a hill, the Water Train vehicle slows down; going down the hill it regains speed with virtually 100 percent efficiency. Climbing up a 500 foot high hill, the speed of the Water Train will decrease from 150 mph at the base of the hill to 75 mph at the top, and then speed back up to 150 mph when it descends to the hill's base. This is a tremendous advantage over pipelines and canals, which require pumping to climb over hills. To go across the Tehachapi Mountains, for example, the Edminston Pumping Plant of the California Aqueduct has to pump the water intended for Southern California over an elevation rise of almost 2,000 feet, taking 835 megawatts of electrical power to do so (7). Much of this input power is lost through inefficiencies and frictional losses in the canal channels, as it flows down to the users.

How much water can the Water Train deliver and how much would it cost, both for construction and per 1,000 gallons delivered? Table 2 gives the principal features and capabilities for a Reference Water Train system design capable of delivering 1 Billion gallons of water per day. Considerably larger volumes of water can be delivered by the system, if desired, and for considerably longer distances than the assumed 300 miles.

Table 2

Reference Design for the Maglev Water Train System

- 1 Billion gallons of water delivered per day.
- 300 mile delivery distance (600 miles round trip).
- 150 mph Water Train average speed.
- 75,000 gallons of water (270 metric tons) per vehicle.
- 70 Maglev vehicles per train.
- 30 meter long Maglev vehicles; 2.1 kilometer long train.

- 5 round trips of a train per day.

- 26 million gallons delivered per day per train.

- 40 trains operating on Maglev guideway.

- 3.4 meter (11 feet) diameter water bladder.

- 165 kWh average propulsion power per trip per vehicle (flat terrain).

- zero propulsion power for guideway downgrade of 22 feet per 10 miles.

- 22 cents per 1,000 gallons delivered for propulsion power, assuming flat terrain.

- 87 mile coast distances (no propulsion power) when Water train speed drops from 160 mph down to 140 mph (flat terrain).

- 560 foot coast uphill when water Train speed drops from 150 mph down to 75 mph.

- 15 million dollars construction cost per 2 way mile for on-grade Maglev guideway (1 guideway for outbound vehicles, 1 guideway for return vehicles, and 1 spare guideway for maintenance and other operations).

- 1 million dollars capital cost for Maglev vehicle

- 24 cents per 1,000 gallons vehicle amortization costs (30 year period).

- 40 cents per 1,000 gallons guideway amortization costs (30 year period)

- 86 cents per 1,000 gallons total cost in flat terrain.

- 64 cents per 1,000 gallons for down grade of 22 cents per 10 miles.

What is the status of the other 2 options for water transport, canals/aqueduct and pipelines? The largest present canal/aqueduct systems are in California, the State Water Project (SWP) and the Central Valley Project (CVP) shown by the accompanying map (Figure 2). (8)

Figure 2

California gets a lot of water and needs a lot of water. In normal years it gets 200 million acre feet of water (1 billion gallons per day equals 1.2 million acre feet per year). 5 to 10 million acre feet of water come from Colorado, Oregon, and Mexico; 60 percent of this is used directly, evaporates, or flows to the ocean, saline aquifers, and the Salton Sea. (9) About 34 million acre feet are used for irrigation and 9 million acre feet for urban and industrial uses.

The SWP and CVP canals and aqueducts convey a large fraction of California's water supplies from areas where it is surplus to areas where it is needed, both agricultural and urban. Normally, on the order of 10 million acre feet per year would be conveyed southward from the Sacramento-San Joaquin Delta via the Aqueduct. (9)

However, due to the record California droughts and drop in precipitation over the 2 years 2007 and 2008, the state received only 70% of its normal annual rainfall, which severely strained water supply.(10) Water shortages will probably get much worse in the coming decades. California is overpumping its aquifers at a rate of 2 million acre feet each year. (9) Scientists at Livermore National Laboratory and Scripps Institute of Oceanography predict that by 2040 AD most of the snow pack in the Sierras and Colorado Rockies would melt by April 1, because of global warming. Moreover, the amount of snow pack has decreased by 20% in the past few years. (11) California faces a much worse water crisis in the years ahead.

The Water Train can help alleviate this coming crisis by bringing large amounts of water from the Columbia River and other sources in Oregon down to the Sacramento-San Joaquin Delta, then to be delivered throughout California by the existing aqueduct/canal system. The delivery distance from Dalles, Oregon on the Columbia River to the Delta is approximately 600 miles.

Doubling the delivery rate of the Water Train Reference Case to 2 Billion gallons per day would deliver 2.4 million acre feet of water per year to the California Delta, a major help in meeting its water needs. The same guideway could be used, with the only modification being the addition of more Maglev Water Transport vehicles. The projected total delivery cost would be about 1.30 dollars per 1,000 gallons. The cost is higher than the Reference case cost, because the guideway is 600 miles long, compared to 300 miles for the Reference case. Because the water delivery rate is doubled, the guideway amortization cost per 1,000 gallons per mile is cut in half, meaning that total cost is not itself doubled.

Will Oregon and Washington allow the diversion of water from the Columbia River to California? Not certain. The States around the Great Lakes have signed a compact that forbids the export of water from the lakes. A similar compact could occur for the Columbia River. On the other hand, on average, the Columbia River discharges 165 Billion gallons of water per day (7500 cubic meters per second) into the Pacific Ocean (12). One would hope that diverting 1 or 2 Billon gallons per day to California would not be a big deal – better California than the Pacific

Much bigger aqueduct/canal projects than the California Aqueduct system are already being planned and executed in China to transport 44.8 Billion cubic meters of water per year (31 Billion gallons per day) through the 3 branches of the project. (13) Figure 3 is a NASA satellite image of China. The Eastern Route across China will deliver 10 Billion gallons per day, the Central Route 9 Billion gallons per day, and the Western Route 12 Billion gallons per day.

There are many environmental concerns about China's Project, particularly about pollution of the diverted water. In addition, construction of the Western Route poses many major engineering challenges. The Route starts at high altitude (9,000 to 15,000 feet above sea level) on the Qinghai-Tibet Plateau to bring water from the 3 tributaries of the Yangtze River hundreds of miles across high mountains to Northwest China. The Water Train appears to be a very promising option for the Western Route. Not only would it be better suited to the mountainous terrain, but it could also generate massive amounts of electric power as it delivered the water.

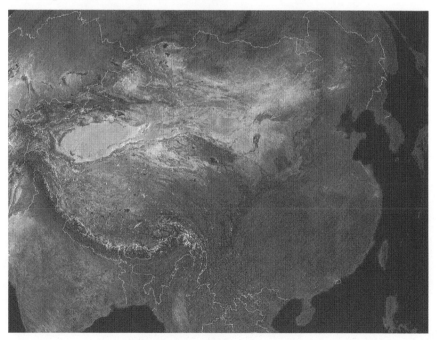

Figure 3

The 3rd water transport option, by pipeline, is exemplified by the World's largest water pipeline system, the Great Man Made River in Libya (14). Fresh water is pumped from underground aquifers in the Sahara Desert and transported through large diameter concrete pipes located underground. Figure 4 shows the scale of the concrete pipes used for the Great Man Made River (15). 85 million cubic meters (113 million cubic yards) were excavated for the first phase, which delivered more than 500 million gallons per day of fresh water to Benghazi and Sirt, over a distance of about 700 miles. This phase was inaugurated in 1991 for a cost of 14 Billion dollars. In 2010 dollars, it probably would cost well over 30 Billion dollars.

Figure 4

In comparison to the first phase of the Man-Made River, the Reference Water Train would deliver twice as much water for the same 700 miles construction cost. The Libyan Project did not involve importing across mountainous terrain with frequent up and down grades. Building a pipeline in such terrain would be much more expensive, and the pumping energy requirements much greater, due to the upgrade and downgrade siting of the pipeline.

In summary, while large scale canals/aqueduct and pipeline projects have transported massive amounts of water at acceptable cost, they can be limited in their application to locations where the terrain is favorable to their use. The Water Train, on the other hand, can be applied to a much wider range of terrains that involve hilly and mountainous terrain, and still deliver water at an acceptable cost. In doing so, the Water Train can alleviate drought in a much greater number of areas of the World.

Chapter Thirteen

Finale - Which Song Will the Fat Lady Sing?

Rather than focus only on Maglev as a transport system, its technology and potential benefits, we have broadened the scope of the book. We describe the historical development of transport in America and how American transport innovations have benefited our Nation and the rest of the World. We then describe the present problems and deficiencies in transport that America and other countries are experiencing, and how Maglev can help to solve them. Along the way we describe our personal fight to develop Maglev as a major mode of transport for the 21st Century, and the many benefits it will provide, including the use of Maglev to launch payloads into space at a cost that is much less than using chemical rockets, the use of Maglev to store electrical energy from intermittent renewable energy sources like wind and solar, and the use of Maglev to transport very large amounts of fresh water to drought stricken areas.

Most importantly, however, we discuss the crucial decision that now faces humanity. Should humans continue to consume very large amounts of fossil fuels for transport, or transition to transport system that do not use them? Continuing with transport based on fossil fuels will almost certainly lead to environmental disaster, and possibly even the extinction of the human species.

Modern society and a high standard of living require large amounts of high speed, low cost, efficient transport of people and goods. We cannot return to the horse and wagon World we left behind 200 years ago.

Humanity will have to make this decision soon, before we reach the point of no return, when global warming starts a runaway process in which the warming oceans and permafrost regions release more methane and carbon dioxide. These emissions in turn will cause more warming and further methane and carbon dioxide releases, producing a situation that cannot be stopped and that will result in the mass extinction of much of the life on Earth, possibly including humans. This could be very ironic – humans start the 6th Extinction, and are in turn made extinct.

How much time before the Earth reaches this tipping point? We don't know; nobody knows. We may have already reached it and as yet have not realized it. No matter what experts say, whether they say it will never happen, or that it will happen in X years, it's all guesswork at this point. A large scale experimental effort is vitally needed to provide a better idea of what are the conditions and times involved in the process.

We also vitally need to explore and develop in much greater depth what are the practical options for transport that does not depend on fossil fuels – their capabilities and limitations for civilization's future transport needs, what they will cost, how soon and at what scale can they be implemented, how they will affect the environment and living standards, how safe and reliable they are, and so on.

Today to meet our future transport needs we mostly have lots of talk, goals pulled out of the air – 80% reductions of carbon dioxide emissions by year Y, and so forth – platitudes, and exhortations, with very little in the way of specific plans and actions. This must change soon, before we reach the point of no return.

We hope that you find our book informative and useful, and look forward to seeing you on a high speed Maglev vehicle someday.

A final thought: In the sad event that humanity does become part of the 6th extinction, there is one small bright note. Millions of years from now, an intelligent species digging through Earth's sediments will find lots of fossilized automobiles. Hopefully our successors will be intelligent enough to understand what happened, and not repeat our mistakes.

James Powell, Franklin Award Ceremony

Gordon Danby, Franklin Award Ceremony

James Jordan

That's All Folks

Acknowledgement

Researching and writing a book is not done in isolation. We had the benefit of discussing, with many of our Maglev colleagues, the strategy and opportunities for implementing Jim Powell and Gordon Danby's 2nd generation superconducting Maglev transport system, the subject of this book.

The book was born from our frustration with the opposition to implementing superconducting Maglev in the United States. If Senator Moynihan's R&D legislation had not been blocked in the U.S. House of Representatives, Americans would now be riding in comfort in an all-electric, all-weather Maglev travel system that is extremely energy efficient, does not need oil, and just lightly sips electrons.

What does the future hold for Maglev in America? Will our leaders seize the opportunity to make America the World leader in 21st Century transport, or will the U.S. end up buying it from abroad? Will this book help to achieve the goal of a National Maglev Network? Nobody knows. This we do know, however, the book would not have come to pass without the dedicated support and assistance of many thoughtful people who are concerned about the economic, energy, and environmental security of human society. The book tells the story of 50 years of effort and commitment by the inventors of superconducting Maglev and their colleague, James Jordan. The book also benefitted tremendously from the efforts of Bob Coullahan, President & Chief Operating Officer of Readiness Resource Group, Inc. of Las Vegas, Nevada and Douglas Rike, a great industrial designer who did a lot of the graphics in this book.

The research and fact-checking for the book was greatly helped by the use of the Internet, Wikipedia, and Google. We were also assisted by wonderful people who work in the Senate library, who kept a watchful eye out for publications relevant to the book's examination of environmental, energy, and economic issues. We are especially grateful to Tamara Elliott, who commutes by rail, and quickly saw the benefits of superconducting Maglev. Her ability to find publications of interest was unfailing. A few doors from the Senate library is the Congressional Research Service Information Center for support of the Senate. Jack Swartz, who worked in this office when the book was launched, is a wonderful resource because his knowledge of government policy and history is legendary. Discussions with Jack provided enough stimulus for 10 books. The Center is also the workplace for Audrey Crane-Hirsch, an excellent reference research specialist, who cheerfully guided Jim Jordan through the great data search resources in the Center.

Jim Jordan's fellow Doorkeeper, Myrna Webb, and Chaplain of the U.S. Senate, Admiral Barry Black, offered moral encouragement and spiritual guidance during the writing of this book. Myrna Webb, a former school teacher and a former aide to several Senators, daily posed questions and promoted discussion about the policy issues relevant to our proposal for a National Maglev Network. The questions and discussions were invaluable in laying out the book. Myrna had the experience of taking a 17 hour Amtrak trip from her home in Indianapolis to Washington, DC and spurred the campaign of Jim Jordan to seek the Presidency of Amtrak for the purpose of evolving Amtrak to Maglev. Jim's campaign failed but he attracted supporters for the concept. Chaplain Black, an exceptional Biblical scholar and successful author, was a great role model for how to write a book while carrying out a very busy schedule.

A special thanks to Jim Jordan's workmates in the Senate and their sincere interest and pride in his participation in the GE Ecomagineering competition and granting the time off for Jim's trip to GE's Global Research Center in Schenectady, NY. Even though we did not win the prize, it felt good to read about the selection of our Maglev Energy Storage System, which is described in Chapter 11, as a finalist, and publication of an article in the Senate Sergeant at Arms Newsletter about our trip to G.E.

In the category of educational encouragement, we give our appreciation to the teachers and students from the Middle Schools on Long Island, who hold the annual science and engineering Maglev contest at Brookhaven National Laboratory, featuring as guests, Dr. Powell and Dr. Danby. The interest and enthusiasm of the students and the teachers make us all very proud.

References

Prologue

1. O'Toole, R., "Gridlock: Why We Are Stuck in Traffic and What to do about it", CATO Institute (2009)

2. Shapoun, H., Duffield, J., Wang, M."The Energy Balance of Corn Ethanol: An Update" USDA, Report AER 814 (2002)

3. http://www.eia.doe.gov/bookshelf/brochures/greenhouse/Chapter1.htm

4. http://www.physorg.com/print 183231158.html

5. http://www.nytimes.com/2010/03/05/science/earth/05methane.html

6. http://guardian.co.uk/environment/2010/jun/14/arctic-permafrost-methane

7. http:/en.wikipedia.org/wiki/Chevrolet_Volt

8. Census Bureau, 2008 U.S. Statistical Abstracts

9. http:/www.mrdowling.com/800density.html

10. Powell, J. and Danby G., "High Speed Transport by Magnetically Suspended Trains", Paper 66-WA/RR-5, Presented at 1966 Winter ASME Meeting, NYC. NY (November 1966)

11. http://www.digitalworldtokyo.com/500 kph_Maglev_flying trains_get_green_light_to burn_up_Japan

12. "Benefits of Magnetically Levitated High Speed Transport for the United States", Maglev Technology Advisory Committee Reports, Executive Summary (June 1989); The Technical Report (March 1992); James Powell and Gordon Danby, Co-Chairmen

Chapter One:

1. http://en.wikipedia.org/wiki/erie_canal

2. http:/www.hrmm.org/steamboats/fulton.html

3. http:/en.wikipedia.org/wiki/first_transcontinental_railroad

4. Amtrak System Timetable, Fall/winter 2007-2008, Amtrak.com

5. http://en.wikipedia.org/wiki/panama_canal

6. http://en.wikipedia.org/wiki/Ford_ModelT

7. http://en.wikipedia.org/wiki/wright_brothers

8. http://www.fhwa.dot.gov/pressroom/dot0795.html

The Fight for Maglev   References

9. http://en.wikipedia.org/

10. http://en.wikipedia.org/wiki/Apollo_program

11. Powell, J. and Danby, G. "High Speed Transport by magnetically suspended trains" paper 66-WA/RR-5 presented at 1966 Winter ASME Meeting, NYC, NY (Nov 1966)

12. "Govt May OK Direct Tokyo-Osaka Maglev line", the Yomiuri Shimbun, October 21, 2010, http://www.youmiuri.co.jp/dy/business/T101020005605.htm

13. "Benefits of Magnetically Levitated High Speed Transport for the United States", Maglev Technology Advisory Committee Reports; Executive Summary (June 1989); The Technical Report (March 1992; James Powell and Gordon Danby, Co-Chairmen

Chapter Two: Today and Tomorrow in America's Transport Hell

1. http://en.wikipedia.org/wiki/inferno_(Dante)

2. New York Times Discussion Blog May 27, 2010, *8:46 pm* "Do We Tolerate Too Many Traffic Deaths?"

3. Miller, T. and Zaloshnja, E., "On a Crash Course", Pacific Institute for Research and Evaluation", study conducted for the Transportation Construction Coalition (TCC) (May 2009) http://www.artba.org/mediafiles/pirestudy.pdf

4. "Transportation Costs and Benefits", Table 15; TDM Encyclopedia Victoria Transport Policy Institute, http:/www.vtpi.org/tdm/tdm66.htm

5. http://www.publicpurpose.com/ut-6995 commute.htm

6. http://www.fhwa.gov/pressroom/dot0795.htm

7. http://en.wikipedia.org/wiki/airbus_A380

8. Marsa, Linda, "A Wing and a Prayer", DiscoverMagazine.com (September 2009)

9. O'Toole, R., "Gridlock: Why we are stuck in traffic and what to do about it", CATO Institute (2009)

10. Census Bureau, 2010 Statistical Abstracts

11. http:/www.mrdowling.com/800density.html

Chapter Three: The Message: Avoiding the 6th Extinction

1. Extinction Event- Wikipedia, http://enwikipedia.org/wiki/extinction_event

2. The Sixth Extinction, Richard Leakey and Roger Lewin, Doubleday (1995)

3. Eldridge, Niles, The Sixth Extinction http://www.actionbioscience.org/newfrontiers/eldridge2.html

4. Harden, Garrett, the Tragedy of the Commons, Science, 162 p. 1243-1248 (1968)

5. http://earthobservation.nasa.gov/features/maya/

6. http://en.wikipedia.org/wiki/greenhouse_gas

7. http://en.wikipedia.org/wiki/file:vostok-ice-core-petit.png

8. http://cdiac.ornl.gov/trends/co2/lawdome-graphics.html

9. http://en.wikipedia.org/wiki/global_warming

10. http://en.wikipedia.org/wiki/Carbon_cycle

11. Figure 10-55, "Emissivity of Carbon Dioxide, in Heat Transmission, Section 10 of Perry's Chemical Engineers Handbook, 6th edition McGraw-Hill (1984)

12. Statistical Abstracts of the United States: 2010. Table 1351. U.S. Department of Commerce

13. http://www.eia.doe.gov/oiaf/1605/ggrpt/carbon.html

14. http://www.eia.doe/conference/2010/sessions5/sieminski.pdf

15. Statistical Abstracts of the United States 2010 Table 1346, U.S. Department of Commerce

16. http://en.wikipedia.org/wiki/peak_oil

17. http:/en.wikipedia.org/wiki/automobile_industry_in_China

18. U.S. Statistical Abstracts 2010, Table 1060, U.S. Department of Commerce.

19. Bandivadekar, Anup P., Heywood, John B., Coordinated Policy Measures for Reducing the Fuel Consumption of the U.S. Light-Duty Vehicle Fleet, June 2004

Chapter Four: The Maglev America Project – Our Highways to the Future

1. Highway Research Board, NAS, 1962. http://www.saferoads.org/issues/fs-trucks.htm

2. "Comparison of Cost for Maintaining Highway and Waterway Freight Transport Systems" U.S. DOT, April 9, 2001

3. Table 1-32 "U.S. Vehicles miles, Research and Innovative Technology Administration," Bureau of Transportation Statistics

4. Table 1046, "2006 Statistical Abstracts of the United States," U.S. Census Bureau

5. Table 3, "Resident Population Projections, 2006 U.S. Statistical Abstracts", U.S. Census Bureau

6. "Measuring Worth", http://www.measuringworth.org/usgdp/

7. National Highway Traffic Safety Administration (2008);http://www-nrd.nhtsa.dot.gov/pubs/811162pdp

Chapter Five: Global Maglev: The Big Winners in a Much Smaller World

Ocean Shipping Section

1. Evans, Paul, "Big Polluters: one massive container ship equals 50 million cars", http:www.gizmag.com/shipping-pollution/11526

2. "U.S. warns of pollution from merchant ships off the Florida Coast", www.guardian.co.uk/environment/2009/Mar/31/noaa-pollution -Florida-freighters-tankers-cruise ships.

3. "International Shipping and World Trade: Facts and Figures", IMO Library Services, February 2006

4. http://en.wikipedia.org/wiki/emma_maersk

5. http://wiki.answers.com/Q/How_Much_fuel;_does_a_container_ship_burn

Trans-Siberian Railway

1. "Trans-Siberian Railway", Wikipedia, http://wikipedia.org/wiki/Trans-Siberian Railway

Bering Strait

1. "Bering Strait Crossing", Wikipedia, http://en.wikipedia.org/wiki/bering_strait_crossing

2. "Czar Authorizes American Syndicate to Begin Work" New York Times, August 2, 1906

3. Discovery Channel's "Extreme Engineering", http://dsc.discovery.com/convergence/engineering/beringstrait/interactive/interactive.html

4. "Bering Strait", Wikipedia, http://en.wikipedia.org/wiki/bering_strait

Pan American Highway

1. Pan American Highway, Wikipedia, http://en.wikipedia.org/wiki/Pan_American_Highway

Strait of Gibraltar

1. "Strait of Gibraltar", Wikipedia, http://en.wikipedia.org/wik/Strait_of_Gibraltar

2. "Strait of Gibraltar Crossing", Wikipedia, http://en.wikipedia.org/wiki/strait_of_Gibraltar_crossing

3. "Gibraltar Bridge", http://www.opacengineers.com/projects/gibraltar

The Fight for Maglev   References

4.   "Strait of Gibraltar Floating Bridge", http://www.tdrin.com/gibraltar.htm

5.   "Channel Tunnel", http://en.wikipedia.org/wiki/Channel Tunnel

Indian Railways

1.   "Indian Railways", Wikipedia http//en.wikipedia.org/wiki/Indian_Railways

2.   "France offers to help India modernize railways including Post trains, " 13 May
     2008 Agence France Presse http//www.skyscrapercity.com/showthread – php?t =
     435076&page=2

3.   "Mumbai's deadly trains claim a dozen daily", 26 June 2008 Agence France Presse.
     Same website as (2)

4.   http://wapedia.mobi/en/Mumbai_Suburban_Railway

5.   "India: Transport at a Glance", South Asia Energy and Infrastructure (SASEI) Group
     of the World Bank, July 2005

6.   "Economy of India", Wikipedia http://en.wikipedia.org/wiki/Economy_of_India

7.   Pucher, J., et al, "Urban Transport Crisis in India" Transport Policy (2 (2005), 185-
     198

China Railways

1.   K. Richburg, "China is Pulling Ahead in Worldwide Race for High Speed Rail
     Transportation," Washington Post, May 12, 2010.

2.   "High Speed Rail in China", wikipedia.http://en.wikipedia.org?wiki/high-speed-
     rail_in_china

3.   M. Liu, et al, "The New Silk Road", Newsweek May 10, 2010.

4.   "China's High Speed Eurasian Railway Strategy for Central Asia",
     http://volvbilis.wordpress.com/2010/09/09/China's-high-speed-eurasian-railway-
     strategy-for-central-asia/

Chapter Six: How Maglev Works – First and Second Generation

1.   http://en.wikipedia.org/wiki/large_hadron_collider

2.   http://lhc-machine-outreach.web.cern.ch/lhc-
     machine_outreach/components/magnets.htm

Chapter Seven: The Fight for Maglev: First Round

1. Powell ,J., and Danby G., "High Speed Transport by Magnetically Suspended Trains", paper 66-WA/RR-5, presented at 1966 Winter ASME Meeting, NYC, NY (November 1966)

2. Kolm, H., et al, "The Magneplane System",-Cryogenics 15, p.377-384 (1975)

3. Powell, J.R., and Danby, G.T., "The Linear Synchronous Motor and High Speed Ground transport",; Proc.6th Intersociety Energy Conversion Engineering Cont. Boston, MA, p 118-131 (1971)

4. Danby, G.T., Jackson, J.W., and Powell, J.R., "Force Calculations for Hybrid (Ferro-Null Flux) Low Drag Systems', IEEE Trains on Magnetics, Mag 10 p.443 (1974)

5. Powell, JR and Danby GT, "Dynamically Stable Cryogenic Magnetic Suspension for Vehicles in Very High Velocity Transport Systems," Recent Advances in Engineering Science (EAC Eringen), Gordon & Breach, Vol 5, p.159-182 (1970)

6. Powell, J.R. and Danby, GT. Magnetic Suspension for Levitated Tracked Vehicles," Cryogenics 11, p.192-204 (1971)

7. Powell, J.R. and Danby, G.T., "Cryogenic Suspension and Propulsion Systems for 200-2000 mph ground Transport" Proc. Cryogenic Society of America Conf on Applications of Cryogenic Technology, Vol.4 p.299-332 (1971)

8. Danby, G.T. and Powell, J.R., "Integrated Systems for Magnetic Suspension and Propulsion of Vehicles" Proceedings of 1972 Applied Superconductivity Conference, Annapolis, MD, p.120-126

9. http://en.wikipedia.org/wiki/Great_Hanshin_earthquake

10. http://www.rtri.ot.ip/rd/maglev/html/english/maglev-frame_E.html

11. http://magnetbahnforum.de/index.php?speed-records

Chapter Eight: Second Round – Senator Moynihan Climbs into the Ring

1. "Use of the Interstate Highway System Right-of-way for Magnetic Levitation High Speed Transportation Systems" Hearing before the Subcommittee on Water Resources, Transportation and Infrastructure of the Committee on Environment and Public Works, United States Senate, One Hundredth Congress Second Session, February 26, 1988

The Fight for Maglev   References

2. "Benefits of Magnetically Levitated High Speed Transportation for the United States", Maglev Technology Advisor Committee Reports; Executive Summary (June 1989); The Technical Report (March 1992) James Powell and Gordon Danby, Co-Chairmen

3. "The President's Proposal for Magnetic Levitation Transportation" Hearing Before the Subcommittee on Water Resources, Transportation, and Infrastructure of the Committee in Environment and Public Works, United States Senate, one Hundred and First Congress, second Session, March 9, 1990.March 9, 1990, Senate Meeting

4. "Florida Maglev Project Description: Executive Summary", Maglev 2000 of Florida

5. "Maglev 2000, Transportation Technology: Final Report to Florida Department of Transportation and Federal Railway Administration"; Maglev 2000 of Florida, et al (April 2002)

6. "Florida Maglev Deployment Program for Kennedy Space Center Circulator National Demonstration Project" Maglev 2000 of Florida, et al/2004

7. Powell, J., et al, "Fabrication and Testing of Full Scale Components for the 2nd Generation Maglev 2000 System, Maglev 2008 Conference, San Diego, California, December 2008

8. Danby, G. and Powell, J. "Magnetic Levitation: A New Mode of Transport for the 21st Century"; Lecture given at the Award for the Franklin Medal for Engineering, April 2000

Chapter Nine: Third Round – Decision Time for America

1. 600 million dollar proposal to DOT FRA submitted for HSIPR program by James Jordan for Interstate Maglev Project

2. First Tiger Grant proposal to DOT FTA Maglev Research Center at Polytechnic Institute at NYU

Chapter Ten: Maglev Launch: Finally, the Final Frontier

1. Glaser, Peter E, "Power From the Sun: Its Future" Science 162 22(November 1968)

2. Mankins, John, "Hawaiian Power Beaming Experiment" www.space.com – experiment-boosts-space-solar-power.html

3. Angel, Roger "Feasibility of Cooling the Earth with a cloud of Small Spacecraft Near the Inner Lagrange Point (L1) www.pnas.org/cgi/doi/10.1703/pnas.0608163103

The Fight for Maglev   References

4. Powell, J., Maise, G., and Paniagua, J. "Maglev Launch: A New Concept for Very Low Cost Earth to Orbit Transport Using Ultra High Velocity Magnetic Launch", *paper IAF-01-S.6.04, 52nd International Astronautical Congress, Toulouse, France, Oct. 1-5 (2001).*

5. Powell, J., Maise, G., and Paniagua, J. "Maglev Launch: A Maglev System for Ultra Low Cost Launch of Cargo to LEO, GEO, and the Moon", *Paper IAC-03-IAA.13.1.04, 54th International Congress, Bremen, Germany.*

6. Powell, J., Maise, G., and Paniagua, J. "Maglev Launch: An Ultra Low Cost Launch System to Enable Large Scale Exploration of the Solar System", *Space Technology and Applications International Forum (STAIF-2006), Albuquerque, NM, February 12-16 (2006).*

7. Powell, J., Maise, G., Paniagua, J., and Jordan, J., "Maglev Launch – An International Facility to Magnetically Launch Payloads at Ultra Low Unit Cost"; *Paper IAC-06-D3.2.7; 57th International Astronautical Congress, Valencia, Spain, October (2006).*

8. Powell, J., Maise, G., Paniagua, J., and Rather, J. "Magnetically Inflated Cable (MIC) System for Large Scale Space Structures", NIAC Phase 1 Report, May 1, 2006, NIAC Subaward No. 07605-003-046. Also, "MIC – A Self Deploying Magnetically Inflated Cable System", *Acta Astronautica, 48, No 5-12, p 331-352.(2001)*

Chapter Eleven: Maglev Energy Storage – The Good Sisyphus

1. Hamilton, Edith, "Mythology: Timeless Tales of Gods and Heroes"

2. Painting By Titian, 1549

3. Powell, J,; Danby, G; Coullahan, R; Griffis, F.H.; and Jordan, J. "Maglev Energy Storage and the Grid", 2010 Advanced Energy Conference, Nov 8-9, New York City, NY

4. http://en.wikipedia.org/wiki/racoon_mountain_pumped_storage_plant

Chapter Twelve: Maglev Water Transport – A Billion Jugs A Day

1. http://en.wikipedia.org/wiki/David_Blaine

2. The Water Issue, National Geographic, April 2010

3. Kranhold, K :Water, Water, Everywhere", Wall Street Journal, January 17, 2008 (http: //online.wsj.com/article/SB 12005 369 8876396483.html

362

The Fight for Maglev   References

4. http://en.wikipedia.org/wiki/desalination

5. Miller, J.E. 2003 "Review of Water Resources and Desalination Technologies, Sandia National Laboratories, Albuquerque, NM 49 pp. http://www.Sandia.gov/Water/docs/MillerSAND 2003_0800.pdf.

6. Powell, J, and Danby G, "The Water Train: Long Distance Delivery of Water by Maglev", Report DPMT 3, DP Maglev Technology, Inc., December 1997

7. http://en.wikipedia.org/wiki/Edmonston_Pumping_Plant

8. http://www.mwdh2o.com/mwdh2o/pages/publications/other/large/conveyance_map_ly.jpg

9. http://westernfarm press.com/environment/califronia-water-supply-demand-0226/

10. http://www.matternetwork.com/2009/1/Sacramento-san-joaquin-delta-san.ctm

11. Melvilie, Kate, "California's water supply Dwindling Science Express, http://www.scienceagogo.com/news/20080103202904data_trunc_sys.shtml

12. http://en.wikipedia.org/wiki/Columbia_River

13. http://www.water-technology.net/projects/south_North/

14. http://www.water-technology.net/projects/gmr/

15. http://en.wikipedia.org/wiki/Great_Manmade_River

Chapter Thirteen: The Finale

No Reference

From left to right, top to bottom: Redwood Forest; coal ash sludge from a Dec 22, 2008 breech of a fly ash dam at a TVA coal power plant in Tennessee; beach on the Gulf of Mexico; the April 20, 2010, explosion and fire on the Deepwater Horizon rig site of the largest marine oil spill in the history of the petroleum industry; Illinois corn field: Illinois coal mine, artist drawing of the Interstate Maglev system; a typical Interstate Highway near a major metropolitan area.

Index (Names)

A

Allinger, Joe, Coworker with Gordon Danby, *177*

Armstrong, Neil, First man to walk on Moon, *29, 298*

Ausubel, Jesse, Analysis of past and future transport systems, *269*

B

Baker, Howard, Ambassador to Japan, *266*

Benedict, Manson, MIT Professor, 169

Bishop, Tim , Representative, New York, meeting with, *257, 258*

Blow, Larry, MTAC Member, *195*

Bright, Anthony, MTAC Member,, *195*

C

Card, Andrew, Chief of Staff, President Bush,, *267*

Carr, Robert, Representative, Detroit, Chairman House Transportation Committee, *199*

Choate, Pat, author, "Dangerous Business", *271*

Clinton, Governor, NY, pioneered Erie Canal, *22*

Coffey, Howard, MTAC Member, *195*

Coffey, Howard, Stanford Research Institute Maglev Program, *156*

Cuomo, Mario, Governor, NY, *199, 244, 245, 246*

D

Darman, Richard, Director OMB, *198*

E

Eisenhower, Dwight, US President, Initiated Interstate Highway System, *9, 10, 28, 187*

F

Fair, Harry, MTAC Member,, *195*

Ford, Henry, Pioneered U.S. Auto Industry, *xv, 9, 25, 35, 156, 228, 247, 265, 355*

Frankel, Emile, Deputy Secretary of Transportation, meeting with, *249*

Friedman, Thomas L., columnist and author, quote from New York Times column, Invent, Invent, Invent, published June 27, 2009, *v*

Fulton, Robert, Inventor of Steamboats, *23, 279*

G

Gargano, Charles, Chairman, Empire State Development Corporation, *259*

Gibbon, Edward, Author, "Decline and Fall of the Roman Empire,", *227*

Gibbs, Richard, MTAC Member, *195*

Graham, Bob, Senator Florida, Moynihan Maglev Hearing, *193*

The Fight for Maglev   Index (Names)

Gran, Richard, MTAC Member, *195*

Griffis, F.H. "
   Trip to Japan, *262*

Griffis, F.H., Provost, Polytechnic
   Institute of NY
   meeting with Empire State
      Development Corporation:, *260*

Griffis, F.H., Provost, Polytechnic
   Institute of NY,
   meeting with Senator Schumer, 263

Guthrie, Woody, singer, "This Land is
   My Land, This Land is Your Land, *77*

H

Hardin, Garret, author, "The Tragedy of
   the Commons", 54

Henry, John, MTAC member, *195*

Holder, Nick, assistant to Rep. Bishop,
   257

Hoopengardner, R, FTA Report on
   Maglev, *222*

Hughes, Vernon, Colleague of Gordon
   Danby, *179*

J

Jackson, David, Professor, McGill
   University, *174*

Jackson, John, Colleague of Gordon
   Danby, *177*

Johnson, Larry, Argonne National
   Laboratory, witness at 1st
   Moynihan Hearing on Maglev,, *193*

Johnson, Larry, MTAC Member, *195*

K

Kasai, Yoshiyuki, President, Japan
   Railways, *268*

Keever, D, FTA Report on Maglev, *222*

Kelly, General Patrick, Witness, 2nd
   Moynihan Hearing on Maglev, *197*

Kennedy, John, U.S. President, Apollo
   Moon Program, *10,28*

Kitagawa, Takashi, Washington
   Representativef of Japan Railways,
   meeting with, *265*

Kolm, Henry, M.I.T, co-inventor of
   Magneplane, *156*

Kolm, Henry, MTAC Member, *195*

L

LaTourette, Steve, Representative,
   Ohio, Chairman of Subcommittee
   on Railroads,, *245*

Lederman, Andrew, Assistant to
   Senator Schumer, Meeting with on
   Maglev, *262,264-265*

Leung, Edward, MTAC Member, *195*

Lincoln, Abraham, President of U.S.,
   Transcontinental Railroad, *24*

Lohneiss, Andrea, Economic
   Development, Riverhead, Meeting
   about Maglev Test Facility at
   Riverhead, *257*

Lundine, Stanley, Lt. Governor of New
   York, Addressed NY Maglev
   Workshop on NY Maglev Report,
   199

Lynch, Tim, MTAC Member, *195*

M

Mineta, Norman, Secretary of
   Transportation, *249*

Morena, John, Principal in Maglev
   2000, *203*

The Fight for Maglev

Index (Names)

Morse, Samuel, Inventor of telegraph, *138*

Moynihan, Daniel Patrick, Senator, New York, *159, 189-199,259-260*

N

Nakayama, Osamu, representative Japan Railways, meeting with in Washington, *265*

O

Obama, Barack, President U.S., speech about Japanese Maglev, *275-276*

Oberstar, James, Representative, Ranking Member of Transportation Committee, letter for Maglev Test Facility on Long Island, *247*

Olson, Mancur, author, "The Rise and Decline of Nations", *270*

Ott, Kevin, MTAC member, *195*

P

Page, Robert, Witness at 2nd Moynihan Hearing on Maglev, *197*

Pataki, George, Governor of New York, founded Empire State Development Corporation, *259*

Pressler, Larry, Senator, attended Moynihan meeting on Maglev, *194*

Proise, Mike, MTAC member, *195*

R

Ramsey, David, MTAC Member, *195*

Ray, Mrs. Teacher for James Powell, *167*

Reich, Robert, author, "Supercapitalism, The Transformation of Business, Democracy, and Everyday Life ", *271*

Reid, Harry, Senator Nevada, attended 1st and 2nd Moynihan hearings on Maglev, *194*

Rike, Douglas, GE Ecomagination Challenge, *285*

Robertson, Fred, Consultant to MTAC, *195*

Roosevelt, Theodore, President of US, Panama Canal, *24*

Rosner, Carl, MTAC Member, *195*

S

Salter, Bob, Consultant to MTAC, *195*

Schumer, Charles, Senator, New York, meeting with for support of Maglev test Facility on Long Island, *259, 262-264*

Schwartz, Mel, colleague of Gordon Danby, *176*

Schwarzenegger, Arnold, Governor, California, proponent of High Speed Rail System in California, *237*

Smith, Charles, expert on Maglev and High Speed Rail, *184*

Symms, Steve, Senator, Attended 2nd Moynihan Meeting on Maglev, *197*

T

Thornton, Richard, MIT, co-inventor of Magneplane, *156*

Thornton, Richard, MTAC Member, *195*

Twain, Mark, author, "Life on the
Mississippi, *1, 23*

V

Von Karman, Theodore, famed
aerodynamist, *163*

W

Wagner, Tom, President of Maglev
2000, *203*
Welch, Richard, witness at 1st
Moynihan Hearing on Maglev, *193*
Williams, Clarke, Chairman of Nuclear
Engineering Department,

Brookhaven National Laboratory,
170
Wright, Wilbur and Orville, inventors
of the airplane, *26*

Y

Yachmetz, Mark, Associate
Administrator of Federal Railroad
Administration, *250*

Z

Zavadowski, Richard, MTAC Member,
195

Index (Places and Topics)

Prologue: Why Maglev is Inevitable
- Electric cars, *17, 256, 369*
- Chevrolet Volt, *6, 17, 80, 355, 369*
  - Limited to short trips, 17
  - Transported by Maglev for long trips, 17
  - Weather impacts, cold & hot, on range of electric cars, 17
- Greenhouse gases, emitted by,1, 9,10,17, 20
  - Automobiles and trucks,9,17-18, 77
  - Methane hydrates in oceans, warming of, 5-6
  - Synfuels, future projections for emissions, 18, 77-80
- High Speed Rail travel, 18, 88-89
  - High Speed Rail per capita travel mileage much smaller than highway travel mileage even in France and Japan, 18,80
  - Only carries passengers, not autos, trucks, and freight, 18,80
  - Requires massive government subsidies for construction and operation. 18,30
  - US government proposed HSR program, 9
  - US per capita rail passenger travel mileage is only 18 miles per year, 18

Chapter 1: America: Once the Leader in World Transport
- U.S. Transport Revolutions, *21-32*
- Erie Canal, 21-*22*
  - Governor DeWitt Clinton, *22*
- Steamboats, *23*
  - Robert Fulton, inventor of, *23*
- Transcontinental Railroad, *24*
  - President Abraham Lincoln and, *24*

- Chinese workers, *29-30*
- Panama Canal, *24-25*
  - President Theodore Roosevelt and , *24-25*
- Model T automobiles, *25-26*
  - Henry Ford and, *25-26*
- Airplanes, *26-27*
  - Wright Brothers, Inventors of, *26-27*
- Interstate Highway System, *28*
  - President Dwight Eisenhower and, *28*
- Apollo Moon Project, *29*
  - President John Kennedy and , 29
- Steel industry in US, *31-32*
  - Sale of J&L Technology to Japan, *31-32*
- Japanese 1st Generation Maglev System, *10,33, 147-153,159-160, 183,229,241*
  - Based on Powell-Danby Maglev inventions, *33*
  - Design of Japanese Maglev guideway, *148*
  - Discussions on Maglev with Japanese engineers and scientists, 33,146
  - Tests of Japanese Maglev vehicle, *203*
  - Test facility at Yamanashi, 33
  - Tokyo to Osaka route, *33*
  - World Speed record, *33*
- Superconducting Maglev inventions by Powell and Danby
  - 1966 paper for ASME on 1st generation Maglev System, *32,156*
  - Basis for Japanese Maglev system, *33-34*
  - 2nd Generation Maglev 2000 System, *33-34*

- o Description of 2nd Generation Maglev-2000 System, *35*

Chapter 2: Transport Hell
- Highway travel, 37-40
  - o Annual US deaths & injuries on highways, 38
  - o Cost of highway deaths and injuries, 39
  - o Cost of highway travel, 39
  - o Congestion delays, 39
  - o Future congestion on US highways, 39
- Airway travel, 41-42
  - o Air travel discomfort,41
  - o Delays due to weather & congestion, 41-42
  - o Failure of air travel, 42
  - o Safety concerns, 42
- Public Transit travel, 43-45
  - o Discomfort of public transit travel, 43-44
  - o Decline in public transit ridership, 45
  - o Future of Public Transit travel, 44-45
  - o High fares, 45
  - o Slow travel speeds, 44-45
- Rail travel, 46-48
  - o Amtrak ridership, 47
  - o Foreign High Speed Rail ridership, 47
  - o Government subsidies, 47-48
  - o High fares, 47-48
- Fossil fuels for transport, 49-51
  - o Dependence on oil fueled transport, 49
  - o Environmental damage from synfuels, 51
  - o Peak oil and transport, 50-51
  - o US oil consumption for transport, 50
- Public transit, 43-45
  - o Almost all American commuters (87%) take automobiles to work, only 5% take public transit, 44
  - o Fares very high per passenger mile, 45
  - o Large government subsidies required, 45

Chapter 3: The Message: Avoiding the 6th Extinction
- Mass extinctions on Earth, 52-56
  - o Previous 5 mass extinctions, 52-53
  - o 6th mass extinction underway caused by humans, 53-54
- Tragedy of the Commons, 54-56
  - o Garrett Hardin essay, 54-55
  - o How selfish exploitation of the Commons causes societies to collapse, 55-56
  - o Collapse of the Mayan civilization, 55-56
  - o Today's global commons, ocean acidification and atmospheric carbon dioxide, 56
- Global warming causes, 58-68
  - o Atmospheric carbon dioxide concentration increase since start of the Industrial Revolution, 58-59
  - o Correlation of World temperature increases with increased carbon dioxide concentration, 58-59
  - o Physical reasons why increased carbon dioxide increases World temperature, 60-63
- Global warming deniers, 64-67
- Capture and sequestration of carbon dioxide from vehicle emissions is not practical, 70
- Carbon dioxide emissions from oil fueled vehicles, 71-74
  - o Impact of synfuels on vehicle carbon dioxide emissions, 71-73

- o Projections of future emission rate and atmospheric carbon dioxide levels from vehicles using synfuels, 73
- Biofuels for vehicle transport, 68-69
  - o Land area needed to meet US transport fuel needs, 69
  - o Net energy from gallon of ethanol, 69
- Hydrogen fuel for vehicle transport, 69
  - o Number of 1000 megawatt reactors needed to produce hydrogen fuel for US vehicles, 69
  - o Safety concerns for hydrogen fueled vehicles, 69
  - o Terrorists using hydrogen autos as bombs, 69
- Synfuels for vehicle transport, 69
  - o Doubles carbon dioxide emissions per gallon of fuel used in vehicles, compared to gasoline, 69
  - o Manufactured from coal, oil shale, tar sands, etc., 69
  - o World carbon dioxide emissions in future from Synfuels, 69
- Ocean acidification, 74-76
  - o Absorption of increased atmospheric carbon dioxide in the ocean are making it more acidic, 75
  - o Death of ocean life when ocean becomes too acidic, 75
  - o Experiments described to determine when ocean life will die due to increased acidification, 19,75
- Runaway global warming, 75
  - o Carbon dioxide stored in permafrost and methane in ocean hydrate beds is released when the oceans and

permafrost become warmer world, 76
- o Release cannot be stopped when temperature reaches certain level, will cause runaway global warming and mass extinctions, 74-76
- o Runaway point can be predicted by experiments on permafrost and ocean methane hydrates, 76
- Oil production and reserves, 11-12,67-68
  - o Current world oil production, 67
  - o Future cost of oil, 12
  - o World oil reserves, 12, 68
- Oil consumption, 3-4, 73-74
  - o American per capita consumption, 3
  - o Percentage consumed by transport, 73
  - o Rest of World per capita consumption, 3, 73-74
- World population, 3,18, 73-74
  - o Current World population, 3,18, 73-74
  - o Prediction for 2050 World population, 3,18, 73-74

Chapter 4: The Maglev America Project – Our Highways to the Future
- National Maglev Network, Advantages 81,86,90
  - o Can be privately financed, 90
  - o Carries trucks, autos, & freight as well as passengers, 81
  - o Does not use expensive scarce oil, biofuels, or hydrogen fuel, 81
  - o Eliminates highway congestion and maintenance problems, 86
  - o Much cheaper than passenger only High Speed Rail, 80,275

- National Maglev Network, description of, 90-99
  - Cost of, 96
  - Intercity 300 mph Maglev routes, maps of, 90-93
  - Metropolitan areas connected to 300 mph Network, 90-93
  - Service by Maglev on existing RR tracks inside metropolitan area, 94
  - US population served by Maglev Network, fraction of, 91-94
- National Maglev Network, environmental, economic, and social benefits, 81
  - Economic savings in cost of transport, 81
  - Environmental benefits, 81
  - Reduced highway deaths, injuries, and health damage, 81
- American highways, problems of, 93-98
  - Cost of highway damage from cars and trucks, 86
  - Highway congestion, present and future, maps of, 85
- Federal Highway Administration (FHA) projections of future highway traffic and congestion, 84-87
  - Maps of US highway freight traffic for 2002 and 2025, 85
  - Maps of US peak period congestion for 2002 and 2025, 84
  - Map of ton-miles of truck shipments by State, 88
- Highway truck traffic, 86
  - 50,000 trucks daily on some highways, 86
  - US expenditures on truck transport, 86
  - A single truck does as much damage as 9600 autos, 86
  - Trucks cause 60 Billion dollars per year of highway damage, 86

Chapter 5: Global Maglev: The Big Winners in a Much Smaller World

- Global Maglev Transport, 101-134
  - Advantages of global Maglev freight transport over conventional ship transport, 101-108
  - Bering Strait Maglev route, 112-116
  - China Maglev routes, 130-134
  - India Maglev routes, 126-130
  - Pan American Highway route, 116-121
  - Trans-Siberian Railway Maglev route, 109
- Trans-Siberian Railway Maglev route
  - Maglev route capital cost, 111
  - Map of route, 109
  - Travel time and cost for Maglev freight transport, Asia to Europe, compared to ships, 109-111
- Bering Strait Maglev route, 112-116-
  - Early conventional bridge & tunnel designs, 112-113
  - Floating undersea Maglev tube, concept and cost, 114
  - Maglev transport cost across Bering Strait, 116
- Pan American Highway Maglev route, 116-121
  - Alaska highway section of Maglev route, 120
  - Darien Gap in Columbia, S.A. 117
  - Maglev system built alongside Pan American Highway, 118
  - Total cost of 15,000 mile Pan American Highway Maglev route, 120
- Strait of Gibraltar Maglev route, 121-125
  - Early conventional bridge & tunnel designs, 123

The Fight for Maglev   Index (Places and Topics)

- o Floating undersea Maglev tube concept and cost, 124-125
- o Maglev trip time and cost across Strait of Gibraltar, 125
- India Maglev routes, 126-130
  - o Enormous passenger traffic on India railroads, 126-128
  - o India railroad travel is very crowded, slow, and cheap, 126
  - o India railroad gauge is not standard 4 feet 6 wide gauge, 128
  - o Total cost for conversion of 40,000 mile railroad system & to Maglev, using existing RR tracks, 130
- China Maglev routes, 130-134
  - o China now building very large High Speed Rail Network, 133
  - o First generation Shanghai Maglev System not being expanded in China, 133
  - o Potential for converting China High Speed Rail trackage to 2nd Generation Maglev, 133

Chapter 6: How Maglev Works – First and Second Generation

- Magnets, basic types for Maglev, 139-142
  - o Electromagnets, 140
  - o Permanent magnets, 140
  - o Superconducting magnets, 141
- Superconducting Magnets, 142-144
  - o Application for Maglev, 142-144
  - o Application for MRI medical machines, 142
- Large Hadron Collider, 143
- Maglev 2000 Superconducting Quadrupole magnet, 150-153
  - o 4-pole magnets compared to 2 pole magnets, 150
  - o Allows Maglev 2000 vehicles to travel on elevated monorail guideways, flat planar

guideways, and existing RR tracks, and transition between them, 150
  - o Enables high speed electronic switching to off-line stations, 151-152
  - o Quadrupole magnets enable Maglev 2000 vehicles to carry heavy trucks & autos, 153
  - o Very low magnetic fringe fields from quadrupoles, 152

Chapter 7: The Fight for Maglev: First Round

- Invention of superconducting Maglev, 155-188
  - o First published concept of superconducting Maglev, the 1963 "Magnetic Road" paper, 164
  - o Collaboration with Gordon Danby on design using aluminum loops in guideway instead of superconducting cables, 164
  - o Publication of "High Speed Transport by Magnetically Suspended Trains: at 1966 ASME Conference, 156,164
  - o Visits by Japan and other countries/organizations that start to work on 1966 Maglev design, 157
- German 1st generation electromagnetic Transrapid Maglev System, 158-161
  - o Clearance between vehicle and guideway is very small, 159
  - o Commercial Maglev system in Shanghai, China, 133
  - o Electromagnetic suspensions are inherently unstable, rapid servo control of magnet current at thousandths of second, 146

- Testing of Transrapid vehicles, 160-161
- Innovation, conditions for, 186-188
  - Avid micro-management of innovators 187
  - Do not teach to tests 187
  - Emphasize creativity and critical thinking,, 186
  - Innovation is an emotional drive, not a logical procedure that can be ordered and taught, 163
  - Stop outsourcing America's science and engineering jobs to other countries, 187
- Powell, James life and educational experiences leading to the invention of superconducting Maglev, 165-172
- Danby, Gordon, life and educational experiences leading to the invention of superconducting Maglev, 173-186

Chapter 8: Second Round – Senator Moynihan Climbs into the Ring

- Maglev Technology Advisor Committee (MTAC), 195-197
  - Established by Senator Moynihan in 1988 with Powell and Danby as Co-Chairmen, 195
  - Issued reports on technology and benefits of Maglev to Senator Moynihan's Subcommittee on Water Resources, Transportation, and Infrastructure, 196
  - MTAC members, 195
- Maglev 2000 components, fabrication of, 203-223
  - Aluminum guideway loop panels, 212-216
  - Guideway beam, 217-218
  - Superconducting quadrupole magnets, 208-212
  - Vehicle fuselage, 218-219

- Very low funding level for Maglev 2000 components, 202
- Response to FTA Report on Maglev 2000 Levitation Test, 220-223
- Funding for 2nd Generation Maglev 2000 development, 203
- Maglev 2000 laboratories in Florida and Long Island, 203
- Maglev 2000 route studies, 199-202
  - Cape Canaveral to Titusville, Florida route, 200
  - Kennedy Space Center to Saturn V visitor center route, 202
- Franklin Institute Award of 2000 AD medal for engineering to Powell and Danby, 224
  - Previous awardees, 224
- Yamanashi Facility for Testing of 1st generation Maglev passenger system, 223-224
  - Dedication in April 1997, 223
  - Guideway design, 148
  - Participation of Powell at dedication, 223-224
  - World speed record of 361 mph, 223

Chapter 9: Third Round – Decision Time for America

- Gathering Storm report from the National Academy of Engineering, 274
  - Concluded that US innovation and competitiveness is declining 274
- Energy efficiency by Transport Mode, 253
- Annual expenditures, current and future, for US transport modes, 254
- US transport demand in 2025, oil use and carbon dioxide emissions for Maglev and Synfuel options, 256
- Tiger Grant Proposal to FTA (Federal Transit Administration), 235-236

The Fight for Maglev   Index (Places and Topics)

- o Facility at Riverhead, Long Island, would test and certify Maglev 2000 vehicles for operation on existing RR tracks, 236
- o Proposed 60 million dollar program not funded by FTA, 236
- o "Shovel ready" existing technology proposals favored, not new technologies,236
- Department of Transportation (DOT) actions on Maglev, 200-201, 275
  - o Begin US Maglev programs after Powell/Danby invention of superconducting Maglev, 34
  - o Cancellation of US Maglev programs, 34
  - o Funding of 6 Maglev route studies in US by Federal Railroad Administration –5 were German Transrapid Maglev routes, 6th was Maglev 2000 – FRA finalists were Transrapid routes, 242
  - o Testing and certification program proposal for 300 mph Maglev 2000 system 234-235
  - o TIGER proposal for Maglev 2000 system using RR tracks, 235-236
- Florida Maglev 2000 Project, 199-223
  - o Initial funding by Florida Department of Transportation in 1996, 199
  - o More funding by Federal Railroad Administration, 200
  - o Map of 20 mile Cape Canaveral to Titusville Maglev route, 200
  - o More funding by Federal Railroad Administration, 202
  - o Participant organizations n Florida study, 201
  - o Route not selected as FRA finalist, 202

- Department of Transportation (DOT) meetings with, 249-250
  - o Meeting with Deputy Secretary of DOT, Emile Frankel, 249
  - o Meeting with Associate Administrator of Federal Railroad Administration(FRA), 249-250
- US Congress, meetings with and letters to Senators and Representatives, to describe Maglev 2000 benefits, 257-281
  - o Meeting with staff of Representative Timothy Bishop, 257-258
  - o Meeting with Senator Schumer & Staff, 262-264
  - o Meeting with Senator Reid, 278-281
- SUMMIT proposal for Maglev Test & Certification Facility in Nevada, 282-284
  - o Demonstrate Maglev 2000 systems for long distance truck transport, energy storage, and water transport, 282-284
  - o Proposal written by Robert Coullahan, James Powell, and Gordon Danby, 284
- Maglev Energy Storage proposal to General Electric, 285-290
  - o Presentation of Maglev energy storage technology to GE Ecomagination Challenge in Schenectady, NY, 285-290
- 2nd Generation Maglev 2000 system, unique capabilities of 149-154
  - o Ability to travel on monorail and planar guideways and transition smoothly between them, 149-151
  - o Carries heavy trucks, autos, & freight in addition to passengers, 149-154

375

- Electronic, no-mechanical, switching at high speed to off-line stations for loading/unloading, 149-151
- Levitated travel on existing RR tracks, 151-152
- Very low magnetic fringe fields at natural Earth background levels, 152-153
- China,, potentially the World leader in Maglev, 291-296
  - China already operates first commercial Maglev system based on 1st generation German Transrapid technology, 295
  - China can quickly transition to 2nd generation Maglev technology, 291
  - Container ships can transport 20 miles of prefabricated Maglev 2000 guideway beams and vehicles to anywhere in the World, 291-292
  - National Maglev Network of 28,800 miles could all be prefabricated in China and shipped to America at half the cost compared to building it in America,, 291-296
  - Strategic and political aspects of China building U.S. National Maglev Network 291-296

Chapter 10: Maglev Launch: Finally, the Final Frontier
- Space launch applications, 300-336
  - Beaming power to Earth, 301
  - Colonies on Mars, 303
  - Discover Alien life, 304
  - Hotels in Space, 305
  - Protect Earth from asteroids, 300

- Sunshields against global warming, 302
- Space Maglev launch systems, 307-319
  - Cargo launch Gen-1 system, 307-319
  - Cost of Maglev Space Launch, 316-319
  - Human launch Gen=2 System, 307-316
  - Potential launch sites, 322-324
  - Technology of Maglev launch, 308-316

Chapter 11: Maglev Energy Storage – The Good Sisyphus
- Energy storage application, 327-336
  - Acronym for Maglev Energy Storage (MAPS), 328
  - Advantage of MAPS over pumped hydro storage, 334
  - How MAPS works, 328-334
  - MAPS storage capability, efficiency and cost, 334
  - Storage of Wind & Solar power, 333

Chapter 12: Maglev Water Transport – A Billion Jugs a Day
- Water transport applications, 337-350
  - California Water Train, 347-348
  - China water train, 349
  - How Maglev Water Train Works, 341-346
  - Reference design of water train, 342
  - Several times without food and water,336
  - Water requirements to grow food, 338

Index (Illustrations & Credits)

Front Cover - Doug Rike
p. v. Photo of Drs. Danby and Powell
p. vi. Photo of Senator Patrick Moynihan
from U.S. Senate Internet Files

Preface
p.x Maglev 2000 Scenes Jordan & Doug
Rike
p.xvi Maglev 2000 Scene of delivery van
loading Jordan & Doug Rike

**Foreword – How Much Time Has
Humanity Got?**
Prologue - Why Maglev is Inevitable
p. 8. pteropod, *Limacina helicina*
Photo/NOAA
p.13. Decision Tree Powell & Doug Rike
p.19. Maglev Mt. Fuji scene Japan
Railways (JR)
p.20. Maglev 2000 Drawing, Maglev 2000

**Chapter 1 - America- Once the World
Leader in Transport**
p.22. Watercolor Erie Canal by John
William Hill, 1829 Public Domain (PD)
p.23. Pen and Ink Sketch of Robert
Fulton's "Clermont" PD
p.24. Linking Transcontinental Railroad at
Promontory, Utah *Photo* by Andrew
Russell, 1869. PD
p.25.Panama Canal Scenes. Wikipedia, PD
Theodore Roosevelt at the controls of
steam shovel. Library of Congress PD
p.26. Henry Ford. Library of Congress PD
p.26 Wright Brothers 1st Flight from
Library of Congress, PD
p.28 Interstate Highway System Map from
US DOT
p.29 Neil Armstrong on Moon NASA
p.30. Engraving 19th Century Chinese
Railway workers, Wikipedia, PD

p.31. Rendering of High Speed Rail in
California, CHSRA, PD
p.32. Watercolor of Steel Mill in PA, PD
p.33. Photo of superconducting Maglev
on Yamanashi Test Track. JR
p.36. Scene of U.S. Postal Service Truck
loading on Maglev 2000 RORO vehicle.
Jordan and Doug Rike

**Chapter 2 – Today and Tomorrow in
America's Transport Hell**
p.37 Stradano's visualization of the 5th
Circle of Hell
p.38 Highway Crash Scene from
www.nrd.nhtsa.dot.gov/Pubs/811402.pdf
p.40 6th Circle Etching by Paul Gustave
Doré
p.41 Interior of Airbus 380 Wikipedia PD
p.43 7th Crcle etching by Paul Gustave
Dore
p.44 photo of NY Subway from
Metropolitan Transit Authority
p.46 Doré illustration of Dante's Inferno
8th Circle Fraud
p.47 Photo of high speed train Taiwan
Wikipedia PD
p.49. Doré illustration for Dante's Inferno
9th Circle Betrayal
p.50. Photo of Dark Lake from Wikipedia,
PD

**Chapter 3 – The Message: Avoiding
the 6th Extinction**
p.57 Figure 1 420,000 years of ice core
data from Vostok, U.S.Antarctica
Research Station
p.59 Figure 2 Atmospheric Carbon Dioxide
from Law Dome Ice Cores, CSIRO, PD and
Figure 3 Global Temperatures, NASA
p.60 Figure 4 Carbon Cycle Wikipedia, PD
p.62 Figure 5 Engineering Data derived
from Perry's Chemical Engineers
Handbook, Powell

The Fight for Maglev

Index (Illustrations & Credits)

p.68 Figure 6 Per Capita Oil Consumption Relative to GDP Wikipedia, Presented at US EIA 2010 Conference, A. Sieminski
p.71 Fuel Consumption Trends Bandivadekar, Anup P., Heywood, John B., Coordinated Policy Measures for Reducing the Fuel Consumption of the U.S. Light-Duty Vehicle Fleet, June 2004
p.73 Table 2 Carbon Dioxide Emitted by Transport. Powell

Chapter 4 – The Maglev America Project – Our Highways to the Future
p.82. Scene of Maglev 2000 elevated guideways built on ROW in I-5. Doug Rike
p.84 Fig.1A 1B maps of congestion on Interstate Highway System. DOT
p.85 Fig 2A, 2B maps of truck usage of Interstate Highway System. DOT
p.88. Fig 3. Ton miles of truck shipments by state. DOT
p.89. Fig 4. Population distribution of the US 2000 US Census
p.91. Fig 5. 1st 5years of Maglev America Project. Doug Rike
p.92. Fig 6. 2nd 5 years of Maglev America Project. Doug Rike
p.93. Fig 7. 3rd 5 years of Maglev America Project. Doug Rike

Chapter 5 – Global Maglev: The Big Winners in a Much Smaller World
p.100. Montage of global citizens Doug Rike from PD photos
p.104. Fig.1. TEU drawing. Rike & Powell
p.105. Fig. 2. Hanjin Container Ship in San Francisco bay. PD Wikipedia
p.109. Fig, 3. The Trans-Siberian Railway. PD Wikipedia
p.110. Fig. 4. Trans-Siberian railroad track near the town of Ust' Katay in the Ural Mountains. PD Wikipedia
p.113. Fig.5. The Bering Strait, NASA
p.117. Fig.6. Pan American Highway Map. PD Wikipedia

p.118. Fig. 7. Pan-American Highway in Argentina PD Wikipedia
p.119. Fig.8 Pan-American Highway in San Martin, El Salvador PD Wikipedia
p.120. Fig.9. Signpost at Delta Junction, Alaska, PD Wikipedia
p.122. Fig 10 & 11.Strait of Gibraltar, PD Wikipedia
p.129. Map of India. PD
p.131. Map of China. PD Wikipedia

Chapter 6 – How Maglev Works – First and Second Generation
p.139.Fig 1 Maglev 2000
p.140. Fig 2. Maglev 2000
p.141. Fig 3. Maglev 2000
p.143. Fig 4. Photo LHC PD Wikipedia
p.145. Fig 5. Diagram PD Wikipedia
p.147. Fig 6. Photo JR
p.148. Fig 7. Drawing JR
p.150. Fig 8. & Fig 9. Maglev 2000
p.152 Fig 10. Animation Sequence of Interstate Maglev Doug Rike
p.153 Fig.11. Scene of RORO Maglev vehicle loading produce truck Doug Rike

Chapter 7 – The Fight for Maglev: First Round
p.156. Fig.1. Cover page of 1966 Maglev Paper. Powell and Danby
p.157 Fig 2. Photo of TACV U.S. DOT
p.160. Fig 3,4,5, JRTRI, Fig 6 PD Wikipedia

Chapter 8 – Second Round – Senator Moynihan Climbs Into the Ring
p.196. MTAC Report Cover Powell & Danby
p.200 Fig 1a. Maglev 2000
p.201 Fig 1b. Maglev 2000
p.204 Fig 2. Maglev 2000
p.205 Fig 3. and Fig 4 Maglev 2000
p.206 Fig 5. Maglev 2000
p.207 Fig 6. Maglev 2000
p.208 Fig 7. Maglev 2000
p.209 Fig 8. & Fig 9. Maglev 2000

p.210 Fig 10. Maglev 2000
p.211 Fig 11. Maglev 2000
p.212 Fig 12. & Fig 13. Maglev 2000
p.214 Fig 14. & Fig 15. Maglev 2000
p.215 Fig 16. Maglev 2000
p.216 Fig 17. Maglev 2000
p.217 Fig 18. Maglev 2000
p.218 Fig 19. & Fig 20. Maglev 2000
p.219 Fig 21. Maglev 2000

Chapter 9 – Third Round – Decision Time for America
p.226 Meccano Magazine PD Doug Rike
p.251 Slide Powell and Jordan
p.253 Slide Powell and Jordan
p.254 Slide Powell and Jordan
p.256 Slide Powell and Jordan
p.258 Google Map of Calverton Site
p.260 Photo Andrea Mohin/ New York Times/REDUX w permission
p.263 Photo James Jordan
p.270 Slide. Jordan with acknowledgement to Jesse Ausubel
p.280 Photo James Jordan
p.281 Golden Spike Drawing traced on U.S. map of high traffic congestion Jordan

Chapter 10 – Maglev Launch: Finally, the Final Frontier
p.300 Fig.1 NASA
p.301. Fig 2 NASA
p.302. Fig 3 NASA
p.303. Fig 4 NASA
p.304. Fig 5 NASA
p.305. Fig 6 NASA
p. 307 Table 1 Powell
p. 308 Table 2 Powell
p.310 Fig. 7 Powell & Fig. 8 PD Wikipedia
p.312 Fig 9 StarTam launch rendering Wikipedia PD
p.313 Table 3 Powell
p.318 Table 4 Powell
p.319 Figure 10 Powell
p.321 Figure 11 Powell
p.322 Figure 12 Slide Powell

p.324 Table 5 Powell

Chapter 11 – Maglev Energy Storage – The Good Sisyphus
p.326 Cover Illustration Robert Coullahan & Doug Rike
p.327 Titian painting PD
p.329 MAPS concept drawings Powell Robert Coullahan & Doug Rike
p.331 MAPS Concept graphic captured from animation by Doug Rike
p.332 MAPS Stability System Powell
p.335 MAPS Concept graphic captured from animation by Doug Rike

Chapter 12 – Maglev Water Transport – A Billion Jugs A Day
p.336 Drought Montage Introduction Doug Rike from U.S. Gov't and PD sources
p.338 Table 1 Powell
p.342 Fig. 1. Water Train Concept Powell & Doug Rike
p.345 & 346 Table 2 Powell
p.347 Fig.2. Map of California canal and aqueduct system PD Wikipedia
p.349 Fig 3. China Map PD Wikipedia
p.350 Fig 4. Photo Great Man Made River PD Wikipedia

Chapter 13 – Finale – Which Song Will the Fat Lady Sing?
p.352 Authors' Photos, PD

Back Cover – Doug Rike

*PD = Public Domain

The Fight for Maglev

About the Authors

James R. Powell, Ph.D. is a Director of the MAGLEV 2000 of Florida Corporation

Dr. Powell and his colleague, Dr. Gordon Danby are the recipients of the 2000 Benjamin Franklin Medal in Engineering for their invention of superconducting Maglev. The medal was awarded to by The Franklin Institute "for their invention of a magnetically-levitated transport system using super conducting magnets and subsequent work in the field." The Franklin Institute awards medals annually in recognition of the recipients' genius and civic spirit and in memory of the Institute's namesake, Benjamin Franklin, who exhibited those same qualities. Some noted past recipients of the Franklin Institute medals include Alexander Graham Bell, Thomas Edison, Neils Bohr, Max Planck, Albert Einstein and Stephen Hawking.

He was a senior scientist at Brookhaven National Laboratory (BNL) from 1956 through 1996. His experiences have led to significant advances in the design and analysis of advanced reactor systems, cryogenic and super conducting power transmission, plasma physics, mine safety, fusion reactor technology, electronuclear (accelerator) breeder systems, transmutation of nuclear wastes, space nuclear thermal propulsion, electromagnetic hypervelocity guns, hydrogen and synthetic fuels, and transportation infrastructure.

He holds patents for the Particle Bed Reactor (PBR) for nuclear rocket propulsion, the use of aluminum structure in fusion reactors; blankets employing solid lithium ceramics and alloys for tritium breeding; and, demountable super conducting magnet systems and the Advanced Vitrification System (AVS) for high-level nuclear and toxic wastes. He and Dr. Danby are the holders of the first patent for superconducting Maglev in 1968, as well as many recent patents on their 2nd generation advanced maglev system.

Dr. Powell holds a Bachelor of Science in Chemical Engineering from the Carnegie Institute of Technology and a Doctor of Science in nuclear engineering earned in 1958 from the Massachusetts Institute of Technology. Dr. Powell has published almost 500 professional papers and reports. He is a member of the American Nuclear Society.

Gordon Danby, Ph.D. is a Director of the MAGLEV 2000 of Florida Corporation , together with Dr. Powell, he was awarded the Franklin Institute Medal 2000 for Engineering for their Maglev inventions. He retired from Brookhaven National Laboratory where he worked on the theory and experimental development of accelerators and magnetic detectors for the study of basic properties of matter. Dr. Danby, together with Dr. Powell, is directing the development of advanced 2nd generation Maglev by their company Maglev 2000 of Florida.

Gordon Danby is widely respected for his contribution to the practical application of theoretical science to technology. His achievements are recognized by his peers as changing Magnetic Resonance Imaging and Transportation Industries.

From the Franklin Award citation, *"Danby's pioneering research efforts in magnetic technology led to the production of open Magnetic Resonance Imaging (MRI) machines that are better, faster and more patient friendly than their tunnel-style predecessors. Danby, along with James Powell, also invented the Superconducting Maglev, a magnetically levitated, high speed train system. The practical and efficient design of the Maglev provides mixed freight and passenger service and interfaces easily with other transport modes."*

Dr. Danby received his B.S. in physics and math from Carleton University in Ottawa, Canada, and his Ph.D. in nuclear physics from McGill University in Montreal, Canada. He is a fellow of the American Physical Society. In 1983, the New York Academy of Sciences honored Danby with the Boris Pregel Award for Applied Science and Technology.

James Jordan is the founder and President of the Interstate Maglev Project and Executive Vice President of Maglev 2000.

The energy crises of the 1970s focused the Navy career of James Jordan. The new era of scarce oil and rapid increases in oil prices dramatically introduced Commander Jordan to the national military and economic security consequences of America's growing dependence on oil. Commander Jordan served as the first director of the Navy Energy R&D program office in the Pentagon. As director, he developed strategies and technologies aimed at sustaining military and national economic security in the new oil reality.

In 1979, Mr. Jordan retired from the Navy and became a senior policy advisor to the late Senator John C. Stennis, Chairman, Armed Services Committee and Defense Appropriations Committee. In this capacity, Mr. Jordan was a Senate staff leader in energy, transportation, environment, and agricultural policy.

In 1988, after leaving the U.S. Senate, Mr. Jordan founded several entrepreneurial ventures directed toward development of environmentally sustainable energy, and economic growth: efficient electric Maglev (**mag**netic **lev**itation) transportation, carbon capture and storage, nuclear waste isolation, hydrogen and electric power co-generation, advanced nuclear power generation and earth science data management.[4]

Education: MBA, Harvard Business School, Cambridge, MA; Distinguished Graduate, Industrial College of the Armed Forces at the National Defense University, Washington, DC; B.A., University of North Carolina, Chapel Hill, NC, Student Body President and Graduate of Senior High School, Greensboro, NC.

Mr. Jordan is the managing co-author of The Fight for Maglev and can be reached at james.jordan@magneticglide.com

---

Consortium International Earth Science Information Network, (www.ciesin.org), now located at Columbia University. In 1992, Mr. Jordan introduced CIESIN to the U.N. Conference on Environmental Development (UNCED) in Rio.

Made in the USA
Charleston, SC
07 February 2012